Learning Magazine's
DAY By DAY
All-Year-Long
BOOK

illustrated by Bob Walsh

TEACHER CONTRIBUTORS

Thomas Balchak, Glenn Coats, Laurie Cooper, Rick Crosslin,
Deborah Delisle, Linda Froschauer, Marian Kirberg, Debbie Lerner, Marilyn Kay Nance, Gerry Parmet,
Rose Reissman, Ann Walser

Project Director..............................Jeanette Moss
Managing Editor......................................John Ziff
Art Director.................................Kathleen Cuddihy
Developmental Editor.....................Karen Hansen
Associate Editor.......................................Rose Foltz
Research Editor..........................Jeanne Humphrey
Production Manager..................Katherine Murphy
Production Designer...............................Bob Perry
Production Artists................................Ann Raphun,
                              Robert Wieder, Anet Oakes
Typographer...........................Valerie Rosenberger
Proofreader..Nancy Papsin
Administrative Assistants.....................Denise Lee,
                                              Lisa Shomper

Editorial Director...........................Charlene Gaynor
Design Director................................Edward Rosanio
Director of Production ....Bacil Guiley

INTRODUCTION

In this book, you'll find a page for every day of the year. And on each of those pages, you'll find:

- a list of famous and fascinating people born on that day
- a list of important and intriguing events that happened on that day
- several timely, date-based activities developed by *Learning* magazine's award-winning staff of classroom-teacher field editors.

If you're always looking for new activities to liven up the curriculum, or intriguing tidbits to kick off a project or get the day off to a stimulating start, then this is the resource for you. The 384-page DAY-BY-DAY BOOK extends and expands on *Learning*'s popular Calendar feature. In all, it contains more than 4,500 facts and over 1,000 brand-new activities.

Plus! An introductory page for each month includes a list of "Monthlong Observances," "Weeklong Events," and "Special Days and Celebrations," as well as a suggested "Project of the Month" to do with your students throughout the month.

Learning's DAY-BY-DAY BOOK will never be dated because every day of the year is included. No matter what your school's schedule—August to May, September to June, or year-round—the DAY-BY-DAY BOOK will be there for you. Enjoy this helpful, energizing resource today—and throughout your years of teaching.

On the pages of this book, you'll find the following symbols, which link the activities to the events or subjects on which they're based. The symbols will help you make connections at a glance between the dates, the activities, and your curriculum.

KEY

- 🎭 **The Arts**
- 📖 **Authors & Books**
- 🌐 **Countries Near & Far**
- 🖋 **Historic People & Events**
- 🪶 **Holidays & Observances**
- 💡 **Inventions & Inventors**
- 📋 **Popular Culture**
- ❀ **Potpourri**
- 🏅 **Records & Firsts**
- ⚗ **Science & Health**
- 🏈 **Sports**
- 🇺🇸 **The United States**

Table of contents

SEPTEMBER

☆ Project of the Month: Breakfast Book

Celebrate All-American Breakfast Month throughout September. Start by having your students compare breakfast favorites. What are common likes and dislikes? Then ask each child to survey five people (including himself or herself) with the following questions: Do you eat breakfast every morning? Does your breakfast usually contain a bread item? A meat item? Any fruits or vegetables? Is your weekend break-fast different from your weekday breakfast? Does anyone else in your family eat breakfast with you? How long do you stay at the table during breakfast? Do you take a vitamin at breakfast? After the surveys are completed, discuss what your class learned.

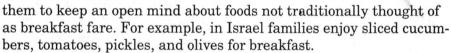

Throughout the month, ask your students to cut out magazine pic-tures of breakfast foods. Remind them to keep an open mind about foods not traditionally thought of as breakfast fare. For example, in Israel families enjoy sliced cucum-bers, tomatoes, pickles, and olives for breakfast.

At the end of the month, display the pictures. Discuss each food's nutritional value and visual appeal. With all the pictures in view, ask each child to create a nutritious breakfast menu. Compile all the menus in a "Class Breakfast Book."

EXTENDER: Ask your students to bring empty cereal boxes to class. Have them work in small groups to study the nutritional panels on any four boxes. After they list the serving size (in grams) and the amount of sucrose and other sugars (in grams), challenge the groups to calculate the percent-age of sugar. Which brands had the least sugar? What sugges-tions do your students have to warn cereal eaters of high sugar content?

SEPTEMBER 1
activities

✒ Young monarch

At the age of 9 months, Henry VI succeeded his father, Henry V, as king of England. In 1431, he succeeded his grandfather, Charles VI, as king of France. Quite a job—for a 10-year-old! Ask your students what they think would be some of the advantages and disadvantages of being a member of a royal family. In what ways might the lives of royal children be similar to and different from your students' lives?

⚗ Fabulous flocks

Very few bird species were as numerous as the passenger pigeon. For hours on end, flocks numbering 1 billion to 2 billion would darken the sky. One breeding colony in Michigan covered a $2 \times 1/2$-mile area. Have your students look at a road map of their hometown and pick a location about 28 miles away. About how long would it take to drive to that location? Next, have them pick a place that's about $3^1/_2$ miles away. How long would it take to ride a bicycle to that place? Invite your students to read more about the passenger pigeon and the mystery of its disappearance.

❀ The "unsinkable"

The *Titanic* measured 882 feet in length. Have your students develop their own scale to compare the length of the *Titanic* with that of their classroom or gym. As a special homework challenge, ask them to take an 882-foot walk. Have the walkers compare how they kept track of the distance they covered.

If placed upright, the *Titanic* would have been taller than any building of her day. Have your students compare her in an upright position to the Washington Monument, the Empire State Building, the Sears Tower, the Pyramid of Cheops, the Eiffel Tower, a local monument.

SEPTEMBER 2
activities

📖 Dino-mite author

Children's author and illustrator Bernard Most was born in New York City. From age 4, he wanted to be an artist. After completing his training, he became an artist for an advertising agency. But he also wanted to write and illustrate children's books. When his 6-year-old son Glenn said that he wished dinosaurs would return, Most got the idea for his first book, *If the Dinosaurs Came Back*. Since then, he has written many other dinosaur books.

Tell your students that when Bernard Most visits classrooms, he urges kids never to give up on their dreams. He points out that some of his books were published after many rejections. Ask your students to share situations that forced them to "hang in there" and try again.

Most calls himself a "fishaholic"—he has six tropical fish tanks and keeps as many as 88 fish at once. How would your students describe themselves—"computerholics," "dogaholics," "stampaholics," "tall taleaholics," "teddy bearaholics"?

📝 Milestones

After George Bush was rescued by the U.S. submarine *Finback*, he remained on board for a month, censoring mail during the day and serving as lookout during the midnight-to-4 a.m. shift. Bush's ordeal was certainly a milestone in his life. Ask your students to read different biographical accounts about Bush and select other milestones in his life. Then have a committee review each student's selections and pick the 10 most important milestones. Write these on flat "stones" made from construction paper, and mount them on a bulletin board.

BIRTHDAYS

1850 • **EUGENE FIELD**, American poet and author of "Wynken, Blynken, and Nod"

1917 • **CLEVELAND AMORY**, champion of animal rights

1937 • **BERNARD MOST**, children's 📖 author and illustrator

1952 • **JIMMY CONNORS**, American tennis player who became the first man to win 100 singles titles

EVENTS

1666 • **THE GREAT FIRE OF LONDON** destroyed four-fifths of the city.

1789 • Congress organized the U.S. **DEPARTMENT OF THE TREASURY.**

1944 • **GEORGE BUSH**, the navy's 📝 youngest pilot, parachuted from his burning plane during World War II. After paddling for hours in the Pacific Ocean, he was rescued.

1945 • **JAPAN FORMALLY SURRENDERED** to the United States aboard the USS *Missouri* in Tokyo Bay.

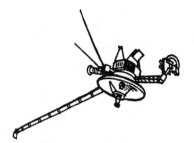

SEPTEMBER 3
activities

BIRTHDAYS

1856 • LOUIS SULLIVAN, American architect who pioneered the skyscraper

1920 • ALIKI (full name: Aliki Liacouras Brandenberg), children's author

1923 • MORT WALKER, American cartoonist and creator of "Beetle Bailey"

EVENTS

1189 • RICHARD THE LION-HEARTED was crowned king of England.

1609 • ENGLISH EXPLORER HENRY HUDSON sailed his vessel, *Half Moon,* into New York Harbor.

1783 • The United States and Britain signed the TREATY OF PARIS, which officially ended the Revolutionary War.

1894 • LABOR DAY first became a legal holiday.

1895 • THE FIRST PROFESSIONAL FOOTBALL GAME took place in Latrobe, Pa.

1940 • COLOR TELEVISION was demonstrated for the first time.

1970 • HAILSTONES THE SIZE OF GRAPEFRUITS fell on Coffeyville, Kan.

1976 • THE U.S. SPACECRAFT *VIKING 2* landed on Mars and took the first close-up color photographs of the planet's surface.

Athletic inflation

When the Latrobe YMCA and the Jeannette Athletic Club played the first professional football game, each player was paid $10. Today, some NFL stars make $125,000 or more per game. Have your students use their calculators to figure out a ratio comparing the two salaries.

Labor Day tie-in

President Grover Cleveland signed a bill making Labor Day a legal holiday honoring American workers. Have your students list the different kinds of workers they meet in the course of a school day. As a special challenge, ask teams to list occupations for every letter of the alphabet—architect, brick mason, calligrapher, disc jockey, engraver, florist, genealogist, and so on. Which team developed the list with the most unusual jobs?

Wacky weather measure

Ask your students to draw what they think is a life-size grapefruit. Then compare everyone's drawing with an actual grapefruit. Whose picture was the closest? Next, introduce the term *circumference.* Use a tape measure to find your grapefruit's circumference. Cut the grapefruit in half and define the terms *diameter* and *radius.* Then give everyone a section to eat. During writing workshop, encourage interested students to write about what it might be like to get caught in a hailstorm with grapefruit-sized stones. Or they might want to write about another wacky weather day.

Fictional families

When Aliki was growing up, she loved to draw pictures of her family—and Peter Rabbit's. She thought it was fun that both families had three girls and a boy named Peter. Ask your students to draw their favorite fictional family. Is it the Berenstain Bears? The Stupids? George and Martha? Curious George and the man with the yellow hat? Gilly Hopkins and her foster family? Horton and his babies?

SEPTEMBER 4
activities

🏳 The (town or city) name game
Spanish settlers named their village *El Pueblo de Nuestra Senora la Reina de los Angeles,* which means "The Town of Our Lady, the Queen of the Angels." Do any of your students know how their town got its name? Invite them to give fictional explanations in their journals.

✿ First jobs
Ten-year-old Barney Flaherty got his job delivering papers by answering the following classified ad in the New York *Sun:* "To the Unemployed—a number of steady men can find employment by vending this paper." What are some ways your students earn extra money? What do they do with the money they earn?

📖 Dear Peter Rabbit
Beatrix Potter had many pets when she was growing up. She called one of her rabbits Peter Piper, a name she later used for the hero of a picture letter she sent to Noel Moore, her best friend's son. This get-well letter began, "I shall tell you a story about four little rabbits whose names were Flopsy, Mopsy, Cottontail, and Peter...." Ask your students to create their own "get-well picture letters" to send to the children's ward at a local hospital.

⁂ Calculated lengths
The *Graf Zeppelin* was 776 feet long. Take your students to the gym, hallway, or parking lot and mark off the airship's length. Today's airships—seen on TV panoramas of major sports events—measure about 192 feet long. Have your students use their calculators to compare the lengths.

BIRTHDAYS
1846 • **DANIEL BURNHAM,** architect and city planner
1848 • **LEWIS H. LATIMER,** co-developer of the electric light bulb
1912 • **SYD HOFF,** children's author

EVENTS
1609 • Henry Hudson discovered the island of MANHATTAN.
1781 • Spanish settlers founded LOS ANGELES.
1807 • ROBERT FULTON began operating his first steamboat on the Hudson River.
1833 • Barney Flaherty became the FIRST NEWSBOY IN THE UNITED STATES.
1883 • THE FIRST SELF-SERVE RESTAURANT opened in New York City.
1888 • George Eastman received a patent for the KODAK CAMERA.
1893 • BEATRIX POTTER sent a get-well letter about a rabbit family to 5-year-old Noel Moore.
1920 • THE FIRST BOY SCOUT RALLY was held in London.
1929 • THE *GRAF ZEPPELIN* completed the only round-the-world trip by an airship.
1972 • U.S. swimmer Mark Spitz won his SEVENTH GOLD MEDAL at the Munich Olympics, becoming the first person to win that many in a single Olympics.

NEWSPAPER CARRIER DAY

SEPTEMBER 5
activities

Keeping tabs on TV

The rating system developed by Arthur C. Nielsen's marketing research company in 1950 is used to determine who's watching what television programs and for how long. Ask your students to poll five people for their favorite weekly programs. Compare your class findings with those publicized in the newspaper (check *USA TODAY*). Then ask your class to suggest factors that might affect the ratings (age, geographic region, gender, ethnic background).

Tunnel trip

Help your students get a sense for the distance of Switzerland's St. Gotthard Tunnel by having them use road maps or atlases to find locations that are 10 miles from their homes. Get out the calculators and find out how long it would take to travel through the tunnel at various speeds—15 mph, 35 mph, 55 mph. Encourage the students to graph their findings.

Procrastination time

The Procrastination Club of America has declared Sept. 5 as a day to put away watches and forget about the stresses and strains of being on time. Get in on the fun by covering your wall clock with a piece of cloth. Ask your students to discuss what makes them late. What types of events or activities are they most likely to be late for? At the end of the day, ask the kids how they felt about a clock-free day. In what ways was it inconvenient?

SEPTEMBER 6
activities

✎ Volunteers then and now

The Marquis de Lafayette served in the U.S. Continental Army as a volunteer. He didn't want money. Ask your students what they can do as volunteers in their community or school. Brainstorm for a list of potential projects—raking leaves, taking a younger child for a walk, collecting items for recycling, organizing games for younger children, walking an invalid neighbor's dog, collecting canned food for neighborhood shelters, tutoring a non-English-speaking child, forming a crew to clean up the school grounds, becoming a pen pal with a retiree or hospitalized child, collecting books and magazines for distribution at shelters or hospitals.

🇺🇸 Looking at leaders

When the Founding Fathers established a 4-year term for the president of the United States, they didn't specify the number of terms a president could serve. After Franklin Roosevelt died in office during his fourth term, a constitutional amendment was ratified that limited the presidential terms to two. Ask your students to research the length of terms for other elected government officials—senators, representatives, mayors, school board members, tax collectors, and so on. What service terms do they suggest for officers in their classroom?

BIRTHDAYS

1757 • **THE MARQUIS DE LAFAYETTE,**
✎ Revolutionary War hero

1766 • **JOHN DALTON,** English chemist, physicist, and developer of atomic theory

1860 • **JANE ADDAMS,** American social worker and humanitarian who founded Hull House

EVENTS

1628 • **THE MASSACHUSETTS BAY COLONY** was established in Salem, Mass., by 100 English Puritans.

1787 • **THE CONSTITUTIONAL CONVEN-TION** adopted a 4-year term for president.

1866 • **FREDERICK DOUGLASS** became the first black delegate to a national political convention.

1927 • **THE HARLEM GLOBETROTTERS** were organized.

1954 • **Groundbreaking ceremonies** were held in Shippingport, Pa., for the world's **FIRST NUCLEAR POWER PLANT.**

SEPTEMBER 7
activities

BIRTHDAYS

1829 • **FERDINAND VANDEVEER HAYDEN, American geologist who was instrumental in the creation of Yellowstone National Park**

1860 • **GRANDMA MOSES (full name: Anna Mary Robertson Moses), American primitive painter**

1936 • **BUDDY HOLLY, American singer, guitarist, and songwriter**

EVENTS

1502 • **AMERIGO VESPUCCI, the Italian navigator for whom America was named, returned to Lisbon after his third trip to the New World.**

1813 • **THE NICKNAME "UNCLE SAM" first appeared in print, in a Troy, N.Y., newspaper.**

1822 • **BRAZIL DECLARED ITS INDEPENDENCE from Portugal.**

1936 • **BOULDER DAM, now known as Hoover Dam, began operation.**

1958 • **Mary Davis set the WOMEN'S RECORD FOR NONSTOP TALKING—110 hours, 30 minutes, 5 seconds—on a New York radio station.**

1977 • **Cindy Nicholas became the first woman swimmer to complete A ROUND-TRIP, NONSTOP CROSSING OF THE ENGLISH CHANNEL.**

ICE CREAM MONTH

"Uncle Sam" and other nicknames

The real "Uncle Sam" was Samuel Wilson, inspector of provisions for the United States Army in New York and New Jersey during the War of 1812. An employee at Wilson's meat-packing plant jokingly told visitors that the "US" stamped on each barrel of meat stood for "Uncle Sam" Wilson. (These initials actually stood for "United States.") By the end of the War of 1812, "Uncle Sam" was widely used as a nickname for the U.S. government. Invite your students to share the stories behind their nicknames, or those of family or friends. If they could select nicknames for themselves, what would they choose and why?

TO CELEBRATE ICE CREAM MONTH

Tell your students that the average American eats about 15 quarts of ice cream each year. Ask the kids to guess how many flavors of ice cream there are (over 200) and which is the most popular (vanilla). As a homework assignment, have your students ask five people to name their favorite flavor. Graph the results as a class. Did vanilla turn out to be the most popular in the survey?

Dam dimensions

Hoover Dam, located in the Black Canyon of the Colorado River, is 726 feet high and 1,244 feet long. Have your students compare its height with that of the school flagpole, and its length with that of a school bus. Tell your students that Hoover Dam's concrete base is 660 feet deep and contains $3\frac{1}{4}$ million cubic yards of concrete—enough to pave a two-lane highway from New York to San Francisco. Ask the kids to use a map scale to figure out that distance.

SEPTEMBER 8
activities

📖 Summer memories

Jack Prelutsky's poems are full of humor. Read several from *What I Did Last Summer*. Then have your students write a poem or story centered on a funny summertime moment.

📖 Artists' viewpoints

The Velveteen Rabbit, written by Margery Williams Bianco in 1922, has been interpreted by a number of illustrators, including Michael Hague, David Jorgensen, and S.D. Schindler. Ask your class to discuss the different media used by these artists to complement this tender story. Which illustrations do your students prefer and why?

🇺🇸 Honors to the flag

The first flag salute read: "I give my heart and my hand to my country—one country, one language, one flag." Some people thought this salute was "too juvenile and lacking in dignity." Ask your students to compare and contrast the first flag salute and today's pledge. How do they feel about the original?

✑ Worldwide readers

The United Nations Educational, Scientific and Cultural Organization (UNESCO) uses International Literacy Day to call attention to the problem of adult illiteracy. Ask your students to estimate the percentage of the world's adults who don't know how to read (about 25%). Have them figure out how many people this represents. To emphasize the number, have the kids calculate 25% of the adults in their school, their town, their state, and the United States.

BIRTHDAYS

1940 • **JACK PRELUTSKY**, children's 📖 author and illustrator

1948 • **MICHAEL HAGUE**, children's 📖 author and illustrator

EVENTS

1565 • Spaniards founded ST. AUGUSTINE, FLA., the oldest city in the United States.

1892 • **NATIONAL PLEDGE OF ALLE-** 🇺🇸 **GIANCE DAY**—The "Pledge of Allegiance" was first published in the magazine *Youth's Companion*.

1921 • Margaret Gorman became the **FIRST MISS AMERICA** at age 15; she's still the youngest ever crowned.

1930 • The comic strip "BLONDIE" first appeared.

1960 • American track star **WILMA RUDOLPH** won her third gold medal of the Rome Olympics.

1966 • The first "STAR TREK" episode aired.

1971 • **THE JOHN F. KENNEDY CENTER FOR THE PERFORMING ARTS** opened in Washington, D.C.

✑ **INTERNATIONAL LITERACY DAY**

SEPTEMBER 9
activities

BIRTHDAYS

1754 • **WILLIAM BLIGH,** English captain of the HMS *Bounty* at the time of the famous mutiny

1903 • **PHYLLIS WHITNEY,** children's author

1906 • **AILEEN FISHER,** children's author

EVENTS

1689 • **PETER THE GREAT,** age 17, took power in Russia.

1776 • **THE CONTINENTAL CONGRESS** made the name "United States" official.

1836 • **ABRAHAM LINCOLN** received a license to practice law.

1850 • **CALIFORNIA** became the 31st state.

1851 • **A WEEKLY BUDGET of $10.37** was proposed for the average working-class family of five.

1893 • **PRESIDENT GROVER CLEVE-LAND's** wife became the mother of a baby girl, the first child born to a First Lady in the White House.

1908 • **ORVILLE WRIGHT** made the first flight that exceeded 1 hour.

• **NEW YORK MOUNTED POLICE** went on duty for the first time.

1963 • **A GIANT PANDA** was born in captivity for the first time.

📖 Writer's inspiration

Phyllis Whitney wrote her first book, *A Place for Ann,* after viewing the ruins of an old colonial house. Take students on a neighborhood walk to look for interesting buildings, or have them bring in photographs of homes, storefronts, construction sites, or other structures. Then ask the kids to tell or write fictional stories about the families who are living—or have lived—at these sites.

❀ Pocketbook shock

Ask your students to survey their families to find out how much it takes per week to feed, clothe, and house the family. Students can then compare and contrast these present-day budgets with the 1851 amount of $10.37. (They'll have to adjust the figures to fit the size of their own family.) They also might want to conduct an oral history survey by asking seniors in their families or communities to recall the cost of a movie ticket, a visit to the doctor, oil or gas, a candy bar, a bus or train ride, a car, and so on. What surprised them the most?

❁ White House kids

In honor of the anniversary of the birth of President Grover Cleveland's daughter, challenge your students to name other presidential children and do some research to discover more. What would be some of the advantages and disadvantages of being a "presidential progeny"?

❁ Taking flight

In 1908 Orville Wright made 57 complete circles over Fort Myer, Va., at an altitude of 120 feet. The flight lasted 1 hour and 2 minutes and set several records. Ask your students to guess where a flight of 1 hour and 2 minutes could take today's passengers. Then have them check their atlases.

SEPTEMBER 10
activities

✎ Sewing celebration

Elias Howe's first sewing machine—which imitated the human arm sewing—was a failure. But he didn't give up. With his father's financial support, he developed a second machine that could sew 250 stitches a minute. Ask your students how many stitches they think a human can sew in a minute. Set a timer and ask a few volunteers to sew. Use calculators to figure out the average, then compare it with the machine's rate. Finally, have your students write about someone they know who, like Elias Howe, wouldn't give up.

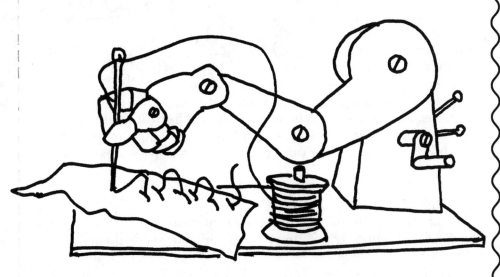

❀ Coast to coast

When the Lincoln Highway was officially dedicated, groups of Boy Scouts across the country simultaneously put up the road signs. Have your students use their atlases to find other geographic locations named in honor of President Lincoln. Ask teams of students to write the grid coordinates or latitude-longitude readings for the various locations so others can find them. Challenge students to find locations named after other U.S. presidents.

✑ Doggie graph

Ask your students to list what they like to put on a hot dog—onions, relish, ketchup, mustard, chili, cheese, and so on. Then have everyone predict what the class's most popular hot dog fixin' will be. Tally the results in bar graph form.

SEPTEMBER 11
activities

▣ Personalized parks

After New York City bought an 843-acre tract of land for development into a public park, it announced a competition for the park design. The winner was "Greensward," a landscape plan that included groves, rock outcroppings, foot and bridle paths, carriage drives, and bridges. Have your students create maps— complete with paths, recreation trails, bodies of water, playgrounds, entrances, and exits—of an imaginary park. After the designs are finished, ask your students what they think landscape architects must keep in mind as they work to plan—or improve—a park.

☞ Comic relief

Ask your students to list their favorite comic strips. Why do they like them? Are all comic strips funny? Do any of your students identify with a particular comic strip character? Look at several comic strips to see how cartoonists use frames to tell a story. Then have your students create their own version of one of these favorites or devise a new comic strip in which characters from one strip interact with characters from another.

✐ Baseball bonanza

Commemorate Pete Rose's record-breaking 4,192nd base hit by having teams of students select another baseball milestone and illustrate it—commemorative plate style—on a paper plate.

SEPTEMBER 12
activities

⊘ Olympic flashback

Jesse Owens deflated Adolf Hitler's "Aryan race" theory by winning gold medals in the 100 meters, 200 meters, 400-meter relay, and long jump at the 1936 Summer Olympics in Berlin, Germany. Have a group of students research Hitler's "Aryan race" theory and report its basic premise to the class. Then discuss the flaws in Hitler's argument. Can your students think of current examples of racial or ethnic prejudice?

📺 Artists then and now

The Lascaux Cave paintings depict a variety of animals important to people who lived 10,000 to 35,000 years ago. Show your students pictures of the paintings. Then divide the class into groups and ask each to create its own cave painting on a piece of large, brown butcher paper. Tell the groups to include pictures of animals that are important in their lives. To create a stonelike effect, crumple the paper. Display the "cave paintings" in the hallway.

BIRTHDAYS

1812 • **RICHARD MARCH HOE,** American inventor of the rotary press used in modern newspaper printing

1913 • **JESSE OWENS,** American track star who won four gold medals at the 1936 Berlin Olympics ⊘

EVENTS

1846 • English poets **ROBERT BROWNING AND ELIZABETH BARRETT** were married.

1910 • **ALICE STEBBINS WELLS,** the first woman police officer in the United States, was sworn in by the Los Angeles Police Department.

1940 • **THE LASCAUX CAVE PAINTINGS** 📺 in France were discovered by four boys and a pet dog.

1959 • The USSR's *LUNA 2* was launched. It became the first space probe to land on the moon.

1974 • **SHIRLEY TEMPLE,** former child movie star, became U.S. ambassador to Ghana.

SEPTEMBER 13
activities

BIRTHDAYS

1851 • **WALTER REED, American army**  **surgeon who proved that yellow fever is transmitted by the bite of a mosquito**

1857 • **MILTON HERSHEY, founder of the Hershey candy empire**

1916 • **ROALD DAHL, British children's author**

EVENTS

1788 • **NEW YORK was selected as the capital of the United States.**

1826 • **A RHINOCEROS was first exhibited in the United States.**

1845 • **The Knickerbocker Club of New York set down the FIRST BASEBALL RULES.**

1922 • **Al-'Azizyah, Libya, recorded an all-time high of 136.4° F IN THE SHADE.**

1948 • **MARGARET CHASE SMITH was elected to the U.S. Senate, becoming the first woman to serve in both houses of Congress.**

1987 • **FRED ROGERS of "Mister Rogers' Neighborhood" left for Moscow to appear on a Soviet children's TV program.**

Wonderful rhinoceros

The rhinoceros dates back 20 million years. Today, there are five species left, and they're all on the endangered list. Your students might be surprised to hear that a 5,500-pound adult rhino can gallop 24 mph. Ask them to use record books to compare the rhino's speed with that of other animals—including man.

Famous Americans

Walter Reed Hospital in Washington, D.C., is named in Dr. Walter Reed's honor. Have your students list places in their community—parks, schools, buildings, streets—that were named after prominent people.

Chocolate feast

Milton Hershey would be amazed to learn that Americans eat 5.8 million pounds of chocolate each day. That's enough chocolate to make a 2-foot-thick candy bar the size of a football field. Have your students use their calculators to figure out how many cubic feet of chocolate that is. Then plan a chocolate-tasting party. Choose four different types of chocolate bars cut into bite-sized portions. Provide each child with a paper plate divided into four sections. After sampling each kind, the kids must select a favorite. Graph the results.

SEPTEMBER 14
activities

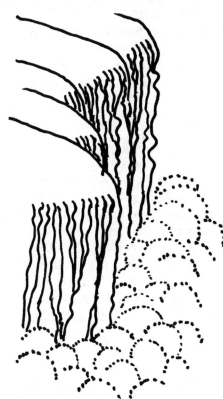

 Niagara Falls math

Create a three-dimensional Niagara Falls bulletin board with construction paper and ribbon. Post extra-credit math problems around the paper falls. For example, your students could use almanacs and reference books to find out how many gallons of water flow over the falls in 1 minute, 1 hour, 1 day, their lifetime. They could compare the falls' height with their school's or their classroom's.

✐ Thank you, Mr. Roosevelt

In 1902 President Teddy Roosevelt took a 5-day bear-hunting trip. Newspapers made fun of Roosevelt when he refused to shoot a small cub. But a candy-store owner in Brooklyn, N.Y., admired the president's decision. In Roosevelt's honor he sewed a plush toy bear, which he called a "Teddy Bear," and placed it in his window display. Read *The First Teddy Bear* by Helen Kay. Then have a teddy bear picnic—with your students' favorite furry friends as guests of honor. Some students may want to dress a bear as their favorite storybook character.

📖 Newbery honors

William H. Armstrong's book *Sounder* received the Newbery Medal in 1970. Ask your students to investigate the history of this book award. Have a group of volunteers make a list of other Newbery Medal recipients. Go over the list and invite any student who's familiar with one of the books to give a talk about it for the class.

BIRTHDAYS

1769 • **ALEXANDER VON HUMBOLDT,** German scientist after whom a Pacific current was named

1914 • **WILLIAM H. ARMSTRONG,** children's author

1950 • **JOHN STEPTOE,** children's author

EVENTS

1741 • **GEORGE FREDERICK HANDEL,** the German composer, finished the *Messiah* after 23 days of work.

1778 • **BENJAMIN FRANKLIN** was appointed American minister to France.

1814 • **FRANCIS SCOTT KEY** wrote "The Star-Spangled Banner" as the British shelled Fort McHenry.

1860 • **NIAGARA FALLS** was illuminated for the first time.

1886 • George Anderson patented the **TYPEWRITER RIBBON.**

1901 • **THEODORE ROOSEVELT** became the 26th president of the United States.

1940 • Congress passed the Selective Service and Training Act, providing for the **FIRST PEACETIME DRAFT** in U.S. history.

SNACK-A-PICKLE TIME

14

SEPTEMBER 15
activities

📖 Kids' choices

Upon retiring from the navy, James Fenimore Cooper began writing novels. Many of his books, including *The Deerslayer, The Last of the Mohicans,* and *The Pathfinder,* are classics. Invite the children in your class to make a list of books they'd call classics.

BIRTHDAYS

1789 • **JAMES FENIMORE COOPER,** American novelist
1857 • **WILLIAM HOWARD TAFT, 27th** president of the United States
1890 • **AGATHA CHRISTIE, English** detective novelist
1914 • **ROBERT McCLOSKEY, children's** author
1934 • **TOMIE DEPAOLA, children's** author and illustrator

EVENTS

1789 • **Congress changed the name of the Department of Foreign Affairs to the DEPARTMENT OF STATE.**
1821 • **COSTA RICA gained its independence from Spain.**
1949 • **THE FIRST COMPUTER CALCULATION OF PI was made.**
1971 • **THE FOREST SERVICE introduced Woodsy Owl and the slogan "Give a Hoot; Don't Pollute."**
1984 • **Montague, Mich., dedicated the WORLD'S LARGEST WEATHER VANE—48 feet high and 3,500 pounds.**

RESPECT FOR THE AGED DAY IN JAPAN

📖 Mystery bags

Agatha Christie's mysteries have been translated into more languages than any other books. In honor of this prolific writer, have your students create their own mysteries—with paper bags. Ask each cooperative group to put two to four objects that are related in some way in a paper bag. The groups should then write a set of clues to help others figure out the contents of the bag.

✿ A piece of pi

The first computer-generated calculation of pi produced 2,037 decimal places in 70 hours. Today's supercomputers have reached 1,011,196,691 digits. If printed on a line, this calculation would stretch nearly halfway across the United States. Have your students figure out how many miles that would be.

🌐 Special honors

In Japanese culture, elderly people are looked upon with esteem and reverence. Ask your students to interview an older relative or family friend. Brainstorm for possible questions that will help your students better know "old friends" in their family.

SEPTEMBER 16
activities

🇺🇸 Name that school

Ask your students how they'd feel if the name of their town were changed. What alternative names would they suggest? Then invite them to give their school a new name for a day. What names would they offer and why? Select several new names and have teams of students design a school logo, letterhead, and a flag for each. Invite the principal to hear the suggestions and select one as the official "Name of the Day."

Spending spree

Ask students to bring in a catalog from J.C. Penney. Have a contest to see how much money groups of students can spend in 20 minutes using the catalog. Tell the students that they must keep track of the name of each item, the price, and the page number. At the end of the time, pass out calculators to determine which group is the winner.

📖 Monkey business

Celebrate H.A. Rey's birthday by having your students describe how Curious George could get into trouble in their classroom, gym, library, cafeteria, and principal's office. Of course, they'll need to explain how they'd rescue the mischievous monkey and return him to the man in the yellow hat.

BIRTHDAYS

1875 • **J.C. PENNEY**, American merchant and founder of the J.C. Penney Co.

1898 • **H.A. REY**, children's author

EVENTS

1492 • **COLUMBUS** and his men first saw patches of seaweed in mid-ocean on their first voyage to America.

1620 • **THE PILGRIMS** left Plymouth, England, on the *Mayflower*.

1630 • The village of **SHAWMUT, MASS.**, changed its name to Boston.

1787 • Printers prepared 500 copies of the **CONSTITUTION** for the official signing ceremony.

1919 • **THOMAS EDISON** explained in a letter that he and his assistants worked in the lab about 18 hours each day.

1926 • **CHARLES LINDBERGH** parachuted safely in Ottawa, Ill., when his airmail plane ran out of gas.

SEPTEMBER 17
activities

BIRTHDAYS

1730 • **BARON VON STEUBEN**, German soldier who helped the Americans in the Revolutionary War

1907 • **WARREN BURGER**, U.S. Supreme Court chief justice

1916 • **MARY STEWART**, children's author

EVENTS

1787 • **CONSTITUTIONAL CONVENTION** 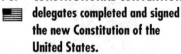 delegates completed and signed the new Constitution of the United States.

1796 • President George Washington delivered his **FAREWELL ADDRESS**.

1930 • New York governor Alfred E. Smith laid the cornerstone for the **EMPIRE STATE BUILDING**.

1988 • Solectria V, a **SOLAR-POWERED CAR** built by the Massachusetts Institute of Technology, won the first U.S. solar-car race.

CITIZENSHIP DAY

17

Constitutions then and now

After the Constitution was drafted, George Washington wrote in his diary: "I...returned to meditate the momentous work...." Have student teams react to these questions: Why was the Constitution "momentous work" to Washington? What changes came about as a result of the Constitution? Did it protect every American's rights? How about the rights of women, Native Americans, and blacks?

Take the discussion a step further by composing a class constitution. On a large piece of paper, draw a scroll, labeling it "Our Constitution." Have your students brainstorm for the rights and responsibilities they want to include, and write them on the scroll. After all your students add their "John Hancock" to the class constitution, post it in a prominent place.

Bye, George!

George Washington's farewell address included this message: "Observe good faith and justice toward all nations. Cultivate peace and harmony with all...." What a powerful charge to the country! Ask your students to think about how today's leaders would react to these words. How can the kids take these words to heart in their community or school? Invite students to share essays or posters that reflect their thoughts and ideas.

SEPTEMBER 18
activities

 Dictionary update

Lexicographers can never rest. They must continually work at finding appropriate terms and definitions to include in their dictionaries. Sometimes they even include slang words and phrases that are generally not accepted as formal English. Have students compile a list—with their own definitions—of current slang. Then have them look up the terms in their dictionaries. Can they find all the terms?

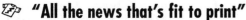 "All the news that's fit to print"

Ask your students to list the many jobs associated with newspaper publishing. Did they remember the reporters, editors, copy editors, photographers, advertising sales representatives, graphic artists, and distributors? How about the cartoonists and columnists?

Tell your students that more than 500,000 trees are harvested to make the newspapers Americans read each Sunday. Ask a team of students to find out how their local newspaper is reducing, reusing, and recycling newsprint. Challenge them to find out about the process of recycling newsprint.

Mission to Mars

The United States and the Soviet Union had many cooperative space projects, including Apollo-Soyuz. When a cosmonaut and an astronaut met in Mars, Pa.—a town near Pittsburgh—they told school groups about their experiences in space and the U.S.-Soviet space efforts. Have your students use atlases to find other towns named for planets and other celestial bodies (Venus and Jupiter, Fla.; Earth and Mercury, Tex.; Neptune, N.J.).

ENTERING MARS PA

BIRTHDAYS

1709 • SAMUEL JOHNSON, English lexicographer and critic who compiled the first dictionary of the English language

1908 • HAROLD COURLANDER, children's author

EVENTS

1793 • President George Washington laid the cornerstone of the U.S. CAPITOL in Washington, D.C.

1851 • The *NEW YORK TIMES* was first published.

1889 • Social reformer Jane Addams moved into Hull House, AMERICA'S FIRST SETTLEMENT HOUSE.

1937 • NIGHTTIME SKYWRITING was displayed for the first time.

1947 • THE UNITED STATES AIR FORCE was created as a separate department.

1981 • BILL COSBY became an honorary national chairman for Pets Are Wonderful.

1983 • Adventurer George Meegan completed a 19,021-MILE WALK from the tip of South America to Prudhoe Bay, Alaska.

1989 • A U.S. astronaut and a Soviet cosmonaut met with "MARTIANS."

SEPTEMBER 19

activities

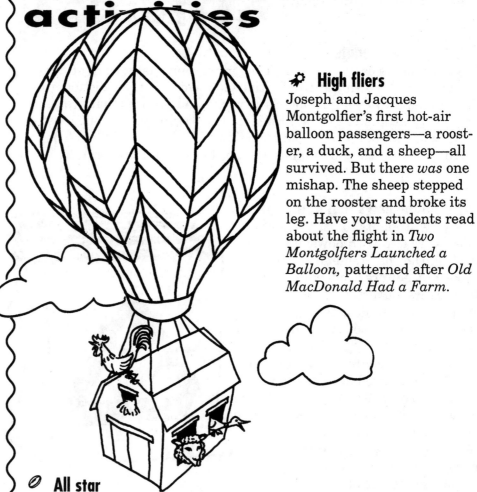

BIRTHDAYS

1894 • **RACHEL FIELD**, children's author and poet

1967 • **JIM ABBOTT**, one-handed baseball pitcher

SLIMEY THE WORM, "Sesame Street" character

EVENTS

1783 • **JOSEPH AND JACQUES MONTGOLFIER** selected a rooster, a duck, and a sheep as the first passengers for their hot-air balloon.

1859 • **THE CONFEDERATE WAR SONG** "Dixie" was sung for the first time.

1881 • **VICE PRESIDENT CHESTER ARTHUR** succeeded James Garfield as the 21st president of the United States.

1957 • The U.S. bathyscaphe *Trieste* reached a **RECORD DEPTH** of 3,200 meters.

• The United States conducted its first **UNDERGROUND NUCLEAR TEST.**

1988 • Twenty-five American mothers and children returned from an **EXCHANGE PROGRAM WITH THE SOVIET UNION.**

1990 • The Library of Congress selected 25 movies for the **NATIONAL FILM REGISTRY.**

✿ High fliers

Joseph and Jacques Montgolfier's first hot-air balloon passengers—a rooster, a duck, and a sheep—all survived. But there *was* one mishap. The sheep stepped on the rooster and broke its leg. Have your students read about the flight in *Two Montgolfiers Launched a Balloon,* patterned after *Old MacDonald Had a Farm.*

⊘ All star

Pitcher Jim Abbott is one of the few baseball players to go straight from college to the major leagues. And he achieved this despite having only one hand. Ask your students to draw an outline of their hand. On each finger, have them write a personal quality that they think helps others overcome a disability.

☞ Movie buffs

The Library of Congress selected 25 outstanding movies for its National Film Registry. A committee considered over 1,000 movies before selecting such favorites as *The Wizard of Oz, Snow White and the Seven Dwarfs,* and *Star Wars.* The Library of Congress will add a high-quality print of each selected movie to its collection of over 75,000 films and TV shows. What movies would your students nominate—and why?

SEPTEMBER 20
activities

 Fateful trip

Magellan's voyage around the world began in Spain with 241 men and five ships. The 50,000-mile voyage ended 3 years later with only 18 men and one ship. Magellan himself was one of the casualties. Have your students make a list of risks involved with travel today.

Safety first

Elisha Graves Otis invented a safety elevator that would operate automatically in case the lifting rope or chain broke. Discuss other safety devices, such as seat belts, air bags, and smoke and burglar alarms. Then have groups prepare safety rules for various places and situations: on the playground, in the classroom, at home, while bike riding. Have the groups make posters to show their safety rules.

Breaking gender barriers

Belva Lockwood, an early leader in the struggle for equal rights for women and an 1884 U.S. presidential nominee, believed that women should be able to pursue careers. She acted on this belief by becoming a lawyer. One of her accomplishments was to gain equal pay for women government workers. Have students interview working women who are in careers once considered "men's work."

SEPTEMBER 21
activities

BIRTHDAYS

1756 • JOHN McADAM, Scottish inventor of the macadam road-making system

1866 • H.G. WELLS, British science fiction writer

1908 • TARO YASHIMA, children's author

1947 • STEPHEN KING, American novelist noted for his horror stories

EVENTS

1893 • Frank Duryea drove the FIRST SUCCESSFUL GASOLINE-POWERED CAR in America on the streets of Springfield, Mass.

1897 • "YES, VIRGINIA, THERE IS A SANTA CLAUS," proclaimed a now-famous New York *Sun* editorial.

1937 • J.R.R. TOLKIEN published *The Hobbit.*

1969 • Steve O'Neal of the New York Jets kicked the LONGEST PUNT—98 yards—in a professional football game.

1990 • BIOSPHERE II, the world's largest totally enclosed environment, began its experiments.

WORLD GRATITUDE DAY
FALL ARRIVES
(Sept. 21 or 22)

Ecosystems under glass

Biosphere II is a 2$\frac{1}{2}$-acre, glass-enclosed structure in Oracle, Ariz., that simulates five ecosystems: desert, marsh, ocean, savanna, and rain forest. The eight participants in the 2-year study were supposed to raise their own food and recycle everything they used. Divide the class into groups, and have each organize a suitcase of essentials for the 2-year stay. Give each group the opportunity to present its "must-haves" to the class. Then discuss what would be some of the positive and negative aspects of being a part of this experiment.

A world of thanks

Businesswoman Edna Fuerth Lemle established World Gratitude Day in 1965. Her concept was for people of all nations and religions to unite in an expression of gratitude. Have your students design "peace cards"—postcards with an illustration about gratitude or human rights and a message of peace for a student in another classroom.

Welcome, fall!

During the autumnal equinox, the sun is in the plane of the earth's equator, and day and night are of equal length throughout the world. Celebrate this celestial event by inviting your students to make a list of what they especially like to hear, smell, taste, and touch in fall. Then ask them to create an acrostic poem based on the word *fall* or *autumn.* Encourage volunteers to share their poems with other classes.

SEPTEMBER 22
activities

🇺🇸 Mail call

Celebrate the establishment of the post office by having your students track the family mail for a week, then graph the results in these categories: personal letters or cards, bills, magazines, and "junk mail."
Figure out the class averages in each category.

❀ Peacemakers

Mark the anniversary of the establishment of the Peace Corps by asking students to interview someone who has served as a volunteer. Invite the volunteers to speak about their experiences. Perhaps your students could develop activities for a neighborhood peace corps and undertake such projects as organizing a cleanup drive, tutoring, and working at senior centers.

✎ Gone to the dogs

Celebrate Dog Week by inviting your students to select favorite dog stories to share. Then set up "canine clubs" to research a specific dog breed. Each club must label on a map its breed's country of origin and supply you with facts and stats about the breed—information that will appear in math problems. Finally, invite the kids to share a photograph of their dog or a friend's dog. As a homework assignment, have them write a biography of the dog.

BIRTHDAYS

1927 • **TOMMY LASORDA, professional baseball player and manager**
1960 • **JOAN JETT, singer and musician**

EVENTS

1776 • **NATHAN HALE, American patriot and Revolutionary War spy, was hanged by the British.**
1789 • **THE U.S. POST OFFICE was 🇺🇸 established.**
1862 • **President Abraham Lincoln issued the EMANCIPATION PROCLAMATION.**
1903 • **Italo Marchiony invented the ICE CREAM CONE.**

1911 • **CY YOUNG, baseball's winningest pitcher, won his 511th and last game.**
1961 • **THE PEACE CORPS became a permanent agency of the U.S. government.**
1976 • **The U.S. *Viking* spacecraft discovered that the planet MARS HAS A POLAR ICE CAP.**
1981 • **THE WORLD'S FASTEST TRAIN made its inaugural run, reaching speeds of 156 mph on the 300-mile route from Paris to Lyon, France.**

✎ **DOG WEEK (last full week in Sept.)**

SEPTEMBER 23
activities

BIRTHDAYS
63 BC • **AUGUSTUS CAESAR, the first Roman emperor**

1838 • **VICTORIA CLAFLIN WOODHULL, the first woman presidential candidate**

1932 • **RAY CHARLES, American pianist, singer, and composer**

1949 • **BRUCE SPRINGSTEEN, American singer, guitarist, and songwriter**

EVENTS
1492 • **COLUMBUS'S CREW sighted a dove, leading them to think land was near on the first voyage to America.**

1806 • **THE LEWIS AND CLARK EXPEDITION came to an end as the explorers completed their homeward trip to St. Louis. The expedition took 2 years, 4 months, and 10 days.**

1846 • **Johann Galle, a German astronomer, discovered the planet NEPTUNE.**

1938 • **A TIME CAPSULE, to be opened in 5,000 years, was buried on the grounds of the New York World's Fair.**

1985 • **THE WORLD'S LARGEST JIGSAW PUZZLE—15,520 pieces—was completed by the Monadnock United Way of Keene, N.H.**

☞ That's entertainment!
Tell your class that Ray Charles, who lost his eyesight as a small boy, has been a successful musician in jazz, rhythm and blues, country, and pop. Undoubtedly, many of your students have seen him in finger-snapping soda commercials. Poll the class to determine favorite singers. Then poll a class with students 3 or 4 years older or younger. Have your students display the results in a Venn diagram. What favorite entertainers did both groups have in common? For homework, your students could poll a parent or other adult and do another Venn diagram. What do they think *this* Venn diagram will show?

✐ Decisions, decisions
The time capsule buried on the grounds of the 1938 New York World's Fair included a Bible, a mail-order catalog, and films of President Roosevelt and of a football game. Ask teams of students to agree on four items they believe are representative of today's times, and have them explain their rationale. After all the teams have presented their selections to the class, vote for the top four choices.

⁂ Puzzler
As a homework assignment, have your students find out how many pieces are in the largest jigsaw puzzle they own. Have them calculate the class mean, median, and mode, then figure out the ratio between the number of pieces in their puzzle and the number of pieces in the world's largest puzzle.

SEPTEMBER 24
activities

✿ Up and away
The first dirigible flew over Paris at a speed of 6 mph. Ask your students whether they think that is faster or slower than most birds fly. Then check an almanac. Next, have them figure out how many minutes it would take for the dirigible to fly 1 mile, 2 miles, and 4 miles.

🏴 Farsighted thinking
President Theodore Roosevelt was a champion of preserving beautiful areas of our country. Survey your class to determine how many students have visited a national park. Name the states where these parks are located, then find them on a map.

✐ Not welcome
In Arkansas in 1957, school integration was the law—yet black students were far from welcome in white schools. When angry whites prevented nine black students from entering high school, President Eisenhower ordered troops to escort the students and guarantee their safety. Ask your students to imagine themselves as one of the nine and write a letter describing how they felt as they entered a place where they knew they wouldn't find many, if any, friends.

✍ Courtesy counts
Celebrate National Courtesy Month by making a class list of what your students could do—as groups or individuals—to brighten someone else's day. Keep a running total of the courteous gestures your class extends throughout the month.

BIRTHDAYS
1755 • JOHN MARSHALL, fourth Supreme Court chief justice

1913 • WILSON RAWLS, children's author

1936 • JIM HENSON, American puppeteer and creator of the Muppets

EVENTS
1789 • Congress established the SUPREME COURT and the office of attorney general.

1852 • THE FIRST DIRIGIBLE was flown ✿ over Paris at 6 mph.

1906 • President Theodore Roosevelt 🏴 established DEVILS TOWER in Wyoming as the first national monument.

1929 • JAMES H. DOOLITTLE made the first "blind" airplane flight, relying entirely on automatic instruments.

1957 • President Dwight Eisenhower ✐ dispatched U.S. troops to Little Rock, Ark., to enforce SCHOOL INTEGRATION.

1960 • The USS *Enterprise,* the FIRST ATOMIC-POWERED AIRCRAFT CARRIER, was launched.

✍ NATIONAL COURTESY MONTH

SEPTEMBER 25
activities

BIRTHDAYS

1807 • **ALFRED VAIL**, American inventor who helped develop Morse code

1931 • **BARBARA WALTERS**, American television newscaster and interviewer

EVENTS

1493 • **CHRISTOPHER COLUMBUS** left Cadiz, Spain, on his second voyage to America.

1513 • **VASCO NUNEZ DE BALBOA** sighted the Pacific Ocean.

1690 • **AMERICA'S FIRST NEWSPAPER,** *Publick Occurrences,* was published.

1882 • **THE FIRST MAJOR LEAGUE DOUBLEHEADER** was played between the Providence and Worcester teams.

1890 • Congress established **YOSEMITE NATIONAL PARK** in California.

1981 • **SANDRA DAY O'CONNOR** was sworn in as the nation's first woman Supreme Court justice.

1988 • **THE DAY BUTTERFLY CENTER** in Pine Mountain, Ga., opened.

• **THE FIRST CHILDREN'S BANK—** the first bank especially for kids—opened at the F.A.O. Schwarz toy store in New York City.

EMERGENCY CARE MONTH

Claim game

Four days after sighting it from a mountain peak, Vasco Nunez de Balboa waded into the Pacific Ocean with his sword drawn and symbolically claimed it for Spain. Who do your students think owns the Pacific Ocean? Ask them to put themselves in the place of the native peoples living along the coast, whose ancestors had probably named the ocean thousands of years before Balboa arrived. Have your students write to Balboa in care of the king of Spain and explain the "mistake" that Balboa made. Then ask your students to list places that have yet to be "claimed" by a country. Who do they think has the right to claim these places?

Budget blast

Celebrate the opening of The First Children's Bank with a math game for teams of three to five students. Give each team a catalog and see which one can select the greatest number of items without exceeding $100. Next, instruct the teams to pick the fewest number of items totaling $100.

Lifesavers

September is Emergency Care Month. Discuss emergency situations that have occurred in the classroom, at recess, on the bus, at home. Then have teams design charts that provide the telephone numbers of the local police, fire department, and ambulance corps. The charts should also include illustrated steps to take in the event of an emergency.

SEPTEMBER 26
activities

BIRTHDAYS

1774 • **JOHNNY APPLESEED** (real name: John Chapman), American pioneer, farmer, and folk hero

1898 • **GEORGE GERSHWIN,** American composer noted for such works as *Rhapsody in Blue* and *Porgy and Bess,* the most popular opera ever written by an American

1985 • **SHAMU,** the first killer whale born in captivity

EVENTS

1580 • **SIR FRANCIS DRAKE** returned from his round-the-world voyage, the second such trip in history.

1772 • **THE NEW JERSEY COLONY** made it illegal to practice medicine without a license.

1789 • Thomas Jefferson was appointed the **FIRST SECRETARY OF STATE.**
      • John Jay was appointed the **FIRST CHIEF JUSTICE** of the United States.

1907 • **NEW ZEALAND** became a self-governing dominion within the British Commonwealth.

1926 • The St. Louis Browns beat the New York Yankees in the **SHORTEST NINE-INNING AMERICAN LEAGUE BASEBALL GAME.** It lasted 55 minutes.

1988 • Marc Batard finished his **CLIMB OF MT. EVEREST** in record time—$22\frac{1}{2}$ hours.

Animal groups
Killer whales, which can reach 31 feet in length and weigh 11,000 pounds, are known for their striking black and white coloration. They prey on seals, walrus, dolphins, fish, and squid, and their conical teeth are designed for grasping and tearing food. Killer whales hunt in packs—called pods. Ask your students to list collective nouns—such as a pride of lions, a gang of elk, a litter of pups, a gaggle of geese—for other animals.

Record-setters
Marc Batard climbed Mt. Everest alone and without oxygen. Ask your students to use record books to find facts and other records about Mt. Everest. Then have them list other time-based records that caught their eye. What do they think motivates people to break records like these? Use the discussion as a way to help kids set personal goals for the year. Make a chart with Mt. Everest as the backdrop on which students can list their school goals. Encourage them to refer to it as they progress.

SEPTEMBER 27
activities

BIRTHDAYS

1722 • **SAMUEL ADAMS, American revolutionary patriot**

1840 • **THOMAS NAST, American political cartoonist who popularized the Democratic donkey and the Republican elephant symbols**

1924 • **BERNARD WABER, children's author**

1956 • **MARTIN HANDFORD, children's author and creator of Waldo**

EVENTS

1777 • **LANCASTER, PA., became the capital of the United States for a day.**

1825 • **In England A LOCOMOTIVE was used for the first time to pull a passenger train.**

1904 • **A woman was ARRESTED FOR SMOKING A CIGARETTE in New York City.**

1937 • **THE FIRST SANTA CLAUS SCHOOL opened.**

1979 • **Congress approved the creation of the DEPARTMENT OF EDUCATION.**

1986 • **PARAPLEGIC JIM MCGOWAN attempted to swim the English Channel.**

1988 • **Canadian sprinter Ben Johnson became the FIRST OLYMPIC GOLD MEDALIST TO BE DISQUALIFIED for illegal drug use.**

✵ Keep on tracking

To commemorate the first use of a locomotive to pull a passenger train, ask children to bring in toy trains, books about trains, or pictures of trains. Have the kids describe similarities and differences between trains of different eras. Then read aloud a railroad folktale about John Henry.

☞ Nast-y

Thomas Nast's political cartoons were so effective that President Lincoln called him the North's "best recruiting sergeant." Celebrate this talented cartoonist by having your students examine current political cartoons from the editorial pages of the local newspaper. What or who are the subjects of these cartoons? How have the cartoonists exaggerated their subjects? Invite the kids to select a current issue and depict their feelings about it in a political cartoon.

⟂ Channel challenge

Ask your students to find the English Channel in their atlases. Where do they think most swimmers cross? Why? (The narrowest point—21 miles—is between Dover and Cape Gris-Nez.) Have the kids use their calculators to figure out how many times they'd need to walk up and down the hall or around the school parking lot or gym to equal 21 miles.

SEPTEMBER 28
activities

 Marathon maps

According to legend, a Greek soldier ran 26 miles from Marathon to Athens to inform people of the Greeks' defeat of the Persians. Have your students use their atlases to check the distance of the alleged run. Then have them use an almanac to find out the host cities for the 10 most recent Olympics, and locate the cities on a map.

Tickling funny bones

As a tribute to Al Capp, creator of the comic strip "Li'l Abner," ask your students to share their favorite comic strip. Have them examine the comic strips in small groups, then compile a list of what they think makes one successful and humorous. What are some possible subjects for their own comic strips?

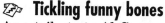 Skate stats

In the United States, over 30 million people roller-skate each year. Have your students use their calculators to find out what percentage of the total U.S. population this figure represents. Then see how many students in the class have roller-skated in the past year. What percentage of the class is represented? How does this compare with the national statistic?

BIRTHDAYS

1839 • **FRANCES ELIZABETH WILLARD,** American reformer and women's rights advocate

1909 • **AL CAPP,** creator of the comic strip "Li'l Abner"

EVENTS

490 BC • **A GREEK SOLDIER RAN 26 MILES** from Marathon to Athens with news of the Greek victory over the invading Persians. This is how the word *marathon* originated.

1781 • American soldiers under George Washington began the **SIEGE OF YORKTOWN,** the last major battle of the Revolutionary War.

1869 • Aristide Berges became the first person to transform a waterfall's **MECHANICAL ENERGY INTO ELECTRICAL ENERGY.**

1892 • **THE FIRST NIGHT FOOTBALL GAME** took place.

1919 • New York beat Philadelphia, 6-1, in the **SHORTEST NINE-INNING MAJOR LEAGUE BASE-BALL GAME.** It lasted just 51 minutes.

ROLLER SKATING WEEK (last full week in Sept.)

28

SEPTEMBER 29
activities

BIRTHDAYS

1758 • HORATIO NELSON, British admiral

1901 • ENRICO FERMI, Italian-American physicist who produced the first sustained nuclear chain reaction

1923 • STAN BERENSTAIN, children's author and illustrator, cocreator of the Berenstain Bears

EVENTS

1650 • THE FIRST MARRIAGE BUREAU was established in London.

1789 • The United States established a REGULAR ARMY with a strength of 700 men.

1829 • SCOTLAND YARD was established.

1988 • Stacy Allison became the FIRST AMERICAN WOMAN TO CLIMB MT. EVEREST.
• THE U.S. MINT issued coins to commemorate the launch of the shuttle *Discovery*.

1990 • Construction was completed on the WASHINGTON NATIONAL CATHEDRAL.

⊕ Wordplay addresses

Tell your students that the cable address of Scotland Yard—the headquarters of London's metropolitan police—is "Handcuffs, London." What other cable addresses can they invent for other famous places? (How about "U.S. Boss" for the White House?)

📖 Writing tips

Stan Berenstain, coauthor of the beloved Berenstain Bears series, believes in the importance of getting young readers excited about books. He and his wife, Jan, try to make things perfectly clear to the reader. They realize that "learning to read well is a difficult job, and most children need all the help they can get." Ask your students to think about books they enjoy reading. Can they picture the scenes in their minds? Then have them take out the piece they're writing. What can they do to make it clearer to readers?

✺ Commemorative coins

Children from the Young Astronauts Council designed coins to commemorate the space shuttle *Discovery,* the first shuttle launched after the *Challenger* tragedy. The gold coin shows a space shuttle in flight, the silver coin depicts an astronaut on the moon, and the bronze coin shows a shuttle combined with a section of the American flag. Ask your class to name some recent events that might merit the minting of special coins. Have the kids draw up some plans.

SEPTEMBER 30
activities

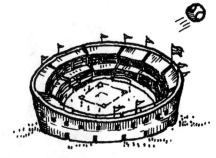

 Community close-up

William Penn was the owner of the largest land area, Pennsylvania, ever held by one citizen. In 1681 he wrote a letter describing the layout of Philadelphia, his "City Beautiful." He wanted to convince others to move to his colony. Have your students make a list of reasons why people might want to live in their community.

⚗ Tooth truth

Divide your students into cooperative groups. Give each group a large construction paper tooth on which to draw pictures that illustrate good dental care.

⁂ Frisbee free-for-all

Take a break from your routine—and celebrate the Frisbee—with some outdoor activities. Set up a variety of events, such as a long-distance Frisbee throw and a toss-the-Frisbee-through-the-Hula-Hoop game. You could also blindfold a student, have another child toss the Frisbee, and ask others in the group to direct the blindfolded child to the fallen disk. When your students get back inside, ask them to describe or draw a toy of the future. In what ways is it similar to and different from today's toys?

BIRTHDAYS

1861 • **WILLIAM WRIGLEY, founder of the Wrigley Chewing Gum Co.**

1882 • **HANS GEIGER, coinventor of the Geiger counter**

1916 • **ALVIN TRESSELT, children's author**

EVENTS

1681 • **WILLIAM PENN wrote a letter describing the layout of Philadelphia, his "City Beautiful."**

1841 • **Samuel Slocum patented THE STAPLER. He called it a "machine for sticking pins into paper."**

1846 • **William Morton became the first dentist to extract a tooth with the help of ANESTHESIA.**

1927 • **BABE RUTH hit his record-setting 60th home run of the season in New York's Yankee Stadium. The record lasted 34 years.**

1958 • **THE FRISBEE was patented.**

1960 • **"THE FLINTSTONES" debuted on television.**

1963 • **A GERENUK (a member of the antelope family) was first born in the United States.**

OCTOBER

☆ Project of the Month: Family History Awareness Festival

Celebrate Family History Awareness Month with a project that involves kids, parents, and grandparents. Give each student a world map and some "peel-and-stick" colored dots. Have the students interview their parents or grandparents about their countries, regions, cities, or towns of origin. Also have the kids find out where other family milestones took place, such as where they and their siblings were born or where their parents and grandparents were married. They should mark each location of interest on their map with a colored dot, then explain its significance on an accompanying paper. (Some kids might want to write numbers on the dots so they can easily refer to the corresponding descriptions.) Throughout the month, students can "dig" into their family's "geohistory" by gathering stories, photos, memorabilia, videos, letters, postage stamps, wedding or christening announcements, and background on the sites marked on their map. In addition, have the kids work with an older family member to develop a family tree that includes, when possible, birthplaces and approximate birth dates.

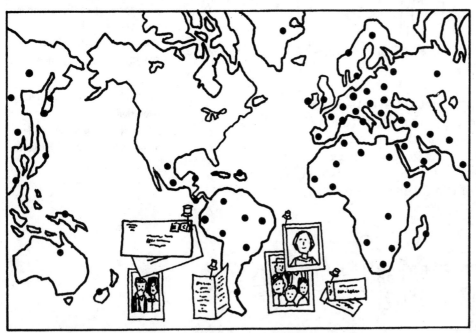

At the end of the month, invite parents, grandparents, and other family members to a Family History Awareness Festival in your classroom. Have volunteers bring in traditional family foods to share while the guests peruse the maps and displayed items.

EXTENDER: Encourage students and their families to repeat this project with a nursing-home resident or with someone who frequents a neighborhood senior center.

MONTHLONG OBSERVANCES

Apple Month
Clock Month
Computer Learning Month
Dessert Month
Family History Awareness Month
Kid's Fitness Month
National Pizza Month
National Stamp Month
Popcorn Poppin' Month
Pretzel Month

WEEKLONG EVENTS

Fire Prevention Week (first full week)
National Metric Week (first full week)
National Newspaper Week (first full week)
National School Lunch Week (begins with the second Sunday)
International Letter Writing Week (second week)
National Pet Peeve Week (second full week)
Dental Hygiene Week (third week)
Magic Week (Halloween week)
National Cleaner Air Week (last full week)
Peace, Friendship, and Goodwill Week (last week)

SPECIAL DAYS AND CELEBRATIONS

Child Health Day (first Monday)
Columbus Day (Oct. 12)
National Storytelling Festival (second weekend)
The World Series
Great Teddy Bear Jamboree (third weekend)
Sweetest Day (third Saturday)
Mother-in-Law's Day (fourth Sunday)
Standard time resumes (last Sunday)
Halloween (Oct 31)

OCTOBER 1
activities

※ Confounded collectors

Tell your students these unusual words for collectors of different things: deltiologist (postcards), numismatist (coins), comiconomen-caricaturist (funny names of people), bibliophile (books). Have students investigate the root words for these terms. Next, ask them what *they* collect. Is there a special term for people with those collections? If not, what words can your class make up? For example, how about "fluffacritterologist" for the person who collects stuffed animals?

✐ Variations on a theme park

Disney World boasts many special areas, called "lands," where all the rides, attractions, and characters follow a theme. These areas include Fantasyland, Frontierland, and Tomorrowland. What new "lands" would your students want to include? How about "Retroland," with a back-in-time theme? Or "Computoland," where computers do everything? Invite the kids to draw and write about their suggested new "land."

✎ Menu check

Ask your students to list all the foods they eat in a day. Tell them to include everything—even the butter or mustard they put on a sandwich. Then have them circle the items that a vegetarian would eat. Remind them that a true vegetarian doesn't eat any foods that come from animals—including eggs, milk, ice cream, mayonnaise, cheese, and soups with beef stock. What did the kids learn about the kinds of foods they're eating? What foods might appear on a vegetarian menu? Compile a meatless recipe book.

BIRTHDAYS

1781 • JAMES LAWRENCE, U.S. naval captain remembered for his exhortation "Don't give up the ship"

1924 • JIMMY CARTER, 39th president of the United States

EVENTS

1814 • "THE STAR-SPANGLED BANNER" was sung for the first time.

1847 • American astronomer MARIA MITCHELL discovered a comet that was later named after her.

1869 • PRESTAMPED POSTCARDS were
※ first put on sale.

1903 • THE FIRST WORLD SERIES began as the Boston Pilgrims hosted the Pittsburgh Pirates.

1940 • THE PENNSYLVANIA TURNPIKE, the nation's first superhighway, opened.

1961 • ROGER MARIS of the New York Yankees hit his 61st home run of the season, breaking the record held by Babe Ruth.

1971 • WALT DISNEY WORLD opened in
✐ Lake Buena Vista, Fla.

1978 • Steve McKinney reached the HIGHEST SPEED FOR ANY SKIER on snow, 124.412 mph.

1982 • EPCOT CENTER at Walt Disney World opened.

✎ WORLD VEGETARIAN DAY

OCTOBER 2
activities

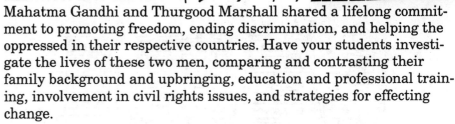

BIRTHDAYS

1800 • **NAT TURNER**, slave insurrection-
    ist
1869 • **MAHATMA GANDHI**, leader of
    the Indian independence move-
    ment
1890 • **GROUCHO MARX**, comedian
1950 • **CHARLIE BROWN**, cartoon char-
    acter

EVENTS

1535 • **French explorer JACQUES CARTI-
    ER landed at what is now
    Montreal.**
1810 • **THE FIRST HARVEST FAIR took
    place in Pittsfield, Mass.**
1866 • **THE FIRST TIN CAN WITH A KEY
    OPENER was patented by J.
    Osterhoudt in New York City.**
1967 • **THURGOOD MARSHALL became
    the first black justice on the U.S.
    Supreme Court.**
1988 • **Bobby McWaters and Ed
    Vantright completed 146.25
    HOURS OF NONSTOP TENNIS.**

    PREVENT-A-LITTER MONTH

Heroes near and far

Mahatma Gandhi and Thurgood Marshall shared a lifelong commit-
ment to promoting freedom, ending discrimination, and helping the
oppressed in their respective countries. Have your students investigate the lives of these two men, comparing and contrasting their
family background and upbringing, education and professional training, involvement in civil rights issues, and strategies for effecting
change.

"Peanuts" gallery

The first "Peanuts" comic strip appeared in just nine newspapers.
Today, the trials and tribulations of Charlie Brown, Lucy, Snoopy,
and Woodstock can be found in 2,000 papers worldwide. Challenge
your students to calculate the percent increase in the strip's distribution. Then ask them to follow the strip for a week. Have them list
any topics or ideas covered that have relevance to their lives. Invite
them to create their own comic-strip character based on one of the
topics or ideas they've listed.

Pet care

October is Prevent-A-Litter
Month, and here's a valuable
lesson for your students. Tell
the class that adult female
cats can have up to four litters
each year, with each litter
averaging about six kittens.
Then have the kids use calculators to do some figuring. To
find out how many kittens just
10 adult females could produce in a year, have them
punch in this sequence:
10×6×4. What ideas do your
students have to encourage
people to be more responsible
pet owners?

OCTOBER 3
activities

▤ Total fitness

George Bancroft is known as "the Father of American History" because he was the first American to write a history of the United States from its beginnings to the ratification of the Constitution. He also helped establish the United States Naval Academy at Annapolis. Tell your class that all students at the Naval Academy live by an honor code that says, "We will not lie, steal, or cheat, nor tolerate among us anyone who does." Then have your kids create an honor code for their classroom.

✐ What's in a name?

Chubby Checker, a rock-and-roll star of the 1950s, popularized a dance called the twist. His real name was Ernest Evans, but he wanted a catchy name that his audiences could easily remember. So he made up a name with repeating beginning sounds, or alliteration. Have your students give themselves an alliterative name for the day. What are the reasons for their choices?

✑ Yum!

Survey your class and make a list of the 15 favorite desserts. Make sure your students are specific—for example, "strawberry ice cream" instead of "ice cream," "chocolate chip cookies" instead of "cookies." Then divide the class into teams and have each team think of a way to organize the desserts. Some might do it by types of desserts—fruit, cake, dairy products. Others might use calories per serving or their own "luscious" rating. Have each team explain its model to the rest of the class.

BIRTHDAYS

1800 • GEORGE BANCROFT, American diplomat and historian called "the Father of American History"
1844 • SIR PATRICK MANSON, British physician who discovered the mosquito's role in the spread of malaria
1916 • JAMES HERRIOTT, author
1918 • MOLLY CONE, children's author
1941 • CHUBBY CHECKER (real name: Ernest Evans), rock-and-roll singer who found fame with "The Twist"

EVENTS

1632 • The Massachusetts Bay General Court forbade PUBLIC USE OF TOBACCO.
1851 • A BOA CONSTRICTOR at the London Zoo swallowed a blanket, which it disgorged more than 3 weeks later.
1951 • BOBBY THOMSON'S NINTH-INNING HOME RUN in the final playoff game against the Brooklyn Dodgers lifted the New York Giants to the National League pennant.
1990 • EAST AND WEST GERMANY were formally reunified after 45 years of division.

✑ DESSERT MONTH

OCTOBER 4
activities

BIRTHDAYS

1822 • RUTHERFORD B. HAYES, 19th president of the United States

1858 • MICHAEL I. PUPIN, American physicist and producer of the first X-ray photograph

1861 • FREDERIC REMINGTON, American painter of the western frontier

1905 • MUNRO LEAF, children's author 📖

EVENTS

1777 • George Washington's troops fought the British at THE BATTLE OF GERMANTOWN in Pennsylvania.

1824 • THE REPUBLIC OF MEXICO was proclaimed.

1915 • DINOSAUR NATIONAL MONUMENT was established in northwestern Colorado and northeastern Utah.

1931 • The comic strip "DICK TRACY" was first published by the New York *Daily News*.

1954 • CAPTAIN KANGAROO made his first TV appearance.

1957 • The Soviet Union launched *Sputnik I*, the FIRST MAN-MADE SATELLITE.

1987 • THE MALLARD FAMILY SCULPTURE, in honor of Robert McCloskey's story *Make Way for Ducklings*, was dedicated in Boston.

TEN-FOUR DAY

📖 Safety-first stick figures

Many of Munro Leaf's books—including *Manners Can Be Fun*—are illustrated with simple, childlike stick figures. Leaf commented, "I drew some scratchy pencil indications of what an artist was supposed to draw in the book and finally wound up by doing them myself." Leaf was surprised that "anybody would dignify them by calling them illustrations." Have your students use Leaf's stick-figure technique to make their own manners booklets, giving pointers on good behavior in various settings, such as a movie theater, restaurant, playground, or bus.

Honors to Mrs. Mallard

Robert McCloskey spent months studying ducks—even sharing his apartment and bathtub with them. The result was his award-winning picture book *Make Way for Ducklings*. A bronze sculpture commemorating Mrs. Mallard and her eight ducklings can be seen at the Boston Public Garden. What suggestions do your students have for commemorating their favorite animal stories?

Code capers

Celebrate Ten-Four Day—the fourth day of the tenth month. Tell your students that U.S. police have developed a series of codes—called the Ten Code—to stand for specific phrases. "Ten-four" means that a message was received and understood. Other codes include 10-31 (crime in progress) and 10-47 (road repair needed). When have your students used codes? Invite your students to develop their own codes and use them throughout Ten-Four Day.

OCTOBER 5
activities

⚗ Rocket launcher

As a boy, Robert Goddard dreamed of space travel. Later on, he made his dreams come true by devoting his life to rocket technology. Have your students make paper rockets by wrapping a 2×8-inch strip of paper tightly around a pencil to create a tube. They should tape their tube at a couple points before removing the pencil, then tape closed the point. After they add fins, they can launch their rockets by inserting a drinking straw into the open end and blowing. Your students might have suggestions for paper rocket contests, such as the farthest distance traveled, the highest trajectory, the best in-the-trash-can landing.

Robert Goddard was known as "the Father of the Space Age." As a research challenge, ask your students whom they would select as the father—or mother—of the automobile, electricity, blue jeans, basketball, television, the zoo, the Frisbee, the computer, and so on.

⚙ Savers

During the first presidential telecast from the White House, President Truman asked Americans to reduce their consumption of meat, eggs, and poultry—to build up stockpiles of grain for war-ravaged Europe. Have your students think of an item or items that they could "do without" for a day to help a cause. Perhaps you could include other classrooms in a plan to designate one day each month as Do-Without-for-a-Cause Day.

BIRTHDAYS

1829 • **CHESTER A. ARTHUR,** 21st president of the United States

1882 • **ROBERT GODDARD,** American ⚗ physicist and rocket pioneer, called "the Father of the Space Age"

1892 • **ROBERT LAWSON,** children's author

1924 • **DONALD SOBOL,** children's author

EVENTS

1502 • **CHRISTOPHER COLUMBUS** landed in modern-day Costa Rica.

1921 • **A WORLD SERIES GAME WAS FIRST BROADCAST ON RADIO.** The New York Giants beat the New York Yankees, 5-3.

1947 • President Harry Truman made ⚙ the **FIRST PRESIDENTIAL ADDRESS TELECAST** from the White House.

1953 • **EARL WARREN** was sworn in as the 14th chief justice of the United States.

1988 • President Ronald Reagan dedicated the cornerstone of the **UNITED STATES HOLOCAUST MEMORIAL MUSEUM.**

5

OCTOBER 6
activities

The world's greatest inventor

Thomas Edison's Kinetoscope projected a clearer, steadier image than other projectors and screen devices. During his lifetime, Edison developed an incredible number of inventions. Have your students graph his contributions according to the following categories: electronic light and power, 389; phonograph, 195; telegraph, 150; storage battery and related items, 141; ore separation, 62; telephone, 62; railroad, 26; motion pictures, 9; automobile, 8; mimeograph, 6; typewriter, 3.

Movie first

The Jazz Singer, called the first talking motion picture, was actually more silent than talking. Al Jolson, a popular singer who was the movie's star, belted out three songs and spoke the words "You ain't heard nothin' yet, folks," giving the film a total of 291 spoken words. The rest of the film was silent with captions. The first all-talking movie, *The Lights of New York,* came out the following year, 1928.

Tell your students that when *The Jazz Singer* premiered, some people predicted that talking pictures would never succeed. Similar views have been expressed about the automobile, the computer, and the automatic teller machine. Lead a discussion on why people often turn away from new ideas and technologies. Ask your students to list things that they believe won't become an accepted part of our culture.

OCTOBER 7
activities

✒ Peacemaker

Bishop Desmond Tutu was awarded the Nobel Peace Prize in 1984 for his role in the nonviolent campaign to end apartheid in South Africa. Discuss apartheid with your class. In what ways do your students think people are discriminated against in *this* country? What changes can the kids suggest?

🏴 Rosy pick

Before the rose was selected as the national flower, 70 bills proposing other flowers were introduced. How do your students feel about the choice of the rose? What flowers would they have suggested, and why? Have them prepare a brief informational report, with an illustration, for their nominations. Take a vote.

🍃 October delight

Celebrate Popcorn Poppin' Month by making a popcorn cake with your class. You'll need the following ingredients: 1 stick of margarine; ½ cup cooking oil; 1 cup miniature marshmallows; 1 cup small gumdrops; ½ cup shelled peanuts; 8 quarts popped popcorn. In one bowl, melt the margarine, add the oil, and stir in the marshmallows. In another bowl, mix the peanuts, gumdrops, and popcorn. Combine the marshmallow and popcorn mixtures and press firmly into two 9×13 greased pans. Bake at 350°. Enjoy the snack while you share Tomie dePaola's *The Popcorn Book*. As a journal assignment, have your students describe something new they learned about popcorn.

BIRTHDAYS

1849 • JAMES W. RILEY, author of *The Little Orphant Annie Book*

1893 • ALICE DALGLIESH, children's author

1931 • DESMOND TUTU, South African ✒ human-rights activist and Nobel Peace Prize winner

EVENTS

1765 • THE STAMP ACT CONGRESS convened in New York to draw up colonial grievances against Britain.

1911 • Only 66 people, the LOWEST PAID ATTENDANCE AT A MAJOR LEAGUE BASEBALL GAME, saw the St. Louis Browns play the Detroit Tigers.

1916 • Cumberland University suffered the WORST DEFEAT IN THE HISTORY OF INTERCOLLEGIATE FOOTBALL, losing to Georgia Tech by the score of 222-0.

1957 • The TV show "AMERICAN BANDSTAND," hosted by Dick Clark, premiered.

1968 • The motion picture industry adopted its FILM-RATING SYSTEM.

1986 • President Ronald Reagan signed 🏴 a bill making the rose our NATIONAL FLOWER.

🍃 POPCORN POPPIN' MONTH

OCTOBER 8
activities

BIRTHDAYS

1870 • **J. FRANK DURYEA**, coinventor of the gasoline-powered automobile

1890 • **EDDIE RICKENBACKER**, American aviator and World War I flying ace

1936 • **SUZANNE NEWTON**, children's author

1941 • **JESSE JACKSON**, American civil rights leader and politician

EVENTS

1871 • **THE GREAT CHICAGO FIRE**, which claimed 250 lives and destroyed most of the city, started in Mrs. O'Leary's barn.

• **THE MOST DISASTROUS FOREST FIRE** in recorded history destroyed Peshtigo, Wis., killing 1,182 people.

1895 • Engelbert Humperdinck's opera *HANSEL AND GRETEL* premiered in the United States.

1956 • Don Larsen of the New York Yankees pitched the **ONLY PERFECT GAME IN A WORLD SERIES** as New York beat the Brooklyn Dodgers, 2-0.

▤ Fire stoppers

The Great Chicago Fire destroyed 18,000 buildings and left 100,000 people homeless. Have your students identify potential fire hazards in their home and school. If any students don't have the local fire department's number on their home phone, have them write it on a self-adhesive label, take it home, and put it there.

▦ Fairy tales, opera style

Tell your students that an opera is a story told in song. Then play some of Engelbert Humperdinck's opera *Hansel and Gretel.* Have the kids select a favorite fairy tale or story and divide the plot into three acts. Challenge them to select popular music that would be appropriate for the plot, rewriting the lyrics if they want. Then they could perform the fairy tale as a puppet show for younger students.

✒ Believe and achieve

Reverend Jesse Jackson is an advocate for education and a promoter of positive self-esteem. When he speaks to children, he encourages them to repeat, "If I believe, then I can achieve." Have your students list their personal goals, then share them with a partner. Ask each pair to create its own "morale booster" saying.

⚾ A perfect day

In 1956 Don Larsen realized a baseball pitcher's ultimate dream when he pitched a perfect game. Invite your students to describe their perfect day. For some, this "day in the sun" might already have happened. For others, it might be a cherished dream.

OCTOBER 9
activities

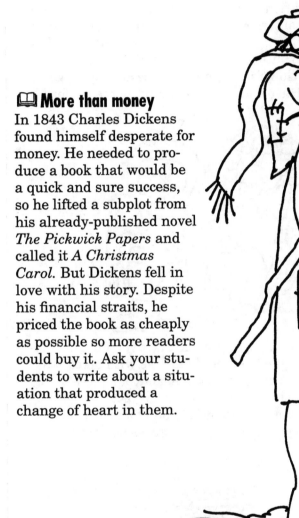

📖 More than money
In 1843 Charles Dickens found himself desperate for money. He needed to produce a book that would be a quick and sure success, so he lifted a subplot from his already-published novel *The Pickwick Papers* and called it *A Christmas Carol*. But Dickens fell in love with his story. Despite his financial straits, he priced the book as cheaply as possible so more readers could buy it. Ask your students to write about a situation that produced a change of heart in them.

BIRTHDAYS
1937 • **JOHANNA HURWITZ**, children's author
1940 • **JOHN LENNON**, English musician, singer, songwriter, and member of the Beatles rock group

EVENTS
1492 • **COLUMBUS PROMISED HIS CAPTAINS** that he'd turn back if land wasn't spotted within 3 days.
1843 • Charles Dickens began writing 📖 *A CHRISTMAS CAROL*.
1888 • **THE WASHINGTON MONUMENT** opened.
1915 • The International Association for Criminal Identification, one of the first **FINGERPRINTING ORGANIZATIONS**, was established.

ALPHABET DAY (Korea)
NATIONAL SCHOOL LUNCH WEEK (week beginning with the second Sunday)

🔍 To fingerprint or not to fingerprint
Fingerprinting has been around for at least 3,000 years. The ancient Chinese used fingerprints as official seals on documents. More recently, law-enforcement agencies have used fingerprinting to identify crime suspects. Your students may be aware of an even-newer trend: Certain local police departments, parent groups, clubs, and schools have begun fingerprinting children to help locate these children should they become missing. Some people feel this is a violation of children's civil rights, especially if the prints are controlled by an official agency. What do your students think? Have them list pros and cons—and alternatives.

OCTOBER 10
activities

BIRTHDAYS
1813 • **GIUSEPPE VERDI**, Italian composer of operas
1909 • **JOHNNY MARKS**, composer of "Rudolph the Red-Nosed Reindeer"
1942 • **JAMES MARSHALL**, children's author

EVENTS
1826 • **DAVY CROCKETT** was elected to the House of Representatives.
1845 • **THE U.S. NAVAL ACADEMY** was founded in Annapolis, Md.

1886 • Englishman Griswold Lorillard introduced **THE TUXEDO** in Tuxedo Park, N.Y.
1899 • **THE LUGGAGE CARRIER** was patented by John Butts.
1935 • **GEORGE GERSHWIN'S PORGY AND BESS** opened on Broadway.
1976 • Dimitrion Yordanidis of Greece became the **OLDEST MAN TO COMPLETE A MARATHON.** He was 98.
1985 • **HUMPHREY THE HUMPBACK WHALE** entered San Francisco Bay. He stayed for 26 days before finding his way back to the ocean.

✿ Costume party
Instead of wearing the traditional white tie and dress coat with tails, Griswold Lorillard wore a tailless jacket and a scarlet satin vest to a ball in Tuxedo Park, N.Y. This new look was dubbed the tuxedo. Ask your students to think of an outfit they'd like to rent for a day. It might be a suit of armor, a clown's costume, a spacesuit, scuba gear, or a fire fighter's uniform. Have each child explain the reason for his selection in his journal.

🔦 In the bag
Years ago, the bicycle was an important mode of travel. For this reason, the luggage carrier, designed especially for use with bikes, was quite popular. Have each student sketch the outline of a piece of luggage and inside draw four items a favorite book character might pack. Divide the class into groups, and have group members take turns showing their drawings while the others guess who would carry the luggage.

📖 Illustrator's comeback
When James Marshall was in 2nd grade, his teacher laughed at his artwork. Embarrassed and disheartened, he quit drawing. (He later modeled his character Viola Swamp after this unsympathetic teacher.) Marshall started drawing again while teaching high school. Soon after, George and Martha, the Stupids, Miss Nelson, and other popular characters were born. What do your students think makes an illustration appealing? Invite them to show some of their favorites.

OCTOBER 11
activities

✿ Historical fiction

Your students might not have heard of Parson Weems, but they've certainly heard of his work. He presented fictitious stories as historical fact and is responsible for the tale of George Washington chopping down his father's cherry tree. This legend, or yarn, wasn't based on fact, yet it became a part of every schoolchild's knowledge. Ask your class to suggest how the expression "to spin a yarn" might have originated. (In the lexicon of sailors, the task of repairing rope was referred to as "spinning," and "yarn" was the term for "rope." To pass the time while doing this laborious task, sailors would tell stories.)

🖋 Famous First Lady

In *This Is My Story*, Eleanor Roosevelt wrote, "No one can make you feel inferior without your consent." Ask your class what she meant by that remark. Can your students remember when someone damaged their self-confidence or tried to put them down? How did they feel, and what did they do about it?

As a young girl, Eleanor Roosevelt was extremely shy. When have your students felt that way? What did they do to overcome their shyness?

📰 Concocted quiz

Legend has it that in the late 1700s, an Irishman named Jim Daly bet that he could introduce a completely meaningless word within 24 hours. He hired local children to chalk the word *quiz* all over Dublin. Daly won his bet: Dubliners were buzzing about the strange word for days. Challenge your students to find the stories behind these words: *denim, honeymoon, sideburns.*

BIRTHDAYS

1759 • **PARSON WEEMS** (full name: ✿ Mason Locke Weems), clergyman and bookseller who popularized legends about George Washington

1844 • **HENRY JOHN HEINZ**, food-products manufacturer

1884 • **ELEANOR ROOSEVELT**, humani-🖋 tarian and wife of Franklin D. Roosevelt

EVENTS

1868 • Thomas Edison applied for a patent for his first invention, an **ELECTRIC VOTE RECORDER.**

1887 • The first **ADDING-MACHINE PATENT** was issued.

1910 • Theodore Roosevelt became the **FIRST PRESIDENT TO FLY** in an airplane.

1936 • "Professor Quiz," the FIRST 📰 **NATIONAL QUIZ PROGRAM** on radio, premiered.

1963 • **ELEANOR ROOSEVELT** became the first First Lady to appear on a commemorative postage stamp.

1984 • Kathy Sullivan became the FIRST **AMERICAN WOMAN TO WALK IN SPACE.**

OCTOBER 12
activities

Consider Columbus

As your class studies Christopher Columbus, have your students keep a two-column chart. In one column, they should put any information that supports the view of Columbus as a master mariner; in the other, any information that bolsters the view of him as a pirate and plunderer. Ask your students to combine their facts to make a master chart for the entire class. Then set up debate teams and have the kids use the chart as they develop their strategies.

Singer, and so much more

Luciano Pavarotti was born in Modena, a small town in northern Italy. Have your class locate his birthplace on a world map. Your students might be surprised that this world-famous tenor was an all-around athlete whose favorite sport was soccer. Have each student vote for his favorite sport on a slip of paper. Collect the papers, then ask the kids to guess how many classmates voted for soccer. Who came closest?

Home of the bard

The Globe Theatre, the largest open-air theater in London, held about 2,500 people. Shakespeare's plays appealed to a diverse audience, so the theater was built to accommodate members of the upper and lower classes. Ordinary people stood in the "pit" area below the stage, while the wealthy sat in tiered galleries. Do your students think they live in a society that has a class system? Why or why not?

OCTOBER 13
activities

 Junior architects

James Hoban was the architect whose design was selected for the Executive Mansion, now called the White House. Divide your class into teams charged with suggesting changes to your classroom's design. Invite each team to present its ideas—and reasoning—to you and the rest of the class. How does everyone feel about the various suggestions?

✿ New perspective

Have your students pretend they're in a balloon hovering above the school. What would the building look like? What about the shrubs and trees? The jungle gym and swings? Students at play during recess? Challenge the kids to draw an aerial view of the school. Then have them discuss their illustrations in small groups.

 Who's the boss?

Margaret Thatcher was the first woman to become prime minister of Britain. The United States has never had a woman president. Do your students think that might change someday? How do they feel about the possibility? Have your class discuss whether a woman chief executive might have a different perspective on certain issues, such as education, war, drug abuse, jobs, environmental protection, medical insurance, and homelessness. Did your class uncover any biases or prejudices during this discussion? Ask your students to write an essay about having a woman as president.

A WOMAN FOR PRESIDENT

BIRTHDAYS

1754 • **MOLLY PITCHER** (real name: Mary Ludwig Hays), Revolutionary War heroine

1769 • **HORACE HAYDEN,** founder of the first dental college

1925 • **MARGARET THATCHER,** prime minister of Great Britain

EVENTS

1775 • The Continental Congress ordered construction of a naval fleet, thereby launching the **AMERICAN NAVY.**

1792 • Construction began on the **WHITE HOUSE.**

1860 • The **FIRST AERIAL PHOTOGRAPH** of part of the United States was taken from a balloon over Boston.

1903 • Boston defeated Pittsburgh in the **FIRST WORLD SERIES.**

1913 • **THE NATIONAL SAFETY COUNCIL** was organized.

1932 • The cornerstone was laid for the **SUPREME COURT BUILDING.**

1982 • The International Olympic Committee announced its decision to restore the two gold medals won by **JIM THORPE** at the 1912 Olympics.

1988 • The United Nations sponsored a "BEARLIFT," flying donated teddy bears to orphaned children in South America.

OCTOBER 14
activities

Nicknames

Theodore Roosevelt had many nicknames, including Bull Moose, Driving Force, Dynamo of Power, Four Eyes, Man on Horseback, Old Lion, T.R., Hero of San Juan Hill, and Meddler. Challenge your students to find out the origins of these nicknames. Then invite them to share the stories behind *their* nicknames.

Pooh party!

Celebrate the debut of Winnie the Pooh with a theme party. Invite your kids to make Pooh-related decorations. Encourage them to bring a stuffed Pooh character or a favorite stuffed animal dressed like Pooh or one of his friends from the Hundred Acre Wood. Read one of the Pooh stories while your students enjoy a special snack, such as Kanga Kupcakes or Piglet's Popcorn.

Up and away

Major Charles E. Yeager became the first person to travel faster than the speed of sound. His flight, at an altitude of 43,000 feet above sea level, was clocked at 700 mph. How does that speed compare with the speed of a jogger, a bicycle rider, an Indy 500 race car, and a charging rhinoceros? Tell your students that the first time Yeager flew, he got very sick. But he loved the feel of flight so much that he forced himself to overcome this sensitivity. Did any of your students keep plugging away at something until they got better at it? Invite them to share their personal stories.

OCTOBER 15
activities

 **Balloon ride**

Ask your students to find out the difference between a hot-air balloon and a dirigible. (A dirigible has a hard internal framework and is kept aloft by lighter-than-air gases, whereas a hot-air balloon relies on heated air and does not have an infrastructure.)

Trillion tickler

Here's how to make 293 trillion more comprehensible to your students. Have them use calculators to determine their approximate age in days, then in hours, then in minutes. When they figure out their age in seconds, they'll be working with numbers in the hundreds of millions! Challenge them to figure out how many years old they'd be at one trillion seconds. (319.7.) Can anyone figure out how many round trips to the sun would equal 293 trillion miles? (5,376 trips.) For younger students, pass out 12 large zeroes plus a one and have them line up to form one trillion.

Big birds

You'd expect to find ostriches—the world's largest living birds—in Africa, but how about in Oklahoma? When profits from traditional farm products such as cattle and wheat dropped, some ranchers in southern Oklahoma turned to a new industry—ostriches. Getting started isn't cheap; people have spent up to $10,000 for one breeding pair. Ostrich meat tastes like a combination of pork and turkey, and ostrich hide is used to make boots, gloves, and purses. Do your students believe that ostriches really stick their heads in sand? Ask them to list other animal myths.

BIRTHDAYS

1608 • **EVANGELISTA TORRICELLI,** Italian mathematician and physicist who developed the barometer

1942 • **BEATRICE GORMLEY,** children's author

1953 • **TITO JACKSON,** American singer

EVENTS

1789 • **GEORGE WASHINGTON** began a 29-day tour of the country. He traveled by coach throughout New England.

1928 • The German dirigible *GRAF ZEPPELIN* arrived in the United States on its first commercial flight.

1984 • The first **PHOTOGRAPHIC EVIDENCE OF ANOTHER SOLAR SYSTEM** was displayed by astronomers in Pasadena, Calif. This solar system is estimated to be 293 trillion miles from earth.

1986 • The **OKIE OSTRICH RANCH** opened in Marlow, Okla.

1990 • **MIKHAIL GORBACHEV** won the Nobel Peace Prize.

NATIONAL GROUCH DAY
WHITE CANE SAFETY DAY
WORLD POETRY DAY (in honor of the poet Virgil's birthday)

15

OCTOBER 16
activities

16

Mr. Dictionary

After about 6 years of work, Noah Webster published his first dictionary, *A Compendious Dictionary of the English Language*. It contained 37,000 entries, including almost 5,000 new words. Among these new entries were "skunk," "hickory," "chowder," and "applesauce." Recent dictionaries have included "ain't," "radar," and "litterbug." Ask your students to develop a list of new words that might not appear in the latest edition of the dictionary. How about new terms used in science and technology, such as "dark matter," "brown dwarf," or "palmtop" (computer)? And what about slang words, such as "heavy metal" or "retro"? Make a class list of these words and have your students write their own definitions.

Stopping hunger near and far

In order to call attention to the issues of hunger, poverty, and malnutrition, the Food and Agriculture Organization of the United Nations established World Food Day. Ask your students to list possible reasons why many countries in the world can't produce enough food to feed their people. What ideas do the kids have for helping hungry families in their community?

OCTOBER 17
activities

Helping hands

Mother Teresa's religious order, the Missionaries of Charity, provides food, shelter, and medical care for the needy in about 30 countries. Ask the kids to comment on the saying "Charity begins at home." What are some suggestions they have for helping the less fortunate of their community?

Earthquake sense

In the future, seismologists hope to be able to predict earthquakes. They have identified three signs that frequently portend a major quake: The water level in the area changes; small earthquakes occur; and animals behave in strange ways. Encourage your students to investigate how dogs and farm animals behave before earthquakes.

Gone to the bears

The Great Teddy Bear Jamboree is celebrated the third weekend in October. How about holding a jamboree in your classroom? Have the kids write an invitation to their favorite stuffed animal. Pass a bear-filled morning reading bear books—both fiction and nonfiction. Have the students compare and contrast the foods, habitats, and habits of different species of bears.

Kindness is contagious!

Sweetest Day began when a resident of Cleveland, Ohio, decided to help some of the underprivileged in his community. He delivered small gifts to orphans and shut-ins. The idea soon spread to other communities, with people remembering both friends and the less fortunate with small gifts and kindnesses. Celebrate Sweetest Day by having each student secretly draw a classmate's name and do whatever possible to show that child special kindness.

BIRTHDAYS

1912 • POPE JOHN PAUL I (Albino Luciani), head of the Roman Catholic church for only 34 days

1938 • EVEL KNIEVEL, motorcycle daredevil

EVENTS

1855 • The English engineer Sir Henry Bessemer patented his STEEL-MAKING PROCESS.

1933 • ALBERT EINSTEIN ARRIVED IN THE UNITED STATES as a refugee from Nazi Germany.

1960 • RACIAL INTEGRATION OF VARIETY-STORE LUNCH COUNTERS began in more than 100 Southern cities.

1974 • The Oakland A's won their THIRD STRAIGHT WORLD SERIES.

1979 • MOTHER TERESA was awarded the Nobel Peace Prize for 30 years of work on behalf of the destitute in Calcutta, India.

1984 • President Reagan launched the YOUNG ASTRONAUTS PROGRAM.

1989 • THE LOMA PRIETA EARTHQUAKE hit San Francisco, registering 7.1 on the Richter scale.

GREAT TEDDY BEAR JAMBOREE (third weekend)

SWEETEST DAY (third Saturday)

OCTOBER 18
activities

Women's rights advocate

Even as a young girl, Lucy Stone was aware of the unequal status of women. When she married Henry Blackwell in 1855, she became the first woman to keep her maiden name. Nowadays, many women choose not to use their husband's last name. They're called "lucy stoners." Can your students think of other common nouns based on personal names?

Queen of the court

Tennis superstar Martina Navratilova was born in Prague, Czechoslovakia. Have your students locate her birthplace on a world map. In 1981 she became a citizen of the United States. A year later she became the first woman to earn more than $1 million from tennis prize winnings. She has since set up the Martina Foundation in order to share some of her wealth with poor children. Do your students think that wealthy people have an obligation to share their fortunes with others? Why or why not?

Mr. October et al

Reggie Jackson was called Mr. October. Ask your students why this nickname was appropriate. Then have them think of other baseball players' nicknames—for example, the Sultan of Swat (Babe Ruth), the Say Hey Kid (Willie Mays), the Splendid Splinter (Ted Williams), the Iron Horse (Lou Gehrig). Have the kids draw a picture that illustrates a baseball nickname literally. For example, an illustration of Dwight Gooden's nickname, Dr. K, might show the letter *K* adorned with a stethoscope and surgical mask.

OCTOBER 19
activities

💡 Sandwiches then and now

In ancient times, the Romans put meat and other foods between pieces of bread. They called their treat "offula." The word *sandwich* caught on when James Montagu, the earl of Sandwich, began eating meat on bread during his card games. Have your students think of interesting—and healthful—sandwich combinations.

🎲 Child adviser

While campaigning for the presidency, Abraham Lincoln received baskets of mail every day. And he took the advice of 11-year-old Grace Bedell, whose letter suggested that he grow a beard because "your face is so thin" and "the ladies like whiskers." After the election, Lincoln stopped in Westfield, N.Y., to meet his young adviser. Ask your students why Lincoln is such a recognizable president. Which other presidents are physically distinctive? Then compare political cartoons with photos of today's leaders. How do the cartoonists make their subjects so recognizable?

⚗ Rocket man

When Robert Goddard was a boy, he'd climb an oak tree at night, look at the moon, and imagine he could travel there on a rocket. His imagination was fired by two of H.G. Wells's books, *First Men on the Moon* and *War of the Worlds,* which were filled with imaginative predictions of space travel. Invite your students to share book titles and stories that have fired their imaginations.

BIRTHDAYS

1931 • ED EMBERLEY, children's illustrator

EVENTS

1744 • THE EARL OF SANDWICH, inventor of the sandwich, told friends in London, "Sandwiches should be eaten with a civilized swallow, not a barbarous bolt."

1752 • Benjamin Franklin proved that LIGHTNING IS ELECTRICITY.

1781 • GENERAL CORNWALLIS SURRENDERED AT YORKTOWN, marking the end of the Revolutionary War.

1814 • THE STAR-SPANGLED BANNER WAS SUNG FOR THE FIRST TIME, in Baltimore, Md.

1860 • AN 11-YEAR-OLD ADVISED PRESIDENT LINCOLN to grow a beard.

1873 • FOOTBALL RULES were formulated in New York City.

1899 • Robert Goddard, at 17, began to speculate in his journal about A SPACESHIP THAT COULD TRAVEL TO MARS.

1983 • The U.S. Senate passed a bill making the BIRTHDAY OF MARTIN LUTHER KING, JR., a federal holiday.

19

OCTOBER 20
activities

⌀ Mickey across the curriculum

Tell your students that the bases on a baseball diamond are arranged 90 feet apart in a square. Have the kids use their calculators to figure out how far a player must run after hitting a home run. Next, tell them that Mickey Mantle hit 536 career home runs, and have them compute the total distance he ran after hitting these homers.

Mantle was a switch hitter, which means he batted right- and left-handed. Have students try various tasks using their dominant hand, then their nondominant hand. Which tasks were hardest to do equally well with both hands? Which were easiest?

Mantle moved from his birthplace, Spavinaw, Okla., to Commerce, Okla., when he was 3 years old. Commerce has since named its main street after him. What streets in your students' hometown are named for local heroes? If your kids could name a street in their town after someone, whom would they choose, and why?

⬱ Pizza fractions

Divide your class into small groups, giving each group an 8-inch construction-paper circle. Have the groups fold their "pizza" circle to create four equal parts. Next, have them cut 16 small circles to represent pepperoni, and 24 shapes for shredded cheese, 8 for green pepper bits, and 12 for mushrooms. Tell the groups to place one-quarter of each ingredient on each quarter of their "pizza." Ask them how many pieces of each ingredient they'd eat as they consumed one-quarter, one-half, three-quarters, and finally the entire "pizza."

BIRTHDAYS

1632 • SIR CHRISTOPHER WREN, English architect

1859 • JOHN DEWEY, American philosopher and educator

1891 • SIR JAMES CHADWICK, English physicist who discovered the neutron

1931 • MICKEY MANTLE, baseball star

EVENTS

1873 • P.T. Barnum opened "THE GREATEST SHOW ON EARTH" at the Hippodrome in New York City.

1910 • A CORK-CENTER BASEBALL was used for the first time in a World Series game.

1964 • HERBERT HOOVER, 31st president of the United States, died at the age of 90.

1967 • Roger Patterson photographed what he claimed was BIGFOOT.

⬱ NATIONAL PIZZA MONTH

20

OCTOBER 21
activities

▦ With-it song

Give teams of students a copy of the lyrics to the patriotic song "America," written by Samuel Francis Smith. Challenge the teams to update these lyrics. Allow 10 to 15 minutes, then give each team a chance to sing its version. Invite the singers to perform different versions at your school's next assembly.

⬛ Museum in the round

Architect Frank Lloyd Wright used right angles in most of his building designs, but he was in a "circular mood" when he planned the Solomon R. Guggenheim Museum. Wright's finished design looked like a giant spiral sculpture. Show your students a picture of the Guggenheim Museum. Tell them that some people call the building a "giant snail," whereas others think it's "the most beautiful building in New York." How do your students feel? What other buildings or structures do they think of as giant works of art?

🍎 Appealing apples

Celebrate Apple Month by asking your class to share favorite apple stories, poems, songs, puns, jokes, and sayings. Then tell the kids that only about 20 of the more than 7,500 varieties of apples are grown in the United States. These include Golden Delicious, Granny Smith, pippin, Wealthy, Northern Spy, Rome Beauty, McIntosh, Delicious, Transparent, and Duchess. How many can your students name? Invite the kids to write a riddle about one of the varieties. For example, which apple wears a raincoat? (McIntosh.) Which apple would the Pope enjoy? (Rome Beauty.)

BIRTHDAYS

1808 • **SAMUEL FRANCIS SMITH,** American poet who wrote the words to the patriotic song "America"

1833 • **ALFRED NOBEL,** Swedish manufacturer, philanthropist, and inventor of dynamite

1944 • **JANET AHLBERG,** children's author

EVENTS

1520 • **FERDINAND MAGELLAN** entered the strait now called the Strait of Magellan.

1805 • Britain's Lord Horatio Nelson defeated the Franco-Spanish fleet at **TRAFALGAR** but was mortally wounded.

1879 • Thomas Edison successfully tested the **INCANDESCENT ELECTRIC LIGHT BULB.**

1929 • New York City established the **FIRST AIR AMBULANCE SERVICE.**

1959 • **THE GUGGENHEIM MUSEUM,** New York City's famous modern art museum, opened.

1976 • **FIVE NOBEL PRIZES**—in chemistry, economics, literature, medicine, and physics—were awarded to Americans.

🍎 **APPLE MONTH**

21

OCTOBER 22
activities

✇ Geronimo!
Hundreds of years ago, Chinese acrobats entertained crowds by jumping with parachutes made of paper and bamboo. In the late 15th century, Leonardo da Vinci sketched a pyramid-shaped parachute consisting of a large cloth fixed to a wooden framework supported by ropes. Today, skydiving is a popular sport. Divide your class into teams, and ask each team to make a list of sports, arranging them from most dangerous to least dangerous. Why are potentially dangerous sports popular?

⚡💡 Copy king
As a law student, Chester Carlson spent hours copying information from library books. And he worked in a patent office, where making multiple copies of patents was a laborious task. To find an easier way to get copies, he built his own laboratory and developed xerography. Years after investing in Carlson's process, the Haloid Company changed its name to Xerox Corporation. The corporation is proud of its name and history and objects when people use "xerox" as a synonym for "photocopy." How do your students feel about Xerox's point of view? Can they think of other trade names—such as Kleenex and Plexiglas—that are misused as common nouns?

🌐 Rain, rain, come this way
Have your students locate South Africa on a map. Tell them that the queen of the Lovedu people, a South African tribe, is also their official rainmaker, their "Transformer of the Clouds." When rain is needed, she consults with her weather lore experts. Have your students guess how much annual rainfall their area of the country gets. Then check an almanac to find out who came closest.

OCTOBER 23
activities

✿ First flying female

Seven years after the Wright brothers flew a heavier-than-air machine, Blanche Scott became the first woman to fly solo. She later became the first woman test pilot. Blanche Scott entered a field that had been "for men only." Today, women pursue a wide range of careers in aviation. Ask your students to list these careers. What jobs are still for men only or women only?

🇺🇸 A right for all

From colonial times on, groups of women worked to gain the right to vote, often in the face of great opposition. Why, do your students think, were some men opposed? And why were some women opposed? Invite your students to pretend they've joined the "march for suffrage." Have them design a poster they could carry, compose a song they could sing, or write a slogan they could shout as they march.

❀ Departure day

Today is the traditional day for swallows to leave San Juan Capistrano in California and begin their migration to Peru. According to *Animal Superstitions* by Thomas G. Aylesworth, swallows have been linked to a variety of misfortunes. In England, low-flying swallows portend bad weather; in France, stealing a swallow's eggs will make your horse lame; in Germany, destroying a swallow's nest will make your house burn down. Can anyone think of other animal superstitions?

Have your students locate San Juan Capistrano in their atlases. Using their map scale, ask them to figure out how far it is from the northernmost part of Peru. How about the southernmost part?

BIRTHDAYS

1920 • **BOB MONTANA,** comic-strip artist and creator of "Archie"
1925 • **JOHNNY CARSON,** talk-show host
1940 • **PELE** (real name: Edson Arantes do Nascimento), Brazilian soccer star
1941 • **P.J. PETERSEN,** children's author

EVENTS

1910 • **Blanche Scott became the FIRST WOMAN TO FLY SOLO** in a plane, reaching a height of 13 feet.

1915 • **The first NATIONAL HORSE-SHOE-PITCHING CHAMPIONSHIPS** took place in Kellerton, Kan.
• **25,000 WOMEN MARCHED** in New York City to demand the right to vote.
1983 • **A terrorist driving a truck filled with explosives made a SUICIDE ATTACK on the U.S. Marine Corps barracks in Beirut, Lebanon, killing 239 marines.**

❀ **SWALLOW DEPARTURE DAY**

23

OCTOBER 24
activities

A closer look
After he constructed his microscope, Anton van Leeuwenhoek saw things that no one had ever seen before, including mosquito wings, lice legs, human skin cells, and single-cell animals (protozoa). Have your students construct water-drop microscopes. Give them an index card, cellophane tape, a 2-inch square of transparency film, and scissors. Have them cut a small hole—about 1-inch square—in the card, and tape the transparency film over the opening. Next, have them place the card on a piece of newspaper. Using an eyedropper or soda straw, they should put drops of water on the transparency film, then read the letters underneath. What happens when they move the card away from the newspaper or add more water drops?

Fall gal
Annie Edson Taylor wanted to prove how daring she could be. She placed a 100-pound blacksmith's anvil (for ballast) at the bottom of a wood barrel and squeezed herself inside. Attendants packed pillows around her, screwed the lid on tight, and pushed the barrel toward Niagara Falls. The barrel plummeted 158 feet straight down and disappeared beneath the turbulent water. It finally popped up hundreds of yards below the falls. When rescuers recovered her, Taylor said, "Nobody ought ever to do that again." Have your students figure out how many desks they'd need to stack to match the distance of Taylor's fall. As a special challenge, give pairs of students a paper bag and a raw egg. Have them devise a way to prevent the egg from breaking in a fall. Test their ideas by dropping their inventions from various heights.

OCTOBER 25
activities

🎴 Abstract art

Among the many artistic media in which Pablo Picasso excelled was collage, the process of gluing various materials to a surface to express a mood, feeling, or theme. Have your students follow these steps to create their own collages:

✳Collect flat materials of different colors and textures—foil, plastic wrap, labels, corrugated cardboard, tissue, food trays, packing material, burlap, buttons, scraps of cloth.

✳Select items that look interesting together and cut or tear them into a variety of sizes.

✳On a piece of cardboard, arrange the shapes to create a feeling, mood, or message. Overlap some of the materials to help create balance.

✳Use empty spaces as part of the design. Decide what to emphasize, determine a center of interest, then glue everything in place.

✳Create a title to reflect the idea or message of the collage.

🦟 Bitten by the love bug

A bull moose in Vermont spent over 10 weeks following a Hereford cow named Jessica. Thousands of sightseers watched the moose woo and nuzzle its bovine sweetheart. Tell your class that a moose in the woods is well camouflaged: Its legs blend with the tree trunks; its brown body fades into the shadows; and its antlers look like branches. Ask your students to draw other animals that rely on camouflage.

1825 • **JOHANN STRAUSS, JR.,** Austrian composer known as "the Waltz King"
1881 • **PABLO PICASSO,** Spanish artist 🎴
1888 • **RICHARD BYRD,** American polar explorer

EVENTS

1870 • **A POSTCARD WAS FIRST MAILED** in the United States.
1931 • **The GEORGE WASHINGTON BRIDGE,** which connects New York and New Jersey, opened.

1940 • **NYLON STOCKINGS** first went on sale in America.
1986 • **THE WORLD'S LARGEST OMELET** was cooked in a 30-foot-wide skillet with 54,763 eggs.
• **A BULL MOOSE BEGAN A 76-DAY COURTSHIP** of a Hereford cow in Shrewsbury, Vt.
1992 • **The Toronto Blue Jays became the FIRST TEAM FROM OUTSIDE THE UNITED STATES TO WIN A WORLD SERIES,** defeating the Atlanta Braves in six games.

25

OCTOBER 26
activities

Backbreaker
The Erie Canal was completed after 8 years of construction. Using wheelbarrows, shovels, and other hand tools, the crew dug a ditch 4 feet deep, 40 feet wide at ground level, and 28 feet wide at the base. Eighty-three locks were built to enable ships to make the climb from the Hudson River to Lake Erie. Have your students use a map scale in their atlas to figure out the length of the canal, which runs from Albany to Buffalo, N.Y.

Class charity
Raise money for a Red Cross charity by holding a used-toy sale. Ask your students to collect old toys, and arrange them by price—25¢, 50¢, $1, and so on. Have committees make posters advertising the event, send invitations, produce a video about the event and its purpose, and speak about the event over the school's public-address system.

Book math
After outgrowing its 88 miles of stacks, the New York Public Library began building an underground extension. Books stored there will be brought to the main library when needed. The extension, which will hold 3.2 million books, should fill up fast because the library acquires over 150,000 books each year. Ask your students to estimate the number of books in *their* library. Collect enough books to make a stack 1 meter high. Then have the kids use this information to estimate how many meters high all the books in their school library stacked together would reach. Can your students think of other ways to solve this problem? Ask your school librarian to check your class's estimate.

OCTOBER 27
activities

 **President's hobbies**

Theodore Roosevelt was an avid hunter and naturalist. When he was growing up, his room always contained a pet mouse or a collection of stuffed birds. When he was president, zoologists recognized him as one of the best field naturalists in the country. He was also an authority on North American big game. What animals do your students think would be called North American big game? What are some big game animals on other continents?

In 1902, during one of Roosevelt's hunting trips, a bear cub wandered into the campsite. The president's friends rushed for their guns, but Roosevelt insisted that the cub be left alone. Have any of your students ever found themselves in a situation in which their opinion was different from everyone else's? Ask them to describe the situation and what happened. Is it always fair for the majority to rule?

Determined record-breaker

Pole-sitter Mellissa Sanders was determined to raise $100,000 for cancer research. Her sister Rebecca was a cancer patient. Tell your class that Mellissa's pole-top "home," which was a 42-square-foot box, included a telephone, a television, and a small plastic pool for baths. Ask your students what they would take with them if they were attempting to break Mellissa's record. Have them use grid paper to determine some possible shapes for a 42-square-foot "home."

BIRTHDAYS
1728 • **CAPTAIN JAMES COOK**, British navigator and explorer of the Pacific Ocean
1811 • **ISAAC MERRIT SINGER**, American sewing-machine inventor and manufacturer
1858 • **THEODORE ROOSEVELT**, 26th president of the United States

EVENTS
1829 • **THE FIRST PATENT FOR A BABY CARRIAGE** was issued in the United States.
1904 • **THE FIRST SUBWAY** opened to the public in New York City.
1938 • Dupont chemists announced the invention of **NYLON**.
1945 • Harry Truman became the **FIRST PRESIDENT TO APPEAR ON TELEVISION.**
1959 • *Luna 3* transmitted the **FIRST PICTURES OF THE DARK SIDE OF THE MOON.**
1986 • Mellissa Sanders began **POLE-SITTING** to raise money for cancer research. She went on to break the world record of 488 days.
1989 • Karen Lindsay of Norcross, Ga., was **ARRESTED FOR FAILING TO RETURN OVERDUE LIBRARY BOOKS.** She spent a night in jail and was released.

OCTOBER 28
activities

BIRTHDAYS

1798 • **LEVI COFFIN**, American abolitionist and founder of the Underground Railroad

1914 • **DR. JONAS SALK**, American physician and developer of the polio vaccine

EVENTS

1492 • Christopher Columbus landed on the island of **CUBA.**

1636 • **HARVARD COLLEGE was founded.**

1886 • **THE STATUE OF LIBERTY** was unveiled in New York Harbor.

1904 • The St. Louis Police Department became the **FIRST POLICE DEPARTMENT TO ADOPT A FINGERPRINTING SYSTEM.**

1945 • **SHOE RATIONING** in the United States ended.

1962 • **THE CUBAN MISSLE CRISIS** ended as Soviet leader Nikita Khrushchev agreed to remove ballistic missiles from Cuba.

Masses welcome

The sonnet "The New Colossus," by Emma Lazarus, is inscribed on a bronze plaque inside the Statue of Liberty's pedestal. Read it to your students, then have them write their own inscriptions for the Statue of Liberty in their journals.

Peeking at prints

Try some dactyloscopy (fingerprinting) with your class. Have your students rub a sharpened #2 pencil on a piece of paper until they've produced a dark, shiny patch. Next, they should lightly rub their index finger over the patch, then cover that finger with a piece of clear adhesive tape. Place the tape on an index card or on an overhead transparency. Have your students compare fingerprints and make observations. Tell them that a police computer can examine over 600 prints per second. How many is that per minute? Per hour?

A scientist's day

Dr. Jonas Salk developed a vaccine for polio and, with funding from the March of Dimes, tested it on 1,830,000 people—including himself and his family. While completing his research, he worked 16-hour days. Ask your students to figure out what percentage of the day that represents. Then have them make a circle graph reflecting the percentage of the day they spend working in school, sleeping, eating, watching TV or relaxing, completing homework, and so on.

OCTOBER 29
activities

🐾 Monster in everyone

In honor of Bela Lugosi's birthday, have your students create masks depicting themselves in a rotten mood. On the back, they should write how they feel when this "monster mood" comes out. Maybe they're embarrassed and lonely, not just grumpy! Discuss the different feelings that might bring on a "monster mood."

🧪 Cloud capers

Throughout history, people have tried to change the weather. They've chanted, danced, and even fired rockets. Modern technology has enabled scientists to modify the weather somewhat. With cloud seeding, dry ice or silver iodide is added to very cold clouds to promote the formation of ice crystals. This method can clear fog over airports and increase precipitation by up to 30 percent in certain circumstances. Ask teams of students to illustrate other ways humans have successfully dealt with the weather (heaters, air conditioners, humidifiers, irrigation systems, landscaping techniques).

Next, follow this simple procedure to create a cloud for your students. Pour about an inch of very hot water into a large glass jar. Then fill a metal cake pan with ice cubes and place it on top of the jar. Take the jar into a darkened room and shine a flashlight on it. Your students will see a small cloud and, if they're observant, drops of precipitation on the bottom of the pan.

BIRTHDAYS
1740 • **JAMES BOSWELL,** Scottish writer whose *Life of Samuel Johnson* is considered a masterpiece of biography

1884 • **BELA LUGOSI,** actor noted for his
🐾 roles in horror films

EVENTS
1682 • **WILLIAM PENN,** the founder of Pennsylvania, landed in Chester, Pa.
1929 • **THE STOCK MARKET CRASHED,** plunging the country into the Great Depression.
1940 • The United States began its **FIRST PEACETIME DRAFT BY LOTTERY.**
1947 • Dry ice was used for the first
🧪 time in **CLOUD SEEDING,** a technique for producing rain, in Concord, N.H.

OCTOBER 30
actiities

BIRTHDAYS
1735 • **JOHN ADAMS,** second president of the United States

1893 • **CHARLES ATLAS,** self-described "97-pound weakling" who became a famous body builder

EVENTS
1485 • King Henry VII of England started a group of royal attendants, called the **YEOMEN OF THE GUARD.** They later became known as the Beefeaters.

1888 • **THE BALLPOINT PEN** was patented.

1938 • Orson Welles's radio dramatization of the H.G. Wells science-fiction classic *THE WAR OF THE WORLDS* caused a nationwide scare.

1989 • **THE WONDERS OF LIFE PAVILION** at Walt Disney World's Epcot Center opened.

🎈 Honored group
The Beefeaters, as the Yeomen of the Guard are now called, serve as official bodyguards to the king or queen of Great Britain for formal occasions. They are not trained fighters, however. Rather, they are chosen for this honorary position because they are honest, hardworking, and considerate. Discuss these qualities with your students. Then establish a group called the Yeomen of the Classroom. Every month, select students who have demonstrated honorable qualities.

Vice presidents then and now
John Adams served as vice president during George Washington's administration. In those days, the candidate with the greatest number of votes became president, and the runner-up became vice president. How do your students feel about that method of selection? What are its advantages and disadvantages? How is the vice president selected today? What are his major responsibilities?

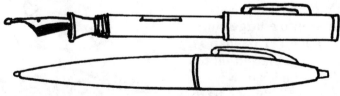

Power of the pen
As a journal assignment, have your students compare and contrast a fountain pen and a ballpoint pen. (Ask your art teacher for some fountain pens.) Encourage the kids to write a letter—from the fountain pen's perspective—describing its feelings about being obsolete. What do your students own that might be obsolete by the time they're adults?

OCTOBER 31
activities

▰ Black Hills stone faces

Sculptor Gutzon Borglum needed to select four presidents to memorialize on Mount Rushmore. He looked for leaders who practiced the ideal "Man has a right to be free and to be happy." His first three choices—Washington, Jefferson, and Lincoln—were obvious. For the fourth, President Calvin Coolidge suggested Theodore Roosevelt, who, he believed, had established the United States as an industrial giant with a backbone of dedicated workers. With this endorsement, Borglum's group was complete. Have your students nominate and vote on four present-day leaders they'd memorialize on a Rushmore-like monument.

⁂ Kid power

On Halloween morning in 1987, the pickup truck driven by Rocky Lyons's mother hit a pothole. It flipped over and rolled down an embankment. Five-year-old Rocky pushed his dazed mother out of the truck. She'd sustained bad cuts on her face and two broken shoulders. With Rocky pushing his mother from behind, the two began to crawl up the embankment. Rocky's mother didn't think she could make it, but the boy kept repeating a line from *The Little Engine That Could:* "I think I can, I think I can." Once they reached the road, a truck driver stopped and took them to the hospital. Have the famous words "I think I can" ever gotten your students through a tough situation?

✎ Halloween dos and don'ts

Trick-or-treating is a fun-filled Halloween tradition. But kids must be careful so that the fun doesn't turn into tragedy. Discuss Halloween safety with your students. Have them make up a "dos and don'ts" list and poster for trick-or-treaters.

BIRTHDAYS

1795 • JOHN KEATS, English poet
1860 • JULIETTE GORDON LOW, founder of the American Girl Scouts
1931 • DAN RATHER, American TV journalist
1932 • KATHERINE PATERSON, author of *Bridge to Terabithia*

EVENTS

1864 • NEVADA became the 36th state.
1886 • Arthur Conan Doyle's FIRST SHERLOCK HOLMES STORY, "A Study in Scarlet," was bought for 25 pounds.
1926 • MAGICIAN HARRY HOUDINI died of acute appendicitis.
1941 • MOUNT RUSHMORE MONUMENT was completed.
1987 • Rocky Lyons, age 5, SAVED HIS MOTHER'S LIFE.

✎ HALLOWEEN
NATIONAL MAGIC DAY
NATIONAL UNICEF DAY

NOVEMBER

☆ Project of the Month: Doll Days

Celebrate Doll Collection Month by having your students list different categories of dolls—such as rag dolls, paper dolls, action figures, fashion dolls, baby dolls, and celebrity dolls—along with brand names of commercially sold versions. Ask them to organize their information in an outline. What are the favorite dolls in each category? What is the most popular category? Do students think this information might vary by age level? Have the kids organize their own fact-finding groups to poll children from other grades. Report the findings in your school newspaper.

Throughout the month, ask your students to bring in doll ads. What doll is the "hot" gift for the upcoming holiday season? Does its price vary from store to store? Do prices change as the holidays get closer? Why?

Encourage the kids to bring in family dolls, including commercial, homemade, vintage, and antique varieties. Have each contributor write the doll's name, history, and actual or sentimental value on a card. Then display the dolls, museum style. Invite students from other classes to tour your doll museum.

EXTENDER: How do your students feel about the following questions: Should boys play with dolls? If no, why not? If yes, what kind and up to what age? When should girls stop playing with dolls?

MONTHLONG OBSERVANCES

Aviation History Month
Child Safety and Protection Month
Doll Collection Month
Good Nutrition Month
International Drum Month
Model Railroad Month
National Diabetes Month
National Epilepsy Month
National Ice Skating Month
What's in the News Month

WEEKLONG EVENTS

Cat Week (first full week)
Children's Book Week
  (third full week)
American Education Week
  (first full week preceding the
  fourth Thursday)
Farm-City Week
  (week ending with Thanksgiving)
National Geography Awareness Week
  (third full week)
National Family Week
  (Thanksgiving week)
Latin America Week (last full week)

SPECIAL DAYS AND CELEBRATIONS

Election Day (first Tuesday)
World Community Day (first Friday)
Veterans Day (November 11)
Sadie Hawkins Day
  (first Saturday after November 11)
Great American Smokeout
  (third Thursday)
Thanksgiving (fourth Thursday)

NOVEMBER 1
activities

✎ White House living
Ask how many of your students have visited the White House. Invite them to share photographs and memories of their trip. Make a list of some of the White House's rooms, and assign groups to each research one. Ask each group to use a shoe-box display to depict the room it studied.

🧪 Weather reporters
Start the day with a report from a class weather forecaster. Students can get their information from the daily local newspaper or from "The Weather Channel" on television. Invite them to use *USA TODAY* to expand their forecast to other regions of the country—especially states they're studying or states favorite authors hail from. Invite kids to note daily high and low temperatures in a weather journal. Do they notice any patterns after a few weeks?

🎎 Historical dolls
For Doll Collection Month, have pairs of students trace each other on large sheets of paper. They can then decorate these "paper dolls" as the historical figures they're studying and write a brief biographical sketch of each. Display the finished figures and bios in the hallway so other classes can enjoy them!

BIRTHDAYS
1818 • JAMES RENWICK, American architect who designed the Smithsonian Institution

1871 • STEPHEN CRANE, American author who wrote *The Red Badge of Courage*

EVENTS
1755 • AN EARTHQUAKE destroyed Lisbon, Portugal, killing 50,000.

1765 • THE STAMP ACT went into effect in the American colonies, provoking widespread resistance.

1800 • President John Adams and his ✎ wife, Abigail, became the FIRST RESIDENTS OF THE WHITE HOUSE, which was still unfinished.

1870 • THE U.S. WEATHER BUREAU 🧪 made its first weather observation.

1962 • THE SOVIET UNION launched the spacecraft *Mars 1* to study the Red Planet.

1973 • THE WORLD'S TALLEST BARBER POLE, a towering 50 feet 3 inches, was put up in Alexander, N.Y.

NATIONAL AUTHORS DAY
WORLDWIDE PEACE DAY
🎎 DOLL COLLECTION MONTH

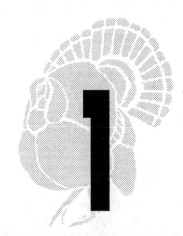

1

NOVEMBER 2
activities

BIRTHDAYS

1734 • DANIEL BOONE, American pioneer

1755 • MARIE ANTOINETTE, queen of France

1795 • JAMES K. POLK, 11th president of the United States

1865 • WARREN G. HARDING, 29th president of the United States

☞ COOKIE MONSTER, sweet-tooth Muppet

EVENTS

1889 • NORTH DAKOTA AND SOUTH DAKOTA became the 39th and 40th states, respectively.

1920 • THE FIRST COMMERCIAL RADIO NEWS BROADCAST originated from station KDKA in Pittsburgh, Pa. It reported the presidential election returns.

1936 • THE BRITISH BROADCASTING CORPORATION began regular TV broadcasts in England.

1948 • PRESIDENT HARRY S. TRUMAN WON REELECTION despite polls predicting a landslide victory for his opponent, Thomas E. Dewey.

1959 • Jacques Plante became the FIRST GOALIE TO WEAR A MASK during a professional hockey game.

BROADCAST JOURNALIST DAY

CAT WEEK (first full week)

▓ Welcome, Dakotas!

Complete a class "K-W-L" chart about North and South Dakota. (Kids start out by listing what they <u>k</u>now about the states and what more they <u>w</u>ant to know.) During free reading, ask a team of students to research the states, with the class "W" list in mind. Later, they can report on what they <u>l</u>earned.

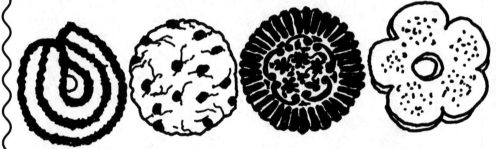

☞ Munch and graph

It's Cookie Monster's birthday! Plan a cookie-tasting party! Choose four different types of cookies. Set up a serving table with bite-sized portions on labeled plates. Give each child a paper plate to divide into four sections and label. Then have the kids take one sample of each cookie to taste. Ask them to write down which cookie is their favorite and which they think will be the class favorite. How many guessed right?

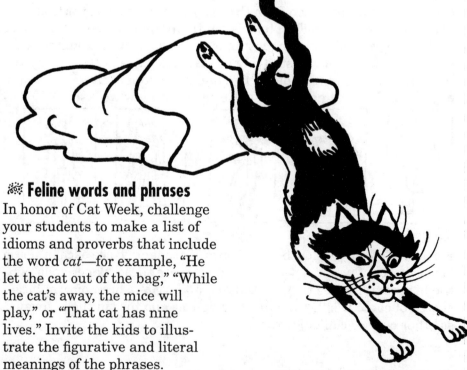

▒ Feline words and phrases

In honor of Cat Week, challenge your students to make a list of idioms and proverbs that include the word *cat*—for example, "He let the cat out of the bag," "While the cat's away, the mice will play," or "That cat has nine lives." Invite the kids to illustrate the figurative and literal meanings of the phrases.

NOVEMBER 3
activities

✒ The noble appetite

In honor of the earl of Sandwich's birthday, brainstorm for titles of nobility (king, queen, duke, duchess, earl, lady, baron, baroness, and so on). Have your students consult an encyclopedia to put their list in order from the lowest rank to the highest. Then invite the kids to create cartoon characters that combine nobility and food—such as the duke of Pizza or Queen Candy Bar.

▦ Today's treaty

Give your students a chance to develop their own treaty, as the Sauk and Fox Indians and the United States did in 1804. First, have two groups of students identify a problem they're having with each other. Then, for the treaty, have them list what each group would do separately and together to make the agreement work. Use black permanent marker to print the final text of the treaty on butcher paper or paper sacks, rubbed with linseed oil to resemble parchment. Tear the edges of the paper to make it look even more authentic. Discuss the treaty with the groups involved and ask if they're satisfied with it. Post the treaty for reference.

❊ Prices then and now

Have your students guess today's prices for a pound of butter, a dozen eggs, and a pound of beef. Get actual prices from a nearby supermarket. Whose guesses were closest? In addition to comparing today's prices for these items with the 1837 prices, the kids could suggest how food packaging, distribution, and advertising have changed since then.

BIRTHDAYS

1718 • JOHN MONTAGU, 4th earl of
✒ Sandwich, credited with the invention of the sandwich for eating at the gaming table

1793 • STEPHEN AUSTIN, colonizer and leader in Texas's fight for independence from Mexico

EVENTS

1679 • PANIC SWEPT EUROPE as a comet approached.

1804 • THE SAUK AND FOX INDIANS
▦ signed a treaty ceding 50 million acres of present-day Illinois to the United States.

1837 • Housewives in Illinois staged a
❊ protest against THE HIGH COST OF FOOD (including butter, 8¢ per pound; eggs, 6¢ per dozen; and beef, 3¢ per pound).

1900 • THE FIRST AUTO SHOW in the United States was held in New York City.

1942 • THE ALASKA HIGHWAY, running from Dawson Creek, British Columbia, to Fairbanks, Alaska, was completed.

1957 • A dog named Laika became EARTH'S FIRST SPACE TRAVELER, on board the Soviet satellite *Sputnik 2.*

1964 • RESIDENTS OF WASHINGTON, D.C., VOTED for the first time in a presidential election.

1992 • BILL CLINTON was elected the 42nd president of the United States.

NOVEMBER 4
activities

BIRTHDAYS

1876 • **JAMES FRASER,** American sculptor

1879 • **WILL ROGERS,** American humorist, humanitarian, and cowboy philosopher

1891 • **FREDERICK BANTING,** Canadian researcher and codiscoverer of insulin

1916 • **WALTER CRONKITE,** American TV journalist

EVENTS

1841 • **THE FIRST IMMIGRANT WAGON TRAIN** arrived in California.

1842 • **ABRAHAM LINCOLN** married Mary Todd.

1879 • James Ritty received a patent for the **CASH REGISTER.**

1922 • English archaeologist Howard Carter discovered steps leading to **THE ENTRANCE GALLERY OF KING TUTANKHAMEN'S TOMB.**

1924 • Nellie Tayloe Ross, the nation's **FIRST WOMAN GOVERNOR,** was elected in Wyoming.

1979 • **MILITANT IRANIAN STUDENTS** seized the U.S. embassy in Tehran and took its staff hostage, an ordeal that lasted 444 days.

MISCHIEF NIGHT IN ENGLAND, AUSTRALIA, AND NEW ZEALAND

🇺🇸 A nickel's story

Sculptor James Fraser's buffalo nickel—which featured a buffalo on one side and an American Indian's head on the other—was issued by the U.S. Treasury in 1913. The design commemorated the importance of the buffalo to the Plains Indians' way of life. Have your students design a coin that commemorates something from contemporary life.

Tell your students that another famous piece by Fraser, the sculpture *The End of the Trail,* depicts an exhausted American Indian at the end of the Trail of Tears, the forced relocation of about 17,000 Cherokees by the U.S. government in 1838. About one in four died during this journey from Georgia to the Indian Territory, west of the Mississippi River. This territory later became the state of Oklahoma. Have your students locate cities and towns in Oklahoma with names that reflect Native American culture.

🔆 A cash register's story

James Ritty designed the first cash register so he could have a record of transactions in his restaurant. His first model looked like a clock, with one hand showing the dollars and the other hand showing the cents. There were rows of keys along the base. Today's electronic cash registers indicate the category and price of each item, the total sale, the amount tendered, and the amount of change. Have students collect grocery tapes and make bar graphs of the different types of purchases—produce, meat, cleaning supplies, and so on. Then have the kids transfer this information to pie graphs showing the percentage of purchases from each category.

NOVEMBER 5

activities

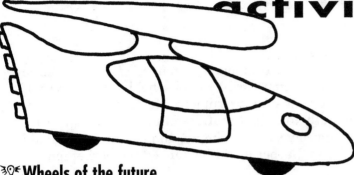

☼ Wheels of the future

Celebrate the automobile with your students. Invite them to draw the car of the future—or their dream car—labeling any unique features and unusual capabilities.

As a journal assignment, ask your students to ponder one of these questions: What would the automobile industry be like without mass production? What would the world be like without cars? What are some of the pros and cons of automobile travel? What could you do to cut back on car use in your family?

✈ Flying time

The first transcontinental airplane flight covered the 2,320-mile distance from New York to Pasadena in 82 hours and 4 minutes. Have the class use calculators to figure out the plane's air speed. Then challenge the kids to determine how long it would take a modern jet (560 mph), a supersonic plane (800 mph), and an orbiting satellite (25,000 mph) to make that trip.

⚗ Nap time!

Scientists studied the grizzly's "long winter nap" by placing a radio transmitter around the bear's neck. Ask your students to list other animals that hibernate throughout the winter. What animals are true hibernators? What animals are partial hibernators? What animals remain active throughout the winter? Ask your students to make bookmarks depicting animals' winter habits. Give the finished products to the school librarian for use in animal or winter books.

BIRTHDAYS

1855 • **LEON PHILIPPE TEISSERENC DE BORT,** French meteorologist who used balloons to investigate the upper atmosphere and who discovered the stratosphere

1912 • **ROY ROGERS,** motion-picture cowboy

EVENTS

1639 • **THE FIRST COLONIAL POST OFFICE** was established in Boston, Mass.

1872 • **SUSAN B. ANTHONY** was arrested and fined $100 for trying to vote in a presidential election.

1895 • George Selden received a patent ☼ for a **GAS-POWERED AUTOMOBILE.**

1911 • **THE FIRST TRANSCONTINENTAL** ✈ **AIRPLANE FLIGHT** arrived in Pasadena, Calif., from New York.

1924 • **THE FIRST CROSSWORD PUZZLE BOOK** was published.

1940 • **FRANKLIN D. ROOSEVELT** became the first U.S. president elected to a third term.

1963 • **THE FIRST RADIO-TRACKED** ⚗ **GRIZZLY BEAR** began its hibernation.

GUY FAWKES DAY, during which British children celebrate the foiling of a 1605 plot to blow up the Houses of Parliament

NOVEMBER 6
activities

BIRTHDAYS

1814 • **ADOLPHE SAX,** Belgian instrument-maker who invented the saxophone

1854 • **JOHN PHILIP SOUSA,** American composer of "Stars and Stripes Forever"

1861 • **JAMES NAISMITH,** Canadian educator who invented the game of basketball

EVENTS

1792 • **GEORGE WASHINGTON WAS REELECTED** by unanimous vote of the electoral college.

1860 • **ABRAHAM LINCOLN** defeated three other candidates for the presidency.

1869 • Rutgers defeated Princeton, 6-4, in the **FIRST INTERCOLLEGIATE FOOTBALL GAME.**

1871 • **ANNA SEWELL** began writing *Black Beauty.*

1928 • Jacob Schick received a patent for **THE ELECTRIC SHAVER.**

• **CHARLES CURTIS,** whose mother was a Native American of the Kaw tribe, became the 31st vice president of the United States.

1987 • American sailor Tania Aebi completed a 2$\frac{1}{2}$-year, 27,000-mile voyage around the world, thus becoming the **FIRST WOMAN TO CIRCUMNAVIGATE THE GLOBE SOLO.**

Inventive musicians

Tell your students that the saxophone was named after its inventor, Adolphe Sax. Then ask them to bring in household items that could be used to create a new musical instrument. Next, have them work in teams or individually to do just that. Remind them to name their instrument after themselves. For example, an instrument created by a student named Jenny Barber might be dubbed the barberophone.

Animal "authors"

In commemoration of the day Anna Sewell began writing *Black Beauty,* ask your students to select an animal—real or fictional—and write a diary entry in that animal's voice. They should focus on a particular incident in the animal's life (for example, giving birth, winning a race, moving). Encourage the kids to consult science books for information that will lend authenticity to their work.

Let the games begin!

In honor of James Naismith, who invented basketball so his students could play a sport indoors, have students work in teams to design a game that meets their needs. Ask the teams to decide: 1) where the game should be played (indoors or outdoors), 2) the number of players on each team, 3) the necessary equipment, and 4) the emphasis of the game (accuracy, speed, strength, endurance, or some combination of these). Have the teams try out their games, then demonstrate them to the rest of the class.

A close shave

Have your students compare the electric shaver with the product that preceded it, the razor. What special needs does the electric shaver meet that the razor does not? In their journals, have the kids list ways products they use could be improved and sketch what the new versions might look like.

NOVEMBER 7
activities

🧪 Determined scientist

Marie Curie had to overcome many obstacles. Her mother died when Marie was 10. Because Poland was ruled by Russia, she had to do all her schoolwork in Russian, not her native tongue. And she had to leave her homeland to get a college degree because women weren't allowed to attend college in Poland. Ask your students to think of accomplishments—large or small—that they've made despite obstacles.

🖋️ Meticulous observers

President Thomas Jefferson, who authorized the Lewis and Clark expedition, asked the explorers to keep careful notes of their journey. Lewis and Clark filled notebooks with detailed descriptions and drawings of the 24 Native American tribes, the 122 animal species, and the nearly 200 plant species they encountered. Take your students for a walk around the school. Have them sketch plants or animals they find, then consult field guides for more information.

✤ Would-be records

A world record is set when a person does something longer, bigger, faster, more often, than anyone else. Ask your students to think of a world record they'd like to set. Then have them draw a picture of themselves setting that record. Add to the fun by asking the kids to give themselves a nickname that describes their special performance. For example, Arden Chapman's nickname could be "the Great Grapecatcher," "Grape Man," or "Gotcha Graper." The kids can make nickname nametags to wear when they share their pictures and tell their record-breaking stories.

BIRTHDAYS

1867 • **MARIE CURIE, Polish-born physicist and chemist who became the first person to win two Nobel Prizes**

EVENTS

1504 • **CHRISTOPHER COLUMBUS** arrived in Sanlúcar, Spain, ending his fourth and last voyage to America.

1805 • **THE LEWIS AND CLARK EXPEDITION** sighted the Pacific Ocean at the mouth of the Columbia River.

1874 • The elephant was first used as a **SYMBOL OF THE REPUBLICAN PARTY**, in *Harper's Weekly*.

1929 • **THE MUSEUM OF MODERN ART** opened in New York.

1940 • **THE TACOMA NARROWS BRIDGE COLLAPSED** in a windstorm. It was the nation's third-largest suspension bridge.

1944 • President Franklin D. Roosevelt was elected to an unprecedented **FOURTH CONSECUTIVE TERM**.

1966 • **NBC BECAME THE FIRST NETWORK** to broadcast all of its programs in color.

1977 • **BY CATCHING A GRAPE** thrown 259 feet in his mouth, college student Arden Chapman established a new world record.

NOVEMBER 8
activities

AMERICAN · LIBRARY · ASSOCIATION · 1876

BIRTHDAYS

1656 • **EDMUND HALLEY,** English astronomer and mathematician

1836 • **MILTON BRADLEY,** American games manufacturer

1847 • **BRAM STOKER,** English-Irish author of *Dracula*

1900 • **MARGARET MITCHELL,** American novelist who wrote *Gone with the Wind*

1922 • **CHRISTIAAN BARNARD,** South African surgeon who performed the first successful human heart transplant

1949 • **BONNIE RAITT,** American singer

EVENTS

1783 • **THE FIRST CIRCULATING LIBRARY** in America was founded in Philadelphia.

1793 • **THE LOUVRE MUSEUM** in Paris opened.

1889 • **MONTANA** became the 41st state.

1895 • **X-RAYS** were discovered by the German physicist Wilhelm Roentgen.

1910 • A patent for a **"BUG ZAPPER"** was issued to W.W. Frost of Spokane, Wash.

1970 • Placekicker Tom Dempsey kicked an NFL-record **63-YARD FIELD GOAL** to propel the New Orleans Saints over the Detroit Lions.

AID AND ABET PUNSTERS DAY
DUNCE DAY

8

The name of the game

When game maker Milton Bradley opened his own print shop, his first big job was for thousands of lithographs of Abraham Lincoln. But the president grew a beard, making the lithographs outdated and impossible to sell, and Bradley faced financial ruin. So he decided to try something different: He developed a board game called The Checkered Game of Life. Today, the Milton Bradley Company is the largest games manufacturer in the country, making such favorites as Life, Stratego, Battleship, and Candyland. What are your students' favorite board games? Graph the class results.

Welcome, Montana!

Ask your students to speculate on the origin of Montana's name (it comes from the Latin term for "mountainous"). Do they think the state's nickname, "Big Sky Country," is appropriate? Montana ranks fourth among the states in land area. Which states do your students think are larger than Montana? How does Montana's total area of 147,046 square miles compare with the area of your state?

The power of the pun

Celebrate Aid and Abet Punsters Day by asking your students to define the term *pun*. Challenge them to illustrate examples. How about a sketch of an inviting bed-and-breakfast establishment, with the sign "Dewdrop Inn." Or a picture of an unhappy chef who's telling his friends that he'd start a bakery if he could raise some dough. Encourage the kids to think about homophones and words with multiple meanings when they're creating puns. Ask them to display their best puns on a bulletin board, which you'll maintain for the entire month.

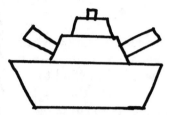

NOVEMBER 9
activities

🧪 Gender bender

Tell your students that Florence Sabin thought science should have no gender identification. Ask them to explain what they think Sabin meant when she said, "The important thing is the progress of knowledge and not which individual is the relay runner who for a brief span carried the torch."

Blackout!

Most people take electricity for granted—until the power goes out! History's most celebrated blackout put 30,000,000 East Coast residents in the dark for up to 13 hours. Almost 1,000,000 people were trapped in elevators and subways. Ask your students to list other aspects of modern life that people frequently take for granted. Have them write a short story that explores the consequences of one or more of these assumptions.

🐾 Forest fire policy

Smokey the Bear was a badly burned cub that survived a fire in the Lincoln National Forest in New Mexico. With a cartoon Smokey as its mascot, the U.S. Forest Service supported a no-burn policy. This led to overgrown "old" forests that inhibited new growth. In the 1970s, a policy allowing natural fires to burn was instituted in order to help rejuvenate forests. This policy was questioned after tremendous fires burned much of Yellowstone National Park in 1988. Show your students pictures of Yellowstone immediately after the fires and a year later. Have small groups design posters depicting the ways in which fire is a natural part of the ecological process.

BIRTHDAYS

1731 • **BENJAMIN BANNEKER,** African-American astronomer and mathematician

1871 • **FLORENCE SABIN,** American 🧪 physician and teacher

EVENTS

1906 • Theodore Roosevelt became the **FIRST U.S. PRESIDENT TO LEAVE THE COUNTRY** while in office, sailing for the Panama Canal Zone.

1938 • Nazis roamed the streets of Germany, destroying Jewish homes, businesses, and synagogues in what came to be known as the **"CRYSTAL NIGHT."**

1965 • **A POWER BLACKOUT** covering 80,000 square miles stranded almost a million East Coast residents in elevators and subways for up to 13 hours.

1976 • **SMOKEY THE BEAR** died at the age of 26.
• The United Nations General Assembly approved 10 **RESOLUTIONS CONDEMNING APARTHEID** in South Africa.

1984 • **THE STATUE** *THREE SERVICEMEN* was unveiled at the Vietnam Veterans Memorial in Washington, D.C.

1989 • **EAST GERMANY OPENED THE BERLIN WALL** and its border with West Germany as thousands celebrated.

activities

BIRTHDAYS

1483 • **MARTIN LUTHER, German the-
ologian and religious reformer**

1879 • **VACHEL LINDSAY, American poet**

EVENTS

1775 • **THE U.S. MARINE CORPS was
established.**

1801 • **Tennessee outlawed DUELING.**

1855 • *THE SONG OF HIAWATHA,* **by
Henry Wadsworth Longfellow,
was published.**

1871 • **REPORTER HENRY M. STANLEY
found Dr. David Livingstone in
central Africa.**

1885 • **THE WORLD'S FIRST MOTORCY-
CLE—a $\frac{1}{2}$-horsepower engine
mounted on a wooden bicycle
frame—was invented by a
German named Gottlieb Daimler.**

1903 • **THE WINDSHIELD WIPER was
patented by Mary Anderson of
Massachusetts.**

1938 • **American writer PEARL BUCK
was awarded the Nobel Prize in
literature.**

1951 • **COAST-TO-COAST DIRECT-DIAL
PHONE SERVICE began.**

1954 • **THE IWO JIMA MEMORIAL was
dedicated in Arlington, Va.**

1969 • **"SESAME STREET" debuted.**

✐ Quite a hike, I presume

Henry Morton Stanley traveled for 236 days and covered 975 miles to find Dr. David Livingstone. Have your students use an atlas to identify an area they're unfamiliar with that's about 975 miles from their hometown.

💡 Everyday things

The windshield wiper, invented on this day in 1903, is an uncompli-cated device that helps drivers avoid accidents. Ask the kids to sug-gest some other simple yet helpful items that make a big difference in their daily lives. What about the bottle opener, the pocket knife, the colander, the staple remover, and thumbtacks? Invite students to write a tribute to one of these devices, such as "Ode to a Hand-Held Orange Juice Squeezer."

☎ Phone fun

Play a map game using area codes. Call out a code (check the front of the telephone book for a list) and the state or country that uses it. Have a volunteer point to the place on the wall map.

Have the kids make wallet-sized cards that contain important phone numbers— such as the police and fire departments, the poison control center, and parents' work numbers. Encourage the kids to keep this information handy.

📑 Muppet moments

To celebrate the 1969 debut of "Sesame Street," have your students make a list of its stars—both human and muppet. Invite the kids to make anniversary cards for their favorite characters. Send them in care of Children's Television Workshop, One Lincoln Plaza, New York, NY 10023. Continue the party by asking your kids to share their favorite "Sesame Street" book with classmates or with a class of younger students.

NOVEMBER 11
activities

 Keep on trackin'

Celebrate the anniversary of the first indoor track meet by organizing a similar event at your school. Once you get the principal's approval, meet with the gym teacher to design activities. Include such favorite events as the broad jump and relays. But also try some nontraditional events, such as a walking race in which students must keep one foot on the ground at all times and may not bend their knees, a backward race, or a hopping race. Vary the distances of the races so "tortoises" as well as "hares" have a chance to show their stuff.

Hats off to vets

Tell your students that Veterans Day is a time to honor the men and women who've served in our country's armed forces. Have each student make a list of relatives who are veterans, including the branches of the armed forces in which these relatives served. Then compile a class list. Referring to the class list, ask the kids to think about the best way to visually represent the percentages who served in each branch. Would it be a bar graph? A pie chart? Groups of stick figures?

Next, have your students make bookmarks and cards honoring veterans. Send them to a local veterans hospital or ask volunteers to deliver them in person. If possible, arrange for a veteran to speak to your class.

BIRTHDAYS
1885 • GEORGE PATTON, U.S. general

EVENTS
1647 • Massachusetts passed the FIRST COMPULSORY SCHOOL LAW in America.
1868 • The New York Athletic Club held the FIRST INDOOR TRACK MEET.
1889 • WASHINGTON became the 42nd state.
1909 • Work began on the U.S. NAVAL BASE AT PEARL HARBOR.
1918 • AN ARMISTICE was signed ending World War I.
1919 • BRITAIN OBSERVED 2 MINUTES OF SILENCE to honor those who died in World War I.
1921 • AMERICA'S UNKNOWN SOLDIER of World War I was interred at Arlington National Cemetery.
1933 • THE GREAT BLACK BLIZZARD, a storm that kicked up a mile-high wall of dust, ravaged thousands of acres of the Great Plains.
1981 • Fernando Valenzuela of the Los Angeles Dodgers became the FIRST ROOKIE TO WIN BASEBALL'S CY YOUNG AWARD.

VETERANS DAY

11

NOVEMBER 12
activities

BIRTHDAYS

1815 • **ELIZABETH CADY STANTON,** American suffrage leader

1840 • **AUGUSTE RODIN,** French sculptor

1928 • **MARJORIE SHARMAT,** children's author

1941 • **ALMA HEFLIN,** first female American test pilot

EVENTS

1799 • **A DAZZLING METEOR SHOWER** was observed in South Africa by the German naturalist Alexander von Humboldt.

1859 • Jules Leotard, a French acrobat, introduced **THE FLYING TRAPEZE** at a circus in Paris.

1912 • **THE FIRST MOVIE STUNTMAN** jumped from a dynamited balloon into the Hudson River.

1927 • **THE HOLLAND TUNNEL,** which runs under New York's Hudson River, was opened.

1954 • **ELLIS ISLAND,** which since 1892 had processed more than 20 million immigrants to the United States, was closed.

1980 • *VOYAGER 1,* an unmanned U.S. spacecraft, passed Saturn and transmitted new information about the planet's rings.

1981 • The second launching of the **SPACE SHUTTLE** *COLUMBIA* marked the first time a space vehicle was reused.

📖 Family matters

Marjorie Sharmat has written more than 60 books, including the popular Nate the Great series. Many of her characters are named for people in her own family. Ask your students to be detectives (like Nate the Great) and find characters whose names are based on the following members of Marjorie Sharmat's family: her parents, Anna and Nathan Weinman; her sister, Rosalind; her uncle, Harry; her husband, Mitchell; her sons, Craig and Andrew; and her dog, Fritz. Encourage your kids to incorporate some family names in the next story they write.

🎖 Just plane fun!

Celebrate Alma Heflin and other women fliers with these facts and activities:

1. Amy Johnson flew from London to Australia in 1930. The trip took 19 days. Use the scale on your classroom map to calculate the distance she flew in miles and kilometers.

2. Tell your students that in 1917 freight trains were thought to be faster than any airplane. Pioneer aviator Katherine Stinson decided to race a train, and her airplane won. Challenge your students to find out the speed of the fastest train and the fastest commercial airplane of today.

3. Anne Morrow Lindbergh was the first woman in America to get a glider license. Her flying experiences were the inspiration for many of her poems and books. Read aloud passages from *North to the Orient* to your class. Then ask your students to write their own poem or story dealing with flight.

NOVEMBER 13
activities

📖 Happy thoughts

Robert Louis Stevenson, author of the famous book *Treasure Island*, is also known for his poetry. Copy his short poem "Happy Thought" on the chalkboard:

> *The world is so full of a number of things,*
> *I'm sure we should all be as happy as kings.*

Tell your students that this is an example of a rhymed couplet—a two-line poem with rhyming words at the end of each line. Challenge them to express their happy thoughts in a couplet of their own.

📺 The wall

The Vietnam Veterans Memorial is one of the most visited sites in Washington, D.C. Its black, reflective surface is engraved with the names of over 58,000 Americans killed or missing in action in Vietnam. The memorial was designed by Maya Yang Lin, an architecture student at Yale University. A panel of artists, architects, designers, and members of the Fine Arts Commission selected her design from among 1,421 entries, including one from her professor. The ideas, in model form, filled a large warehouse.

Many visitors leave mementos, including stuffed animals, photos, flags, flowers, letters, and poems, at the base of the panel where the name of a relative or friend appears. Ask your students what mementos they would leave. Then share Eve Bunting's powerful book *The Wall*.

BIRTHDAYS

1850 • **ROBERT LOUIS STEVENSON,** 📖 Scottish author who wrote *Treasure Island*

1856 • **LOUIS BRANDEIS,** U.S. Supreme Court justice

EVENTS

1851 • *MOBY-DICK* was published.

1865 • **GOLD CERTIFICATES,** used in place of money or gold to pay debts, were first issued.

1933 • **THE FIRST RECORDED SIT-DOWN STRIKE** in the United States took place at the Hormel Packing Co. in Austin, Minn.

1939 • **THE ROTOLACTOR,** a rotating milking machine capable of milking 1,680 cows in 7 hours, was demonstrated by its inventor, Henry Jeffers.

1940 • **WALT DISNEY'S** *FANTASIA,* the first film with stereophonic sound, premiered in New York.

1946 • **THE FIRST ARTIFICIAL SNOW** was produced at Mt. Greylock, Mass.

1956 • The U.S. Supreme Court declared **RACIAL SEGREGATION ON PUBLIC BUSES UNCONSTITUTIONAL.**

1982 • **THE VIETNAM VETERANS** 📺 **MEMORIAL** was dedicated in Washington, D.C.

13

NOVEMBER 14
activities

BIRTHDAYS

1765 • ROBERT FULTON, American steamboat inventor

1840 • CLAUDE MONET, French painter

1900 • AARON COPLAND, American composer

1907 • WILLIAM STEIG, children's author and illustrator

• ASTRID LINDGREN, Swedish author who created Pippi Longstocking

1908 • JOSEPH McCARTHY, U.S. senator

1930 • EDWARD WHITE, American astronaut who became the first man to walk in space

1948 • CHARLES, PRINCE OF WALES (Charles Philip Arthur George Windsor)

1966 • RONALD McDONALD, corporate mascot of McDonald's fast-food restaurants

EVENTS

1732 • THE FIRST PAID LIBRARIAN, Louis Timothee, was hired by the Library Company of Philadelphia.

1836 • FIBERGLASS WAS PATENTED by a Frenchman named Dubus-Bonnel.

1889 • Journalist Nellie Bly set out on AN AROUND-THE-WORLD TRIP she hoped to complete in less than 80 days.

1963 • SURTSEY, a volcanic island near Iceland, was born.

First impressionist

When Claude Monet first displayed his paintings, most critics—as well as the general public—were scornful. They weren't used to his informal scenes, bright and sparkling colors, bold brush-strokes, and rough surfaces. The artistic movement called impressionism took its name from Monet's 1872 painting *Impression: Sunrise.*

Monet recognized that light changes all the time, so he painted the same scenes at different times of day and under different weather conditions. Have your students go outdoors to observe and sketch an object at different times. What changes do they note?

Nervous author

William Steig didn't write his first children's book until he was 60. Two years later, he won the Caldecott Medal for *Sylvester and the Magic Pebble.* Not accustomed to being in the spotlight, he felt intimidated about giving an acceptance speech for this award. Chances are that many of your students also get anxious about public speaking. To help them overcome this anxiety, create several silly awards each week, and have the recipients give brief acceptance speeches.

Up in smoke

The volcanic island Surtsey was named in honor of Surtur, the fire-possessing giant of Norse mythology. Have your students research other mythical characters— Thor, Atlas, Perseus, Neptune, Aphrodite, Cyclops, Mercury, Pygmalion, Medusa—and describe make-believe islands bearing the names and reflecting the traits of these characters.

NOVEMBER 15
ctivities

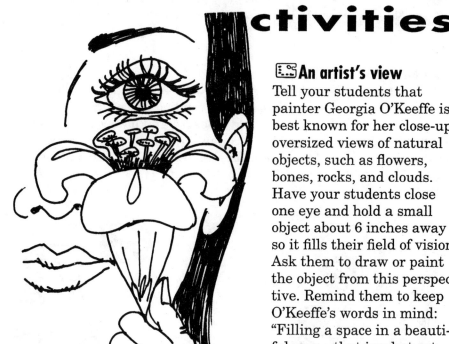

An artist's view

Tell your students that painter Georgia O'Keeffe is best known for her close-up, oversized views of natural objects, such as flowers, bones, rocks, and clouds. Have your students close one eye and hold a small object about 6 inches away so it fills their field of vision. Ask them to draw or paint the object from this perspective. Remind them to keep O'Keeffe's words in mind: "Filling a space in a beautiful way—that is what art means to me."

Mountain man

Pikes Peak was named for Zebulon Pike, an army officer and explorer who sighted it in 1806. He wrote in his journal an impressive description of the mighty mountain. Ask your students to write a description of a natural wonder in their area. Remind them that natural wonders can be common, like a bird hunting for food, the shadow cast by a bare tree, a new snowfall, or the changing shapes of the clouds.

Making changes

The Jefferson Memorial is a tribute to our third president, who was also the writer of the Declaration of Independence. Jefferson believed that there should be less formality in the White House. As president, he began the practice of having guests sit at a round table so everyone would feel equally important. He also preferred his guests to shake his hand instead of bowing, which had been the practice. Ask your students to list practices they think are too formal and what changes they'd make.

BIRTHDAYS

1738 • **WILLIAM HERSCHEL,** German-born English astronomer who discovered the planet Uranus.

1887 • **GEORGIA O'KEEFFE,** American artist

1891 • **ERWIN ROMMEL,** German general

1898 • **DAVID McCORD,** poet and children's author

EVENTS

1777 • The Continental Congress adopted the **ARTICLES OF CONFEDERATION.**

1806 • Zebulon Pike sighted **PIKES PEAK** in Colorado.

1864 • Union soldiers under the command of General William Sherman **BURNED THE CITY OF ATLANTA.**

1896 • **NIAGARA FALLS** was first used to generate power, for the city of Buffalo, N.Y.

1907 • **THE "MUTT AND JEFF"** comic strip first appeared.

1920 • **THE LEAGUE OF NATIONS** held its first meeting in Geneva.

1939 • President Franklin D. Roosevelt laid the cornerstone for the **JEFFERSON MEMORIAL** in Washington, D.C.

NOVEMBER 16
activities

BIRTHDAYS

1873 • **WILLIAM C. HANDY,** African-
American musician and composer
known as "the Father of the
Blues"
1915 • **JEAN FRITZ,** children's author
1964 • **DWIGHT GOODEN,** baseball
pitcher

EVENTS

1864 • **GENERAL WILLIAM SHERMAN**
started his Civil War "March to
the Sea" from Atlanta.
1901 • An automobile was first driven
FASTER THAN A MILE A MINUTE.
1907 • **OKLAHOMA** became the 46th
state.
1933 • The United States established
**DIPLOMATIC RELATIONS WITH
THE USSR.**
1969 • **MOON ROCKS** first went on
 public display, in New York
City's Museum of Natural
History.
1973 • President Richard M. Nixon
signed a bill authorizing construction of a **TRANS-ALASKAN
OIL PIPELINE.**
• **THE RECORD FOR MOST BINGO
CARDS** played simultaneously
was set by Robert Berg, who
had 30 seconds between calls to
check his 346 cards.

CHILDREN'S BOOK WEEK

⚗ Moon rocks

In 1969, astronaut Neil Armstrong collected 48 pounds of soil and
rocks from the moon. Scientists eagerly studied these samples. They
discovered a rock mineral not found on earth and named it
Armalcolite after the Apollo 11 astronauts—Armstrong, Buzz Aldrin,
and Michael Collins. Have groups of students figure out what they'd
name rocks they discovered.

📖 Hurray for books!

Children's Book Week is sponsored by the Children's Book Council.
Its founder, Franklin Mathews, the official librarian for the Boy
Scouts of America, toured the United States from 1913 to 1915 to
promote higher standards in children's books. Compile a class book
list of your students' personal favorites. Ask the kids why they like
these books, then develop a set of class criteria for excellent books.
When new books are introduced to your class library, have a committee of student reviewers rank each one according to the class criteria

Celebrate Children's Book Week with a class party. Start by having
your students design a place mat based on their favorite book. It
should include the book's title and author and an illustration of the
student's favorite scene. Then have the class design a menu for the
party, including foods that favorite characters would enjoy. For
example, how about gingerbread (in honor of The Gingerbread Boy)
with honey (in honor of Winnie the Pooh)? Before eating, ask the
kids to go to the front of the class and hold up their place mats.

NOVEMBER 17
activities

✒ Names and nouns

The Mobius strip is named for mathematician and astronomer August Ferdinand Mobius. Has anyone in your class ever made one? Can your students think of other scientists whose names are readily associated with their contributions, such as Richter and Jarvis? How about scientists whose names are used as common nouns, such as Diesel, Watt, Ampere, and Bunsen?

🍞 Healthy eating

In honor of Homemade Bread Day, ask your students to collect favorite family recipes for breads. Can they think of any substitutions to make the breads more healthful (for example, egg beaters for egg whites, margarine for butter, skim milk for regular milk)? Ask parent or student volunteers to prepare homemade breads, then cater a classroom bread-tasting festival.

✳ Stamp of approval

Show your students a picture of the bald eagle. Why do they think this bird appealed to our Founding Fathers as a symbol for the country? Where besides postage stamps have they seen this symbol used? Have each student design a class stamp, then hold a vote for the favorite. Have a local stationery store make the winning design into a traditional ink-pad stamp, which you and the kids can use to adorn papers, tests, and classroom correspondence.

✦ Hot statistics

To produce synthetic diamonds, pure carbon is subjected to temperatures above 5,000° F and pressures exceeding 2,500,000 pounds per square inch. Challenge your students to compare this temperature with that of the human body (98.6° F) and this pressure with that of the atmosphere at sea level (14.7 pounds per square inch). Also have the kids compare and graph other temperatures, such as molten lava (2,200° F), a car engine (700° F), and the surface of the sun (10,000° F).

BIRTHDAYS

1790 • AUGUST FERDINAND MOBIUS, German mathematician and astronomer

1918 • BILLY GRAHAM, American clergyman

EVENTS

1800 • CONGRESS convened for the first time in Washington, D.C.

1851 • THE FIRST POSTAGE STAMPS depicting the American eagle were issued.

1855 • Dr. David Livingstone came across VICTORIA FALLS along the Zambezi River.

1869 • THE SUEZ CANAL opened.

1959 • SYNTHETIC DIAMONDS were first commercially manufactured by De Beers in South Africa.

1966 • During a huge meteor shower, 50,000 METEORS WERE OBSERVED over Arizona in a 20-minute period.

1970 • The Soviet Union's Lunokhod 1, a solar-powered eight-wheel robot, became the FIRST VEHICLE TO TRAVEL ALONG THE MOON'S SURFACE.

🍞 HOMEMADE BREAD DAY

NOVEMBER 18
activities

BIRTHDAYS

1789 • **LOUIS DAGUERRE, French painter and inventor of the daguerreotype, the first practical method of photography**

1899 • **EUGENE ORMANDY, Hungarian-born conductor**

1923 • **ALAN SHEPARD, U.S. astronaut who became the first American in space**

1928 • **MICKEY MOUSE, famous cartoon character**

EVENTS

1307 • **According to legend, WILLIAM TELL was forced to shoot an apple off his son's head by an Austrian bailiff.**

1820 • **ANTARCTICA WAS DISCOVERED by a U.S. navy captain, Nathaniel B. Palmer.**

1865 • **MARK TWAIN published his first fiction, "The Celebrated Jumping Frog of Calaveras County."**

1870 • **MAIL WAS CARRIED BY PIGEON from England to France.**

1883 • **STANDARD TIME ZONES were adopted in the United States.**

1894 • **THE FIRST SUNDAY NEWSPAPER COMIC SECTION appeared in the New York *World*.**

1971 • **THE HUNTING OF ANIMALS FROM AIRPLANES was made a federal crime.**

Clock confusion

Until late in the 19th century, there was no national standard time. People would set their watches by the position of the sun, and even if they were off by a little bit, they didn't care. But as the country grew and communication—and railways—expanded, it became necessary to establish standard times. That's when American railroad companies adopted a system of four time zones: eastern, central, mountain, and Pacific. Display a U.S. map that's divided into time zones. Set four watches according to time zone and clip them to the appropriate section of the map. Throughout the day, refer to the watches and talk about what people might be doing at that moment in various parts of the country.

Strike up the band

Celebrate Eugene Ormandy's birthday by asking your students to name the four main sections of an orchestra. Can they list some instruments for each section? Ask a group of young musicians to discuss the seating plan for most orchestras.

Top mouse

Mickey Mouse first appeared in the film cartoon *Steamboat Willie*. Walt Disney attended the premiere in New York so he could see firsthand the audience reaction. He was delighted to hear the laughter. Each Mickey Mouse cartoon Disney made was a hit, and before long, the leading rodent was a star. Your students might be surprised to learn that every day Americans buy at least 5 million things that are shaped like Mickey Mouse or have a picture of Mickey Mouse on them. Ask the kids to list other cartoon characters used in the same way.

NOVEMBER 19
activities

Lefty lore

Like James Garfield, presidents Harry Truman, Gerald Ford, George Bush, and Bill Clinton were all left-handed. Other famous lefties include Julius Caesar, Napoleon, Michelangelo, Albert Einstein, Benjamin Franklin, and Leonardo da Vinci. Martina Navratilova, Boomer Esiason, and Will Clark are recent sports stars who are left-handed. Tell your students that about 10% of the population is left-handed. Compare your class percentage of lefties with this national figure. Then conduct a schoolwide survey to determine if your school fits the average. Report your findings in the school newspaper.

Quality, not quantity

President Lincoln and Edward Everett, a former governor of Massachusetts, secretary of state, and U.S. senator, spoke at a ceremony dedicating a national cemetery at Gettysburg, Pa.—where 3,100 Union soldiers and 3,900 Confederate soldiers died in battle. Newspaper editors throughout the country failed to recognize the importance of Lincoln's speech, relegating the 270-word address to inside pages while covering Everett's 2-hour speech on front pages. Read the Gettysburg Address—now regarded as one of the greatest speeches of all time—to your students. Do they think it's a powerful speech? Why? Challenge them to write a speech of 100 words or less on a topic that evokes strong feelings in them.

Junior architects

Primary students from the Abraham Lincoln School in Chicago gave architect Robert Leathers pictures of their ideal playground. Using their ideas, he designed a fantasy playground of castles, spaceships, mazes, and tunnels. Ask your students to design, draw, and label a diagram of their dream playground.

BIRTHDAYS

1752 • **GEORGE ROGERS CLARK,** frontiersman and Revolutionary War military leader

1805 • **FERDINAND MARIE DE LESSEPS,** French diplomat who masterminded the Suez Canal

1831 • **JAMES GARFIELD,** 20th president of the United States

1905 • **TOMMY DORSEY,** American musician and bandleader

1917 • **INDIRA GANDHI,** Indian prime minister

1921 • **ROY CAMPANELLA,** baseball star

EVENTS

1493 • **COLUMBUS,** on his second voyage to the New World, landed on the island of Puerto Rico and claimed it for Spain.

1850 • **THE FIRST INSURANCE POLICY ON A WOMAN'S LIFE** was issued.

1863 • Abraham Lincoln delivered **THE GETTYSBURG ADDRESS.**

1872 • A patent for the **ADDING MACHINE** was issued to E.D. Barbour of Boston.

1969 • The Brazilian soccer star **PELE SCORED HIS 1,000TH CAREER GOAL,** in Rio de Janeiro.

1987 • Architect Robert Leathers met with Chicago elementary students **TO DESIGN A PLAYGROUND.**

19

NOVEMBER 20
activities

BIRTHDAYS

1858 • **SELMA LAGERLOF**, Swedish writer who became the first woman to win the Nobel Prize in literature

1889 • **EDWIN POWELL HUBBLE**, American astronomer

EVENTS

1789 • New Jersey became the **FIRST STATE TO RATIFY THE BILL OF RIGHTS.**

1820 • The whaling ship *Essex* was **SUNK BY A SPERM WHALE.**

1873 • The cities **BUDA AND PEST WERE UNITED** to form Hungary's capital.

1923 • Garrett Morgan, an African-American inventor, patented **THE TRAFFIC LIGHT.**

1947 • **QUEEN ELIZABETH II** of England married Lieutenant Philip Mountbatten.

1959 • The United Nations adopted the **DECLARATION OF THE RIGHTS OF THE CHILD.**

1969 • The U.S. Department of Agriculture **BANNED THE USE OF THE PESTICIDE DDT** in residential areas.

1976 • **THE LONGEST BANANA SPLIT** ever made—over a mile long— was served in Queensland, Australia.

1987 • **TWIGLET BANK**, the first bank founded by children, run by children, and for children only, opened.

20

⊕ Twin cities
Locate Budapest on a world map. Then have your students search atlases, globes, and maps for other twin cities that could be combined and given new names. List these places on the board. The kids could even combine two states or countries. How about a state called Arkansasaw or a country called Sportugal?

⇗ Stop, look, listen
Ask your students to guess how many traffic lights they pass on their way home from school. Have them keep a tally to see how close they came. If there's a traffic light near your school, your kids can make some observations. How long is the light in its red, yellow, and green phases? How many cars go through the light during a 15-minute period? Will that number vary according to the time of day? How many cars do your students think go through the light each day? Each week?

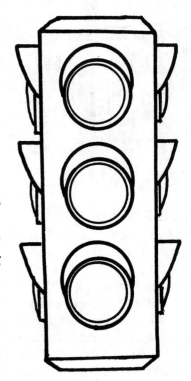

⁂ Rights rally
The Declaration of the Rights of the Child states that all children are entitled to an opportunity to develop in a healthy, normal manner; a name and a nationality; adequate housing and nutrition; recreation and medical services; special care if handicapped; love and understanding; free education; protection in times of disaster; and protection from cruelty, neglect, and discrimination. Encourage your students to write a classroom Declaration of the Rights of the Student. Publish the finished document in your class newsletter.

NOVEMBER 21
activities

✿ What a crowd!

During the first manned balloon flight, Frenchmen Pilatre de Rozier and Marquis Francois d'Arlandes drifted 8 kilometers over Paris before landing. The trip lasted 25 minutes. Parisians got so excited by the news of this event that 300,000 people—half the population of the entire city—showed up 10 days later to watch the second flight. Have your students figure out how many school buses it would take to transport a crowd of that size. Ask the kids whether any of them have ever been part of a big crowd. What kind of event was it? Did they like the experience?

📖 Book awards

Tell your class that Elizabeth George Speare received Newbery Awards for her books *The Witch of Blackbird Pond* and *The Bronze Bow*. Ask a student to check these books out of the school library and read some of the jacket information to the class. What other Newbery Award winners have your students read? If they were to develop their own award, what would they name it and what criteria would they establish for selection?

✺ Underwater president

Harry Truman rode on board U-2513, a captured German submarine, during U.S. naval exercises off Key West, Fla. Show your students a cutaway view of a submarine. (You should be able to find one in an encyclopedia.) Then ask them to draw a cutaway view of their lunch bag, backpack, or toy chest—with contents, of course.

BIRTHDAYS

1785 • **WILLIAM BEAUMONT,** American surgeon and pioneer in research on digestion
1908 • **ELIZABETH GEORGE SPEARE,** children's author
1920 • **STAN MUSIAL,** baseball star

EVENTS

1620 • **THE PILGRIMS SIGNED THE MAYFLOWER COMPACT** before disembarking near Provincetown, Mass.
1783 • **THE FIRST MANNED BALLOON FLIGHT** was made by two Frenchmen.
1789 • **NORTH CAROLINA** became the 12th state to enter the Union.
1864 • **PRESIDENT LINCOLN** wrote a letter of condolence to Mrs. Lydia Bixby, whose five sons had been killed in the Civil War.
1877 • Thomas Edison announced his **INVENTION OF THE PHONOGRAPH.**
1922 • The **FIRST CRUISE SHIP TO CIRCUMNAVIGATE THE WORLD,** the *Laconia,* departed from New York City.
1946 • Harry S. Truman became the **FIRST PRESIDENT TO TRAVEL UNDERWATER ON A SUBMARINE.**
1964 • **THE VERRAZANO-NARROWS BRIDGE,** the suspension bridge with the longest main span in the world, opened.

NOVEMBER 22
activities

BIRTHDAYS

1643 • SIEUR DE LA SALLE, French explorer

1744 • ABIGAIL ADAMS, wife of President John Adams and mother of President John Quincy Adams

1943 • BILLIE JEAN KING, American tennis star

EVENTS

1842 • THE FIRST VOLCANIC ERUPTION RECORDED IN THE UNITED STATES occurred at Mt. Lassen, Calif.

1906 • THE SOS DISTRESS SIGNAL was 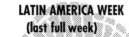 adopted by an international convention in Berlin.

1917 • THE NATIONAL HOCKEY LEAGUE was established.

1927 • THE FIRST SNOWMOBILE PATENT was issued to Carl J.E. Elason.

1931 • Ferde Grofe's *GRAND CANYON SUITE* premiered in Chicago.

1963 • PRESIDENT JOHN F. KENNEDY WAS ASSASSINATED in Dallas, Tex.

1977 • THE CONCORDE JET began service between New York and Paris and London.

1990 • CLIFFORD THE BIG RED DOG made his debut in Macy's Thanksgiving Day Parade.

LATIN AMERICA WEEK (last full week)

Student ciphers

Most people think SOS stands for save our ship, save our souls, or stop other signals. All are wrong. SOS represents the Morse code signal for three short dots, three long dashes, and three short dots. It was adopted by international agreement as a universal call for help because it was easy to understand. Invite student teams to develop their own codes and exchange messages with others. Keep a class code book with decoded messages.

Hockey havens

The National Hockey League was established in 1917. Ask your students to check an almanac to find all the cities that have a professional hockey team. Locate these cities on a map. Which team names seem particularly appropriate? For example, whaling was an important industry in Connecticut during the 19th century, and Hartford's team name is the Whalers.

Canine favorite

Norman Bridwell, the creator of Clifford the Big Red Dog, thinks it's reassuring for kids to see that everyone—even a lovable dog like Clifford—makes mistakes. Have your students bring their favorite Clifford books to class. Invite them to read sections that show the oversized pooch trying to do the right thing but falling just a bit short of his goal.

South of the border

To celebrate Latin America Week, have your students design their own passports, which should include a cover map of that area. Have them use their passports as they keep track of Latin American authors, artists, musicians, and historical figures mentioned throughout the week.

NOVEMBER 23

activities

Funny bones
Explain to those students unfamiliar with the Marx Brothers that Harpo's humor was almost entirely visual and provided a counterpoint to Groucho's verbal humor. Then discuss different types of visual and verbal humor, such as slapstick, exaggeration, sarcasm, irony, putdown, surprise, and misunderstanding. Have your students give examples of these types of humor—from TV shows, movies, books, magazines, or personal experience.

Getting there
Earl Ovington flew the mail between two communities on Long Island: Garden City and Mineola. The distance of his route was 6 miles. On a local road map, mark places that are 6 miles from your school. Have the kids figure out how long it would take a bicyclist to carry mail 6 miles. How about a walker?

Life on the frozen continent
Archaeologists digging near the South Pole found the fossil remains of a Lystrosaurus, a 4-foot reptile that lived about 200 million years ago. Ask your students to make a list of the animals living in Antarctica today. Then have them use this list to sketch a food web that involves at least three of the animals.

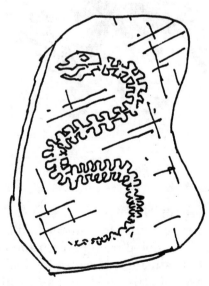

Interplanetary news
In honor of the first space-to-earth news conference, organize your class into teams, and assign each team a planet to investigate. Once research is complete, ask each team to create a news telecast from its planet.

BIRTHDAYS
1804 • FRANKLIN PIERCE, 14th president of the United States
1859 • BILLY THE KID (real name: William H. Bonney), American outlaw
1887 • BORIS KARLOFF, British star of horror movies
1893 • HARPO MARX, American comedian

EVENTS
1876 • Columbia, Harvard, and Princeton formed the FIRST INTERCOLLEGIATE FOOTBALL ASSOCIATION.
1889 • THE FIRST JUKEBOX was installed, in San Francisco.
1897 • J.L. Love received a patent for THE PENCIL SHARPENER.
1911 • The U.S. Post Office's FIRST AIRMAIL PILOT, Earl Ovington, was sworn in.
1945 • WORLD WAR II FOOD RATIONING ended in the United States, except for sugar.
1969 • THE FIRST FOSSIL BONES FOUND IN ANTARCTICA were discovered.
• Apollo 12 astronauts held the FIRST SPACE-TO-EARTH NEWS CONFERENCE.

ZIBELEMARIT (Onion Festival in Switzerland—fourth Monday)

NOVEMBER 24
activities

BIRTHDAYS

1713 • **FATHER JUNIPERO SERRA,** Spanish Franciscan missionary who founded the first mission in California

1784 • **ZACHARY TAYLOR, 12th president of the United States**

1826 • **CARLO LORENZINI (pen name: Carlo Collodi),** Italian writer, author of *Pinocchio*

1849 • **FRANCES HODGSON BURNETT,** American writer, author of *The Secret Garden*

1864 • **HENRI DE TOULOUSE-LAUTREC,** French artist

1868 • **SCOTT JOPLIN,** American composer, known as "the King of Ragtime"

EVENTS

1859 • Charles Darwin published *On the Origin of Species,* which outlined his THEORY OF EVOLUTION through natural selection.

1869 • Women from 21 states met in Cleveland to organize the AMERICAN WOMAN SUFFRAGE ASSOCIATION.

1874 • BARBED WIRE was patented by Joseph Glidden of Illinois.

1896 • Vermont enacted the FIRST ABSENTEE VOTING LAW.

1969 • *APOLLO 12* splashed down in the Pacific to conclude its historic moon mission.

24

Presidential countdown
Zachary Taylor was the 12th president of the United States. See how many of your students can name his 11 predecessors—in order.

Picking a pseudonym
In 1880 Carlo Lorenzini first published *The Adventures of Pinocchio* in a magazine. He selected "Collodi" as his pseudonym because it was the name of the Italian town where his mother was born. Invite your students to use a location-based pseudonym for a day. Ask them each to explain why they selected their name. Then have them write about a toy, doll, or stuffed animal that seemed almost real to them. Invite them to bring it to class and describe its qualities and personality. If possible, read *The Velveteen Rabbit,* another wonderful story about a toy that comes to life.

An artist's eye
Henri de Toulouse-Lautrec had keen powers of observation. He frequently copied from photographs to capture movements and gestures in his paintings. Because he disliked painting professional models, he went to theaters, circuses, and dance halls to paint real performers in action. The posters he created to advertise books, newspapers, and shows also reflect his sense of fun. Ask your students which school activities might have made appealing subjects for Toulouse-Lautrec. Then challenge them to illustrate a scene from one of those activities in the style of this famous French artist.

NOVEMBER 25
activities

🖋 First jobs to top jobs

Andrew Carnegie's early work experience
included stints as a cotton-factory bobbin boy,
telegraph messenger boy, telegraph operator,
and railroad clerk. A humble start for a man
who became one of the world's richest people!
Have your students construct a time line of
Andrew Carnegie's jobs. Then ask them to
interview family members and construct
their employment time lines. Did any of the
interviewees hold similar first jobs? Are any
of those jobs available to young people today?

⚾ The Yankee Clipper

Joe DiMaggio had a lifetime batting
average of .325. He also established one
of the most remarkable records in the
history of baseball: In 1941 he batted
safely in 56 consecutive games. Take
your class outside for a baseball or softball game. Back in the classroom, have
the children use their calculators to compute their batting averages. (Divide the
number of hits by the number of times at
bat; carry it to three decimal places.)

📖 Name change

Crescent Dragonwagon is not the author's pen name. It is a name
she gave herself before her professional career had begun. Crescent
means "the growing," and she selected Dragonwagon because it was
fun and completely frivolous. Let your kids change their names for a
day. Bring a few baby name books to class so they can find out the
meanings and origins of these names.

🇺🇸 Leadership qualities

When John F. Kennedy was a college student, he wrote, "Unless democracy can produce able leaders, its chances of survival are
slight." Ask your students to list qualities of
an able leader. Then have them write a
short essay on the character traits they
think the president of the United States
should have.

BIRTHDAYS

1787 • **FRANZ XAVIER GRUBER,**
Austrian organist and composer
of "Silent Night"
1835 • **ANDREW CARNEGIE,** Scottish-
American industrialist and philanthropist
1846 • **CARRY NATION,** American
temperance leader
1914 • **JOE DiMAGGIO,** baseball star
1946 • **MARC BROWN,** children's author
1952 • **CRESCENT DRAGONWAGON,**
children's author

EVENTS

1817 • **THE FIRST SWORD-SWALLOW-**
ING EXHIBITION in the United
States was given by Senaa
Samma of India.
1952 • Agatha Christie's *THE MOUSE-*
TRAP, the longest-running play
ever, opened in London.
1963 • **PRESIDENT JOHN F. KENNEDY**
WAS BURIED in Arlington
National Cemetery.
1973 • By executive order, the **SPEED**
LIMIT on U.S. highways was
reduced to 55 mph.

NOVEMBER 26
activities

BIRTHDAYS

1895 • **WILLIAM GRIFFITH WILSON,** cofounder of Alcoholics Anonymous

1922 • **CHARLES SCHULZ,** American cartoonist who created "Peanuts"

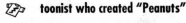

EVENTS

1716 • **A LION WAS FIRST EXHIBITED** in the United States, in Boston.

1783 • **ANNAPOLIS, MD.,** became the capital of the United States.

1818 • **ENCKE'S COMET,** which appears more frequently than any other known comet, was discovered.

1863 • By proclamation of President Abraham Lincoln, **THANKSGIVING DAY** was celebrated on the last Thursday in November.

1864 • **LEWIS CARROLL** sent an early Christmas present to Alice Liddell, a 12-year-old friend: a handwritten manuscript that he later expanded into *Alice's Adventures in Wonderland.*

1883 • **SOJOURNER TRUTH,** a former slave who became a leading abolitionist, died.

1925 • **FORD ANNOUNCED THE PRICE** of its popular roadster: $260.

🏳️ Cavalcade of capitals

Seven cities, besides Annapolis, have been the nation's capital: York, Pa.; Philadelphia; Baltimore; Lancaster, Pa.; Princeton, N.J.; Trenton, N.J.; and now Washington, D.C. Have teams of students research these other capital cities. What do the cities have in common? What do students think is important in choosing a capital? Then challenge the teams to select a new city to be the nation's capital. They could design a poster highlighting the merits of their choice.

📝 Behind-the-scenes with "Peanuts"

After skipping two and a half grades in elementary school, Charles Schulz felt out of place. He disliked being the youngest child in his grade, and he fell behind in his work. Like Charlie Brown, the character he created years later, he felt ignored by other children. Looking back on his school days, Schulz noted, "Now I realize that Charlie Brown's goofs are familiar to everybody." Ask your students to bring in a "Peanuts" strip and write a paragraph explaining why the subject is relevant to readers of all ages.

When Schulz was 13, his family was given a mixed-breed black and white dog that became the inspiration for another famous "Peanuts" character. When he started his comic strip, Schulz intended to name the dog Sniffy, but there was already a cartoon pet with that name. So he changed the name to Snoopy. Ask your students to explain how their families have selected names for pets.

NOVEMBER 27
activities

🧪 Up scale, down scale

Observe the birthday of Anders Celsius by having students use their calculators to convert temperatures from Fahrenheit to Celsius. Using the formula $C=(F-32)\times5\div9$, they can express interesting temperatures—that of the human body, the surface of the sun, the oven setting for a batch of brownies, the record high in Death Valley—on the Celsius scale.

🚲 Wheelers

Those who complained about bicycles on Boston streets also disliked the black tights and handlebar mustaches sported by so many cyclists. Ask your students to describe how cyclists are dressing today. What are some safety rules all cyclists should practice? Challenge the kids to compare the average costs of a bicycle 100 years ago and today.

✦ It's a wonderful life

Ask your students to use almanacs and record books to find average life spans and longevity records for various animals. Then have them make bar graphs to show the results. What kinds of animals seem to live longer? Invite the kids to write biographies of their pets. Encourage them to include photos.

📺 Parent TV favorites

To celebrate the birthday of "Buffalo Bob" Smith, ask your students to interview their parents about the children's TV shows they watched. Beforehand, brainstorm for a list of questions. Students might want to find out about the format of the programs, what times the shows were on, or how they're different from the kids' shows of today.

BIRTHDAYS

1701 • **ANDERS CELSIUS**, Swedish astronomer and inventor of the Celsius scale

1917 • **"BUFFALO BOB" SMITH**, host of the children's TV show "Howdy Doody"

1960 • **KEVIN HENKES**, children's author and illustrator

EVENTS

1582 • **WILLIAM SHAKESPEARE WAS ISSUED A MARRIAGE LICENSE** in the diocese of Worcester, England.

1885 • **A METEORITE** landed near Mazapil, Mexico.

1890 • **A PROTEST AGAINST BICYCLES** took place outside Boston. The demonstrators claimed bicycles made the roads unsafe for horses and buggies.

1903 • Puss, **THE OLDEST CAT ON RECORD**, was born. She lived for 36 years and 1 day.

1910 • Pennsylvania Station opened in New York City. At the time, it was the **LARGEST RAILWAY TERMINAL** in the United States.

1960 • Hockey star Gordie Howe recorded his **1,000TH CAREER POINT**.

1973 • By a vote of 92-3, **THE SENATE VOTED TO CONFIRM GERALD FORD** as vice president, succeeding Spiro Agnew.

27

NOVEMBER 28
activities

BIRTHDAYS

1757 • **WILLIAM BLAKE, English poet whose works include "The Tiger"**

1866 • **HENRY BACON, American architect who designed the Lincoln Memorial**

1931 • **TOMI UNGERER, children's illustrator**

EVENTS

1843 • **France and England recognized the INDEPENDENCE OF HAWAII.**

1895 • **THE FIRST U.S. AUTO RACE began in Chicago. J. Frank Duryea won with an average speed of 7$\frac{1}{2}$ mph.**

1929 • **Ernie Nevers established an NFL SINGLE-GAME SCORING RECORD by running for six touchdowns and kicking four extra points.**

1979 • **Billy Smith of the New York Islanders became the FIRST NHL GOALIE TO SCORE A GOAL.**

📖 Poem, poem

Read aloud William Blake's famous poem "The Tiger." Then invite your students to write their own poem addressing an animal and asking it a question.

🖼 It's monumental

Show your students pictures of the Lincoln Memorial. Ask them to name other monuments that can be found around the Mall in Washington, D.C. Then have them design postcards for some of the monuments in their community.

⚙ Some race!

The first U.S. auto race covered a 54-mile course from Chicago to Evanston, Ill., and back. More than 80 cars entered, but only 6 completed the race. Have your students use their calculators to compute the percentage that finished. Tell the class that it took the winning driver 7 hours and 53 minutes to cover the course, for an average speed of 7$\frac{1}{2}$ mph. Your students might be surprised to learn that a chicken can run faster. Ask them to research how some other animals' speeds compare.

⬭ Football records

Have the kids check the newspaper sports page for current team and individual football statistics. Who are the leading passers, receivers, and scorers? Invite the kids to write their own word problems based on the newspaper stats. What player scored the most points in the the previous week's games? How does his total compare with Ernie Nevers's?

NOVEMBER 29
activities

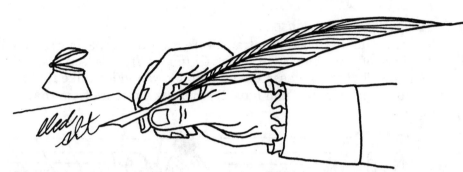

✒ Secret messages

People have sent messages in invisible ink for hundreds of years. Try writing invisible messages with your students. Citrus juice, vinegar, or a mixture of 1 teaspoon of sugar in a glass of water all make fine invisible inks. Have your students write their messages with a small paintbrush, a toothpick, or the head of a small nail. Once the ink is dry, they can exchange messages and take turns carefully holding these near a 150-watt light bulb. Ask them why they think the message reappears. (The heat releases the carbon in the fluid.)
Have your students role-play invisible-ink salespersons. How would they sell this product in 1776 to people who have never used it?

📖 A "must-do"

Madeleine L'Engle called writing an "essential function, like sleeping and breathing." She started writing as soon as she could hold a pencil. And even during the busiest times of her life, she wrote every day. Ask your students what recreational or creative activities they or their family members try to do every day. Create a big book from photographs or drawings of these activities.

⚗ Animals in space

Many animals have blazed their own space trails. Have teams of students research the contributions of animal astronauts and critter cosmonauts. The kids should include the type of animal, the country that sent it into space, and the date of the space flight. Then ask your class to design plaques or citations for each animal. Exhibit them on a bulletin board titled "The Animal Space Explorer Hall of Fame."

BIRTHDAYS

1803 • **CHRISTIAN DOPPLER**, Austrian physicist and mathematician who first explained the Doppler effect
1832 • **LOUISA MAY ALCOTT**, American author who wrote *Little Women*
1876 • **NELLIE TAYLOE ROSS**, first female U.S. governor (Wyoming)
1898 • **C.S. LEWIS**, English writer
1918 • **MADELEINE L'ENGLE**, children's 📖 author

EVENTS

1760 • **THE FRENCH SURRENDERED DETROIT** to the British at the close of the French and Indian War.
1776 • **INVISIBLE INK** was first used in ✖ diplomatic correspondence.
1890 • Navy beat Army, 25-0, in the **FIRST ARMY-NAVY FOOTBALL GAME.**
1929 • Richard Byrd completed the **FIRST PLANE FLIGHT OVER THE SOUTH POLE.**
1961 • A U.S. **MERCURY-ATLAS SPACE** ⚗ **CAPSULE**, along with its passenger, a chimpanzee, was recovered after splashing down.
1963 • President Lyndon Johnson established **THE WARREN COMMISSION** to investigate the assassination of President Kennedy.

NOVEMBER 30
activities

BIRTHDAYS

1667 • JONATHAN SWIFT, Irish-English writer, author of *Gulliver's Travels*

1835 • MARK TWAIN (real name: Samuel Clemens), American writer

1874 • WINSTON CHURCHILL, British statesman

1924 • SHIRLEY CHISHOLM, first black woman to serve in the U.S. House of Representatives

EVENTS

1620 • Peregrine White became the FIRST CHILD BORN TO A PILGRIM FAMILY in the New England colonies.

1782 • England and America signed preliminary peace articles in Paris, marking the END OF THE REVOLUTIONARY WAR.

1875 • A patent for a BISCUIT CUTTER was issued to A.P. Ashbourne of Oakland, Calif.

1887 • THE FIRST SOFTBALL GAME was played in Chicago.

1954 • A METEORITE fell on Ann Hodges of Sylacauga, Ala.

Lilliputians on the loose

Tell your students that Lilliputians were the tiny people encountered by the hero of Jonathan Swift's book *Gulliver's Travels*. Ask the kids to imagine what their classroom or bedroom would look like if they were 2 or 3 inches tall. Then have them draw a picture from that perspective.

Persistent patriot

When Winston Churchill was a boy, he had a hard time in school. However, he could apply himself if he wanted to. He once won a prize for reciting 1,200 lines of poetry from memory without a single mistake! Later, as prime minister of England at the height of World War II, he said, "I have nothing to offer but blood, toil, tears and sweat." Ask your students what this quotation tells about Churchill.

Surprise from space

While resting on her couch, Ann Hodges was jolted to her feet by a tremendous noise. She felt pain in her left hand and hip, saw a large hole in the ceiling, then noticed a rock—still warm to the touch—on the floor. It was a meteorite. Though a meteorite strikes a human only about once every 10,000 years, 200 to 2,000 of them fall to earth each day. Your students might not have seen any meteorites, but they might well have stepped on some micrometeorites: about 20 tons of these dust particles land on earth every day. Can your students explain the difference between a meteor and a comet?

DECEMBER

MONTHLONG OBSERVANCES
Bingo Month
Good Neighbor Month

WEEKLONG EVENTS
Aardvark Week (first full week)
Human Rights Week (week including
   Dec. 10 and Dec. 15)
International Language Week
   (Dec. 15-21)
French Conversation Week
   (third week)

SPECIAL DAYS AND CELEBRATIONS
Hanukkah (8 days, usually in Dec.)
First day of winter (Dec. 21 or 22)
Halcyon Days (7 days before and
   7 days after the winter solstice)
Christmas (Dec. 25)
Kwanzaa (Dec. 26-Jan.1)

☆ Project of the Month: Vive la France!

The third week in December is French Conversation Week. Start preparing your students for this event at the beginning of the month. First, divide your class into teams, and have each select a team name. How about Eiffel's Aces or Paris Players? Next, challenge each team to find English-language words that are derived from French. They can use dictionaries and word-origin books or ask friends or family members for ideas. Develop and post a class list. If possible, recruit a French-speaking staff or community member to provide students with basic conversational vocabulary. Then have the teams make posters in the following categories—breakfast, lunch, dinner, homework, sports, dress, movies, family, seasons. Make sure the students label their illustrations with the appropriate French terms. As their working vocabulary increases, encourage the kids also to label classroom items with their French designations.

At the end of the month, turn your classroom into a French cafe, complete with French music. Make French toast, potage parmentier (potato soup), or mousse au chocolat (chocolate mousse) with your students.

DECEMBER 1
activities

BIRTHDAYS

1912 • MINORU YAMASAKI, American architect who designed the World Trade Center in New York City

1935 • WOODY ALLEN, American actor, writer, and director

1949 • JAN BRETT, children's author and illustrator

EVENTS

1878 • A TELEPHONE was first installed in the White House.

1909 • THE FIRST CHRISTMAS CLUB started in Carlisle, Pa.

1913 • THE FIRST DRIVE-IN AUTOMOBILE SERVICE STATION opened in Pittsburgh, Pa.

1918 • The Kingdom of Serbs, Croats, and Slovenes, later called YUGOSLAVIA, was formed.

1922 • Captain Cyril Turner of the Royal Air Force became the FIRST PILOT TO SKYWRITE IN THE UNITED STATES.

1955 • ROSA PARKS WAS ARRESTED IN MONTGOMERY, ALA., for refusing to give up her bus seat to a white man. The incident helped spark the civil rights movement.

COMPUTER SECURITY DAY
WORLD AIDS DAY

⚡ First-family phone

When the White House first got a phone, few phones were in use anywhere. Telephones were sold in pairs, so each phone could connect with only one other. People couldn't call long distance. Sometimes they couldn't even call across town. Have your students think of reasons the president might need a phone. Whom might he have to call? How could the phone help him in emergencies? Then ask your kids to describe the procedure for making an emergency call.

Crowd-pleasing architect

In addition to the World Trade Center, architect Minoru Yamasaki designed the Dhahran Air Terminal in Saudi Arabia. Saudi officials were so pleased with the building that a picture of it now appears on the nation's currency. Have students identify buildings shown on U.S. currency, then think about other buildings that might merit this honor. Finally, ask the students to draw the reverse side of a $5 bill, replacing the Lincoln Memorial with a building of their choice.

Civil-rights pioneer

In Montgomery, Ala., black bus passengers were required by law to give up their seats and move to the back of the bus if white passengers wanted a seat. When Rosa Parks refused to do this, she was arrested, jailed, and fined. The incident led to a prolonged boycott of city buses and ultimately to a Supreme Court decision declaring racial segregation on buses unconstitutional. Have your students write a journal entry about standing up for what is right. What might the consequences be if the stand is unpopular? Could friendships be lost? In what ways could life be more difficult? Some students might be able to draw on personal experience.

DECEMBER 2
activities

 Get the point?

Georges Seurat wasn't a magician, but his paintings sure fool people! Instead of painting with lines and strokes, he used thousands of dots, a technique called pointillism. Ask your class to stand toward the back of the room while you hold up a print of Seurat's famous *Sunday Afternoon on the Island of La Grande Jatte*. What do they see? What do they see as they move closer? Then show them a color photograph from a magazine or newspaper. Use hand lenses to reveal the dots that form the picture, then discuss the similarities between this technique and Seurat's pointillism. Finally, invite the kids to bring in photos of their families and friends to use as subject matter for a Seurat-like painting. Provide felt-tip markers or tempera paint so kids can stipple their images. Remind them that the closer together they put their dots, the darker the value becomes.

📖 Inner workings

Author David Macaulay has written and illustrated best-selling books about building and how things work. Have your students study his technique. Invite interested kids to make Macaulay-style illustrations to explain the workings of something that interests them.

🏳 This land is your land

The Alaska Lands Act set aside more than 150 million acres—a total area larger than California and Minnesota combined—for parks, wildlife refuges, and conservation areas. Have students use an atlas to locate some of the 26 Alaskan rivers added to the National Wild and Scenic Rivers System by this law. They'll delight in such interesting names as Aniakchak, Salmon, Tlikakila, Selawik, Wind, Fortymile, and Unalakleet.

BIRTHDAYS

1859 • **GEORGES SEURAT,** French artist who developed the technique called pointillism

1863 • **CHARLES RINGLING,** American circus entrepreneur

1906 • **PETER CARL GOLDMARK,** American inventor of the long-playing record and color television

1946 • **DAVID MACAULAY,** children's author and illustrator

EVENTS

1804 • **NAPOLEON BONAPARTE** crowned himself emperor of France.

1816 • The Philadelphia Savings Fund Society, the **FIRST MUTUAL SAVINGS BANK IN THE UNITED STATES,** opened for business.

1916 • Permanent all-over lighting of the **STATUE OF LIBERTY** began.

1942 • The Italian physicist Enrico Fermi and his associates produced the **FIRST SUSTAINED NUCLEAR CHAIN REACTION.**

1980 • **THE ALASKA LANDS ACT** was signed by President Jimmy Carter.

1982 • Barney Clark received the **FIRST PERMANENT ARTIFICIAL HEART.**

PAN AMERICAN HEALTH DAY

BIRTHDAYS

1755 • **GILBERT STUART**, presidential portrait painter

1826 • **GEORGE B. McCLELLAN**, U.S. Civil War general and 1864 Democratic presidential nominee

1838 • **CLEVELAND ABBE**, American meteorologist who was the first weather forecaster for the U.S. Weather Service

EVENTS

1775 • **THE FIRST OFFICIAL AMERICAN FLAG** was raised aboard the naval vessel *Alfred*.

1818 • **ILLINOIS** became the 21st state.

1833 • Oberlin College in Ohio became the **FIRST COED COLLEGE**.

1888 • **THE LONGEST LEASE ON RECORD**—10 million years— was signed in Columb Barracks, Ireland. It was for a plot of land.

1967 • **DR. CHRISTIAAN BARNARD** performed the first human heart transplant.

1973 • *Pioneer 10* made the **FIRST FLYBY OF JUPITER** and transmitted close-up pictures to Earth.

1987 • **KING KONG** welcomed the two millionth visitor of the year to the Empire State Building.

DECEMBER 3
activities

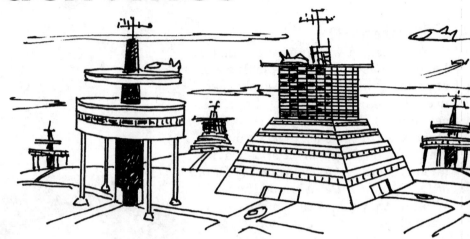

✿ In the year 10,001,888

Have your students write science-fiction stories set on Dec. 3, 10,001,888—the day the Columb Barracks lease expires. Is anyone around to renew the lease? If so, who—or what? What does the land look like? How is it used? How has the rest of the world changed?

⚗ Flyby

Pioneer 10 was traveling thousands of miles per hour as it sped past Jupiter. Even though the encounter was brief, scientists learned much from the data the spacecraft collected. Have your class participate in an information-seeking "flyby." Gather enough photos or posters of interesting subjects for each student to "fly by" one picture. Have the kids return to their seats and list as many things as they can about what they saw. Then place all the photos or posters on the chalk tray for viewing. Ask each student to read his description while the class looks for the picture it matches.

※ Keep on counting

Reinforce the idea of 2,000,000 with this estimation activity. Have your students guess how many people pass through the school cafeteria each day, how many have passed through since school started, and how many will pass through in one school year. They might be surprised to find out that it would take more than 20 years for a school with 600 students to total 2,000,000 cafeteria visitations!

DECEMBER 4
activities

Costs of conflicts

Flags and relics of the Revolutionary War are still on display at Fraunces Tavern in New York City. General George Washington's accounts show that $160,074.00 was spent on the war. Have your students investigate how this compares with the monetary costs of more recent wars.

Abstractions

After seeing an exhibit of Claude Monet's paintings, Wassily Kandinsky gave up his law career to study art. He painted bright designs with no recognizable objects—the first abstract paintings. Kandinsky thought colors had meanings of their own. For example, red was hot and powerful; green was calm and peaceful. Have your students suggest meanings for some of their favorite colors. Then challenge them to use geometric shapes in these colors to create their own abstract pictures.

Peace lovers

Munro Leaf's character Ferdinand the bull would rather smell the flowers then fight. With your students, develop a list of famous individuals or groups who, like Ferdinand, have pursued a nonviolent course.

Critter crimebuster

A burglar broke into a home in Fort Walton, Fla., and stole electronic equipment, cash, and a cockatiel named Coco. The burglar left the squawking bird in a nearby shop. When a local police officer entered the shop, the bird started whistling a TV theme song, and the officer recalled a burglary report mentioning a bird with this special talent. Thanks to Coco, the burglar was arrested. Invite your fledgling authors to compose a script for a new TV show—"Top Critter Cops." How might animals help solve other crimes?

BIRTHDAYS

1866 • **WASSILY KANDINSKY**, Russian artist considered the first abstract painter

1905 • **MUNRO LEAF**, children's author and creator of Ferdinand the bull

MILES, "Sesame Street" character

EVENTS

1776 • **BENJAMIN FRANKLIN LEFT FOR FRANCE** to seek support for the American Revolution.

1783 • **GEORGE WASHINGTON** had a farewell dinner with his officers at Fraunces Tavern in New York City.

1839 • **THE WHIG PARTY** held its first national convention in Harrisburg, Pa., and nominated William Henry Harrison.

1843 • **MANILA PAPER** was patented.

1945 • Congress approved U.S. participation in **THE UNITED NATIONS.**

1990 • **A COCKATIEL NAMED COCO** helped "blow the whistle" on a burglar.

DECEMBER 5
activities

✺ Wild Rose

Rose Wilder Lane, daughter of author Laura Ingalls Wilder, led an active, adventurous life. As a young woman, she flew over San Francisco Bay strapped to the wing of an airplane; at the age of 78, she flew in helicopters as a foreign correspondent during the Vietnam War. And it was Lane who first encouraged her mother to write the Little House books, then edited these books. What family members give your students behind-the-scenes support?

🎞 A Disney tribute

In feature-length animated movies and short cartoons, Walt Disney brought a host of beloved characters to life: Mickey Mouse, Donald Duck, Cinderella, Snow White, Peter Pan, Pinocchio, and Balloo the bear, to name a few.

Your students can create their own short animation. Cut scrap paper into 3×5-inch pieces, and staple together packs of about 30 pieces to form booklets. Distribute one booklet to each student. Next, have each child choose a simple theme that involves movement—changing expressions on a face, a dog wagging its tail and barking, or a short segment of a dance or sporting event, for example. Starting with the first page of the booklet, the kids should draw their picture in pencil, pressing hard enough to make an impression on the next page. (This will enable them to correctly position the image on the next page.) In each succeeding picture, they should change the position of whatever objects are supposed to be in motion. Remind them that anything more than a slight change on consecutive pages will create the appearance of jerky movement. After the kids have completed their drawings, have them exchange their booklets and view one another's work by fanning the edges of the pages with their thumb.

DECEMBER 6
activities

✒A memorial in words

The author Carl Sandburg was a great admirer of Abraham Lincoln. He wrote more than 4,000 pages on our 16th president. Have your students estimate how many words that represents. Then have them count the words on a couple pages from Sandburg's Lincoln biographies and revise their estimates.

🇺🇸 A memorial in stone

In 1783 the Continental Congress unanimously decided to build a national monument to honor George Washington—but it wasn't completed for more than 100 years. By 1864 workers had completed only 152 feet of the 555-foot tower. Have your students estimate what percentage that represents, then check their estimates with calculators. How many of your students have seen the Washington Monument? Can anyone name people honored by monuments in your hometown?

📖 A tree of their own

It is thought that a rock maple tree on the grounds of the Farren Memorial Hospital in Montague, Mass., inspired the poet Joyce Kilmer to write, "I think that I shall never see / A poem lovely as a tree." Seventy years after Kilmer wrote those words, controversy raged when the hospital closed and developers proposed to chop the tree down. Set up a mock debate in your class, with some students speaking on behalf of the developers and others speaking for the tree.

Take your class for an early winter walk around the school grounds. Have each student adopt a tree and draw two pictures of it: one as it looks in December and one as they think it will look in spring. In a few months, take the class outside again to check the spring illustrations against the actual trees.

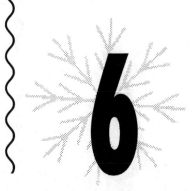

BIRTHDAYS

1876 • **FREDERICK DUESENBERG,** American automobile manufacturer

1886 • **JOYCE KILMER, American** 📖 poet

EVENTS

1534 • Spaniards founded the city of **QUITO, ECUADOR.**

1790 • **CONGRESS MOVED** from New York City to Philadelphia.

1847 • **ABRAHAM LINCOLN TOOK HIS** ✒ **SEAT IN CONGRESS** as a representative from Illinois.

1884 • **THE WASHINGTON MONUMENT** 🇺🇸 was completed when a 3,300-pound capstone was placed atop it.

1924 • **THE U.S. BORDER PATROL** was founded.

1941 • President Franklin Roosevelt made **A PERSONAL APPEAL FOR PEACE** to Japan's Emperor Hirohito. Japan attacked Pearl Harbor the next day.

1973 • **GERALD FORD,** a longtime congressman from Michigan, was sworn in as vice president of the United States, replacing Spiro Agnew.

ST. NICHOLAS DAY

6

DECEMBER 7
activities

BIRTHDAYS

1761 • MARIE TUSSAUD, creator of Madame Tussaud's Wax Museum in London
1873 • WILLA CATHER, American writer
1956 • LARRY BIRD, basketball star

EVENTS

1787 • DELAWARE became the first state when it ratified the U.S. Constitution.
1842 • THE NEW YORK PHILHARMONIC SOCIETY, the oldest symphony orchestra in the United States, was formed.
1877 • THOMAS EDISON demonstrated the first phonograph.
1941 • PEARL HARBOR WAS ATTACKED by the Japanese.
1945 • Percy Le Baron Spencer patented the MICROWAVE OVEN.
1968 • A LIBRARY BOOK OVERDUE FOR 145 YEARS was returned to the University of Cincinnati Library. The $22,646 fine was waived.
1970 • American cartoonist RUBE GOLD-BERG died.
1988 • AN EARTHQUAKE registering 6.9 on the Richter scale leveled the city of Spitak, Armenia.

IT'S OKAY NOT TO BE PERFECT DAY

▆ All aboard the United States

Most kids know that Delaware was the first state, but can your students list the first 10 states—in order? Where in the order of admission does their state fall?

✒ "A date which will live in infamy"

Just 3 hours before the Japanese attacked Pearl Harbor, the U.S. army's chief of staff received an intercepted message that an attack would occur somewhere in the Pacific. He notified Manila, the Panama Canal Zone, and San Francisco, but atmospheric conditions prevented him from getting the message to Hawaii. Ask your students to illustrate how today's messages are sent and received.

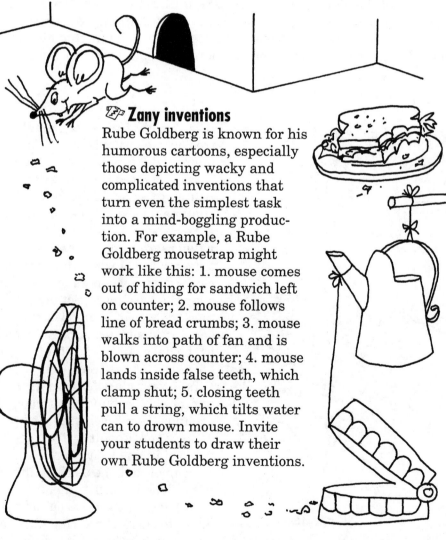

✐ Zany inventions

Rube Goldberg is known for his humorous cartoons, especially those depicting wacky and complicated inventions that turn even the simplest task into a mind-boggling production. For example, a Rube Goldberg mousetrap might work like this: 1. mouse comes out of hiding for sandwich left on counter; 2. mouse follows line of bread crumbs; 3. mouse walks into path of fan and is blown across counter; 4. mouse lands inside false teeth, which clamp shut; 5. closing teeth pull a string, which tilts water can to drown mouse. Invite your students to draw their own Rube Goldberg inventions.

DECEMBER 8
activities

⌨ Fun with doodles

James Thurber told stories with simple drawings. Give a copy of the same scribble to each of your students. Ask the kids to turn the page until an idea for a drawing occurs to them. Post the completed drawings and see all the variations that came from a single scribble.

💡 Lessons from lemons

Celebrate the invention of the lemon squeezer by writing the following phrase on the chalkboard: "When life gives you lemons, make lemonade." What personal stories do you—and your students—have that illustrate how someone made the best of a bad situation?

⚙ Success through failure

By experimenting with lift and drag, aeronautical engineer Samuel Langley built a successful heavier-than-air airplane model. Even though his full-size aircrafts failed to fly, Langley brought respect to the study of mechanical flight, previously an object of ridicule. Invite your students to fly paper airplanes in the gym or cafeteria. Encourage them to hypothesize about why some models fly farther— or higher—than others.

⚗ Strike up the band

Computers at the Bird Banding Laboratory in Laurel, Md., hold six decades of information on over 43 million banded birds. Banders catch birds in fine nets and keep them just long enough to record the band's identification number; the bird's species, age, and sex; the date of banding; and other interesting data. Even though only 3 percent of the bands are ever recovered, scientists can use the information to theorize about migration routes and schedules. Ask your students to name birds that migrate from their community in the fall. Which bird species remain throughout the winter?

BIRTHDAYS

1542 • MARY, QUEEN OF SCOTS
1765 • ELI WHITNEY, American inventor of the cotton gin
1894 • JAMES THURBER, American ⌨ humorist and cartoonist
1925 • SAMMY DAVIS, JR., American singer and dancer

EVENTS

1801 • Ebenezer Cobb, who LIVED IN THREE CENTURIES, died at age 107.
1840 • DR. DAVID LIVINGSTONE set sail for Africa.
1863 • President Abraham Lincoln announced his PLAN FOR THE RECONSTRUCTION OF THE SOUTH.
1896 • J.T. White invented THE LEMON 💡 SQUEEZER.
1903 • A HEAVIER-THAN-AIR FLYING ⚙ MACHINE, designed by engineer Samuel Langley, crashed into the Potomac River.
1909 • THE AMERICAN BIRD BANDING ⚗ ASSOCIATION was formed.
1941 • THE UNITED STATES DECLARED WAR on Japan.
1979 • A cat named Sherry was reunited with her owners after she spent 32 days and TRAVELED 225,000 MILES IN THE HOLD OF AN AIRLINER.

DECEMBER 9
activities

BIRTHDAYS

1848 • **JOEL CHANDLER HARRIS,** American writer and creator of the Uncle Remus stories

1886 • **CLARENCE BIRDSEYE,** American inventor of the process for deep-freezing food

1898 • **EMMETT KELLY,** American circus clown

1899 • **JEAN DE BRUNHOFF,** French author and illustrator who created Babar

1902 • **MARGARET HAMILTON,** American actress who portrayed the Wicked Witch of the West in *The Wizard of Oz*

EVENTS

1842 • **THE FIRST CHRISTMAS CARDS** were created in England.

1884 • **BALL-BEARING ROLLER SKATES** were patented by Levant Richardson.

1926 • **THE FIRST NATIONAL CHRIST-MAS TREE SERVICE** took place in Kings Canyon National Park in California.

1960 • **The Sperry Rand Corporation introduced Univac 1107, the FIRST COMPUTER TO OPERATE IN NANOSECONDS.**

1965 • *A CHARLIE BROWN CHRISTMAS* became the first "Peanuts" TV show.

📖 Oral traditions
Joel Chandler Harris learned about the customs, language, and folktales of African-Americans while working on a plantation in Georgia. Have your students retell a story they've heard from their parents or grandparents.

Fad fun
One hundred years ago, roller skating was a national fad. Have your students list some current fads. Do they think these fads will last? As a special assignment, ask students to quiz their parents and grandparents about fads *they* remember.

Chilly relay
To mark the birthday of Clarence Birdseye, divide your class into teams of three or four. Have each team write the letters A to Z on a sheet of paper. Then have one child at a time write a food that can be frozen next to the appropriate letter. The team with the longest list after 5 minutes wins.

Top clown
Emmett Kelly became famous for his act as a sad-faced hobo clown. Many clowns design their own faces, which they sometimes copyright so no other clowns can use them. Have each student design a clown face without showing anyone. Then pair up the kids and have them take turns giving oral directions to their partner on how to draw their clown face. (The child giving the directions should not look at the partner's evolving drawing.) Afterward, have them compare the originals with the reproductions to see how well they gave and followed directions.

Sizable circumference
President Calvin Coolidge designated a 2,000-year-old giant sequoia called the General Grant the first national Christmas tree. This 267-foot colossus has a circumference at its base of 107.5 feet. Have your students measure 107.5 feet of string and form it into a circle.

DECEMBER 10
activities

🧪 Measurement mischief

On the chalkboard, draw a line 1 meter long. Then have your students estimate, in meters, the length of the classroom, the width of a desk, and so on. Next, have them calculate the actual measurements using a metric ruler. Tell the kids that early units of measurement were based on the human body. The earliest known unit was the cubit, an Egyptian measure referring to the length of an arm from the elbow to the tip of the middle finger. The mile was established in Rome as the distance covered by a Roman legionnaire taking a thousand double steps. The span of a Viking's arms was called a fathom. And King Henry I of England decided that the distance from the tip of his nose to his fingertips was a yard. Ask your students to devise some measurements of their own.

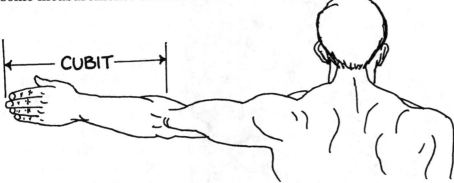

CUBIT

📖 With an artist's eye

Ernest Shepard's subjects included A.A. Milne's famous *Winnie the Pooh* characters and Rat, Toad, Mole, Otter, and Badger from Kenneth Grahame's *The Wind in the Willows*. After Shepard met Grahame and detailed his plans for illustrating the characters, the author said simply, "I love these little people; be kind to them." Read an unfamiliar story aloud to your students and ask them to draw the key character. Have them display their drawings and compare and contrast their interpretations.

🏅 Special honors

In honor of American Nobel Peace Prize recipients Theodore Roosevelt, Jane Addams, and Martin Luther King, Jr., have your students nominate classmates who deserve recognition for their thoughtfulness. Ask a committee to design a special citation for the winners.

BIRTHDAYS

1830 • **EMILY DICKINSON**, American poet

1851 • **MELVIL DEWEY**, American librarian who developed the Dewey decimal system

1879 • **ERNEST HOWARD SHEPARD**, children's book illustrator

EVENTS

1607 • **CAPTAIN JOHN SMITH** was rescued by Pocahontas.

1799 • **THE LENGTH OF A METER** was set to equal 1/10,000,000 of the distance between the North Pole and the equator.

1817 • **MISSISSIPPI** became the 20th state.

1901 • **THE FIRST NOBEL PRIZES** were awarded.

1906 • Theodore Roosevelt became the **FIRST U.S. PRESIDENT TO RECEIVE THE NOBEL PEACE PRIZE.**

1913 • Leonardo da Vinci's masterpiece, the *MONA LISA*, was recovered 2 years after it was stolen.

1931 • Jane Addams became the **FIRST AMERICAN WOMAN TO WIN THE NOBEL PEACE PRIZE.**

1964 • **MARTIN LUTHER KING, JR.,** received the Nobel Peace Prize.

HUMAN RIGHTS DAY
NOBEL PRIZE PRESENTATION DAY

10

DECEMBER 11
activities

BIRTHDAYS
1863 • **ANNIE JUMP CANNON,**
 American astronomer
1954 • **JERMAINE JACKSON, American** singer

EVENTS
1719 • The first recorded sighting of the **AURORA BOREALIS,** the northern lights, occurred in New England.
1816 • **INDIANA** became the 19th state.
1844 • Dr. Horace Wells became the **FIRST DENTIST TO USE AN ANESTHETIC** for a tooth extraction.
1919 • **THE FIRST MONUMENT TO AN INSECT** was dedicated in Enterprise, Ala. It honored the boll weevil, a destructive insect that forced farmers to diversify their crops.
1941 • **GERMANY AND ITALY DECLARED WAR** on the United States.
1946 • The United Nations General Assembly established UNICEF, the United Nations International Children's Emergency Fund.
• Industrialist John D. Rockefeller, Jr., donated land for the **UNITED NATIONS' WORLD HEADQUARTERS.**
1972 • *Apollo 17* **LANDED ON THE MOON.**

⚗ Young observer
As a young girl, Annie Jump Cannon loved to stargaze through a trapdoor in her attic. She also enjoyed holding crystal candlesticks up to the sunlight, which made rainbows on her wall. Use a glass prism to show your class this captivating effect. If a prism isn't available, use a shallow pan about three-fourths full of water. Place the pan near a source of bright light and slant a mirror at the end of the pan opposite the light to create a rainbow on the wall or ceiling. Challenge your students to explain how the ranbow is created.

✎ A donation to the world
When the United Nations selected New York City as the location for its permanent headquarters, delegates met in hotel rooms and college halls for lack of a headquarters building. But Rockefeller's donation of a six-block tract along the East River solved this problem. The UN Headquarters, designed by architects from 11 countries, is one of New York's famous landmarks. Ask your students to name noteworthy structures in your community. What makes them memorable or special? Distribute a map of the United States and have the kids locate and label other human-built landmarks, such as the Gateway Arch, the Mormon Tabernacle, Epcot Center, Hoover Dam, the Sears Tower, Independence Hall, and Mount Rushmore.

DECEMBER 12
activities

✒️ Go with the flow

As a member of the Continental Congress, John Jay opposed the colonies' independence from England, but he wasn't present during the final vote. Once ties were formally severed, however, he became an ardent supporter of independence. Ask your students why they think Jay changed his position. Next, have them write a story in which the main character changes his plans. Tell them to make sure the character's motivation is clear.

🎵 Musical master

At the age of 29, Ludwig van Beethoven began to realize he was losing his hearing. Seventeen years later, he was completely deaf and had to communicate by writing on notepads. Play parts of his Ninth Symphony for your students. Remind them that he was completely deaf when he composed it.

✽ The poinsettia's story

After serving as ambassador to Mexico, Dr. Joel Poinsett returned to his South Carolina home with a colorful plant called "Flame Leaf" or "Flower of the Holy Land." The plant was renamed "poinsettia" in his honor. Challenge your students to research the people for whom these plants were named: zinnia (Johann Gottfried Zinn), begonia (Michel Begon), dahlia (Anders Dahl), fuchsia (Leonhard Fuchs), and Lewisia (Meriwether Lewis).

Many other words in our language honor people. Have your class investigate the etymology of the following: silhouette, sandwich, saxophone, braille, Douglas fir, maverick, zeppelin, volt, and guppy.

BIRTHDAYS

1745 • **JOHN JAY**, first chief justice of the United States

1915 • **FRANK SINATRA**, American singer

1932 • **BARBARA EMBERLY**, children's author

EVENTS

1787 • **PENNSYLVANIA** became the second state.

1792 • **LUDWIG VAN BEETHOVEN**, age 22, paid 19¢ for his first music lesson with Franz Joseph Haydn.

1800 • Congress voted to establish Washington, D.C., as the nation's **PERMANENT CAPITAL.**

1851 • Dr. Joel Robert Poinsett, an American diplomat for whom **THE POINSETTIA** was named, died.

1899 • George Grant received a patent for **THE GOLF TEE.**

1901 • Italian inventor Guglielmo Marconi received the **FIRST TRANSATLANTIC RADIO SIGNAL.**

1925 • **THE FIRST MOTEL**, Motel Inn, opened in San Luis Obispo, Calif.

1953 • Major Chuck Yeager flew a Bell X-1A jet 2.5 **TIMES THE SPEED OF SOUND.**

POINSETTIA DAY

DECEMBER 13
activities

⬚ Where to go, what to do
Tell your students that Sir Francis Drake's around-the-world expedition took plenty of planning. Have groups of students use U.S. highway maps to plan an expedition of their own—a weeklong car trip not to exceed 300 miles each day. Where will they go? What will they see? Ask each group to make an itinerary to share with classmates.

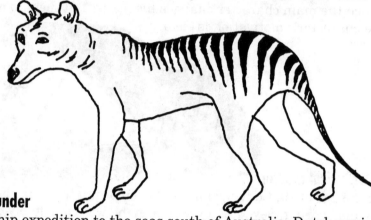

⬚ Down under
On a two-ship expedition to the seas south of Australia, Dutch navigator Abel Tasman became the first European to see New Zealand, but he decided not to land there because of the natives' hostile behavior. Have your students study a map of Polynesia and find locations that bear Tasman's name (the Tasman Sea and Tasmania, for example). Can they name some animals named after this adventurer? (The Tasmanian devil and Tasmanian tiger.)

⬚ Special moments
Observe Yehudi Menuhin's achievement by asking your students how they would celebrate a special feat or event. Would they ask for ice cream, as Yehudi did?

⬚ Class back-patters
Hold a class meeting to get suggestions on how to celebrate Tell Someone They're Doing a Good Job Week. Start by asking the kids to remember times someone complimented them on their work. How did they feel? Maybe your students could design certificates for you to distribute when someone is especially helpful in a cooperative activity, cleans up the class pet's cage, reads an original poem, solves a difficult math problem, and so on.

BIRTHDAYS
1818 • **MARY TODD LINCOLN**, wife of President Abraham Lincoln
1835 • **PHILLIPS BROOKS**, Episcopal bishop who composed the song "O Little Town of Bethlehem"

EVENTS
1466 • The Italian sculptor **DONATELLO** died.
1577 • **SIR FRANCIS DRAKE** left England to sail around the world.
1642 • The Dutch navigator Abel Janszoon Tasman discovered **NEW ZEALAND**.
1927 • Yehudi Menuhin, a **10-YEAR-OLD VIOLINIST**, made his debut at a concert in Carnegie Hall. After his performance, he asked for a dish of ice cream.

ST. LUCIA DAY
TELL SOMEONE THEY'RE DOING A GOOD JOB WEEK

DECEMBER 14
activities

🇺🇸 Monumental honors

When the Revolutionary War was over, the Continental Congress unanimously decided to build a national monument honoring George Washington. Divide your class into groups. Have each group research one former president who is still alive and design an appropriate monument in his honor. For example, a monument to Jimmy Carter might include a dove, commemorating his role in the Camp David accord, a peace treaty between Egypt and Israel. Ask each group to share its ideas. Do all the designs meet the class criteria for a monument?

✒️ Promoting peace

Major goals of the Carnegie Endowment for International Peace were to encourage peaceful settlement of international disputes and to find practical ways of preventing war. What are some peaceful ways your students have settled disputes? Are there winners and losers in a peaceful settlement? Why do your students think it's so hard to get countries to settle disputes peacefully?

🕊️ A special mother

Halcyon Days is observed during the 7 days before and 7 days after the winter solstice, the shortest day of the year. According to legend, the halcyon, a fabled bird, nested at sea around the time of the winter solstice and calmed the waters during this period to protect her young. Point out that mothers often go to extraordinary lengths to protect their children. Have your students create cards depicting times when their mothers protected or nurtured them—for example, by keeping them away from danger or calming them when they were frightened. Then encourage the kids to share the legend of the halcyon, and their cards, with their moms.

BIRTHDAYS

1503 • **NOSTRADAMUS**, French physician and astrologer famous for his predictions

1897 • **MARGARET CHASE SMITH**, first woman elected to both houses of the U.S. Congress

1929 • **LORNA BALIAN**, children's author and illustrator

EVENTS

1799 • **GEORGE WASHINGTON** died at 🇺🇸 Mount Vernon in Virginia.

1819 • **ALABAMA** became the 22nd state.

1910 • Andrew Carnegie's $10 million ✒️ gift established **THE CARNEGIE ENDOWMENT FOR INTERNATIONAL PEACE.**

1911 • The Norwegian explorer Roald Amundsen became the first person to reach the **SOUTH POLE.**

1929 • Amelia Earhart formed an **ORGANIZATION FOR LICENSED FEMALE PILOTS.**

1967 • DNA was created in a test tube.

1990 • Magic Johnson, Chris Evert, and Jackie Joyner-Kersee joined the **PRESIDENT'S COUNCIL ON PHYSICAL FITNESS AND SPORTS.**

🕊️ **HALCYON DAYS**

BIRTHDAYS

1832 • **ALEXANDRE GUSTAVE EIFFEL,** French engineer who designed the Eiffel Tower in Paris

1861 • **CHARLES EDGAR DURYEA,** American inventor who built the first successful gasoline-powered automobile

EVENTS

1791 • **THE FIRST 10 AMENDMENTS TO THE CONSTITUTION—the Bill of Rights—were ratified.**

1886 • **The number of shares traded on the NEW YORK STOCK EXCHANGE in a single day exceeded 1 million for the first time.**

1938 • **Ground was broken for the JEFFERSON MEMORIAL.**

1969 • **THE OLDEST FOSSILIZED FLEA on record was discovered in Australia.**

1970 • **The USSR's *Venera 7* became the FIRST SPACECRAFT TO LAND ON VENUS.**

1989 • **London's BIG BEN WAS SILENCED for 3 hours because of faulty cogwheels.**

BILL OF RIGHTS DAY

NATIONAL CARE AND SHARE DAY

DECEMBER 15
activities

Some hopper!

Fleas are arguably the best jumpers in the world: They can leap 12 inches, or 150 times their length. Have your students calculate how far a jump of 150 times *their* height would take *them*. Fleas live on the blood of host mammals. They use their antennae to sense heat, vibrations, air currents, and carbon dioxide—which signal the presence of a nearby host. Fleas themselves are also hosts—for mites, which live between the plates of their exoskeletons. Ask your students to research and illustrate other host-parasite relationships.

London landmark

Many people think Big Ben is the 22-foot-diameter clock on the clock tower of England's Houses of Parliament. But it's actually the clock tower's 13.5-ton bell. Big Ben chimes every 15 minutes—and has, with few exceptions, since its installation in 1859. Test your students' knowledge of other famous landmarks—and have some fun— by holding a class "Password" tournament. For the passwords, use such famous landmarks as the Taj Mahal, the Sphinx, the Great Wall of China, and the Eiffel Tower. Have two-person teams compete in three-round games, with partners alternating roles (clue giver and clue receiver) after each round. Remind the kids that clues must be one word only and must not contain any form of any word in the landmark. Locations, however, are acceptable clues.

Helping hands

Celebrate National Care and Share Day by helping your students learn about organizations in their community that provide services for others. Have teams of students go through the local telephone directory and list agencies they'd like to learn more about.

DECEMBER 16
activities

📽 Nickname nonsense

Celebrate the birthday of football star William "the Refrigerator" Perry by asking your students how they think he got his nickname. If possible, show them pictures of him. Tell your class that sometimes a nickname expresses the opposite of what the person is really like. For example, a shy, soft-spoken person might get the nickname Gabby. Or a serious person might be nicknamed Giggles. What "opposite" nickname might be appropriate for William Perry? Invite the kids to pick an opposite nickname for themselves, write it on a name tag, and use that nickname for the day.

🎐 Fiesta

In Mexico, candlelit processions of "pilgrims"—traditionally composed of nine families—knock on the door of a different house each night for the nine nights preceding Christmas. After singing a song asking the master of the house for *posada* (shelter), they are admitted, and food, refreshments, games, dancing, and the breaking of a pinata follow. Celebrate the culture of Mexico by holding a fiesta in your classroom. If you have students of Mexican ancestry, perhaps their parents would volunteer to prepare some traditional foods and to talk about their culture. Play a tape of mariachi music to get everyone into the spirit. And, of course, include a pinata in the day's festivities.

BIRTHDAYS
1770 • **LUDWIG VAN BEETHOVEN,** German composer
1775 • **JANE AUSTEN,** English novelist
1893 • **MARIE HALL ETS,** children's author
1901 • **MARGARET MEAD,** American anthropologist
1917 • **ARTHUR C. CLARKE,** science fiction writer
1932 • **QUENTIN BLAKE,** children's author and illustrator
1962 • **WILLIAM "THE REFRIGERATOR"** 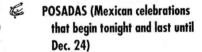 **PERRY,** football player

EVENTS
1631 • **VESUVIUS,** a volcano in Italy, erupted.
1773 • **THE BOSTON TEA PARTY** took place.
1922 • Florence Allen of Ohio became the **FIRST WOMAN JUSTICE OF A STATE SUPREME COURT.**
1953 • **THE DELAWARE WATER GAP BRIDGE** between Pennsylvania and New Jersey opened.
1974 • **THE SAFE DRINKING WATER ACT** became law.

🎐 **POSADAS (Mexican celebrations that begin tonight and last until Dec. 24)**

16

DECEMBER 17
activities

Woman with a cause

At the age of 22, Deborah Sampson decided to take up arms in support of the American cause in the Revolutionary War. Women weren't allowed to serve in the army, so she cut her hair, dressed in men's clothing, and enlisted as Robert Shurtleff. After her secret was discovered by an army doctor, she received an honorable discharge and a military pension. Tell your students that during Operation Desert Storm, the 1991 military campaign to oust Iraqi forces from Kuwait, American women served as combat soldiers for the first time. How do the kids feel about this?

Flight fascination

Orville and Wilbur Wright's fascination with flight began with a planophore—a toy with a rubber band and a windup propeller. Twenty-five years later, Orville piloted the first engine-driven airplane. Use the Wright brothers' historic first flight as a starting point for a class time line about flight. Assign a student research team to each decade from 1903 to the present.

German tradition

During "Knocking Nights," the three Thursday evenings before Christmas, many German children dress up in masks and go from house to house chanting rhymes that begin with the word *knock.* To drive away evil spirits, they also crack whips, ring cowbells, and rattle dishes. The children are rewarded with fruit, candy, or money. Challenge your students to make up rhymes beginning with the word *knock.* Select a Thursday to take your story of "Knocking Nights" to other classrooms. Your students can wear masks, recite their rhymes, and use noisemakers in their parade.

DECEMBER 18
activities

🏳 Ratification graph

New Jersey officially became the third state when its representatives voted unanimously to ratify the Constitution. Have your class graph the ratification votes (for and against) of the original 13 states: Del., 30-0; Pa., 46-23; N.J., 38-0; Ga., 26-0; Conn., 128-40; Mass., 187-168; Md., 63-11; S.C., 149-73; N.H., 57-47; Va., 89-79; N.Y., 30-27; N.C., 194-77; R.I., 34-32.

🎨 Childlike painter

Paul Klee had the talent to be a professional musician or writer, but he decided on a career in art. Klee always thought children expressed themselves freely in their art. So he was flattered when people said that his work resembled children's paintings. Show your students some Klee paintings and ask them to point out any child-like characteristics.

✿ Welcome, Su Lin

Have your students list special habitat considerations they think zookeepers had to keep in mind for Su Lin, the giant panda.

✎ Clown surprise

For International Clown Day, divide your class into groups of three. Give each group a piece of manila paper folded into three equal sections. Have one person from each group draw a clown's head in the top portion of the paper (without showing the other members of the group). With the top section folded down and out of sight, the second person in the group should then draw the clown's body on the middle section. With the first two sections folded back, the third student should draw the clown's legs and shoes on the bottom section. Finally, have each group unfold its paper and take a look at the whole clown, then select a name.

BIRTHDAYS

1879 • PAUL KLEE, Swiss artist
🎨

1882 • ZOLTAN KODALY, Hungarian composer

1886 • TY COBB, American baseball player who has the highest life-time batting average (.367) in major-league history

1947 • STEVEN SPIELBERG, American movie director

EVENTS

1787 • By a vote of 38-0, NEW JERSEY RATIFIED THE U.S. CONSTITUTION.

1865 • THE THIRTEENTH AMENDMENT, which abolished slavery, was ratified.

1936 • Su Lin became THE FIRST GIANT PANDA TO ARRIVE IN THE UNITED STATES.

1956 • JAPAN joined the United Nations.

1957 • THE FIRST COMMERCIAL NUCLEAR POWER PLANT in the United States began supplying electricity to Shippingport, Pa.

✎ INTERNATIONAL CLOWN DAY

18

DECEMBER 19
activities

BIRTHDAYS
1928 • EVE BUNTING, children's author

EVENTS
1732 • BENJAMIN FRANKLIN began publication of *Poor Richard's Almanack*.

1776 • THOMAS PAINE published "The American Crisis," which included the words "These are the times that try men's souls."

1777 • George Washington and 11,000 troops established a CAMP AT VALLEY FORGE, PA.

1787 • Thomas Jefferson received A COPY OF THE CONSTITUTION.

1871 • CORRUGATED PAPER was patented.

1959 • Walter Williams, THE LAST CIVIL WAR VETERAN, died at the age of 117.

1972 • Apollo 17, the sixth and LAST MANNED MOON LANDING MISSION, ended with a splashdown in the Pacific Ocean.

1984 • WAYNE GRETZKY scored his 1,000th point in his 632nd professional hockey game.

❁ Advice from almanacs
Poor Richard's Almanack contained useful information about housekeeping and farming as well as weather forecasts and Franklin's pithy sayings, such as "Early to bed, and early to rise, makes a man healthy, wealthy, and wise." Have your students make a "Class Almanac for Kids." They could write tips for keeping desks neat, taking care of pets, and studying.

🏳 Reminder from Jefferson
Thomas Jefferson was in France at the time of the Constitutional Convention. Although he approved of the Constitution, he was concerned because it didn't include protection for citizens' rights. He wrote letters urging convention representatives to include guarantees for such rights. As a result, James Madison introduced 12 amendments. Ten of these were adopted and became known as the Bill of Rights. Go over these rights with your students, then have them write a letter—as Jefferson did—that explains the importance of one or more of these rights.

🖋 Moonstruck
The moon has inspired writers and storytellers since ancient times. William Shakespeare compared the moon to "a silver bow new-bent in heaven." Ask your students how the moon and a silver bow are alike. Invite them to write a metaphor about the moon in their journals.

⭕ The great Gretzky
Hockey star Wayne Gretzky was the youngest player, at 19, to receive the National Hockey League's Most Valuable Player award. What are some goals your students would like to achieve by the time they're 19? How will they do it?

DECEMBER 20
activities

🏴 A growing nation

The Louisiana Purchase nearly doubled the area of the United States. The territory consisted of more than 800,000 square miles extending from the Gulf of Mexico to Canada and from the west bank of the Mississippi to the Rockies. Have your students draw a map of the United States at the time of the purchase, shading the new lands.

▒ Lending a helping hand

After campaigning for an incumbent city councilman, 7-year-old Teddy Andrews was appointed to Berkeley's Youth Commission, a board that advises the city council on youth issues. Once in office, he developed a "wish list"—a plan to provide clothing, school supplies, and even scholarships to homeless and needy children. Ask your students what their wish list would include.

✎ Games across generations

The popular game bingo was created in 1929 by Edwin S. Lowe, a traveling toy salesman. Have your students brainstorm for categories of games—electronic, board, outdoor, indoor, ball, card, and so on. For each of these categories, have a group of students compile a list of games and write the list on the board. Then have the entire class vote for a favorite in each category.

Next, have each student ask a parent and grandparent or older neighbor what their favorite childhood game was for each category. In certain categories—for example, electronic—they probably had no games. Once the data is collected, have the kids compare the favorite games of their generation with those of the other generations represented in their survey. Report the findings in a newsletter.

BIRTHDAYS

1868 • **HARVEY FIRESTONE**, founder of the Firestone Tire and Rubber Co.

EVENTS

1606 • **CAPTAIN JOHN SMITH** and 120 colonists left London bound for America.

1620 • Samuel Fuller became the **FIRST DOCTOR TO ARRIVE IN NEW ENGLAND**.

1699 • **RUSSIA ADJUSTED ITS CALENDAR** so New Year's Day would be Jan. 1, not Sept. 1.

1803 • **THE LOUISIANA TERRITORY** was  formally transferred from France to the United States, which had purchased the territory for about $20 per square mile.

1820 • Missouri levied a $1 per year **TAX ON BACHELORS** between the ages of 20 and 50.

1860 • South Carolina became the **FIRST STATE TO SECEDE FROM THE UNION**.

1880 • **ELECTRIC LIGHTS FIRST LIT UP BROADWAY** in New York City.

1988 • Teddy Andrews, age 7, was sworn in as **YOUTH COMMISSIONER** for the city of Berkeley, Calif.

1989 • **RENOVATIONS OF THE SISTINE CHAPEL** in Rome were completed.

✎ **BINGO MONTH**

BIRTHDAYS

1879 • JOSEPH STALIN, Russian dictator
1922 • PAUL WINCHELL, American ven-
triloquist
1959 • FLORENCE GRIFFITH JOYNER,
American track star

EVENTS

1620 • THE PILGRIMS landed at
Plymouth, Mass.
1909 • THE FIRST JUNIOR HIGH
SCHOOL was established.
1913 • THE FIRST CROSSWORD PUZZLE
was published.
1937 • Walt Disney's *Snow White and
the Seven Dwarfs,* the FIRST
FULL-LENGTH ANIMATED FILM,
premiered in Los Angeles.
1968 • *Apollo 8* blasted off. The mission
would mark the first time any-
one had seen the DARK SIDE OF
THE MOON.
1987 • Penny-saver Warren Holdread
BOUGHT A NEW CAR USING
PENNIES.

FIRST DAY OF WINTER
(Dec. 21 or 22)
FOREFATHERS DAY

DECEMBER 21
activities

☞ Dummy dialogue

Celebrate the birthday of Paul Winchell by giving your students the chance to perform with a favorite doll or toy. Have them write a dialogue between themselves and their "dummy." Suggest that they try to convince their dummy to do something the dummy might not want to do, such as go to school, eat broccoli, do homework, or take a bath. Have them debut their acts in class.

✒ Step up to the mike

Have the kids use today's talk-show format to interview Pilgrims as they disembark from the *Mayflower.* Encourage them to check Pilgrim diaries and other reference books to gather information for the anniversary interviews.

⁂ A penny saved

When Warren Holdread purchased a new car, he brought his pennies with him—all 284,500 of them. (He also brought his checkbook so he could make up any difference.) For many years, Holdread had been tossing pennies into a 55-gallon drum in his garage. The dealer who sold Holdread the car said the penny collection was fun, but it cut into his profits. Wrapping pennies costs $3\frac{1}{4}$ ¢ per roll of 50. Have your students use their calculators to figure out how much of a possible $1,300 profit was lost because of the pennies.

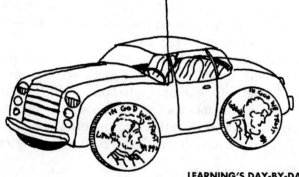

DECEMBER 22
activities

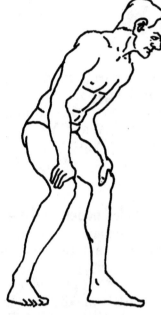

⚙ Grow, gorilla, grow

Tell your students that the gorilla and the chimpanzee are the closest living relatives of man. Have them compare the gorilla's weight—at the following stages—with a human's:

Birth: 4-5 pounds
Age 2: 35 pounds
Adult female: 200-250 pounds
Adult male: 400-450 pounds
Adult male in captivity: 600-700 pounds

⚗ Extinct is forever

Some species become extinct as a result of natural selection. But in other cases, man has disrupted natural cycles by destroying habitats, overkilling, and introducing exotic species. Scientists believe that by the year 2000, species may be going extinct at a rate of 100 per day. Can your students name some endangered plants or animals in their area? Invite them to make posters of these species.

⬡ Fluffy stress-reducer

Ask your students to bring to school the stuffed animal or toy that makes them feel better when they're sad or sick or just need a friend. Divide the class into small groups so that each child can introduce his toy. Then ask the children to think of ways they might be able to help kids who've been traumatized. Perhaps they can raise money to buy stuffed toys for youngsters brought to the emergency room of a nearby hospital.

BIRTHDAYS

1696 • JAMES OGELTHORPE, founder of the Georgia colony
1858 • GIACOMO PUCCINI, Italian composer

EVENTS

1775 • THE BRITISH PARLIAMENT prohibited trade with the American colonies.
• The Continental Congress established the CONTINENTAL NAVY.
1847 • CONGRESSMAN ABRAHAM LINCOLN of Illinois made his first speech in the House of Representatives.
1937 • THE LINCOLN TUNNEL, which connects New York and New Jersey under the Hudson River, opened.
1939 • A coelacanth, a fish THOUGHT TO BE EXTINCT FOR 65 MILLION YEARS, was caught off the coast of South Africa.
1956 • Colo became the FIRST GORILLA
⚙   BORN IN CAPTIVITY.
1973 • THE FIRST ENDANGERED
⚗   SPECIES ACT was passed.
1988 • In Barry County, Mich., POLICE
⬡   CARS AND AMBULANCES STARTED CARRYING TEDDY BEARS to comfort young passengers.

DECEMBER 23
activities

BIRTHDAYS

1732 • **RICHARD ARKWRIGHT, English inventor and manufacturer called "the Father of the Factory System"**

EVENTS

1783 • **GEORGE WASHINGTON, commander-in-chief of the Continental Army, retired to Mount Vernon.**

1788 • **The state of Maryland offered a 10-square-mile tract on the Potomac River as the SITE FOR THE NATIONAL GOVERNMENT.**

1823 • **"A VISIT FROM ST. NICHOLAS," by Clement Clarke Moore, was first published.**

1893 • **THE OPERA** *HANSEL AND GRETEL,* **by Engelbert Humperdinck, premiered.**

1913 • **THE U.S. FEDERAL RESERVE SYSTEM was established.**

1948 • **THE TRANSISTOR was invented by John Bardeen and Walter Brattain.**

1986 • **The experimental aircraft** *Voyager* **completed THE FIRST NONSTOP, UNREFUELED FLIGHT AROUND THE WORLD.**

FEAST OF THE RADISHES (Mexico)

Welcome, Washington

Ask your class to find out how many states were part of the United States at the time Maryland donated land for the nation's capital. Have the kids locate these states on a map. Why do the kids think the District of Columbia was a good choice for the capital? Would they select a different location for the capital now? Why?

A well-traveled paper airplane

The lightweight experimental aircraft *Voyager* made aviation history by completing a nonstop, unrefueled journey around the world. The plane covered the 25,012-mile distance in 9 days. Pilots Jeana Yeager and Dick Rutan were a bit wobbly after their landing—after all, the cockpit they'd traveled in was the size of the backseat of an automobile. *Voyager* is a giant paper airplane made of layers of honeycomb paper and graphite sealed with epoxy resin. Ask your students to draw their own designs for an airliner, military aircraft, or recreational plane of the future.

Radish rally

Every year thousands of visitors flock to the city of Oaxaca in southern Mexico to see sculptures made from radishes. Contestants frequently use several radishes—some up to 2 feet long—to depict familiar landmarks, holidays, famous people, or historical scenes. According to Mexican lore, Zapotec Indian children, who had no formal toys, used radishes as playthings. What everyday items have your students imaginatively turned into playthings?

DECEMBER 24
activities

✐ Kit the illiterate

Christopher "Kit" Carson never learned to read or write. Yet he was a superior trapper and hunter as well as a trusted frontier scout, guide, and soldier. Ask your students whether Carson could succeed today without reading and writing skills.

▰ A second victory

By the end of the War of 1812—often called the second war for independence—Americans felt a renewed pride in their fledgling nation, and countries around the world began to view the United States more seriously. Have your students discuss what might have happened if the British had been victorious in the War of 1812. How do they think U.S. citizens would have been treated? What would the British have done with the leaders of the former United States? Finally, have your students write a story set in the present and based on the premise that England had won the War of 1812. What are some of the ways the kids' lives today would be different?

✎ Gift givers

Christmas Eve and Christmas are a time of great religious celebration in the Christian church. One of the most popular traditions—gift giving—is a commemoration of the Magi's presents to the Christ child. Tell your students that the holiday gift giver has many names throughout the world. In Italy, it's Befana; in Russia, Babouschka; in France, Pere Noel; in Scandinavian countries, Yule men. Have the students write stories about and draw pictures of imaginary gift givers. What are their names? What kinds of gifts do they bring? What do they give to children who have misbehaved?

BIRTHDAYS

1809 • **KIT CARSON,** American frontier scout

1920 • **JOHN LANGSTAFF,** children's author

EVENTS

1492 • Columbus's flagship, the *SANTA MARIA,* was wrecked on a reef off Haiti.

1801 • The American painter and naturalist Charles Willson Peale exhibited A MOUNTED SKELETON OF A MASTODON.

1814 • THE WAR OF 1812 ended.

1818 • Joseph Mohr, a pastor in Oberndorf, Germany, wrote the words for "SILENT NIGHT." Franz Gruber, the schoolmaster and organist, composed the music.

1948 • THE FIRST TOTALLY SOLAR-HEATED HOME was completed in Dover, Mass.

1968 • The Apollo 8 ASTRONAUTS BROADCAST A CHRISTMAS MESSAGE while orbiting the moon.

✎ CHRISTMAS EVE

DECEMBER 25
activities

BIRTHDAYS

1642 • **ISAAC NEWTON, English physicist**

1821 • **CLARA BARTON, founder of the** **American Red Cross**

1880 • **JOHNNY GRUELLE, American cartoonist and author who created Raggedy Ann**

1887 • **CONRAD HILTON, American businessman who built a chain of successful hotels**

1915 • **ETH CLIFFORD, children's author**

1958 • **RICKEY HENDERSON, baseball star**

EVENTS

1620 • **The Pilgrims began CONSTRUCTION OF A MEETINGHOUSE in Plymouth, Mass.**

1818 • **"SILENT NIGHT" was performed for the first time, in the village church in Oberndorf, Austria.**

1831 • **Louisiana and Arkansas became THE FIRST STATES TO OBSERVE CHRISTMAS AS A LEGAL HOLIDAY.**

1887 • **The character SHERLOCK HOLMES first appeared in Beaton's Christmas Annual.**

1930 • **THE FIRST PUBLIC BOBSLED RUN opened in Lake Placid, N.Y.**

CHRISTMAS

When disaster calls

During the Civil War, Clara Barton carried medicines and supplies to soldiers on the battlefield. After the war, she gave lectures and eventually traveled to Europe, where she found out about the International Red Cross. As a result, she returned to the United States and organized the American Red Cross. Contact the nearest office of the American Red Cross and find out how your class can help.

A special toy

Johnny Gruelle, whose comic strip "Mr. Twee Deedle" appeared in the New York *Herald* from 1910 to 1916, also wrote over 50 books for children. His best-known creation was a rag doll named Raggedy Ann, whose adventures with other toys and dolls always took place while humans were asleep or away. Ask your students to write stories about the secret lives of their favorite toys.

Holiday poems

Have pairs of students each select a different country and research its Christmas traditions. Ask each pair to express their findings in a poem. Kids studying Christmas in France wrote this poem:

> *Children leave their shoes*
> *On the front doorstep.*
> *Come morning they rush to see*
> *What "Le Petit Noel" has left.*

A pair researching Australia created this poem:

> *Summer winds*
> *Knock on your door*
> *When Santa Claus*
> *Sails by the shore.*

DECEMBER 26
activities

🔬 Well-rounded scientist

Charles Babbage is credited with the idea for the first automatic digital computer. He had many interests, including astronomy, probability, meteorology, cryptanalysis, and even lighthouse technology. Often frustrated by lack of funds, Babbage believed that national governments should support scientific activities and help promising inventors. Divide your class into two teams, and have them debate the pros and cons of government support of scientific research.

❄ Snow day

Ask your students to share what they enjoy doing on snow days—when school is closed. Then have them write picture books set during a 29-inch snowfall in their community. In more temperate climes, have students write about "the day it snowed" or another winter weather oddity.

🌽 Harvest festival

From Dec. 26 to Jan. 1, many African-Americans celebrate Kwanzaa, the festival of the harvest. They place the *muhindi,* an ear of corn representing children, and the *kinara,* a holder for seven candles, on a straw mat called the *mkeka.* Every day they light one candle. The candles, called *mushumaa,* symbolize the principles of unity, self-determination, responsibility, cooperative economics, purpose, creativity, and faith. On the last day of the festival, parents give gifts, or *zawadi,* to their children. Ask your students to list ways they can demonstrate these seven principles.

BIRTHDAYS

1792 • **CHARLES BABBAGE, English mathematician, scientist, and inventor**

EVENTS

1776 • George Washington and his troops surprised and routed a garrison of Hessians at the **BATTLE OF TRENTON.**

1799 • In a **EULOGY FOR GEORGE WASHINGTON,** Henry Lee described him as "first in war, first in peace, and first in the hearts of his countrymen."

1845 • Marthasville, Ga., changed its name to **ATLANTA.**

1865 • James Mason patented **THE COFFEE PERCOLATOR.**

1898 • Pierre and Marie Curie discovered **RADIUM.**

1947 • Almost 29 **INCHES OF SNOW** fell in New York City.

JUNKANOO (the Bahamas)
KWANZAA begins

DECEMBER 27
activities

Name droppers

Tell your class that the word *pasteurization* comes from Louis Pasteur, the chemist who invented this method of preserving milk and other beverages through heat treatment. Then play the Name-Drop Game. Write the following names on the chalkboard and challenge your students to come up with the terms derived from them: Louis Braille (braille alphabet), Alessandro Volta (volt—unit of electrical potential), James Watt (watt—unit of electrical power), Rudolf Diesel (diesel engine), Amelia Bloomer (bloomers), Sylvester Graham (graham crackers). Can the kids think of other people whose names inspired common terms?

LOUIS BRAILLE
ALESSANDRO VOLTA
JAMES WATT
RUDOLF DIESEL
AMELIA BLOOMER
SYLVESTER GRAHAM

Fact finders

Ingri D'Aulaire and her husband, Edgar, coauthored many books for children. These included biographies as well as fictional stories with characters based on real-life people. In order to be accurate, the D'Aulaires did extensive research, sometimes traveling great distances to get the information they needed. If your students could go anywhere to get information for a book project, where would they go? What subject would they want to investigate first-hand?

DECEMBER 28
activities

⚰ Gum study

Make chewing gum the focus of a class investigation. Purchase four of five different types of gum. Then decide on some questions to study. For example: What is the color of the gum before chewing? What is the color of the gum after chewing? Is it still sticky after 100 chews? What is the cost per stick? Calculate the number of "enjoyable" chews per stick and determine the cost per chew.

⚙ Motion-picture pioneers

The French brothers Louis and Auguste Lumiere invented the Cinematographe, a machine that served as both motion-picture camera and projector. So for the first time, films could be viewed by audiences, rather than simply by individuals looking through peepholes, as with Edison's Kinetoscope. The Lumieres made scores of films, generally short records of daily life such as a train arriving at a station or a street scene. Let student teams try their hands at Lumiere-style filmmaking. First, have them decide on a visually interesting subject to film for about 3 minutes. Next, have them think about where they'll position the camera. After each team has submitted its plans, borrow a video camera from your media center or a parent and buy a blank videotape. Hold a class screening and discuss the young filmmakers' results.

🏳A closer look at the pledge

Ask your students to write the "Pledge of Allegiance," underlining the five words they believe are the most important. Have the kids define the words and explain why they chose them. Then ask small groups to design pictographs of the pledge using symbols and as few letters or words as possible. Display the results near the flag.

BIRTHDAYS
1856 • WOODROW WILSON, 28th president of the United States

EVENTS
1732 • BENJAMIN FRANKLIN first advertised *Poor Richard's Almanack.*
1832 • John C. Calhoun became the FIRST VICE PRESIDENT TO RESIGN FROM OFFICE.
1846 • IOWA became the 29th state.
1848 • GASLIGHTS were first used in the White House.
1869 • CHEWING GUM was patented by William Semple of Mount Vernon, Ohio.
1895 • The Lumiere brothers showed the FIRST COMMERCIAL MOVIE, in the Grand Cafe in Paris.

DECEMBER 29
activities

BIRTHDAYS

1766 • **CHARLES MACINTOSH, inventor of waterproof fabrics**

1808 • **ANDREW JOHNSON, 17th president of the United States**

1891 • **JOHN CLYDE HALL, founder of the Hallmark card company**

1942 • **JAN GREENBERG, children's author**

1943 • **MOLLY BANG, children's author**

EVENTS

1777 • **An army chef at Valley Forge concocted "PHILADELPHIA PEPPER POT," a meal that raised the soldiers' morale.**

1845 • **TEXAS became the 28th state.**

1851 • **THE FIRST YMCA IN THE UNITED STATES opened in Boston.**

1967 • **The term *BLACK HOLE*—for a region in space left by a star that undergoes complete gravitational collapse—was first used.**

1973 • ***Skylab 4* took the FIRST PHOTOGRAPHS FROM SPACE OF A COMET.**

1976 • **Lynn Cox became the FIRST PERSON TO SWIM THE STRAIT OF MAGELLAN.**

1987 • **Soviet cosmonaut Yuri Romanenko completed A 326-DAY STAY IN SPACE.**

Rainwear

Ask your students how animals protect themselves from rain. Promote a little whimsical thinking by having the kids draw rain gear for animals. How about multiple sets of galoshes for a centipede? Or an umbrella that a swinging monkey can hold with its teeth? Keep the fashion ideas in a class book, and bring it out on the next rainy day.

Kid cards

On the birthday of Hallmark's John Clyde Hall, encourage your students to design their own note cards. Decide on a size for the cards, then have each student make enough cards for the whole class. Tie sets—one from each student—with yarn, and give them to parents as a winter pick-me-up.

Bang-up day

Read Molly Bang's book *Ten, Nine, Eight* to your students. Then invite them to create their own backwards counting book, which they can share with a group of kindergarten students.

All alone

Soviet cosmonaut Yuri Romanenko spent close to 11 months aboard *Mir,* an orbiting space station. Counting his other two missions, he was in space longer than anyone—430 days. With an eye to future long space missions, scientists have been studying Romanenko closely. They're concerned about the effect of weightlessness on the body and the psychological consequences of months of relative isolation. Ask your students what they would miss the most if they were in space for 11 months. What would they take with them to make their spacecraft feel more like home?

DECEMBER 30
activities

⌨ Musical hodgepodge

The first public concert featured "music on sundry instruments." What do your students think "sundry" means? Write down their guesses, then check the dictionary. What unusual instruments have the kids heard in concerts? How about a cannon (listen to the *1812 Overture*), a kazoo, a steel drum, castanets, an old-fashioned washboard? What miscellaneous objects could your students use for their own classroom orchestra? Encourage them to recycle things to make unusual-looking and unusual-sounding instruments for a class concert.

⚗ Hold on!

Tell your students that the earth's surface is actually made up of rocky plates that sometimes shift. When these plates move together and hit or rub one another, an earthquake results. Seismographs determine how much the earth quakes when plates meet. Have your students simulate plate movement by gently sliding two desks against each other. Ask the kids to stack some books on top of the desks, then push or slide the desks together with more force. What happens to the books as the desktops collide?

📖 Not so scientific

Rudyard Kipling won the Nobel Prize in literature in 1907. He wrote many books for children, including *The Jungle Book* and *Just So Stories*. Two famous stories in this latter collection are "How the Leopard Got His Spots" and "How the Elephant Got His Trunk." Share these "pourquoi" stories with your students, then ask them to create their own tales explaining how other animals acquired certain characteristics.

BIRTHDAYS

1850 • JOHN MILNE, British geologist
⚗ and developer of the first accurate seismograph

1865 • RUDYARD KIPLING, British novelist and short-story writer

1867 • SIMON GUGGENHEIM, American philanthropist

1943 • MERCER MAYER, children's author and illustrator

EVENTS

1731 • THE FIRST PUBLIC CONCERT was held in Boston, Mass.

1853 • THE GADSDEN PURCHASE was signed, giving the United States 29,640 square miles of Mexican territory.

1877 • RUTHERFORD B. HAYES became the first president to celebate his silver wedding anniversary in the White House.

1922 • THE SOVIET UNION was formed.

1940 • Los Angeles dedicated its FIRST FREEWAY.

1963 • THE JOHN F. KENNEDY HALF-DOLLAR was authorized by Congress.

DECEMBER 31
activities

BIRTHDAYS

1491 • JACQUES CARTIER, French explorer

1869 • HENRI MATISSE, French painter

EVENTS

1862 • THE *MONITOR,* the Union's ironclad warship, sank.

1879 • Thomas Edison demonstrated his INCANDESCENT LAMP to a New Year's Eve crowd.

1904 • A NEW YEAR'S EVE TRADITION began as an illuminated globe descended a pole atop the Times Tower in Times Square, New York City.

1923 • THE CHIMES OF BIG BEN were first broadcast on the radio.

1935 • The Parker brothers received a patent for their game MONOPOLY.

1946 • President Harry Truman officially proclaimed the END OF WORLD WAR II.

1972 • BASEBALL STAR ROBERTO CLEMENTE was killed in an airplane crash while aiding Nicaraguan earthquake victims.

• The pesticide DDT WAS BANNED in the United States.

ANO VIEJO (Old Year celebration in Ecuador)

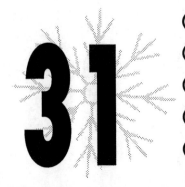

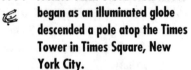

Great works of art, cutout style

Henri Matisse used oil paints during most of his career. When, late in his life, he became confined to a wheelchair, he found a new way to express himself: with paper and scissors. After his assistants painted large sheets of paper with the bright colors he loved, Matisse cut out shapes and arranged the cutouts on canvas. Show your students some of Matisse's cutout works, then ask them to "draw with scissors."

Good-bye to the old year

Tell your students that many superstitions surface on the last day of the year. For example, some people look for a horseshoe to put under their pillow, in hopes that it will bring them good luck in the new year. Others believe that animals speak as the clock strikes midnight. What superstitions have your students heard? Invite them to find out how these superstitions got started.

Countries around the world have their own customs for saying good-bye to the old year and welcoming the new one. For example, in Ecuador, families make a figure of the old year—called Ano Viejo—dress it in an old shirt and pants, and display it in their window. Everyone walks through town and admires the different versions of Ano Viejo, which are burned at midnight. Invite your class to find out what other countries do as part of their New Year's Eve festivities.

JANUARY

☆ Project of the Month: Soup's On

Soup's on all month when your students celebrate National Soup Month. Start the celebration by having your students write, draw, or tell about their favorite soups and when they like to have them. Kids who don't like soup, if there are any, can tell why. How do the soup lovers feel about these negative reviews? Can they think of any ways to change their classmates' minds—and palates?

Throughout the month, ask students to bring in soup labels or, if they eat homemade soup, handwritten descriptions. What brands and types seem the most popular? Keep a frequency graph to show how many kids had soup with their evening meal. Why might some days show a higher frequency than others? Was the weather a factor?

Ask the kids—and their families—to submit a favorite soup recipe Then ask your students to plan a class soup booklet. How do they want to organize it—by country of origin, by family name, by type of soup? Encourage them to develop an index for cross-referencing.

At the end of the month, ask parents to help with a soup-sampling luncheon. Try to include as many varieties as possible.

EXTENDER: Have your students explore the nutritional value of various soups by examining labels. Ask them to list the brands, starring those that are the lowest in fat and putting a check mark next to those lowest in sodium. Students could also investigate soup myths—such as the medicinal properties of chicken soup or the amount of strength provided by hearty meat and barley soup.

JANUARY 1
activities

Congratulations, Thomas and Patty!

In colonial times, it was customary to give a marriage plate to newly-weds. Painted with bright colors, these plates would include a likeness of the couple, their marriage date, and a saying to wish them happiness, health, wealth, and a large family. Have students design a marriage plate for Thomas Jefferson and Martha "Patty" Wayles Skelton. The following descriptions might help the kids: Patty was slender and had auburn hair. She loved music and played the harpsichord and piano. Thomas was tall and had sandy hair. He loved to read, ride, dance, and play the violin.

Sweet-smelling tradition

What started in 1890 as a few carriages with flowers has become the most widely viewed parade in the world—the Tournament of Roses. More than 1.5 million people see the parade in person, while another 150 million or so watch it on television. Some floats are covered with more than 200,000 blossoms. Past themes have included space, fairy tales, and the Old West. Ask your students to vote on a theme for a class parade. Then have them decorate shoe boxes to illustrate the theme.

Fresh starts

Ask the children what they think "turn over a new leaf" means. Tell them that the custom of making New Year's resolutions is the same as turning over a new leaf. Then have them think about resolutions they believe they can keep for at least a month. Help students write their resolutions on leaf-shaped sheets of paper and pin the papers—resolution side in—on a bulletin board. At the end of the month, have those kids who couldn't keep their resolutions remove them from the board. Those who were successful can "turn over their new leaf." Discuss why some of the resolutions were difficult to keep.

"MARY HAD A LITTLE LAMB"

JANUARY 2
activities

🇺🇸 Meaningful mottoes

Celebrate the anniversary of Georgia's statehood by writing its state motto, "Wisdom, justice, and moderation," on the chalkboard. Invite your students to find out the motto of their state. Next, have each child come up with a class motto. Hold a vote for the favorite and have the kids incorporate it into a class seal. Hang the seal over the door to your classroom.

"WISDOM, JUSTICE, AND MODERATION"

✒️ Bridge building

The Brooklyn Bridge is a suspension bridge: Its road surface is supported by cables that hang from its two enormous granite towers. These towers needed a firm foundation, or the bridge would sink and settle. But the East River's bed is composed of sand and loose gravel, with bedrock many feet below. Ask your students to speculate on how the bridge's engineers dealt with this problem. How could work be done underwater? Tell the kids that two half-acre caissons, boxlike structures open at the bottom, were the answer. The caissons, which were made of steel and wood, were sunk by piling masonry on top. When they reached the bottom, the water was pumped out and pressurized air pumped in. Workers could then enter the caissons through a shaft with an air lock and excavate. Demonstrate this idea to your class by taping a piece of paper to the inside bottom of a plastic margarine tub. Turn the tub over and push it to the bottom of a bucket of water. After a minute, carefully lift the tub straight up out of the water. The paper will be dry.

🌐 First writing

In Japan, people celebrate the new year by decorating their front doors with pine branches and bamboo, which symbolize long life and uprightness. Each person in the household uses a brush called a *fude* and special ink to write a favorite poem or proverb—the *kakizome,* or first writing of the year. The most beautiful kakizome is displayed in a place of honor. Have your students write their own kakizomes. Display them near the doorway to your classroom.

BIRTHDAYS

1879 • **SWAN FRITEA, inventor of the Eskimo Pie**

1920 • **ISAAC ASIMOV, American scientist and science fiction writer**

EVENTS

1788 • **GEORGIA became the fourth** 🇺🇸 **state.**

1800 • **THE FREE BLACK COMMUNITY of Philadelphia petitioned Congress to abolish slavery.**

1870 • **Construction began on THE** ✒️ **BROOKLYN BRIDGE, which spans the East River and connects Manhattan and Brooklyn.**

1890 • **Stenographer Alice Sanger became the FIRST WOMAN EMPLOYED IN THE WHITE HOUSE EXECUTIVE OFFICES.**

1893 • **The U.S. Post Office issued the FIRST COMMEMORATIVE STAMPS.**

1929 • **The United States and Canada agreed to preserve NIAGARA FALLS.**

1959 • *Luna 1,* **the FIRST SOVIET MOON PROBE, was launched.**

1974 • **President Nixon signed a bill requiring states to LIMIT HIGHWAY SPEEDS TO 55 MPH.**

🌐 **GOOD LUCK DAY KAKIZOME (Japan)**

JANUARY 3
activities

BIRTHDAYS
1793 • LUCRETIA MOTT, antislavery leader and early advocate of women's rights
1892 • J.R.R. TOLKIEN, English fantasy author
1926 • JOAN WALSH ANGLUND, children's author and illustrator
1934 • PATRICIA LEE GAUCH, children's author

EVENTS
1777 • Mrs. Jinnie Waglum, wearing a soldier's hat and coat, GUIDED WASHINGTON'S ARMY to Princeton, N.J., where the American troops routed the British.
1847 • The California pueblo of Yerba Buena was renamed SAN FRANCISCO.
1871 • MARGARINE was patented.
1888 • THE WAXED PAPER DRINKING STRAW was patented.
1938 • THE MARCH OF DIMES was organized.
1959 • ALASKA became the 49th state.

📖 Hobbit watch

J.R.R. Tolkien's flights of fancy and imagination began when he was a child and wished for dragons. Years later, while telling stories to his children, he made up the term *hobbit* to denote a member of a race of hole-dwelling, beardless little people with fat stomachs, clever fingers, and good-natured faces. Share this description with your students, and invite them to draw their version of a hobbit. Display the finished drawings on the bulletin board, then compare them with the illustration from the front cover of *The Hobbit*. Did any of the students depict the hobbit similarly?

🏳 Welcome to the 49th state

Alaska, the largest state, covers 586,000 square miles. After your students locate Alaska on a map or globe, have them check an encyclopedia for the total area of *their* state. Then they can use their calculators to compare their state's size with Alaska's. About how many times would their state fit inside Alaska? How many times would Rhode Island fit?

The United States paid Russia $7.2 million for all 577.4 million acres of Alaska. Ask the kids to figure out the per-acre cost. Do they think Alaska was a wise purchase? Why or why not? Finally, invite your kids to design a license plate for Alaska, incorporating aspects of the state's economy, culture, climate, or natural resources.

JANUARY 4
activities

📖 Famous folklorists

Jacob Grimm and his brother Wilhelm collected folktales from all over Germany. Your students are probably acquainted with at least some of their most famous work, *Grimm's Fairy Tales*. Divide your class into groups, and have group members take turns reading these tales to one another. As they listen, have the kids write down the following information: title, subject, plot, theme or moral, and relevancy of the tale to their lives. After they've had enough time to see some patterns, have the group members collaborate on fairy tales of their own.

🖋 Back in time

The Old Senate Chamber in Washington, D.C., looks just as it did when Daniel Webster, Henry Clay, John C. Calhoun, and other famous senators met there. It contains 64 mahogany desks and leather armchairs, silver inkwells, and even snuffboxes. Visitors can walk the galleries and look down into the chamber. Ask your students to think of other places they wish had been "frozen in time"—maybe a grandparent's school, a prehistoric cave dwelling, or a medieval city. Have each child draw a picture of one of these "snapshots."

🛞 Global biker

Thomas Stevens left San Francisco and headed east on an "ordinary"—a bicycle with a 50-inch-diameter front wheel and a 17-inch-diameter rear wheel. He rode across the United States, then from England to China. Three years after beginning his journey, he returned to San Francisco, having traveled 13,500 miles on his own power. Challenge the kids to calculate and compare the total revolutions made by the front and rear wheels of Stevens's bike.

BIRTHDAYS

1643 • **SIR ISAAC NEWTON**, English scientist and mathematician

1785 • **JACOB GRIMM**, German folklorist
📖

1809 • **LOUIS BRAILLE**, French teacher who invented the braille system of writing for the blind

1813 • **SIR ISAAC PITMAN**, English inventor of shorthand

EVENTS

1493 • **CHRISTOPHER COLUMBUS** began his return trip to Spain from the New World.

1790 • George Washington delivered the first **STATE OF THE UNION ADDRESS.**

1859 • The U.S. Senate held its **FINAL MEETING IN THE OLD SENATE CHAMBER.**
🖋

1885 • Mary Gartside became the **FIRST AMERICAN TO HAVE AN APPENDECTOMY.**

1887 • Thomas Stevens arrived in San Francisco, Calif., completing the **FIRST AROUND-THE-WORLD BICYCLE TRIP.**
🛞

1896 • **UTAH** became the 45th state.

TRIVIA DAY

BIRTHDAYS

1779 • STEPHEN DECATUR, American naval hero

• ZEBULON PIKE, American explorer for whom Pike's Peak is named

1855 • KING CAMP GILLETTE, American inventor of the safety razor

EVENTS

1895 • The German physicist Wilhelm Roentgen announced the DISCOVERY OF THE X RAY.

1905 • THE NATIONAL ASSOCIATION OF AUDUBON SOCIETIES was founded.

1914 • Automobile manufacturer Henry Ford announced the adoption of a MINIMUM WAGE OF $5 A DAY.

1925 • Nellie Tayloe Ross became the FIRST FEMALE GOVERNOR in the United States of Wyoming.

1943 • American botanist GEORGE WASHINGTON CARVER died.

1972 • President Nixon ordered NASA to begin work on a MANNED SPACE SHUTTLE.

1973 • U.S. airlines began using MAGNETOMETERS, metal-detecting devices, to scan passengers.

BIRD DAY

JANUARY 5
activities

Where human eyes can't see

When Wilhelm Roentgen discovered X rays, he launched the fields of medicine and physics into a new era. This invisible radiation could travel through items opaque to visible light, such as wood, cardboard, and skin. Ask your students how X rays are used in airports. Then challenge them to find out how they are used in modern medicine. Why are X rays so important in hospital emergency rooms? What is MRI (magnetic resonance imaging)? Why is it safer than X rays? Ask a local emergency room or radiology lab for sample X rays to show to your class.

Peanut power

When the botanist and teacher George Washington Carver went to work at Tuskegee Institute in Alabama, many farmers in the South were encountering severe difficulties. Year after year of cotton cultivation had depleted the soil. Carver began searching for solutions. He encouraged farmers to diversify their crops by planting legumes, which helped restore nitrogen to the soil. And he discovered that the sweet potato and peanut would grow especially well under the conditions that prevailed. To make sure farmers had a market for these crops, Carver developed hundreds of uses for them. Peanuts, for example, are used in kitty litter, soap, vinegar, shoe polish, ink, cheese, and face powder.

Have your students make a collage illustrating the variety of products made from peanuts. Then ask the kids if they know of any unusual sandwich combinations that use peanut butter. Designate a day for a class peanut butter picnic, and have the kids bring in finger sandwiches of their unusual combinations. Which were the most popular?

JANUARY 6
activities

📖 Metaphorically speaking

Carl Sandburg was known for his use of metaphors. In his famous poem "Fog," he writes that fog "comes on little cat feet." Share the poem with your class. Then ask your students to close their eyes as you read it again. What pictures do they see in their minds? Read it once more so the kids can act it out. Then ask them to think of animals that might be used to describe thunder, clouds, sleet, wind, rain, high tide, a volcano, or a hurricane. Have them write a short poem modeled after "Fog."

✒️ Freedom in focus

Which of Franklin D. Roosevelt's "four essential human freedoms" do your students think is the most important? Have them work in small groups to decide on a new freedom to add to the list. Finally, ask the kids to suggest freedoms that specific groups should have. For example, what freedoms should children have?

✒️ SOS to a famous detective

The fictional detective Sherlock Holmes regularly gets requests to solve real crimes. Every week about 40 letters arrive at the Abbey National Building Society, a bank occupying the site that would include Holmes's 221B Baker Street home. Have your students draft a class letter to Sherlock Holmes, requesting him to solve a particular mystery. Ask your school librarian to compile a list of detective stories available in your library, then encourage your students to "investigate."

BIRTHDAYS

1878 • CARL SANDBURG, American poet
📖
1919 • VERA CLEAVER, children's author
1957 • NANCY LOPEZ, American golfer

EVENTS

1759 • GEORGE WASHINGTON married Martha Custis.

1838 • Samuel F.B. Morse demonstrated his TELEGRAPH for the first time.

1898 • THE FIRST TELEPHONE COMMUNICATION BETWEEN A SUBMERGED SUBMARINE AND LAND took place.

1912 • NEW MEXICO became the 47th state.

1941 • Franklin D. Roosevelt made his ✒️ FOUR FREEDOMS SPEECH. He advocated freedom of worship, freedom of speech, freedom from want, and freedom from fear.

1942 • Pan American Airlines achieved the FIRST AROUND-THE-WORLD COMMERCIAL FLIGHT.

✒️ SHERLOCK HOLMES'S "BIRTHDAY" (observed by the Baker Street Irregulars on the first Friday after Jan. 1)

JANUARY 7
activities

Galileo and gravitation
In addition to his ground-breaking work in astronomy, Galileo made important contributions to the understanding of gravitation. He theorized that if objects of different weights were dropped from the same height, they would fall at about the same rate, with air resistance accounting for any differences. It is said that he tested this theory by dropping an iron cannonball and a lighter wooden ball from the Leaning Tower of Pisa. Conduct your own test to demonstrate that gravity affects all objects in the same way. Tell your students that you're going to stand on your desk and simultaneously drop a penny and a dictionary. Ask them to predict which will hit the ground first. Many will be surprised when the objects hit at the same time.

Private line
Miles of cable had to be laid on the ocean floor for the first transatlantic phone service. Students can create their own telephones for short-distance transmission of sound. Provide pairs of students each with two paper cups, two paper clips, and about 10 feet of string. Have them poke a hole in the bottom of each cup, thread string through each hole, tie each end to a paper clip, and gently pull until the string is taut. Have a student speak quietly into one cup while his partner listens through the other. Ask the kids to replace the string with fishing line, wire, thread, and yarn. Which conducts sound the best?

Tower challenge
Give teams of students about 20 4-inch-square pieces of paper. Instruct them to build the tallest paper tower possible. They can fold the sheets or cut them in any way, but they can't use any other materials.

JANUARY 8
activities

✎ Elvis lives!
Celebrate Elvis Presley's birthday by playing some of his songs for your class. Afterward, have the kids write their own reviews of "the King of Rock and Roll." How does his music compare with the music your students listen to?

♨ Classifying colors
Divide your class into small groups, and give each group a hole puncher, one crayon (not black) from an eight-color crayon box, and a few old magazines. Ask the groups to punch out holes they think are within the color family of their crayon. How many different shades of the color can they find in 15 minutes? Finish the activity by having each group glue its holes into a pattern that spells the color's name.

🇺🇸 Winter blues-buster
Senator Dirksen's bill to make the marigold the national flower never became law. But the marigold—and other beautiful flowers—can bring a splash of color and a hint of spring to your classroom. Have your students look through seed catalogs and vote for a classroom flower. Hang photos of the winner and other top finishers on the bulletin board. Order seeds, then germinate and grow them in your classroom.

BIRTHDAYS
1935 • **ELVIS PRESLEY,** American rock
✎ and roll singer
1942 • **STEPHEN HAWKING,** English physicist

EVENTS
1800 • **THE FIRST SOUP KITCHENS FOR THE POOR** opened in London.
1815 • **THE BATTLE OF NEW ORLEANS,** the last engagement of the War of 1812, was fought, 2 weeks after a peace treaty had been signed.
1918 • President Woodrow Wilson delivered his **FOURTEEN POINTS ADDRESS,** which outlined his ideas for a "peace of justice" after World War I.
1935 • Professor Arthur Cobb Hardy
♨ invented the **SPECTROPHO-TOMETER,** an instrument that describes over 2 million shades of color.
1965 • Senator Everett Dirksen of
🇺🇸 Illinois introduced a bill to make the **MARIGOLD** the national flower of the United States.

WORLD LITERACY DAY

JANUARY 9
activities

BIRTHDAYS
1870 • JOSEPH BAERMANN STRAUSS, designer of the Golden Gate Bridge
1913 • RICHARD NIXON, 37th president of the United States
1914 • CLYDE ROBERT BULLA, children's author

EVENTS
1493 • CHRISTOPHER COLUMBUS RECORDED SEEING THREE "MERMAIDS," which were probably West Indian manatees.
1788 • CONNECTICUT became the fifth state.
1793 • Jean Pierre Blanchard and his dog made the FIRST SUCCESSFUL BALLOON ASCENT IN AMERICA.
1839 • LOUIS DAGUERRE received France's Legion of Honor award for his contributions to photography.
1929 • THE FIRST SCHOOL FOR SEEING EYE DOGS was founded.
1956 • The advice column "DEAR ABBY" premiered.
1960 • Construction began on the ASWAN HIGH DAM on the Nile River in Egypt.
1968 • SURVEYOR 7 made a soft landing on the moon.

NATIONAL EDUCATION ON SMOKING AND HEALTH WEEK (second full week)

☙ Price break
After performing ballooning feats in Europe, Jean Pierre Blanchard traveled to America. To cover his expenses, he decided to charge spectators at his ballooning exhibition $5. Many protested the high cost, so he lowered the price to $2. Have your students ever balked when they thought something was too expensive? Give the kids some simple problems that illustrate the concept of supply and demand.

☙ Photo fun
Painter and inventor Louis Daguerre developed the first practical system of photography. His experimental work was boosted by an accident—mercury vapor from a broken thermometer came into contact with a silver plate, giving it the ability to hold an image. Daguerre would be impressed by today's cameras, which have extended human vision from microscopic particles to distant planets. Ask your students to search for unusual photographs to use in a special display.

Also try this activity: Use bleach to wipe the images off old slides. Then invite the kids to create new images using thin permanent markers. Show the slides with a projector. Students might be surprised to see how their images look enlarged.

☙ Caretakers
Celebrate National Education on Smoking and Health Week by playing a variation of the popular game "I'm going on a trip and I'm taking...." In this version, the kids must list ways to take care of their bodies. As the game goes around the circle, each child must repeat what everyone has already said, then add a new suggestion. Ask one student to serve as a secretary and write down all the ideas. Review the suggestions periodically.

JANUARY 10
activities

✒ Revolutionary best-seller

By 1776, enthusiasm in the American colonies for separation from England was waning. That's when Thomas Paine wrote *Common Sense,* a 50-page pamphlet advocating independence. In several months, an amazing 500,000 copies were sold. Have your class find out how many copies have been sold of some of today's best-sellers. How does the population of the United States today compare with the population in 1776? Have students compare the percentage of the U.S. population that read *Common Sense* in 1776 with the percentage of today's population that read a recent best-seller.

✿ Black gold

The first oil strike was a gusher called Spindletop. It sent a huge fountain of oil spraying more than 100 feet above the derrick and almost drowned the drilling crew. The gusher could be seen for 10 miles. Have your students use roadmaps to find a location 10 miles from their school.

☞ Off to see the wizard

Scarecrow, played by Ray Bolger, joined Dorothy, Cowardly Lion, Tin Man, and Toto on a trip to Emerald City in the movie version of *The Wizard of Oz.* He wished for a brain. If your students could wish for one thing to better themselves or make a change in themselves, what would it be? Have them weave the idea into a story.

BIRTHDAYS

1738 • ETHAN ALLEN, American soldier who led the Green Mountain Boys during the Revolution
1904 • RAY BOLGER, American actor and dancer who played Scarecrow in *The Wizard of Oz*

EVENTS

1776 • Thomas Paine published his pamphlet *COMMON SENSE.*
1807 • President Thomas Jefferson received the REPORT OF THE LEWIS AND CLARK EXPEDITION.
1845 • The English poets ELIZABETH BARRETT AND ROBERT BROWNING began corresponding.
1901 • THE FIRST OIL STRIKE IN TEXAS was made.
1911 • THE FIRST AERIAL PHOTOGRAPH was taken.
1946 • Delegates from 51 nations met for the FIRST SESSION OF THE UNITED NATIONS GENERAL ASSEMBLY.
       • RADAR SIGNALS WERE BOUNCED OFF THE MOON for the first time.
1985 • Shel Silverstein's *A LIGHT IN THE ATTIC* broke the record (111 weeks) for the longest period on *The New York Times* best-seller list.

HUMAN RELATIONS DAY

JANUARY 11
activities

BIRTHDAYS

1755 • **ALEXANDER HAMILTON, first secretary of the U.S. Treasury**

1885 • **ALICE PAUL, American women's rights leader and founder of the National Women's Party**

EVENTS

1569 • **THE FIRST LOTTERY was held in London.**

1770 • **Benjamin Franklin sent CHINESE RHUBARB to America.**

1878 • **Alexander Campbell became the first milkman to deliver his customers' MILK IN GLASS BOTTLES.**

1935 • **AMELIA EARHART became the first woman to fly solo across the Pacific Ocean.**

1964 • **A report from the U.S. surgeon general declared CIGARETTES HAZARDOUS TO HEALTH.**

    BANANA SPLIT DAY

Top accountant

When Alexander Hamilton became the first secretary of the Treasury, the United States was in financial trouble. The Revolutionary War had been costly. To pay the bills, Hamilton established credit with other countries and set up a bank to handle the government's money. Hamilton's picture is on the $10 bill, a reminder of his contributions to a new nation. Have your kids look at other currency and coins to see what leaders' faces appear. List these on the board. Were any noteworthy leaders left out?

Book buddies

Amelia Earhart loved adventure—and books. She and her sister Muriel often took turns reading aloud to each other while doing chores, such as washing dishes and sweeping floors. Have students make a list of times they could read with others while doing chores or errands. Have them share the lists with their parents.

Ice cream sensation

The banana split is a descendant of the ice cream sundae, which was first served in an ice cream shop in Two River, Wis. Ice cream with chocolate syrup on it became quite popular, but the shop owner served it only on Sunday, hence its name. Have your students conduct a survey of favorite toppings for ice cream. Graph the results. Then invite the kids to write a recipe for the ultimate banana split—complete with the most popular toppings.

JANUARY 12
activities

📖 Rhymes 'n' riddles

French writer Charles Perrault collected and interpreted eight popular fairy tales—including "Cinderella" and "Sleeping Beauty"—in a collection subtitled *The Tales of Mother Goose*. Though most people associate Mother Goose with nursery rhymes, Perrault's book contained no rhymes. Rather, it was the English publisher John Newbery who first used the Mother Goose character in a book of nursery rhymes, called *Mother Goose's Melody*. Have cooperative teams each select a favorite nursery-rhyme character or characters to use as the answer to a riddle they create. Each riddle could begin with the familiar "Hey diddle diddle/The cat and the fiddle." For example:

> *Hey diddle diddle*
> *The cat and the fiddle*
> *Who went rub-a-dub-dub?* (Three men in a tub)

> *Hey diddle diddle*
> *The cat and the fiddle*
> *Whose wife could eat no lean?* (Jack Sprat)

📖 At the library

Jack London came from an impoverished family that included 12 children. As a young child, he had no books of his own. But by age 10, London had discovered his public library and was a frequent borrower of books about adventure, travel, sea voyages, and discoveries. Ask your students to name the most treasured book they own. Then have them ask their parents the same question. Why do the kids think people treasure certain books?

BIRTHDAYS

1628 • 📖 **CHARLES PERRAULT**, French writer who collected such favorite fairy tales as "Cinderella," "Sleeping Beauty," and "Little Red Riding Hood"

1876 • **JACK LONDON**, American author 📖

EVENTS

1773 • **AMERICA'S FIRST PUBLIC MUSEUM** opened in Charleston, S.C.

1812 • The steamboat *NEW ORLEANS* became the first boat to deliver cargo by steam on the Mississippi River.

1896 • Dr. H.L. Smith made the **FIRST X-RAY PHOTOGRAPH IN THE UNITED STATES.**

1915 • The U.S. House of Representatives **REFUSED TO GIVE WOMEN THE RIGHT TO VOTE.**

1932 • Hattie W. Caraway of Arkansas became the **FIRST WOMAN ELECTED TO THE U.S. SENATE.**

1970 • **THE BOEING 747** made its first transatlantic flight.

1990 • The shuttle *Columbia* returned to earth with **TOMATO SEEDS THAT HAD BEEN IN SPACE FOR 6 YEARS.**

JANUARY 13
activities

BIRTHDAYS

1808 • SALMON CHASE, American statesman and Supreme Court chief justice

1926 • MICHAEL BOND, children's author

• RUBBER DUCKY, "Sesame Street" character

EVENTS

1733 • GEORGIA, the last of the original 13 colonies, was established.

1794 • Congress passed legislation increasing to 15 the NUMBER OF STARS AND STRIPES on the flag.

1854 • Anthony Faas patented the ACCORDION.

1864 • Songwriter STEPHEN FOSTER died with only 38¢ to his name.

1888 • THE NATIONAL GEOGRAPHIC SOCIETY was founded.

1943 • "VICTORY SAUSAGES" (meatless hot dogs) were introduced to make rationing easier during World War II.

1966 • Robert Weaver became the FIRST BLACK APPOINTED TO A CABINET POST, secretary of the Department of Housing and Urban Development.

1990 • Soviet leader Mikhail Gorbachev said he was prepared to accept A MULTIPARTY SYSTEM IN THE USSR.

• SILVESTERKLAUSE PARADE (Switzerland)
STEPHEN FOSTER MEMORIAL DAY

13

📖 Buy that bear!

On Christmas Eve in 1957, Michael Bond noticed a lone toy bear left unsold on a store shelf. He bought it for his wife. Because he lived near Paddington Station in London, he named the bear Paddington. Bond began a story about the toy bear, and within 8 days, he'd completed his first children's book. Since then, he's written 10 additional novels and two short-story collections about Paddington. Have your students write a short story about one of their toys.

Special pals

When your students think of Rubber Ducky, the familiar "Sesame Street" character, do they also think of his pal, Ernie? What favorite "pals" (inanimate or animate) do your students link to themselves? Divide the class into groups, and have group members list pals in stories they've read. How about Ira and his teddy bear, Winnie-the-Pooh and Christopher Robin, Wilbur and Charlotte, Peter Pan and Tinkerbell? Make a class list and assign a different pair of pals to each child. Ask each child to draw the pals and write the name of the book and author at the top of the page.

🌐 Unusual parade

People in Urnasch, Switzerland, celebrate St. Sylvester's Day with an unusual parade. They dress in costumes made from twigs, moss, pinecones, straw, nuts, shells, and other natural things. As they walk through the countryside, they yodel a greeting at each farmhouse. Take a winter walk around your school grounds. What do your students see that the Swiss yodelers might use for their costumes?

JANUARY 14
activities

✒ A man for all seasons

Albert Schweitzer identified an incident that occurred when he was 8 as a turning point in his life. He and a friend were stalking birds with slingshots. Although he didn't really want to kill any birds, Schweitzer was afraid his friend would laugh at him if he didn't go along. As he aimed his slingshot, Schweitzer heard church bells. He stopped himself, threw the slingshot on the ground, and scared away the bird. From that day on, he paid little attention to what others thought of him and dedicated himself to helping people and animals. In what ways have your students avoided "buckling under" to peer pressure? Invite them to share their personal stories in their journals.

Schweitzer won the Nobel Peace Prize in 1954. In his acceptance speech, he said there would never be real peace until people realized their unity with one another and with all living creatures. Invite your students to react to this philosophy. Have them make posters depicting ways to protect living things.

🌐 Rice is nice

During the Pongal festival, the people of Singapore honor the sun and the rain, which ripen the rice crop. They cook rice and form it into balls for the birds. Make suet balls or peanut butter-covered pinecones for the birds near your school.

BIRTHDAYS

1741 • **BENEDICT ARNOLD,** Revolutionary War traitor

1806 • **MATTHEW FONTAINE MAURY,** American naval officer and pioneer in modern oceanography

1875 • **ALBERT SCHWEITZER,** German ✒ physician and humanitarian

1886 • **HUGH LOFTING,** English author who wrote the Dr. Dolittle books

EVENTS

1734 • Thermometers in Yeneseisk, Siberia, registered 120° F **BELOW ZERO.**

1914 • Henry Ford's **FIRST AUTOMOBILE ASSEMBLY LINE** went into operation.

1943 • Franklin D. Roosevelt became the **FIRST PRESIDENT TO FLY IN AN AIRPLANE WHILE IN OFFICE.**

1952 • NBC's "TODAY" show premiered.

1969 • Soviet cosmonauts made the **FIRST LINKUP OF TWO ORBITING SPACESHIPS,** *Soyuz 4* and *Soyuz 5.*

🌐 **NATIONAL PRINTING INK DAY PONGAL** (Harvest Festival in Singapore—Jan. 14-17)

14

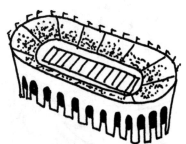

BIRTHDAYS
1891 • RAY CHAPMAN, the only professional baseball player to be killed by a pitched ball
1929 • MARTIN LUTHER KING, JR., 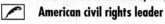 American civil rights leader

EVENTS
1870 • THE DONKEY SYMBOL OF THE DEMOCRATIC PARTY appeared for the first time.
1885 • William Bentley, age 19, MADE THE FIRST SUCCESSFUL PHOTOGRAPH OF A SINGLE SNOWFLAKE.
1927 • George Young, a nearly penniless 17-year-old, won $25,000 in A 16-HOUR SWIMMING MARATHON.
1943 • THE PENTAGON, the headquarters of the Department of Defense and of the United States Army, Navy, and Air Force, was completed.
1967 • The Green Bay Packers beat the Kansas City Chiefs, 35-10, in the FIRST SUPER BOWL.

HUMANITARIAN DAY
 NATIONAL COMPLIMENT DAY

JANUARY 15
activities

Memories of Martin
Make Martin Luther King's legacy real to your students by having them do a "Memories of Martin" oral history project. After they've read some background material on Dr. King, have them develop a set of interview questions, then pose these questions to family and community members. Invite interviewees who have special memories of Dr. King to come to your classroom and share them. Perhaps someone heard him speak, participated in a march with him, or was personally touched by his actions.

Critter symbols
Show your students a picture of the Democratic Party donkey (check the encyclopedia). What characteristics might make the donkey appealing to a political party? Ask the kids to brainstorm for other animals that symbolize a group, club, team, or product. Start them off with Mickey Mouse, the symbol of Disneyland. As a homework assignment, have them look through newspapers and magazines or watch television to find other animal symbols. What animal do they think would be a good symbol for their class? Why? Ask a student artist to draw the animal symbol the kids decide on. Post the picture in a prominent place.

Esteem-boosters in many languages
Ask your students to share compliments that are unique to their cultural backgrounds. Start them off by telling them some ways people are complimented on their good looks in various cultures. For instance, *sheinket* means "good-looking" in German, *sheine madala* is Yiddish for "a pretty girl," and *un hombre guapo* is Spanish for "a handsome man." Invite the kids to ask their parents and grandparents for compliments unique to their cultures.

JANUARY 16
activities

⚗ Incredible incisors

Your students might be surprised to discover that the earliest and most primitive mastodons, which lived some 40 million years ago, were only the size of pigs. But even they had the elongated trunk and incisor teeth (tusks)—two above and two below—that are the main characteristics of all mastodons. They also had molars for grinding food. The best-known mastodons stood about 7 to 9 feet at the shoulders and became extinct around 8,000 years ago, possibly because of overhunting by humans. Ask your students to name animal species that are endangered today because of human practices. Have each student research one of these species and report on what is being done to save it from extinction.

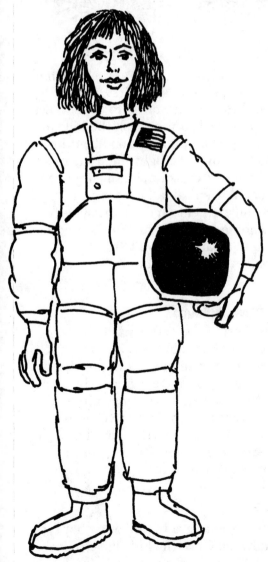

☄ On a whim

While a student at Stanford University, Sally Ride read in the campus newspaper that NASA was accepting applications for astronaut candidates. On a whim, she applied. Ride and five other women were among the 35 applicants chosen from the 8,037 people who applied. Have your students use their calculators to figure out what percentage of the applicants were selected as candidates, and what percentage of the candidates were women. Sally Ride went on to become the United States' first woman in space, aboard the shuttle *Challenger* on June 18, 1983. Ask whether anyone in your class ever did something on a whim and achieved positive results. Invite the kids to share their stories.

BIRTHDAYS

1911 • JAY "DIZZY" DEAN, baseball pitcher
1935 • A.J. FOYT, American race car driver and four-time winner of the Indianapolis 500
1950 • DEBBIE ALLEN, American dancer, singer, and actress

EVENTS

1547 • IVAN THE TERRIBLE was crowned czar of Russia.
1883 • THE U.S. CIVIL SERVICE was established.
1920 • THE EIGHTEENTH AMENDMENT went into effect, making it illegal to make or sell alcoholic beverages.
1962 • TWO MASTODON TEETH were ⚗ discovered by children in Hackensack, N.J.
1967 • Alan Boyd became the FIRST U.S. SECRETARY OF TRANSPORTATION.
1978 • NASA accepted its FIRST ☄ WOMEN CANDIDATES FOR ASTRONAUTS.
1991 • THE GULF WAR, in which a U.S.-led coalition of nations fought to oust Iraqi forces from Kuwait, began with air strikes against Baghdad.

NATIONAL NOTHING DAY

JANUARY 17
activities

BIRTHDAYS

1501 • LEONHARD FUCHS, German botanist

1706 • BENJAMIN FRANKLIN, American statesman, scientist, and philosopher

1925 • ROBERT CORMIER, children's author

1931 • JAMES EARL JONES, American actor

1938 • JOHN BELLAIRS, children's author

1942 • MUHAMMAD ALI, American boxing champion

EVENTS

1773 • The English explorer James Cook became the first person to sail across the ANTARCTIC CIRCLE.

1919 • POPEYE THE SAILOR made his debut as a character in the comic strip "Thimble Theater."

 WHEAT BREAD MONTH

Plant man

The German botanist Leonhard Fuchs studied ways plants could be used as foods and medicines. Fuchsia—flowering shrubs—were named in his honor. Challenge your students to find out where the following plants got their names: iris, poinsettia, forsythia, achillea, begonia, monarda, narcissus, camellia, magnolia, zinnia, wisteria.

Happy birthday, Ben!

Here's an art project that will increase your students' appreciation of Benjamin Franklin. Have them make a kite mobile. First, they should cut out a construction-paper kite and five or more paper bows for the kite's tail. Then, as you read about Franklin, ask the kids to jot in their notebooks interesting or unusual information about his inventions (for example, the Franklin stove, the lightning rod, and bifocal glasses) and his accomplishments (for example, the organization of a postal system, a newspaper, a hospital, an academy, a library, a fire department, a police department, and an antislavery society). Next, have the students choose facts to write on their bows, hang the bows on a piece of yarn, and attach the tail to the kite. They can then hang their kite mobiles above their desks.

Mr. Spinach

As most of your students know, Popeye the Sailor gets his strength from eating spinach. Ask the kids to invent and name a comic-strip character who gets his strength from a different type of fruit or vegetable. Have students work in small groups to create an interesting adventure for the character.

Sandwich snoopers

Have your kids survey students in the cafeteria to find out what type of bread they've used for their sandwich. Once the kids have collected their data, have them make a chart showing the results.

JANUARY 18
activities

🌐 A look at llamas

In Peru llamas are used as pack animals. Tell your class that llamas simultaneously lift both feet on the same side when running. Ask your students to watch their pets run. How do they move their feet? When llamas get angry or tired, they hiss and spit. How do some of your students' pets react when angry or tired?

🇺🇸 Our 50th state

Your students might be surprised to find out that about 80% of Hawaii's population lives in or near the city of Honolulu on the island of Oahu. What are the population centers in your state? Have each student write a paragraph explaining why those areas might have larger populations than other areas. Share the paragraphs in a discussion focusing on the geographic and historical reasons.

📖 Oh, Pooh!

A.A. Milne's son, Christopher Robin, was the inspiration for the Pooh stories. Christopher's stuffed animals were the models for the characters Piglet, Tigger, Eeyore, Kanga, and Roo. Winnie-the-Pooh was Christopher's teddy bear. He named it after a real bear in the London zoo ("Winnie") and a swan that he fed (which he called "Pooh"). Invite the kids to bring in some of their favorite stuffed toys, and ask them to explain how they selected the toys' names.

When Piglet asked Pooh what was the first thing he said to himself when he awoke in the morning, Pooh answered, "What's for breakfast?" Celebrate Pooh Day by planning a Pooh breakfast. What do the kids think would be appropriate? How about English muffins with honey or honey-coated cereal?

BIRTHDAYS

1779 • PETER MARK ROGET, English scholar and thesaurus author
1782 • DANIEL WEBSTER, American orator and statesman
1856 • DANIEL HALE WILLIAMS, African-American surgeon credited with performing the first successful open-heart operation
1882 • A.A. MILNE, children's author 📖 and creator of Winnie-the-Pooh
1934 • RAYMOND BRIGGS, children's author

EVENTS

1535 • LIMA, PERU, was founded by the 🌐 Spanish conquistador Francisco Pizarro.
1778 • English explorer James Cook discovered and named the SANDWICH ISLANDS (now the Hawaiian Islands) after the earl of Sandwich.
1911 • Lieutenant Eugene Ely became the FIRST PERSON TO LAND A PLANE ON A SHIP, the USS *Pennsylvania*.
1943 • Bakers in the United States were ORDERED TO STOP SELLING SLICED BREAD for the duration of World War II.
1944 • E.B. Kan became the FIRST CHINESE PERSON GRANTED U.S. CITIZENSHIP.
1989 • THE ROCK AND ROLL HALL OF FAME inducted Dion, Otis Redding, the Rolling Stones, the Temptations, and Stevie Wonder.

📖 POOH DAY

18

JANUARY 19
activities

BIRTHDAYS

1736 • **JAMES WATT**, Scottish inventor of the modern steam engine

1807 • **ROBERT E. LEE**, commander in chief of the Confederate armies

1809 • **EDGAR ALLAN POE**, American poet and short-story writer

1839 • **PAUL CEZANNE**, French impressionist painter

1941 • **SUSAN DODSON**, children's author

EVENTS

1840 • Lieutenant Charles Wilkes sighted **ANTARCTICA** and claimed it as a U.S. possession.

1861 • **GEORGIA** seceded from the Union.

1898 • Brown shut out Harvard, 6-0, in the **FIRST OFFICIAL COLLEGE HOCKEY GAME.**

1903 • President Theodore Roosevelt sent the **FIRST GREETING TELEGRAM**, to King Edward VII in London.

1955 • President Dwight Eisenhower held the **FIRST TELEVISED PRESIDENTIAL PRESS CONFERENCE.**

• **NATIONAL VOLUNTEER BLOOD DONOR MONTH**

• **SINGAPORE KITE FESTIVAL**

✿ Whimsical telegrams

Ask your students to create telegrams for their favorite athlete, movie star, book or cartoon character, author, singer, politician, or other notable personality, living or dead. Next, pair up your students. While one student plays the role of the telegram recipient, the other student reads, raps, or sings the telegram. Then the kids switch roles.

✑ Southern sojourn

Ask four-member teams each to select an Antarctica-related team name. For example, one team might be the Leopard Seals, another the Queen Maudelanders. Have the teams each make a list of the supplies they'd need for an expedition to Antarctica. Then announce that the teams must limit their lists to the 10 most-essential items and rank the items in order of importance. Have each team share its list. What do the lists have in common? Have the whole class agree on one list.

⚗ F.Y.I.

Invite a member of the local Red Cross to come to your class and speak about blood types, blood donations, and blood transfusions.

⊕ High-flying festival

Everyone who participates in the Singapore Kite Festival must design his own kite. Ask your kids to find Singapore on the globe. Then give them a large sheet of paper so they can design—and paint—their own kites. Display the finished kites in the hallway. Next, ask a committee to research Singapore and compile a list of interesting facts about it. Write the facts on paper kites and hang them at eye level. Invite other classes to see the kite display.

JANUARY 20
activities

⊘ Winter exercise

Basketball was designed as a sport that could be played during the winter and on rainy days. It got its name because the goal was to throw a ball into a peach basket hung on a wall. Early basketball, unlike the modern version, was quite slow. Each time the ball landed in the basket, a player had to climb a ladder and remove it. What are some ways your students get fast-paced exercise during the winter? Have a team of students survey the class and report the results. What suggestions do the kids have to increase their aerobic activity when the weather doesn't cooperate? Consider organizing a lunchtime exercise program.

❈ Emergency!

Eighth-grader Clayton Ary got scared when his 62-year-old grandmother fell and started turning blue. He dialed 911 for help but received only a recorded message saying 911 was not a service in that community. Next, he called the operator, who explained how to give mouth-to-mouth resuscitation. Clayton followed her directions, and his grandmother started breathing on her own. Tell your students that they should always give their address, phone number, and type of emergency if they call 911. Have them make reminders—on peel-and-stick labels—that they can put on their home phone.

BIRTHDAYS

1775 • ANDRE AMPERE, French scientist who made important contributions to the study of electricity and magnetism

1920 • JOY ADAMSON, wildlife conservationist and author of *Born Free*

1930 • EDWIN "BUZZ" ALDRIN, American astronaut

EVENTS

1892 • ⊘ THE FIRST BASKETBALL GAME was played at the YMCA gym in Springfield, Mass.

1945 • President Franklin Roosevelt was inaugurated for AN UNPRECEDENTED FOURTH TERM.

1952 • Patricia McCormack made her debut as AMERICA'S FIRST FEMALE BULLFIGHTER.

1965 • LYNDON JOHNSON BROKE TRADITION by asking his wife, instead of a government official, to hold the family Bible during his presidential inauguration.

1980 • The Pittsburgh Steelers posted their FOURTH SUPER BOWL VICTORY in as many attempts.

• President Jimmy Carter announced that the United States would BOYCOTT THE SUMMER OLYMPICS IN MOSCOW because of the Soviet Union's invasion of Afghanistan.

1987 • ❈ OVER-THE-TELEPHONE ADVICE helped 13-year-old Clayton Ary save his grandmother's life.

1993 • BILL CLINTON of Arkansas was inaugurated as the 42nd president of the United States.

PRESIDENTIAL INAUGURATION DAY

20

JANUARY 21
activities

✿ Around the world under the sea

Conventional submarines are powered by diesel-combustion engines that burn oil. Nuclear subs—such as the *Nautilus*—are run by a fission process requiring uranium. The uranium engine uses less fuel to produce more energy. In fact, a lump of uranium the size of a golf ball can take a nuclear sub around the world seven times! Have your kids use their calculators to figure out that distance. Then challenge them to find out how the *Nautilus* got its name.

❀ High-flying feline

A cat named Felix escaped from her box in the cargo hold of a Boeing 747 while flying from Frankfurt, West Germany, to Los Angeles. She logged 179,000 miles over three continents and made 64 stops before airline personnel discovered her. Ask your students to figure out the average number of miles Felix traveled between stops. Have them write a story about one of her adventures.

✍ Happy hugging!

Tell your students that celebrities voted the most huggable person of the year have included First Lady Barbara Bush and actors John Candy and Dom DeLuise. Ask your kids to think of the most huggable people in their lives. Invite them to show their appreciation to these "huggables" by making special certificates.

JANUARY 22
activities

✿ Just for kids

Ask your students what kinds of items they would include in a kids' museum. Would they pick only older items, or do they think items from today would deserve to be represented? Why? Have the kids tell about the museums they've visited.

📖 Junior critics

Brian Wildsmith's four children frequently helped him evaluate his book illustrations. After pinning an illustration to a wall, Wildsmith would ask his kids what they thought of it. If they were less than enthusiastic, he'd think of ways to improve it. Only when the children were excited about the illustration would he feel satisfied. Do your students' parents have jobs the kids can help with? Why or why not?

🌐 Skating saga

The Elfstedentocht (Tour of the Eleven Towns) is an ice-skating event that began in the Netherlands in the 17th century. Young men in the northern province of Friesland decided to skate, in a single day, over all the frozen canals that connected the province's 11 towns. Every year, thousands of participants skate over the same 129-mile, 483-yard course. Have your students figure out how long it would take them to cover the Elfstedentocht course if they skated at an average rate of 5, 7, or 12 mph.

🍿 Snack sensation

Popcorn comes in more than 40 flavors, including watermelon, tutti-frutti, and pizza. Ask your students to suggest other flavors they'd like to try. Have the class vote for three new flavors, then instruct small groups to compose a letter to a popcorn company suggesting one of the three.

BIRTHDAYS

1561 • FRANCIS BACON, English essayist

1788 • GEORGE GORDON, LORD BYRON, English poet

1930 • BRIAN WILDSMITH, children's book illustrator 📖

EVENTS

1789 • *The Power of Sympathy*, by William Hill Brown—considered by some to be THE FIRST AMERICAN NOVEL—was published.

1926 • The Children's Museum, the ✿ WORLD'S LARGEST MUSEUM FOR KIDS, opened in Indianapolis, Ind.

1930 • Excavation for the EMPIRE STATE BUILDING began.

1987 • A LABRADOR RETRIEVER NAMED COCO saved his $2\frac{1}{2}$-year-old master from freezing to death by curling up on top of him.

🌐 ELFSTEDENTOCHT (the Netherlands)

🍿 NATIONAL POPCORN DAY (Super Bowl Sunday)

JANUARY 23
activities

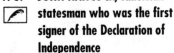

BIRTHDAYS

1737 • JOHN HANCOCK, American statesman who was the first signer of the Declaration of Independence

1832 • EDOUARD MANET, French impressionist painter

EVENTS

1849 • ELIZABETH BLACKWELL became the first American woman to receive a medical degree.

• THE FIRST PRACTICAL ENVE- LOPE-FOLDING MACHINE was patented.

1916 • A 100° TEMPERATURE VARIA- TION (-44° F to 56° F) occurred during a 24-hour period in Browning, Mont.

1960 • The U.S. bathyscaphe *Trieste I* made a RECORD-BREAKING DESCENT to 35,820 feet.

1964 • THE TWENTY-FOURTH AMEND- MENT was ratified, eliminating the poll tax in U.S. elections.

1988 • Bob Benoit became the FIRST PERSON TO BOWL A PERFECT GAME IN A TELEVISED TITLE MATCH.

🌐 BABIN DEN (Grandmother's Day in Bulgaria)

✐ NATIONAL HANDWRITING DAY PIE DAY

✐ The world's most famous signature

When John Hancock signed his name to the Declaration of Independence, he placed it dead center and large enough for the failing eyes of King George III to see. Hancock's name has become synony- mous with any signature. Ask your stu- dents to find out what the following names have come to mean, and why: Benedict Arnold, Einstein, Don Juan, Simon Legree, Florence Nightingale, and Scrooge. What would the kids like associ- ated with their own names? Have them tell why by writing a story about them- selves.

☼ Inspirational doctor

Elizabeth Blackwell pursued a career in medicine when such a path was generally considered unthinkable for a woman. Because of her courage, intelligence, persistence, and desire to help others, she won the respect of her teachers and fellow students. Ask your students to think of someone they respect. Does that person have anything in common with Blackwell?

🌐 A special thank-you

A Bulgarian woman who delivered babies was called a *baba,* or "grand- mother." Tradition held that a baba passed some of her wisdom to each newborn she delivered. Every year par- ents and children showed their appre- ciation by bringing their baba flowers. Ask your students to find out where they were born. Mark the locations on a map. Which child was born farthest from his or her present home?

✐ Handwriting hoopla

Tell your students that in ancient times, most people didn't know how to write and would pay a scribe when they needed a letter or anything else written. Celebrate National Handwriting Day by having your students do the day's lessons in pairs. For the first half of the day, have one person be the scribe and write what the other dictates. Have the kids switch roles for the sec- ond half of the day.

JANUARY 24
activities

📆 Fun food combos

Christian K. Nelson owned an ice cream and candy store in Iowa. One day, a young customer couldn't decide whether to buy ice cream or a chocolate candy bar. His dilemma got Nelson thinking about coating a slice of ice cream with chocolate. After months of experiments, he finally got the chocolate to stick. Nelson initially called his treat the "I-Scream Bar," but later changed the name to "Eskimo Pie." Ask your students to come up with food invention ideas of their own. How about vitamin-filled chewing gum? Or edible spoons made from pressed granola? Have the kids create a slogan or logo promoting their new product. Then invite them to share their ideas in a 1-minute commercial.

⚗ Uniquely Uranus

Tell your students that it takes Uranus 84 years to complete one orbit around the Sun. Have the kids use almanacs to find out what was happening on Earth 84 years ago. What do they think might be happening 84 years from today?

🌐 Bolivian tradition

During the 3-day Alacitis Fair in La Paz, Bolivia's Aymara Indians celebrate their god of prosperity, Ekeko. They make little figurines of the god—a jolly fellow who carries a backpack—and fill his miniature backpack with tiny pots, clothing, food, or other items they need. In turn, they hope that Ekeko will provide *them* with these necessities. What would your students put in Ekeko's backpack?

BIRTHDAYS

1870 • **WILLIAM MORGAN**, American physical education instructor credited with the invention of volleyball

1968 • **MARY LOU RETTON**, American gymnast

EVENTS

1848 • James W. Marshall discovered **GOLD AT SUTTER'S MILL, CALIF.**

1908 • Sir Robert Baden-Powell organized the **FIRST BOY SCOUT TROOP** in England.

1916 • The Supreme Court ruled **INCOME TAX** constitutional.

1922 • Christian K. Nelson patented the 📆 **ESKIMO PIE.**

1985 • The space shuttle *Discovery* was launched in the **FIRST SECRET MILITARY FLIGHT OF THE SHUTTLE PROGRAM.**

1986 • Photos sent from *Voyager 2* ⚗ showed 10 **PREVIOUSLY UNKNOWN MOONS OF URANUS.**

🌐 **ALACITIS** (Bolivian festival, Jan. 24-26)

JANUARY 25
activities

BIRTHDAYS
1759 • ROBERT BURNS, Scottish poet
1914 • JAMES FLORA, children's author

EVENTS
1890 • REPORTER NELLIE BLY completed an around-the-world trip in 72 days, 6 hours, and 11 minutes.

1895 • Tchaikovsky's ballet "SWAN LAKE" premiered in St. Petersburg, Russia.

1905 • THE WORLD'S LARGEST DIA-MOND—3,106 carats—was discovered in South Africa.

1915 • Alexander Graham Bell made the FIRST TRANSCONTINENTAL TELEPHONE CALL, from New York to San Francisco.

1924 • THE FIRST WINTER OLYMPICS began in Chamonix, France.

1945 • Grand Rapids, Mich., became the FIRST CITY TO FLUORIDATE ITS MUNICIPAL WATER SUPPLY.

1983 • THE WORLD'S MOST POWERFUL INFRARED TELESCOPE, called IRAS, was launched into orbit to search for distant stars, comets, and asteroids.

✍ NATIONAL EYE CARE MONTH

✍ Global trip

After reading Jules Verne's *Around the World in Eighty Days,* reporter Nellie Bly decided to go the fictional hero Phileas Fogg one better. She rode ships, trains, carriages, tugboats, sampans, rickshas, horses, and burros—and beat Fogg's time by 7 days, 17 hours, 48 minutes, and 46 seconds. Have your students collaborate on a modern-day travel story. First, create a character and choose an around-the-world route—beginning and ending in your hometown—that the character will travel. (You needn't choose the most direct or even an east-west route.) Then select as many points along the route as there are students in your class, and assign each student one point. Each student will write about how the character gets from his assigned point to the next point along the route. Encourage research so the kids will be able to describe locales, cultures, and customs; discourage kids from having the character merely "take a plane." Put the descriptions in order, add magazine photos when possible, and bind into a book.

⁂ Superstitions in stone

Many myths, superstitions, and legends surround gemstones. For example, opals supposedly bring bad luck to anyone not born in October. It was once believed that people could protect their house from lightning and storms by touching it with a ruby. And early Christians felt that gazing at a sapphire would elevate one's thoughts to heaven. Have the kids create their own superstitions about their birthstones.

✍ The eyes have it

Can your students think of activities that might be harmful to the eyes? How about rubbing them with dirty hands, using power tools without goggles, or looking directly at the sun. Ask the kids to create eye-care "Warning" posters.

JANUARY 26
activities

✒ Flighty about our national symbol

Benjamin Franklin, John Adams, and Thomas Jefferson were the three members of a committee charged with selecting a national symbol. Adams and Jefferson favored the bald eagle, Franklin the wild turkey. In a letter to his daughter, Sarah Bache, Franklin expressed his feelings about the majority's choice: "He is a bird of bad moral character....The Turkey is a much more respectable bird...." How do your students feel about their state bird? What qualities do they think the bird demonstrates? If they could make a change, which bird would they select and why?

🇺🇸 Picture the Wolverine State

Ask your students to sketch Michigan and label the four Great Lakes that touch it—without looking at a map. Once everyone is finished, have the kids take out their atlases. They can give themselves one point for each correctly placed lake and an extra point if they showed Michigan in two sections.

❄ Saving...then and now

During World War I, Americans voluntarily gave up meats and grains on certain days of the week so that overseas troops would be well supplied. Today people are voluntarily taking action to save the environment. With your class, develop a list of daily suggestions to help students and their families "live greener." For example:
* Monday: Turn off the lights, the radio, and the TV when you leave the room.
* Tuesday: Check faucets that might be leaking and set up a repair schedule.
* Wednesday: Save paper by writing on both sides.
* Thursday: Clean the lint catcher in the washer.
* Friday: Turn the thermostat down before going to sleep.

BIRTHDAYS

1831 • **MARY MAPES DODGE,** children's author, creator of *Hans Brinker*

1880 • **DOUGLAS MacARTHUR,** American World War II general

1961 • **WAYNE GRETZKY,** Canadian hockey star

EVENTS

1784 • In a letter, Benjamin Franklin ✒ **DISAPPROVED OF THE BALD EAGLE** as the national symbol.

1788 • English settlers first arrived in **SYDNEY, AUSTRALIA.**

1837 • 🇺🇸 **MICHIGAN** became the 26th state.

1875 • George F. Green patented the **ELECTRIC DENTAL DRILL.**

1918 • ❄ **TO SAVE MEAT AND GRAIN FOR THE WAR EFFORT,** Americans were asked to observe "wheatless Mondays and Wednesdays, meatless Tuesdays, and porkless Thursdays and Saturdays."

1950 • **JESSE OWENS** was voted the top track and field athlete of the first half of the 20th century.

1980 • Frank Sinatra sang before 175,000 people—the **LARGEST CROWD EVER ASSEMBLED FOR ONE PERFORMER**—at the Maracana Stadium in Rio de Janeiro, Brazil.

AUSTRALIA DAY

JANUARY 27
activities

BIRTHDAYS
1756 • **WOLFGANG AMADEUS MOZART,** Austrian composer

1832 • **LEWIS CARROLL (real name: Charles Lutwidge Dodgson),** English author who wrote *Alice's Adventures in Wonderland*

1900 • **HYMAN RICKOVER, U.S. admiral who was instrumental in the development of nuclear-powered ships**

1928 • **HARRY ALLARD, children's author**

1939 • **JULIUS LESTER, children's author**

1948 • **MIKHAIL BARYSHNIKOV, Russian ballet dancer**

EVENTS
1880 • Thomas Edison received a patent for his **ELECTRIC LAMP.**

1948 • **THE FIRST TAPE RECORDER** was sold.

1967 • Three American astronauts, Virgil Grissom, Edward White, and Roger Chaffee, were killed in an **APOLLO LAUNCHING-PAD FIRE.**

1973 • A cease-fire accord was signed in Paris by the United States and North Vietnam, ending direct U.S. involvement in the **VIETNAM WAR.**

Special talents
Wolfgang Amadeus Mozart began his exceptional musical career at the age of 3 and was composing by age 5! Today, Mozart is universally recognized as a musical genius. While such incredible ability is rare, everyone has special talents. Ask your students to make a list of things they do well and describe any special training they've had. Be sure to share *your* talents, too. Then make a class talent poster—a roster of your students' unusual abilities. Shared talents—or curiosity about talents—can form the basis for kids' friendships.

The pleasure of pen names
Charles Lutwidge Dodgson published his famous stories *Alice's Adventures in Wonderland* and *Through the Looking Glass* under the pen name Lewis Carroll. Tell your students that some authors select a pseudonym because their given name is unwieldy. Others might want to conceal their identity or increase the chances of getting their work published. For example, in the past some women authors adopted male names. Ben Franklin had 57 pseudonyms, including "The Busybody" and "Mrs. Silence Dogwood." What pseudonyms would your students select for themselves? Why?

Birthday buddies
Harry Allard, coauthor of the popular Miss Nelson and the Stupids books, was delighted to learn that he had the same birthday as one of his favorite authors, Lewis Carroll. Do your students know of famous people who share their birthdays? Help them find out, and create a class poster listing shared birthdays.

JANUARY 28
activities

✒ Let's communicate

When the first commercial telephone switchboard was installed, the operators were all men. Within 7 months, however, they had all been replaced with women because the phone company thought male operators sounded rude. Discuss sterotypical associations your students may have with male and female voices. For example, do the kids associate strength and authority with male voices, warmth and compassion with female voices? Ask students to pay attention to recorded messages—such as airport announcements, computer phone solicitations, and radio and TV commercials—and describe the type of voice used. If the voice of a person of the opposite sex had been used, would the effect have been the same? Why or why not? Have students list occupations that used to be considered for men only or for women only. Ask them to interview their parents and grandparents to find out how job roles have changed during this century.

📖 Black and white

Ann Jonas used only black and white in her picture book *Round Trip*. Give your students white chalk and a piece of black construction paper and encourage them to create their own black-and-white designs and illustrations.

📺 TV favorites

Ask your students to list their favorite television shows, and write them on the board. Then have the kids bestow their own Emmy awards by voting for their favorite shows in various categories. Broaden the activity by surveying students in other classes and reporting the results schoolwide.

BIRTHDAYS

1887 • **ARTHUR RUBINSTEIN,** Polish-born concert pianist

1912 • **JACKSON POLLOCK,** American abstract painter

1927 • **VERA B. WILLIAMS,** children's author

1932 • **ANN JONAS,** children's author 📖

1936 • **ALAN ALDA,** American actor

EVENTS

1807 • London's Pall Mall became the **FIRST STREET IN THE WORLD ILLUMINATED BY GASLIGHT.**

1878 • **THE FIRST COMMERCIAL TELEPHONE SWITCHBOARD** was installed in New Haven, Conn.

1948 • **THE FIRST TELEVISION EMMY AWARDS** were given.

1973 • Arkansas made the **HONEYBEE** its state insect.

1986 • **THE SPACE SHUTTLE** *CHALLENGER* exploded 74 seconds after lift-off, killing all seven astronauts aboard.

1990 • The San Francisco 49ers won their **SECOND CONSECUTIVE SUPER BOWL.**

NATIONAL DAY OF EXCELLENCE
NATIONAL KAZOO DAY

JANUARY 29
activities

BIRTHDAYS

1737 • **THOMAS PAINE, American political philosopher and author of
*Common Sense***

1843 • **WILLIAM McKINLEY, 25th president of the United States**

1915 • **BILL PEET, children's author and
illustrator**

1930 • **CHRISTOPHER COLLIER, children's author**

1954 • **OPRAH WINFREY, American
talk-show host**

1960 • **GREG LOUGANIS, American
diver who won gold medals at
two Olympic Games**

EVENTS

1845 • **Edgar Allan Poe's poem "THE
RAVEN" was published.**

1861 • **KANSAS became the 34th state.**

1886 • **THE FIRST SUCCESSFUL GASO-
LINE-POWERED CAR was
patented by German engineer
Karl Benz.**

1900 • **BASEBALL'S AMERICAN LEAGUE
was organized.**

1929 • **SEEING EYE, INC., the first
guide-dog foundation, was organized.**

1936 • **THE BASEBALL HALL OF FAME
was established in Cooperstown,
N.Y., and the first five members
were inducted.**

1943 • **Ruth Streeter became the FIRST
WOMAN TO ATTAIN THE RANK
OF MAJOR in the U.S. Marine
Corps.**

Student activists

Thomas Paine's pamphlets *Common Sense* and *The American Crisis* convinced many colonists to join the revolt against England. Read some excerpts. Then ask the kids to work in groups to identify a policy, program, or situation affecting the general public that they'd like to change. For example, perhaps they'd like to see the high school swimming pool opened to the public on weekends. Or maybe they believe the federal or state government should fund after-school recreational and educational programs. Once the teams have decided on their issues, have them create their own "common sense" pamphlets designed to bring about the change they're advocating.

Start with sketches

Tell your students that author/illustrator Bill Peet makes sketches of his characters first, then creates stories about them. Have each student draw characters for a potential story, writing his name on the back of the paper. Collect the finished sketches and redistribute them, making certain that no illustrator receives his own sketches. Next, have the students write stories around the sketches. When the writers are finished, have them collaborate with the artists to turn the project into book form. Encourage writer and illustrator to take turns when they read their story aloud to the class.

JANUARY 30
activities

✒ The country's library

In 1800, President John Adams created a reference library for Congress, ordering the first books from England. In 1814, the collection was destroyed when British troops burned the Capitol. Soon afterward, former president Thomas Jefferson offered to sell his personal library—one of the finest in the United States—to Congress. Jefferson was paid $23,950 for his 6,487 books. Have your students use their calculators to figure out the average price per book.

Today the Library of Congress houses almost 80 million items stored on 532 miles of shelves! That's about the distance between Akron, Ohio, and St. Louis, Mo. Have your kids use their atlases to find a location that's 532 miles from their hometown.

Tell the kids that the Library of Congress acquires 10 new items every minute. How many items would that work out to be during the students' lunch and recess break? If your school library got 10 new books each minute for one school day, how much additional shelf space would the librarian need?

📖 Critter colors

Read Gelett Burgess's classic poem "I Never Saw a Purple Cow" to your students. Ask them to pattern their own odd-colored animal poem after it (for example, "I Never Saw a Fuchsia Turtle" or "I Never Saw an Aqua Horse"). Then have the kids create stick puppets featuring their animals. They can visit other classrooms to share the fun.

BIRTHDAYS

1866 • **GELETT BURGESS,** American
📖   humorist who wrote "I Never Saw a Purple Cow"

1882 • **FRANKLIN D. ROOSEVELT,** 32nd president of the United States

1899 • **MAX THEILER,** South African microbiologist who developed the vaccine for yellow fever

1924 • **LLOYD ALEXANDER,** children's author

EVENTS

1790 • **LIFEBOATS** were first used.

1815 • The Library of Congress pur-
✒   chased **THOMAS JEFFERSON'S BOOK COLLECTION.**

1915 • Congress created the **U.S. COAST GUARD.**

1917 • **THE FIRST JAZZ RECORD** was produced.

1933 • The radio show **"THE LONE RANGER"** premiered.

1940 • **THE FIRST SOCIAL SECURITY CHECKS** were delivered.

1948 • **MAHATMA GANDHI** was assassinated in New Delhi, India.

1972 • Wilt Chamberlain grabbed his 21,734th rebound to become **BASKETBALL'S ALL-TIME REBOUNDING LEADER.**

PURPLE COW DAY

JANUARY 31
activities

K club

Celebrate the birthday of strikeout king Nolan Ryan by examining the history behind the "K"—the symbol for a strikeout. Tell your students that Henry Chadwick, a New York sportswriter, invented the baseball scorebook. He thought the letter S could stand for single, shortstop, or stolen base, so he used the letter K—the last letter in the *word* struck—to indicate a strikeout. Have any of your students ever tracked a baseball game on a scorecard? What other symbols are used?

For and against

A male chimpanzee named Ham was rocketed into space during a test of the Project Mercury capsule that would later carry U.S. astronauts into orbit. The Soviet Union used dogs in its testing of space capsules. Ask your students to describe the rationale for using these animals. How do the kids feel about animal experimentation in general? Make a class list of pros and cons on this issue. Invite the kids to spell out and defend their individual positions in their journals.

Big Mac attack

The world's largest McDonald's restaurant, located in Moscow, has 27 cash registers, employs 630 people, and seats 900 customers. When McDonald's advertised for jobs in its Moscow restaurant, 26,000 people applied. Have your students use their calculators to figure out what percentage of the applicants got positions. Then tell the kids that an average of 12,500 people eat at the restaurant every day. Have your class find out how that number compares with the number of students buying lunch in the school cafeteria.

FEBRUARY ♡

☆ Project of the Month: New-Idea Calendar

Use National New Idea Week to focus your students on creativity and problem solving throughout the month. Start off by showing students the popular "Word-a-Day," "Joke-a-Day," or "Sports-Fact-a-Day" calendars sold commercially. Challenge your class to create a new monthlong calendar modeled after these favorites: the "New-Idea-a-Day Calendar." First, decide on a month—maybe April or a summer month. Then ask the kids to identify tasks and situations that would benefit from some new ideas, such as homework, recess, studying, making new friends, violence, child abuse, the homeless, political reform, pet care, baby-sitting, earning extra money. Assign student committees to each generate ideas for an assigned topic. Remind them to poll parents and other students for suggestions. Ask artists in each committee to make sketches to go with the ideas. After the information is compiled and formatted, raise some money for the class—or a student-selected charity—by selling the calendar to interested kids and parents.

"New-Idea-a-Day Calendar" MAY

FEBRUARY 1
activities

EVENTS

1709 • Scottish sailor Alexander Selkirk was rescued after being STRANDED FOR 4½ YEARS ON A DESERT ISLAND.

1790 • THE U.S. SUPREME COURT held its first session.

1862 • THE "BATTLE HYMN OF THE REPUBLIC," by Julia Ward Howe, was published.

1865 • President Abraham Lincoln approved the THIRTEENTH AMENDMENT, which abolished slavery.

1893 • Thomas Edison completed work on the world's FIRST MOTION PICTURE STUDIO.

1936 • A huge ice floe BLOCKED THE FLOW OF NIAGARA FALLS.

1949 • RCA Records issued the FIRST 45-RPM SINGLE.

1960 • THE FIRST CIVIL RIGHTS SIT-IN DEMONSTRATION was held in Greensboro, N.C.

1978 • HARRIET TUBMAN became the first black woman honored on a postage stamp.

NATIONAL FREEDOM DAY
ROBINSON CRUSOE DAY

1

✒ Lost and found

Alexander Selkirk, the sailor who inspired Daniel Defoe's classic adventure tale, *Robinson Crusoe,* survived alone for 52 months on a South Seas island. For fun and imaginative thinking, have your students play "Stranded," a game in which they're on a desert island that has only a tree and a freshwater spring. In a box, put about 20 index cards, each with the name of an object that may help them survive and eventually leave the island (examples: umbrella, book, bed, mirror, dog, bugle, rope, ax, peanut butter). Have groups of four students draw five object cards and plan how to use the items. Ask them to act out their survival strategies for the class.

✾ Making movies

Celebrate the completion of the first movie studio by making "moving" pictures with your students. Give each child two rubber bands and a cardboard circle about 3 inches in diameter. Have the kids staple one rubber band to the left side and the other rubber band to the right side of their circle directly opposite each other. Next, have them draw unrelated objects on the front and back of their circle. (They could use the center of both sides to draw such objects as an elephant and an empty bird cage or use the top half of one side and the bottom half of the other to draw, for example, a cow and the moon.) Next, have the children work in pairs to view the "movies." While one child holds the rubber bands, one in each hand, the other child winds and releases the cardboard circle. The kids will experience the illusion of motion as they watch the elephant entering the bird cage or the cow jumping over the moon.

FEBRUARY 2
activities

✿ Box mystery

People generally enjoy seeing something unusual—such as the leopard exhibited in the United States in 1802. Tap this tendency in your students. Transform a shoe box into a peep box by cutting an eye opening at one end and a few light holes in the top. Label the box "The Greatest Sight in the World." Put something unique and personal of yours, such as a family photo or a special piece of jewelry, inside the box. Tell your students something they must do to get a chance to look inside. After a while, change the artifact or ask a student to bring something in to be placed inside the box.

📖 Making the most of bad days

Judith Viorst wrote about her son in *Alexander and the Terrible, Horrible, No Good, Very Bad Day*. Ask your students about bad days they've had. Have each child describe and illustrate a "from bad to worse" experience. Create a compilation for your class library. Read the book aloud on days that seem to be spiraling downward.

🐾 How much wood could a woodchuck chuck?

Richard Thomas, a fish and wildlife biologist, was intrigued by the famous groundhog (woodchuck) riddle: How much wood could a woodchuck chuck if a woodchuck could chuck wood? So he decided to figure out approximately how much soil a woodchuck tosses when

digging a burrow. He found that the average groundhog burrow measures 35 cubic feet, and that 1 cubic foot of soil weighs 20 pounds. Have your students complete the calculation. What other "groundhog math" challenges can they develop?

BIRTHDAYS

1931 • JUDITH VIORST, children's author
1962 • GARTH BROOKS, American singer

EVENTS

1802 • Thousands of Bostonians paid 25¢ each to see the FIRST LEOPARD EXHIBITED IN THE UNITED STATES.

1848 • Mexico and the United States signed the TREATY OF GUADALUPE HIDALGO, which formally ended the Mexican-American War. Under the terms of the treaty, the United States paid Mexico $15 million for territory that now forms part or all of the states of California, Nevada, Utah, Arizona, New Mexico, Texas, Wyoming, and Colorado.

1876 • Baseball's NATIONAL LEAGUE was founded.

1887 • Pennsylvania Germans celebrated the FIRST GROUNDHOG DAY.

1935 • THE FIRST LIE DETECTOR TESTS were given.

1956 • Tenley Albright, who overcame polio at age 10, became the FIRST AMERICAN WOMAN TO WIN AN OLYMPIC FIGURE-SKATING TITLE.

1982 • Photos transmitted by the U.S. space probe *Voyager 2* revealed four to six previously UNDISCOVERED MOONS ORBITING SATURN.

🐾 GROUNDHOG DAY

FEBRUARY 3
activities

✒ Dollar description
Test your students' observation skills by having them study both sides of a dollar bill (use the opaque projector). Turn the projector off and ask questions about the bill (for example: How many times does the word or number *one* appear? Are the top and bottom borders identical? What appears at the bottom of the pyramid?).

✒ Famous slogan
Horace Greeley popularized the slogan "Go West, young man!" What other slogans have your students heard? Develop a class list by category—advertising, geography, history, and so on. Then challenge the kids to create some catchy slogans in other categories, including ecology, peace, and friendship. Have your class vote for the best slogans and create posters to display around the school.

📖 Magic spell
Tell your students that one of Joan Lowery Nixon's books is titled *A Deadly Game of Magic*. Can the kids list other stories and fairy tales in which magic is a key ingredient? How about "Jack and the Beanstalk" or "Snow White"? Invite your students to create a story in which magic plays an important role.

◉ Soybean ceremony
The Japanese bean-throwing festival, Setsubun, sprang from a legend in which clever warriors outsmarted their enemies by throwing soybeans into their eyes. Invite your students to describe and illustrate an imaginary celebration—complete with the rituals that accompany it.

FEBRUARY 4
activities

 Counting Confederate states

In 1860 and 1861, 11 U.S. states that favored slavery seceded from the Union. Delegates from six of these states—South Carolina, Mississippi, Florida, Alabama, Georgia, and Louisiana—met in Montgomery, Ala., where they organized the Confederate States of America and set up a provisional government with Jefferson Davis as president. The other states that joined the Confederacy were Texas, Arkansas, North Carolina, Tennessee, and Virginia. Have your students consult a U.S. map and locate the 11 Confederate states.

Gossamer gown

Is a dress made from spiderwebs the ultimate "all natural" fashion statement? Challenge your students to do the empress of Brazil one better by devising and drawing their own outfit made entirely of objects found in nature, such as shells, seaweed, flowers, leaves, cattails, birds' nests, moss, and pinecones.

Civil rights stalwart

Rosa Parks brought the issue of segregation into national focus when she was arrested for refusing to give up her bus seat to a white person in Montgomery, Ala. Because of her actions, she often received harassing telephone calls. Have your students role-play what to do if they are home alone and answer a threatening call.

BIRTHDAYS

1746 • **THADDEUS KOSCIUSZKO,** Polish patriot and aide to George Washington

1902 • **CHARLES LINDBERGH,** American pilot who became the first person to fly solo across the Atlantic Ocean

1913 • **ROSA PARKS,** American civil rights heroine

1925 • **RUSSELL HOBAN,** children's author

EVENTS

1789 • **THE ELECTORAL COLLEGE** named George Washington as president.

1861 • **THE CONFEDERATE STATES OF AMERICA** was formed in Montgomery, Ala.

1877 • The empress of Brazil presented Queen Victoria with **A DRESS WOVEN OF SPIDERWEBS.**

1926 • John Giola became the **CHARLESTON DANCE CHAMP** after dancing $22\frac{1}{2}$ hours straight.

1932 • **THE FIRST WINTER OLYMPICS HELD IN THE UNITED STATES** began in Lake Placid, N.Y.

1957 • **THE FIRST PORTABLE ELECTRIC TYPEWRITER** went on sale.

FEBRUARY 5
activities

WEATHERMAN'S DAY

Weather science and lore

Weatherman's Day commemorates the birth of Dr. John Jeffries, a Boston physician who kept detailed records of weather conditions from 1776 to 1816. In their notebooks, have your students keep daily records of precipitation, temperature, and cloud cover. Have them compare their data with information listed in the local paper.

Tell your students that before people had almanacs, newspapers, or meteorologists, they looked for changes in animal behavior or appearance to foretell changes in the weather. Some thought that if a cat sneezed or a rooster crowed at night, rain was coming; or if the black band on a woolly bear caterpillar was wide or a squirrel's tail was extra bushy, lots of snow was on the way. Although such signs are not always reliable, the folklore is fun. Invite the kids to research other weather superstitions. Some kids might want to ask their grandparents for ideas.

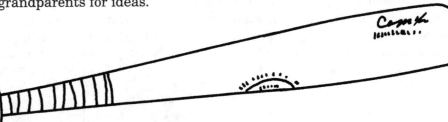

Play ball!

When David N. Mullany cut holes into one side of a polyethylene baseball, he'd invented the Wiffle Ball. Because of the drag created by its many holes, the ball couldn't be thrown or hit far, so it was ideal for backyard or street-corner games.

The Wiffle Ball curves easily when thrown, which makes it hard to hit. Its inventor thought the baseball slang term *whiff*—which means to miss a pitch—captured the essence of his plastic ball. Ask your students to think of new brand names for some of their favorite toys or board games.

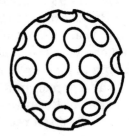

FEBRUARY 6
activities

 Bambino's birthday

George Herman (Babe) Ruth is widely considered the greatest slugger in baseball history. In 22 major league seasons—played in an era when home runs were rare—he hit 714 homers, a total that has only been surpassed by Hank Aaron. Have your students use their calculators to figure out how many homers Ruth averaged per season.

Monkey business

Celebrate Curious George's birthday by sharing a variety of monkey books with your students. While the kids are examining the pictures, have them suggest adjectives that describe monkeys. After the list is complete, ask each child to select one adjective and write it on a card. Then, on brown construction paper, the kids should draw and cut out a monkey that matches their adjective. Meanwhile, cut vinelike spirals from green construction paper and mount them on a bulletin board. Place each monkey—along with its accompanying adjective card—at the end of a vine.

 Hobbies on center stage

Celebrate Hobby Month by asking your students to share their favorite leisure-time activity. First, have them complete a fact sheet on which they describe the materials they use, how they got started, and what they've learned from the hobby. Post the fact sheets along with a schedule for presentations. Encourage your students to read the fact sheets before each presentation so they can prepare questions for the presenters.

BIRTHDAYS

1756 • **AARON BURR,** American political leader who is remembered for his duel with Alexander Hamilton

1895 • **BABE RUTH,** baseball player

1911 • **RONALD REAGAN,** 40th president of the United States

EVENTS

1754 • Benjamin Banneker, a mathematician and inventor, built the **FIRST CHIMING CLOCK IN AMERICA.**

1778 • **FRANCE** agreed to help the United States in its fight against the British in the Revolutionary War.

1788 • **MASSACHUSETTS** became the sixth state.

1865 • **GENERAL ROBERT E. LEE** was appointed commander-in-chief of the Confederate armies.

1933 • **THE TWENTIETH AMENDMENT** went into effect, designating Jan. 20 as the date of presidential inaugurations.

1939 • H.A. Rey's book *Curious George* was published.

1952 • **ELIZABETH II** became queen of England.

MIDWINTER DAY
HOBBY MONTH

FEBRUARY 7
activities

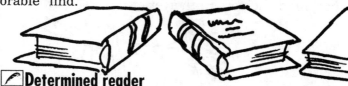

BIRTHDAYS

1812 • **CHARLES DICKENS, English nov-elist**

1817 • **FREDERICK DOUGLASS, American abolitionist lecturer, author, and government official**

1867 • **LAURA INGALLS WILDER, American author**

1883 • **EUBIE BLAKE, American composer and pianist**

EVENTS

1827 • **THE FIRST BALLET PERFORMED IN THE UNITED STATES was presented in New York City.**

1904 • **A FIRE IN BALTIMORE destroyed 1,500 buildings in the city's business section.**

1971 • **WOMEN IN SWITZERLAND WERE GIVEN THE RIGHT TO VOTE in federal elections.**

1984 • **American astronaut Bruce McCandless took the FIRST UNTETHERED SPACE WALK, using a jet pack to move more than 300 feet from the space shuttle *Challenger*.**

1985 • **Bruce Morris of Marshall University made the LONGEST MEASURED FIELD GOAL IN COLLEGE BASKETBALL HISTORY. It was 89 feet 10 inches.**

EAT A PICKLE DAY

📖 Early reader

Charles Dickens was a precocious reader. When he was growing up in Chatham, England, he loved to read Shakespeare and the *Arabian Nights*. He was delighted when he found boxes of novels stashed in the attic of his home. Ask your students to describe their most memorable "find."

✒ Determined reader

Many of Frederick Douglass's accomplishments would have been impossible if he hadn't been so determined to master reading. As a slave, he wasn't supposed to be allowed to read. But when he was 8 years old, the mistress of the house where he served invited him to listen as she read aloud to her son. Douglass later convinced her to teach him to read. All too quickly, however, the master of the house put a stop to the lessons. But Douglass had gotten a start and practiced reading whenever he could. Have your students list things they wouldn't be able to do if they couldn't read.

📖 Pioneer days

At age 65, Laura Ingalls Wilder began writing a series of books about her childhood as a member of a pioneer family. Have your students compare and contrast contemporary life with pioneer life. Have them consider the following: foods and meals, famous people in the news, kids' games, chores, clothing, fears, symbols of wealth. Then have them imagine themselves in an earlier period and write a story including details of that period.

⊘ What a shot!

Take your class to the gym and measure 89 feet 10 inches from the basketball net. What is the longest field goal one of your students—or you—can make? How does it compare with Bruce Morris's record shot?

FEBRUARY 8
activities

📖 Science fiction?

Tell your students that Jules Verne combined scientific fact with fantasy to create his classic stories. Verne's research was remarkably thorough: Data he developed for his novels *From the Earth to the Moon* and *Round the Moon* (rocket weight, 12,230 pounds; speed, 25,000 mph) correspond almost exactly to the 1968 *Apollo 8* spacecraft (weight, 12,392 pounds; speed, 24,200 mph). Verne wrote about many inventions before they existed, including air conditioning, remote control, oxygen tanks, television, dirigibles, rocket capsules, missiles, and submarines. Challenge your students to include a future invention in one of their stories.

🏅 Female phenoms

Have your class brainstorm for a list of sports that women participate in. Then challenge the kids to find out who the top female athletes are in each of those sports. Have them prepare a brief biography for each athlete.

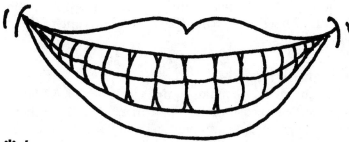

⚗️ Keep on smilin'

For Children's Dental Health Month, have groups of students design posters featuring "Teeth Tips" and "Dental Don'ts." To provide some background information, invite a dentist, dental hygienist, or oral surgeon to talk to your class about dental health. Encourage the kids to ask questions and take notes. Afterward, they can get additional information by checking library books or pamphlets. As the students create their posters, suggest that they include a cartoon character— perhaps a talking tooth or dental mirror. Place the finished posters in community centers.

BIRTHDAYS

1820 • WILLIAM TECUMSEH SHERMAN, American general
1828 • JULES VERNE, French science-fiction writer 📖
1834 • DMITRI MENDELEYEV, Russian chemist who formulated the periodic table of elements
1931 • JAMES DEAN, American actor
1934 • ANNE ROCKWELL, children's author
1940 • TED KOPPEL, American TV journalist

EVENTS

1587 • MARY, QUEEN OF SCOTS was beheaded at Fotheringhay, England.
1910 • The American branch of the BOY SCOUTS was established.
1922 • President Warren Harding had a RADIO INSTALLED IN THE WHITE HOUSE.

🏅 GIRLS AND WOMEN IN SPORTS DAY
NATIONAL INVENTORS DAY
⚗️ CHILDREN'S DENTAL HEALTH MONTH

FEBRUARY 9
activities

BIRTHDAYS

1773 • **WILLIAM HENRY HARRISON,** **ninth president of the United States**

1927 • **DICK GACKENBACH, children's** 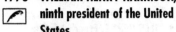 **author**

EVENTS

1825 • **The House of Representatives chose JOHN QUINCY ADAMS as president after none of the four presidential candidates received the required majority of electoral votes.**

1870 • **Congress established the U.S. WEATHER BUREAU.**

1911 • **THE LINCOLN MEMORIAL was approved by Congress.**

1943 • **The World War II BATTLE OF GUADALCANAL ended with a U.S. victory over the Japanese.**

1965 • **Martin Luther King, Jr., met with President Lyndon Johnson to discuss BLACK VOTING RIGHTS.**

1969 • **THE FIRST BOEING 747 took off from Seattle, Wash.**

1975 • **The Jaycees of Liberal, Kan., set a record for the LARGEST PANCAKE FLIPPED ON A GRIDDLE. It was 12 feet in diameter.**

Campaign slogans and shortened terms

William Henry Harrison, ninth president of the United States, became famous as a soldier. He led the U.S. forces at the battle of Tippecanoe during the War of 1812. During his campaign for president, he and his running mate, John Tyler, adopted the slogan "Tippecanoe and Tyler, too!" Discuss the historical significance and effectiveness of this and other presidential campaign slogans, including: "Fifty-four forty or fight" (James K. Polk); "A house divided against itself cannot stand" (Abraham Lincoln); "A square deal all around" (Theodore Roosevelt); "He kept us out of war" (Woodrow Wilson); "I like Ike" (Dwight Eisenhower).

Tell your students that Harrison died of pneumonia 32 days after he was inaugurated, thus serving the shortest term as president. Challenge your students to find out which other presidents failed to serve out their full terms of office, and why. Who was president the longest?

Thumbs down

Children's author Dick Gackenbach dislikes big cities, diets, and flying in airplanes. What would your students put on their "I could do without..." list? Invite them to write about one of these dislikes in their journals.

Fantastic flapjack

Have your students make a yarn circle with a 12-foot diameter to represent the record-setting pancake. Then have them use a small piece of yarn to show an average-size pancake. How many average-size pancakes would fit inside the record-breaker?

FEBRUARY 10
activities

✺ Sticking with the original

When *The New York Times* first adopted its motto, many readers expressed their disapproval. So the publisher offered a $100 prize to anyone who could come up with a better motto. The contest generated 20,000 entries, but the editors decided to stay with their original choice. Ask your students to suggest a motto for their school newspaper.

✿ Tuneful telegrams

In celebration of the first singing telegram, have your students compose and deliver messages to different people in your building. Start by making a list of lucky recipients. How about the school nurse, the custodian, parent volunteers, the secretary, and the lunchroom staff? Next, divide the class into groups. Then have the groups decide on which familiar tune—"London Bridge Is Falling Down" or "Twinkle, Twinkle, Little Star"—they'll use. Finally, have the kids compose lyrics personalized to the recipient—and schedule their delivery.

⊘ Multiple medal winner

Besides winning his Olympic gold medals, Mark Spitz set 35 world records in his career. Despite his success, teammates sometimes criticized Spitz for his aloofness and cockiness. Ask your students if any of their friends ever expressed disapproval of something they did. How did the kids feel? How did they get back in their friends' good graces?

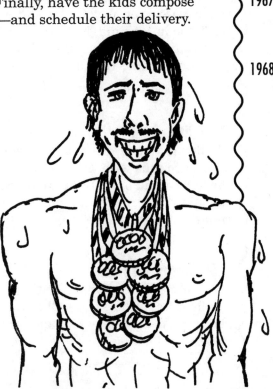

BIRTHDAYS

1930 • **E.L. KONIGSBURG**, children's author
1950 • **MARK SPITZ**, American swimmer ⊘ who became the first athlete to win seven gold medals in a single Olympics
1955 • **GREG NORMAN**, Australian golfer

EVENTS

1863 • Virginia Alanson Crane received a patent for the FIRE EXTINGUISHER.
1897 • *The New York Times* adopted its ✺ motto, "ALL THE NEWS THAT'S FIT TO PRINT."
1933 • **SINGING TELEGRAMS** were ✿ introduced.
1942 • **U.S. AUTO PLANTS STOPPED MAKING CIVILIAN CARS** for the duration of World War II.
1961 • **THE NIAGARA FALLS HYDROELECTRIC PROJECT** began producing power.
1967 • **THE TWENTY-FIFTH AMENDMENT** was ratified. It dealt with vacancies in the offices of president and vice president.
1968 • Figure skater **PEGGY FLEMING** became the only American to win a gold medal at the Winter Olympics in Grenoble, France.

10

FEBRUARY 11
activities

✿ Born not-free

In recent years, the cost of health care has become a national concern. Use one example to bring this complex issue into focus for your students. Ask them to find out the approximate cost of their mother's hospital stay when they were born and, if possible, the costs of their *parents'* births. Then contact a local hospital or a doctor or nurse affiliated with your school and ask what the current cost of a birth would be. Have your students compare the prices. What conclusions can they draw? Do they have any suggestions for controlling the costs of birth?

Pasta person

Thomas Jefferson first sampled macaroni when he visited Paris in the late 18th century. He loved it and wanted to be able to make it at his home in Virginia. Not long afterward, his secretary purchased a macaroni-making machine in Italy and shipped it to America. Poll your students for their favorite pasta dish. Have them graph the results.

◉ A little land

Challenge your upper-grade students to compare the area of your school grounds with the area of Vatican City. They'll need to pace off the length and breadth of the school grounds (and figure out how to calculate any irregularly shaped sections), multiply, and convert square yards to square miles.

📖 Hooray for Hans!

When Jane Yolen started writing books, she drew upon the style of her favorite author, Hans Christian Andersen. Have your students choose an author they like and write a story or poem in that author's style.

FEBRUARY 12
activities

❊ Show time!

Commemorate the first professional puppet show in America by having your students make puppets to dramatize a favorite folktale, tall tale, or poem—or even a current news story or something interesting that's happening in their own lives. Ask the kids to forms groups, write scripts for their characters, and rehearse. Then invite other classes to join the audience.

⚗ Tortoise islands

Tell your students that Charles Darwin did much of his scientific research on the Galapagos Islands. Have the kids locate these islands—off the coast of Ecuador—on a world map. The islands take their name from the Spanish word for tortoises. Galapagos tortoises are giants, weighing up to 500 pounds. Ask the kids to figure out how many classmates it would take to tip the scales at 500 pounds. Note that some tortoises have a life span of 150 years. Then have the kids use almanacs to find other animals that have long lives.

✐ The president on the penny

As your students know, Abraham Lincoln is depicted on the penny. Ask the kids what a penny can buy. Make a list. Then make a list of reasons for continuing or discontinuing the minting of pennies. Use a roll of pennies to give your students practice categorizing, graphing, and computing. First, have the kids separate the pennies into various groupings. You might have them divide the coins by date, by wear, or by degree of shininess. Then help the students make a class graph to show the results. Finally, pass out calculators and have groups of students add the dates of a sample of 10 pennies. Which group has the largest total? Have groups switch penny samples to check the addition.

BIRTHDAYS

1781 • **RENE THEOPHILE HYACINTHE LAENNEC**, French physician who invented the stethoscope
1809 • **CHARLES DARWIN**, English naturalist who formulated the theory of evolution through natural selection
• **ABRAHAM LINCOLN**, 16th president of the United States
1893 • **OMAR BRADLEY**, American general in World War II
1934 • **BILL RUSSELL**, American basketball player and coach
1938 • **JUDY BLUME**, children's author
1958 • **ARSENIO HALL**, American comedian and talk-show host

EVENTS

1738 • **THE FIRST PROFESSIONAL PUPPET SHOW IN AMERICA** was presented in New York City.
1878 • **THE BASEBALL CATCHER'S MASK** was patented.
1908 • **THE FIRST ROUND-THE-WORLD AUTO RACE** began in New York.
1909 • **THE NATIONAL ASSOCIATION FOR THE ADVANCEMENT OF COLORED PEOPLE (NAACP)** was founded.
1914 • Ground was broken for the **LINCOLN MEMORIAL**.
1918 • All **BROADWAY THEATERS** in New York City closed to save coal.

FEBRUARY 13
activities

Sour puss

While driving through Eldon, Iowa, American artist Grant Wood was inspired by a house with a Gothic arch window. He wanted to paint the house and the kind of people who lived there. Not wishing to disturb the residents, he asked his sister and his family dentist to pose as a stern-faced farmer's daughter and her father. He called the painting *American Gothic.* Unfortunately, the painting angered many Iowa farm women who thought Wood was making fun of them. One disapproving writer stated, "That woman's face would sour milk." Show *American Gothic* to your students. Have them write their own hyperboles or metaphors to describe the two famous faces.

Precious find

Quite a surprise awaited a 62-year-old librarian rummaging through her grandfather's trunks, which had been stored in her attic for 30 years. In one of the trunks, she discovered the original handwritten manuscript of part of *Adventures of Huckleberry Finn!* If your students could see an original manuscript from a published author, whose would they choose and why? Have them trade one of their first drafts with a partner. Can they learn anything about their classmate's thinking by looking at that draft?

Snack snooping

During Snack Food Month, survey your class about favorite snack foods. Create two lists—"Favorite healthy snacks" and "Favorite junk-food snacks." Do any of the items on the junk-food list have a healthier alternative? For example, how about saltless popcorn instead of potato chips? Have the students compile and take home a third list containing these healthier alternatives. Ask them to report back on whether their families would try these foods and, if so, whether they liked them.

FEBRUARY 14
activities

🏴 Double anniversary

Oregon and Arizona both gained statehood on this date. Have your students make a chart comparing the two in population, natural resources, tourist attractions, area, climate, elevation, and principal industries.

🦋 Buddies for a day

Celebrate National Have-a-Heart Day by having pairs of kids buddy up as heart mates for the day. To start off, ask the buddies to take each other's resting heart rate. (To get a pulse, kids should gently press their first two fingers on their buddy's wrist for 15 seconds, then multiply the number of beats they feel by four.) Next, the pairs should plan an aerobic exercise they can do safely in the classroom, such as jumping jacks. After they describe their exercise to you, they should do it for 1 minute, then find their after-exercise heart rates. How do the different rates compare?

🦋 Critter cards

Combine your students' love for animals with wordplay and you'll have a new valentine card project. Start by having the kids cut out pictures of animals from magazines. Ask them to pick one animal and think of sounds it makes or special habits or traits it has. Then ask them to think of ways they can incorporate that information into a valentine message. For example, a snow leopard's message might read, "My heart purrs for you, Valentine," or "You make my heart leap and stretch, Valentine." Ask the kids to put the message and picture on construction paper and decorate it as a valentine.

BIRTHDAYS

1859 • **GEORGE WASHINGTON GALE FERRIS,** American engineer who invented the Ferris wheel

1925 • **VALENTINE VALENTINE,** insurance salesman

1944 • **CARL BERNSTEIN,** American journalist who helped break the Watergate story

1946 • **GREGORY HINES,** American dancer and actor

EVENTS

1803 • Moses Coats invented the **APPLE PARER.**

1849 • James Polk became the **FIRST PRESIDENT TO BE PHOTOGRAPHED WHILE IN OFFICE.**

1859 • **OREGON** became the 33rd state. 🏴

1876 • Two rival inventors, Alexander Graham Bell and Elisha Gray, applied separately for a patent for the **TELEPHONE.** Bell applied 2 hours earlier.

1903 • **THE U.S. DEPARTMENT OF COMMERCE AND LABOR** was created.

1912 • **ARIZONA** became the 48th state. 🏴

1931 • The original **DRACULA** movie was released.

1991 • Carrie White, thought to be the oldest living person, **DIED AT THE AGE OF 117.**

🦋 **NATIONAL HAVE-A-HEART DAY**
NATIONAL SALUTE TO HOSPITALIZED VETERANS DAY
🦋 **VALENTINE'S DAY**

14

FEBRUARY 15

activities

15

✒ For men only?

Susan B. Anthony was the first woman depicted on a U.S. coin. However, there is no national holiday commemorating a woman. Ask your students to think of women they might nominate for this honor. Then have them explain the rationales for their choices.

🏴 Slogans then and now

"Remember the *Maine*" became the Americans' rallying cry during the Spanish-American War. Can your students think of other slogans that galvanized popular sentiment? (For example: "Taxation without Representation Is Tyranny," "Liberty! Equality! Fraternity!" "Remember Pearl Harbor," "Never Again.") Ask your students to list catchy public-service slogans, such as "Give a hoot. Don't pollute," "A mind is a terrible thing to waste," and "It's a matter of life and breath." Challenge the kids to create a slogan related to a current topic in science or social studies.

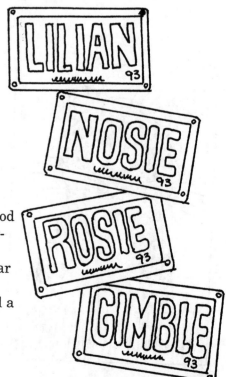

📖 Meet Clifford's creator

When Norman Bridwell was a boy, he dreamed of owning a dog as big as a horse. Though he never got his childhood wish, he did create the bright red, oversized dog Clifford for young readers. Today, Norman Bridwell drives a red car with the personalized license plate "CLIFFORD." Can your students recall a personalized plate they've seen? Invite the kids to design a personalized plate for themselves.

FEBRUARY 16
activities

Let there be music

The first American music festival celebrated the Treaty of Ghent, which ended the War of 1812. Patriotic songs, popular tunes of the day, and classical music were included. Ask groups of students to plan a musical celebration of another American event, but not a national holiday. Have them consider what kind(s) of music would be played and by what orchestras and groups. Then have them list three to five specific songs or selections. Consider working with music teachers to make the celebration a reality.

Just like Indiana Jones

When Howard Carter and Lord Carnarvon opened King Tutankhamen's tomb, they were dazzled by the treasures it contained. Tell your students that King Tut's tomb had remained undisturbed since the 14th century B.C. Have the kids do a little mental math to figure out about how many years ago that was.

Welcome, spring!

Basant Panchami, the Hindu celebration to welcome spring, is also the time to honor Sarasvati, the Hindu goddess of learning and arts. School students place offerings of pens, brushes, and books under pictures of the goddess, in hopes she'll help them do well on tests. Ask your students what they'd name a special U.S. celebration to honor learning. When would this event be?

BIRTHDAYS

1903 • EDGAR BERGEN, American ventriloquist
1957 • LEVAR BURTON, American actor and host of the TV show "Reading Rainbow"
1959 • JOHN McENROE, American tennis player

EVENTS

1814 • THE FIRST AMERICAN MUSIC FESTIVAL was held to celebrate the end of the War of 1812.
1909 • THE FIRST SUBWAY CAR WITH SIDE DOORS began operation.
1923 • British archaeologists opened KING TUTANKHAMEN'S TREASURE-FILLED TOMB.
1937 • Dr. Wallace Carothers received a patent for NYLON.
1959 • FIDEL CASTRO became the premier of Cuba.
1960 • The U.S.S. *Triton* became the FIRST SUBMARINE TO CIRCUMNAVIGATE THE EARTH UNDERWATER.
1965 • *PEGASUS I*, a satellite designed to measure potential hazards of meteoroids to spacecraft, was launched.
1972 • WILT CHAMBERLAIN became the first NBA player to score 30,000 points.

BASANT PANCHAMI (Hindu spring festival)

FEBRUARY 17
activities

Catalog king

In the 1800s, Montgomery Ward, a traveling salesman, realized that people wanted and needed the goods he sold more frequently than he could deliver them. So he created a catalog. The first one, which was distributed in 1872, was a one-page listing of commonly needed items. Ask your students what they think might have appeared in that catalog. By 1944, Montgomery Ward catalog sales reached an annual total of $40 million. Collect some of the hundreds of catalogs available today. Have the kids select one that interests them and pretend they have $100 to spend—including tax and shipping and handling charges. They can use the forms found inside the catalogs. After they've completed their orders, have them trade with a partner to check the math and compare ideas. Finally, discuss the advantages and disadvantages of catalog shopping.

Math race

Celebrate the invention of the electronic calculator by holding math races with groups of three children each. For each round, one of the three does mental math, one does paper-and-pencil figuring, and one uses a calculator. Present one problem at a time. Award 3 points for the first correct answer, 2 points for the second, 1 point for the third, and 0 points for an incorrect answer. Have the kids switch roles after every round, and remind them to note which method was used for each point. What do the results suggest?

Midwinter run

During the Bonten festival, runners carry a *bonten,* a 10-foot pole topped with an animal figure. The first team to reach the finish line—a shrine—gets to display its bonten for the next year. Ask your kids to create an unusual relay to try during recess.

FEBRUARY 18
activities

📖 Current classics

When Mark Twain's *Adventures of Huckleberry Finn* was published, it was banned in Boston. One reviewer claimed it was written in "gutter" language. But the book became a classic and remains one of the most widely read works of fiction. Have your students cooperate to create a class list of books they've read that they think are destined to be favorites in the 2090s. Ask the kids to annotate each selection with a short description of the qualities that make the book timeless. Post the list where other classes can see it.

🧪 Perfect pet names

Clyde Tombaugh selected the perfect name for his cat—Pluto. Have your students make a list of other scientists. What would be appropriate names for their pets? Why?

🐾 Another incredible journey

Tiger the cat arrived home in Dubuque, Iowa, after a 250-mile journey from Wausau, Wis., where he was lost 8 months earlier during his owners' summer vacation. His owners were thrilled to see him again, but they wondered how their pet had crossed the Mississippi River.

Divide your class into groups of three or four students. Give the groups about 15 minutes to develop "Tiger's Tale—The Great Adventure Story," describing just how the cat did find his way home. Ask each group to perform its version of "Tiger's Tale." Then have the kids compile all the scenarios in a class book. If possible, have them share their tales with other classes—and let their audiences decide which version is the most plausible.

BIRTHDAYS

1516 • MARY I, the first queen of England
1957 • VANNA WHITE, TV personality
1964 • MATT DILLON, American actor
1968 • MOLLY RINGWALD, American actress

EVENTS

1688 • The Quakers of Germantown, Pa., made the first formal PROTEST AGAINST SLAVERY in colonial America.
1861 • Jefferson Davis was inaugurated as PRESIDENT OF THE CONFEDERACY.
1884 • Mark Twain's *ADVENTURES OF HUCKLEBERRY FINN* was published.
1930 • American astronomer Clyde Tombaugh discovered PLUTO.
       • Elm Farm Ollie became the FIRST COW TO FLY IN AN AIRPLANE.
1978 • A CAT NAMED TIGER returned home after walking 250 miles.

18

FEBRUARY 19
activities

BIRTHDAYS

1473 • **NICOLAUS COPERNICUS, Polish astronomer**

1865 • **SVEN HEDIN, Swedish scientist and explorer of Tibet**

1876 • **CONSTANTIN BRANCUSI, Romanian sculptor**

1903 • **LOUIS SLOBODKIN, children's author**

1960 • **PRINCE ANDREW, duke of York**

EVENTS

1888 • **A CYCLONE destroyed Mt. Vernon, Ill.**

1942 • **President Franklin Roosevelt ordered Japanese-Americans living on the West Coast to report to INTERNMENT CAMPS in remote areas of the western United States.**

1945 • **U.S. forces in the Pacific began their INVASION OF IWO JIMA.**

1968 • **"MISTER ROGERS' NEIGHBORHOOD" premiered on PBS.**

1989 • **Alfred Furrer, the last survivor of the WORLD WAR I LAST MAN'S CLUB, died at age 97.**

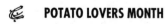 **POTATO LOVERS MONTH**

19

The universe reconsidered

In Copernicus's day, the accepted view—held since the time of Ptolemy in the second century A.D.—was that the earth was the center of the universe, and the planets and the sun revolved around it. Copernicus, however, came to the conclusion that the earth and the rest of the planets actually revolve around the sun. He was right. Challenge your students to name the planets in order from the shortest to the longest orbit around the sun.

Royal family

Prince Andrew, the second son of Queen Elizabeth II and Prince Philip, is a member of Britain's royal family, the Windsors. Create five- or six-student "royal families" in your classroom. Have each family find out a little about castles and design its own. Each family should produce a drawing of its castle's exterior as well as blueprints of the interior that include the dimensions and function of each room. Finally, have each family pick a name, design a crest, and present its castle and crest to the rest of the class.

Grow a spud

During Potato Lovers Month, plant a couple potato eyes in your classroom. At the end of the year, dig up the soil and see if you have any potatoes.

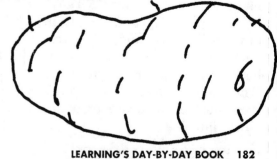

FEBRUARY 20
activities

A special eye

Ansel Adams loved nature and the outdoors. One of his favorite places was Yosemite National Park. Have the kids locate Yosemite on a map. Then make a class list of your students' favorite outdoor places. If possible, show the kids some Ansel Adams photographs. Did they find any from Yosemite?

Mother nature at work

In 1943, in a cornfield outside Parangaricutiro, Mexico, a farmer noticed a 20-inch crack in the ground. The land around it had started to bulge and rise. Throughout that night, horrified villagers watched as ashes, cinders, and fumes spewed forth from the crack. Within 10 days, the Paricutin volcano was 500 feet high, and its explosive sounds could be heard in Mexico City, 200 miles away. Challenge your students to identify the locations of some of today's active volcanoes and mark them on a wall map with yarn and informational cards.

French flower fracas

During the annual 12-day carnival in Nice, France, people bring a healthy supply of flowers and, on a signal, begin throwing them at one another. By the end of the "battle"—which sometimes lasts for hours—the participants can be knee-deep in petals! Challenge your students to write as vivid a paragraph as they can focusing on the sights, sounds, or smells of this event.

Get lost, winter!

People in the Northern Hemisphere go outside today and yell "Hoodie Hoo!" to chase winter away. What suggestions do your students have for their own "Hoodie Hoo!" ceremony? Can they think of a new winter-chasing chant or a chant to entice spring to return early?

BIRTHDAYS

1827 • HIRAM R. REVELS, the first black U.S. senator
1902 • ANSEL ADAMS, American nature photographer
1924 • SIDNEY POITIER, actor who became the first African-American to win an Oscar
1963 • CHARLES BARKLEY, basketball star

EVENTS

1792 • President George Washington signed an act creating the U.S. POST OFFICE.
1839 • Congress prohibited DUELING in the District of Columbia.
1895 • American abolitionist FREDERICK DOUGLASS died in Washington, D.C.
1943 • THE VOLCANO PARICUTIN appeared in a cornfield in Michoacan, Mexico. It eventually buried the village of Parangaricutiro.
1962 • John Glenn became the FIRST AMERICAN TO ORBIT THE EARTH.
1986 • THE WORLD'S LARGEST CAKE was served to 300,000 people celebrating the founding of Texas.

• BATTLE OF THE FLOWERS (France; during the 12-day Nice Carnival, which ends on Shrove Tuesday)

• HOODIE HOO DAY

FEBRUARY 21
activities

BIRTHDAYS
1907 • W.H. AUDEN, English-born American poet
1943 • JIM AYLESWORTH, children's author

EVENTS
1828 • The *Cherokee Phoenix*, the FIRST NEWSPAPER PRINTED IN AN AMERICAN INDIAN LANGUAGE, was published.

1838 • THE FIRST BURGLAR ALARM was installed.

1866 • Lucy B. Hobbs became the FIRST WOMAN TO GRADUATE FROM DENTAL SCHOOL.

1878 • The New Haven, Conn., telephone company issued the FIRST PHONE BOOK. It had 50 listings.

1885 • THE WASHINGTON MONUMENT was dedicated.

1918 • A CHINOOK (a warm wind that blows down the eastern slopes of the Rocky Mountains) changed the temperature in Granville, N.D., from -33° F to 50° F in one day.

1947 • Inventor Edwin Land introduced 60-SECOND PHOTOS with his Polaroid Land camera.

1965 • African-American leader MALCOLM X was assassinated at a rally in New York City.

⊕ TINCUNACO CEREMONY (Argentina)

✎ Open wide!
When Lucy Hobbs became a dentist in 1866, she was entering what had been a man's profession. How far have women come in the medical professions since then? Conduct a class survey to get an interesting, if not completely scientific, perspective on the question. Ask how many students go to a male dentist, and how many go to a female dentist. Then ask the same question about your students' pediatricians. Make a graph of your class results. What conclusions can your students draw from their data?

⁂ The phone has grown
With just 50 listings, the first phone book wouldn't fill a single page today. Show your class a phone book from your community, and ask the kids to estimate how many listings it contains. Have each child write his estimate on a piece of paper. Then ask three kids to count the entries on three different pages. Use a calculator to get the average, then multiply this figure by the number of pages in the book. Which child's estimate was closest?

⊕ For love of kids
In the Calchaqui Valley of Argentina, mothers and godmothers perform the Tincunaco Ceremony during carnival season. They line up on opposite sides of an arch made of willow branches trimmed with flowers, fruit, cheese, lanterns, and candy. After meeting under the arch, the women touch their foreheads together and exchange a child made out of candy. This is their way of honoring the children in their lives. Ask your students to think of ways children are honored in this country. On what occasions do we celebrate love for children here?

FEBRUARY 22
activities

✏️ Big appetite

Your students might be surprised to find out that George Washington was quite an eater. For example, his supper—which might take 2 hours—would include 8 or 10 large dishes of meat and poultry, several kinds of vegetables, and pastries. About how long do your students' families spend at the table for a weekend meal? Poll the kids, then graph the results.

❄️ Taking a loss in stride

Edward Weston bet a friend that Stephen Douglas would defeat Abraham Lincoln in the 1860 presidential election. The stakes? The loser would walk from Boston to Washington, D.C., for the presidential inauguration. Weston lost. After walking for 10 days, he finally arrived at his hotel in Washington. Ask your students to use their atlases to figure out how many miles per day he averaged. Then have them pretend that Weston lived in their hometown and figure out how long it would have taken him at the same pace to walk to Washington, D.C.

⚙️ Nickel power?

With just $315 worth of inventory bought from his former retail employer, 27-year-old Frank Woolworth opened his "Great Five-Cent Store" in Utica, N.Y. To appeal to bargain hunters, he displayed his merchandise on easily accessible counters and sold everything for the same price—5¢. Back then, a nickel could buy a baseball, a handkerchief, even a purse. Can your students think of anything a nickel buys today?

BIRTHDAYS

1732 • **GEORGE WASHINGTON, first president of the United States**

1810 • **FREDERIC CHOPIN, Polish-French composer and pianist**

1892 • **EDNA ST. VINCENT MILLAY, American poet**

EVENTS

1630 • Quadequina, the brother of the Wampanoag Indian chief Massasoit, introduced POPCORN to the New England colonists.

1819 • A treaty was signed whereby SPAIN CEDED FLORIDA TO THE UNITED STATES.

1861 • Edward Weston began A WALKING TRIP FROM BOSTON TO WASHINGTON, D.C., to attend Lincoln's inauguration.

1879 • THE FIRST "FIVE-CENT STORE" opened in Utica, N.Y.

1924 • Calvin Coolidge delivered the FIRST PRESIDENTIAL RADIO BROADCAST FROM THE WHITE HOUSE.

1935 • FLYING AN AIRPLANE OVER THE WHITE HOUSE became illegal.

1980 • THE U.S. HOCKEY TEAM WON THE OLYMPIC GOLD MEDAL by defeating the favored Soviet team, 4-3.

WASHINGTON'S BIRTHDAY

22

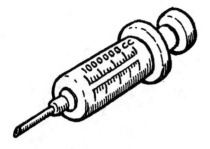

FEBRUARY 23
activities

Disney delights

Have your students make a list of Walt Disney movies they've seen. Ask each child to select one movie and write a plot summary with a contemporary twist. For example: In this story a girl finds some strange but hard-working miners working their claim in a remote forest. She decides to organize their camp for a share of the profits. Later she is given a dangerous drug by a jealous drug dealer and lapses into a coma. Finally, she is resuscitated by a talented young doctor and lives happily ever after. The rest of the class tries to guess which movie the student is describing.

Dolphin doctor

Dr. Spock, a bottle-nosed dolphin at Marine World USA in California, swallowed a 3-inch bolt accidentally left in its tank. A veterinarian tried to remove it from the dolphin's stomach, but his arm was 9 inches too short. Clifford Ray, a professional basketball player, volunteered his 3-foot 9-inch arm for the task. After about $2^1/_2$ minutes of groping inside Dr. Spock's stomach, Ray found the bolt and removed it. What mathematical comparisons can your students make between their arms and Ray's?

Light-years away

A supernova is the explosion of a very large star. Scientists calculated that supernova 1987A occurred about 160,000 light-years from earth. They estimated that the star was "born" about 10 million years ago and was about 40 times as large and 100,000 times as bright as our sun. And it aged about 1,000 times as fast. Have your students use this information along with data found in an encyclopedia to develop a chart comparing 1987A and the sun.

FEBRUARY 24
activities

📖 Fairy-tale tellers

Wilhelm and Jacob Grimm retold in print stories that had been told orally by Gypsies for generations. Ask your students to list their five favorite fairy tales. Which ones did the Grimms write? Tell your students that *Dear Mili* is a Grimm tale that was lost for almost 150 years. If possible, read this tale to the kids and ask them to write letters to the Grimm brothers explaining why they're pleased that the story was found.

📇 Here a scene, there a scene

Before the development of a process for printing photographs, newspapers and magazines had to rely on drawings by illustrators. Winslow Homer began his career as an illustrator. During the Civil War, he sketched soldiers at work or relaxing. After the war, he decided to devote himself to painting. He sketched familiar scenes of people, then painted them back in his studio. Ask your students to draw scenes from their day that they think would interest people 100 years from now.

✿ Fire alarms then and now

On the anniversary of America's first electric fire alarm system, discuss why residential smoke alarms are so important. Have your students draw maps of their homes and indicate where smoke alarms are—or should be—located. Remind them that the batteries should be checked monthly.

BIRTHDAYS

1786 • **WILHELM GRIMM,** German folklorist 📖

1836 • **WINSLOW HOMER,** American artist 📇

1874 • **HONUS WAGNER,** baseball great

1885 • **CHESTER WILLIAM NIMITZ,** commander-in-chief of the U.S. Pacific Fleet during World War II

1947 • **EDWARD JAMES OLMOS,** American actor

1955 • **STEVEN JOBS,** American computer scientist and businessman who cofounded Apple Computer

GORDON, "Sesame Street" character

EVENTS

1839 • **THE STEAM SHOVEL** was patented.

1851 • Boston, Mass., ordered America's **FIRST ELECTRIC FIRE ALARM SYSTEM.** ✿

1863 • **ARIZONA** was organized as a territory.

1949 • **THE FIRST MULTISTAGE ROCKET** was fired.

FLAG DAY (Mexico)

FEBRUARY 25

activities

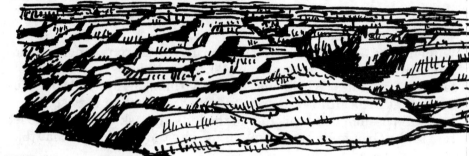

BIRTHDAYS

1841 • **PIERRE AUGUSTE RENOIR,**  French impressionist painter

1873 • **ENRICO CARUSO,** Italian opera tenor

1942 • **CYNTHIA VOIGT,** children's author

1943 • **GEORGE HARRISON,** British singer, musician, songwriter, and member of the Beatles

EVENTS

1540 • The Spanish explorer **FRANCIS- CO VASQUEZ DE CORONADO** embarked from Mexico on a quest for fabled cities of gold.

1793 • President George Washington held his **FIRST CABINET MEET- ING.**

1870 • Hiram R. Revels became the **FIRST BLACK U.S. SENATOR.**

1913 • **THE SIXTEENTH AMENDMENT** went into effect, giving Congress the authority to levy income taxes.

1919 • Oregon became the **FIRST STATE TO TAX GASOLINE.**

1933 • The U.S.S. *Ranger,* the **FIRST AIRCRAFT CARRIER,** was com- missioned.

1990 • Violeta Chamorro was elected president of **NICARAGUA,** ending a decade of government by the Communist Sandinistas.

Failed expedition?

The purpose of Francisco Vasquez de Coronado's expedition was to find the fabled Seven Cities of Cibola, which were said to be filled with gold, silver, and jewels. Coronado found no treasure, but he did discover the Grand Canyon. His 2-year search also led him to the California peninsula, eastward along the Rio Grande, and northward through what is now the Texas Panhandle and Oklahoma into Kansas. Despite all the previously unexplored territory he covered, Coronado's expedition was considered a failure. Have your students make an "explorer chart." One column should list the explorers and their missions; one column, whether or not the original missions were accomplished; and one column, what additional discoveries were made.

Determined artists

In his later years, impression- ist painter Pierre Auguste Renoir was disabled by arthri- tis. His hands were so crippled that he couldn't grip a paint- brush. But that didn't stop him from painting—he painted with a brush strapped to his hand. Help your students understand how hard it was for Renoir to paint with arthri- tis by having them write their names with pencils taped to the backs of their hands. Show the kids examples of Renoir's later work that show the broad brush strokes he made while dealing with his disabling con- dition.

FEBRUARY 26
activities

 Wild west days

William Frederick Cody earned the nickname "Buffalo Bill" because he supplied railroad construction crews with buffalo meat. Can your students name other Old West personalities? How about Billy the Kid, Annie Oakley, Jesse James, Wild Bill Hickock, Wyatt Earp, Butch Cassidy? Invite the kids to research these colorful characters and report their findings to the class.

Subway story

Alfred Ely Beach, a lawyer and inventor, thought New York City needed a subway system. Although his office and home were only 2 miles apart, the trip took an hour on the traffic-choked streets. Beach secretly began construction of a track, railroad car, and station. In 1870, he invited New York City VIPs to the unveiling of his block-long experimental subway. Though some officials were impressed, Beach failed to secure funds for a subway system. New York's subway system finally opened 34 years later. Today, the system is 232 miles long and serves about 750,000 people each day. Have your students list the problems New York would face if all those people drove to work.

Swift skates

Ask your students to figure out the average speed of a skater who covers 100 miles in 6 hours. Then challenge them to compute how far behind a second skater averaging 1.5 mph slower would be when the first skater crossed the finish line.

BIRTHDAYS

1808 • **HONORE DAUMIER,** French caricaturist

1829 • **LEVI STRAUSS,** Bavarian-born creator of the first jeans

1832 • **JOHN GEORGE NICOLAY,** secretary to and biographer of Abraham Lincoln

1846 • **BUFFALO BILL (WILLIAM FREDERICK) CODY,** American frontiersman and Wild West showman

1932 • **JOHNNY CASH,** country singer

EVENTS

1870 • Inventor Alfred Ely Beach demonstrated his **EXPERIMENTAL SUBWAY** in New York City.

1919 • **GRAND CANYON NATIONAL PARK** in Arizona was established by an act of Congress.

1949 • **THE FIRST NONSTOP AROUND-THE-WORLD AIRPLANE FLIGHT** took off from Fort Worth, Tex.

1971 • Kirt Barnes became the **FIRST PERSON TO ICE-SKATE 100 MILES IN LESS THAN 6 HOURS.**

1985 • Thousands of farmers converged on Washington, D.C., to demand **ECONOMIC RELIEF FOR FARMERS.**

26

FEBRUARY 27
activities

☼ New heights
"The Great Snow of 1717"—still considered one of America's worst blizzards—dropped an average of 5 feet of snow on parts of New England. Make a mark on the wall at 5 feet and ask the kids to take turns standing next to it. What is the average difference between their heights and the snow line? Have any of your students been in deep snow? Invite them to share their experiences.

📖 Credit where it's due
In his poem "Paul Revere's Ride," Henry Wadsworth Longfellow failed to mention the contributions of William Dawes (who rode with Revere from Lexington on the night of April 18, 1775, warning of the approach of the British) and Samuel Prescott (who eluded the British when Revere was captured and actually carried the warning to Concord). Have any of your students ever participated in an event without getting credit? How did they feel? Ask them to right a historical wrong by composing a poem about the ride of Dawes or Prescott.

🏳 Presidential power
The Founding Fathers defined the office of president, but they didn't put a limit on the number of 4-year terms one person could serve. George Washington began the two-term tradition, and all presidents followed his example until 1940. Challenge your class to find out who broke the tradition. Divide the class into groups. Then read the Twenty-second Amendment and ask each group to consider the following questions: What is a "lame duck"? Does a two-term limit lessen a president's power in his second term? What are the advantages and disadvantages of a two-term limit? What is a reasonable term length? Would one 6-year term be better than the current system? Why or why not?

FEBRUARY 28
activities

✎ Gold-getters

The first group of California gold-seekers, known as the 49ers, arrived on the steamboat *California*. Within 10 years, San Francisco had grown from a small town to a city of 379,994. Most nearby towns prospered as local businesses and industries grew. Ask your students if they know why people first settled their community. If not, challenge them to find out.

☞ Prolific plastic

After Frank McNamara found himself in a restaurant without enough cash to pay his bill, he decided to set up a club so people could charge meals. He signed up 22 restaurants and one hotel to honor the first Diner's Club card. Within 10 years, there were 1.1 million cardholders. Today, 90 million Americans use 703 million credit cards. Tell your students that when a cardholder doesn't pay off his entire credit-card bill in the given period, he has to pay interest on the unpaid balance. Have the kids use their calculators to figure out and compare how much interest a person would pay on a $596 credit-card balance over 2 months, 6 months, and a full year at interest rates of 12%, 15%, and 18%.

☕ No colds allowed

Astronauts must be in the best possible health for their missions. While in space, their bodies are subjected to various stresses and unusual conditions, so even a common cold could become a severe problem. Ask the kids to compare their performance on days they feel great and days they don't feel so well. Have them help you create a list of ways they can prevent colds and other contagious illnesses.

BIRTHDAYS

1824 • **CHARLES BLONDIN,** French tightrope walker who crossed Niagara Falls many times on a wire

1901 • **LINUS PAULING,** American chemist and two-time Nobel Prize winner

1939 • **TOMMY TUNE,** singer, dancer, and musical theater director

1940 • **MARIO ANDRETTI,** race car driver

EVENTS

1849 • **THE FIRST SHIPLOAD OF CALI-FORNIA GOLD-SEEKERS** arrived in San Francisco.

1854 • **THE REPUBLICAN PARTY** was created at Ripon, Wis.

1901 • **JUPITER'S SOUTH TROPICAL DISTURBANCE** was first observed.

1940 • **THE FIRST TELEVISED BASKET-BALL GAME** took place in New York City's Madison Square Garden.

1950 • **THE DINER'S CLUB** opened for business, and the credit card industry was born.

1969 • *Apollo 9*'s lift-off was post-poned because the **ASTRONAUTS HAD COLDS.**

1984 • Singer **MICHAEL JACKSON** won eight Grammy Awards.

FEBRUARY 29
activities

BIRTHDAYS
1792 • GIOACCHINO ANTONIO ROSSI-NI, Italian composer whose works include *William Tell* and *The Barber of Seville*

1840 • JOHN PHILIP HOLLAND, Irish-born American pioneer in the development of the modern submarine

EVENTS
1288 • Scottish law made it LEGAL FOR WOMEN TO PROPOSE to men.

1940 • The movie *GONE WITH THE WIND* received eight Oscars at the Academy Awards ceremony.

1968 • Dr. Jocelyn Bell Burnell announced the first discovery of a PULSAR, a star that emits regularly pulsating radio waves, X rays, or visible light.

BACHELORS DAY
LEAP YEAR DAY
SAVE THE RHINO DAY

Movie critics
The 1939 movie *Gone with the Wind* won eight Oscars, including best picture, best actress, and best supporting actress. What are your students' favorite movies? Make a frequency graph to tabulate selections. Have the kids describe in their journals what makes a movie a "thumbs up" or a "thumbs down." Then invite children who've seen recent releases to review them in your next school or class newspaper. Or ask the media specialist to videotape your students' "Picks and Pans" program for other classes to see.

Extra day
Tell your students that the earth actually takes 365 days, 5 hours, 48 minutes, and a little over 45 seconds to revolve around the sun. So every fourth year contains 366 days instead of 365. Ask your kids for their suggestions about how to celebrate this "additional" day. Should it be a holiday? Should it be a day on which people could skip or "leap over" whatever they didn't want to do? What would be on your students' list of things to skip? Have the kids list the next seven leap years. From this list, can they formulate a rule for figuring out whether any given year was or will be a leap year?

Wowed by rhinos
Your students might be surprised to find out that the rhinoceros is the second largest land mammal alive today. Can they name the largest? (The elephant.) White rhinos weigh 5,000 to 8,000 pounds. Would the combined weight of you and all your students equal the weight of a single adult rhino? How many more same-size classes would be needed? Tell the kids that white rhinos stay in groups—called crashes—of six or eight. How many names for other groups of animals can your students think of? Challenge them to find out more.

29

MARCH

☆ Project of the Month: Shoe Showcase

Start the month off on the right foot: Spotlight shoes during National Shoe Week. To begin, divide the class into small groups. Have the groups brainstorm for different kinds of media that contain references to shoes—for example, stories, songs, films, print advertisements, and TV and radio commercials. Each group can list specific examples from the various media on a piece of posterboard, then share its list with the class.

Afterward, have each group select a particular "shoe medium" to research and collect material about for a schoolwide "Shoe Showcase Multimedia Fair." For example, a group researching shoe stories could gather a variety of appropriate books, then organize storytelling sessions for primary students. In addition, assign one student in each group to create several "shoe math" problems for the fair. The children can also write letters inviting local shoe experts—shoe salespeople, shoe-store owners, or shoemakers—to speak.

A few days before the fair, have the groups design shoe-shaped catalogs detailing the fair's exhibits and contributors. Invite other classes—and parents—to attend. As people arrive, student greeters can hand out the "Shoe Showcase" catalogs.

BIRTHDAYS

1901 • MARGARET FRISKY, children's author

1921 • RICHARD WILBUR, American poet

EVENTS

1781 • The 13 original states adopted the ARTICLES OF CONFEDERATION, paving the way for federal union.

1790 • Congress authorized the FIRST U.S. CENSUS.

1803 • OHIO became the 17th state.

1867 • NEBRASKA became the 37th state.

1872 • Congress authorized the creation of YELLOWSTONE NATIONAL PARK.

• THE FIRST WOMAN DETECTIVE, Isabella Goodwin, was appointed in New York City.

1912 • Captain Albert Berry made the FIRST PARACHUTE JUMP FROM AN AIRPLANE.

1961 • President John F. Kennedy announced the establishment of the PEACE CORPS.

1966 • The Soviet spacecraft *Venera 3* crashed on Venus, thus becoming the FIRST MAN-MADE OBJECT TO REACH ANOTHER PLANET.

1968 • SEAT BELTS became mandatory in all cars in the United States.

1979 • The U.S. spacecraft *VOYAGER 1* began relaying information as it approached Jupiter.

NATIONAL PIG DAY
PEANUT BUTTER LOVER'S DAY
WHUPPITY SCOORIE (Scotland)

MARCH 1
activities

Everybody counts

The U.S. Bureau of the Census collects billions of pieces of information, then computes and publishes statistics. For example, the census tells us how many people carpool, how many televisions are in the average household, and which state has the most motorcycles. Have your students create a mini census. The class can decide on three questions to ask, then develop a survey sheet. Each child should take home a copy of the sheet and fill in the answers. After collecting the completed sheets, student volunteers can tabulate the results and report to the class.

USA jigsaw

On the anniversary of statehood for Ohio and Nebraska, let your students explore U.S. geography—and have a little fun—with this "hands-on" activity. First, trace a large U.S. map, including the state borders, onto posterboard. Then cut out and laminate each state, tossing the pieces into a shoe box. Have small groups take turns putting the country back together on the floor. Challenge the kids to point out Ohio and Nebraska and to name their capitals.

Nutty menus

Survey your students on which kind of peanut butter—chunky or creamy—they like best. Then challenge them to think of as many foods as they can besides jelly that taste good with peanut butter. Have small groups compile "new and nutty menus" to try at home.

MARCH 2
activities

📰 Who's who at the zoo

The National Zoo had fewer than 200 animals in its first collection. Today, it has more than 2,900. The zoo's kitchen is especially busy. One month's food supply includes 3,500 pounds of apples, 8,400 crickets, 4,400 eggs, 9,600 pounds of fish, and 34,000 pounds of herbivore food. One exhibit features the oldest and most abundant form of life—invertebrates. Ask your students to list animals included in this group.

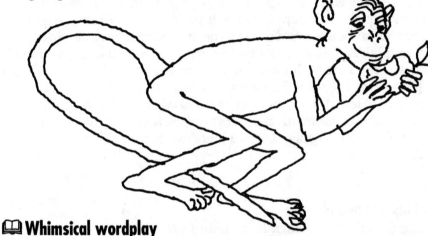

📖 Whimsical wordplay

Dr. Seuss's books are filled with free-spirited verse and wonderful invented words. Ask your students to name a few of these words—for example, Zumble-Zay, Bumble-Boat, Snick-Berry Switch, Zook, Skeegle-mobile. Next, read the verse below to the kids, then challenge them to invent flower names and plant an imaginary wild garden in honor of Dr. Seuss.

> *I shall plant*
> *A garden for Dr. Seuss.*
> *Lots of wild flowers*
> *Will be on the loose.*

📖 Poetic teamwork

Introduce your students to collaboration by sharing the works of Leo and Diane Dillon, husband-and-wife illustrators of *Why Mosquitoes Buzz in People's Ears* and *Ashanti to Zulu*. Next, help students experience the process of collaboration by having them work in pairs to illustrate haiku poems (which typically center on a single image). Afterward, discuss the pros and cons of working collaboratively.

BIRTHDAYS

1793 • **SAM HOUSTON**, American soldier and politician who served as the first president of the Republic of Texas

1904 • **DR. SEUSS** (real name: Theodor 📖 Seuss Geisel), children's author

1931 • **MIKHAIL GORBACHEV**, Soviet leader

1933 • **LEO DILLON**, children's book 📖 illustrator

EVENTS

1776 • **THE U.S. NAVY AND MARINES** fought their first battle of the Revolutionary War.

1877 • In a disputed election, a special electoral commission selected **RUTHERFORD B. HAYES** as president.

1889 • Congress established **THE** 📰 **NATIONAL ZOOLOGICAL PARK** in Washington, D.C.

1899 • **MOUNT RAINIER NATIONAL PARK** in Washington State was established.

1917 • **PUERTO RICANS** became U.S. citizens.

1933 • The movie *KING KONG* opened in New York.

1962 • Basketball superstar **WILT CHAMBERLAIN SCORED 100 POINTS** in one game.

1973 • Eighty countries agreed to **OUTLAW TRADE IN 375 ENDANGERED WILDLIFE SPECIES.**

1988 • The Environmental and Natural History Committee of the Minnesota State Senate approved a bill to make the giant beaver **MINNESOTA'S OFFICIAL FOSSIL.**

MARCH 3
activities

BIRTHDAYS

1847 • **ALEXANDER GRAHAM BELL,** American inventor

1938 • **PATRICIA MACLACHLAN,** children's author

1962 • **JACKIE JOYNER-KERSEE,** American track and field star

• **HERSCHEL WALKER,** American football star

EVENTS

1837 • **CONGRESS INCREASED THE MEMBERSHIP OF THE U.S. SUPREME COURT from seven to nine justices.**

1842 • Massachusetts prohibited kids under 12 from **WORKING MORE THAN 10 HOURS A DAY.**

1845 • **FLORIDA became the 27th state.**

1855 • The U.S. War Department appropriated $30,000 **TO BUY AND TRANSPORT CAMELS.**

1879 • Belva Lockwood became the **FIRST WOMAN TO ARGUE A CASE BEFORE THE U.S. SUPREME COURT.**

1931 • President Herbert Hoover signed a bill making **"THE STAR-SPANGLED BANNER"** the national anthem of the United States.

1988 • A pair of California condors at the San Diego Wild Animal Park produced the **FIRST FERTILE CONDOR EGG EVER CONCEIVED IN CAPTIVITY.**

DOLL DAY (Japan)
NATIONAL DRUG AND ALCOHOL AWARENESS WEEK

State-ly study

Have your students locate Florida on a map of the United States. Then divide the class into groups of three or four, and give each group a large sheet of paper. Ask half the groups to draw the state's outline and mark such features as the state capital, major cities, rivers and lakes, national parks, beaches, and vacation attractions. Encourage the kids to draw or paste on images as well. Ask the other groups to print the word *Florida* in large outline letters. These groups can research Florida's major industries, weather, wildlife, and physical environment, then draw or paste appropriate images within the letters. Display the students' work on a classroom bulletin board.

Signs and sounds

Helping deaf children learn to communicate was of great importance to Alexander Graham Bell, the inventor of the telephone. Bell founded a school in Boston for teachers of the deaf. Ask your librarian for a book on sign language, and challenge your students to learn the Pledge of Allegiance in sign language by the end of the month.

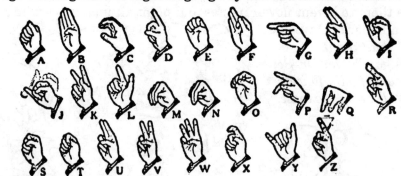

Caring for condors

Molloko (an Indian word for condor) became the first California condor conceived and hatched in captivity. Immediately after the egg was laid, scientists placed it in an incubator, where they monitored it until it hatched 57 days later. Molloko took food from a hand puppet designed to resemble a mother condor. By using the puppet, scientists hoped to prevent the chick from bonding with humans. Ask your students to investigate what brought the California condor to the brink of extinction.

MARCH 4

activities

✒ Presidential architecture

Thomas Jefferson helped plan the city of Washington, D.C., describing it as "a very agreeable country residence." He also selected the architecture for many public buildings and presided over the design competition for the Capitol. Using a pseudonym, Jefferson submitted his own architectural plan for the White House, but it was rejected. Ask your students what might have pleased him about the design of the Jefferson Memorial.

✂ Role models

Have your class discuss the meaning of the saying "It's hard to fill his shoes." Then ask each student to name a person he or she admires. What qualities would be needed to fill that person's shoes? Next, give each student a large sheet of paper, scissors, and colored markers. Have each child draw a large shoe, color it, then cut it out.

Inside their shoes, the kids should write the name of the person they admire and the qualities needed to fill his or her shoes. Display the shoes in the hall for others to see.

⚗ Good eating

List your students' favorite foods on the chalkboard. Then challenge the class to find each food's nutritional value. Afterward, the kids can create jingles or bumper stickers advertising the healthfulness of their favorites.

BIRTHDAYS

1678 • **ANTONIO VIVALDI,** Italian composer
1748 • **CASIMIR PULASKI,** Polish count and American Revolutionary War hero
1906 • **MEINDERT DEJONG,** children's author

EVENTS

1493 • **CHRISTOPHER COLUMBUS** landed at Lisbon, thus completing his first voyage to the New World.
1681 • England's King Charles II granted William Penn a **CHARTER FOR WHAT IS NOW PENNSYLVANIA.**
1789 • **THE FIRST U.S. CONGRESS** convened in New York City.
1791 • **VERMONT** became the 14th state.
1793 • **GEORGE WASHINGTON** was inaugurated for a second term.
1801 • Thomas Jefferson became the ✒ **FIRST PRESIDENT INAUGURATED IN WASHINGTON, D.C.**
1809 • George Clinton became the **FIRST VICE PRESIDENT TO SERVE UNDER TWO PRESIDENTS.**
1928 • **THE FIRST TRANSCONTINENTAL FOOT RACE** began in Los Angeles.
1930 • Emma Fahning became the **FIRST WOMAN TO BOWL A PERFECT 300.**
1933 • President Franklin Roosevelt launched the **NEW DEAL** recovery program.

OLD INAUGURATION DAY
✂ **NATIONAL SHOE WEEK**
⚗ **NATIONAL NUTRITION MONTH**

MARCH 5
activities

First to fall

Crispus Attucks, a former slave who became a sailor, was the first man killed by the British in the Boston Massacre. Challenge your students to develop an in-depth news broadcast describing Attucks's compelling life story.

Updating Currier and Ives

Show your students some Currier and Ives lithographs of 19th-century American life. Then give the kids an understanding of the lithography process—and get them thinking about how life has changed since the last century—with this activity. First, have them use crayons to draw a Currier and Ives-style scene from contemporary American life on white posterboard. Next, have them brush a tacky mixture of dark tempera paint and liquid starch across the picture and place a sheet of vellum over it. Finally, have them roll a rolling pin across the paper to get a print of the picture. When the prints have dried, students can exhibit them alongside the Currier and Ives works. What kinds of changes did the kids include in their updated scenes?

Editorial eyes

During Newspapers in Education Week, give each of your students a recent newspaper. Have each child clip three appealing photos, setting aside the accompanying news stories or captions. Collect all the photos, then redistribute them, making sure no child gets back a photo he clipped. Next, ask the kids to write news stories or captions for the photos. Have each child share his writing with the class. Afterward, the student who clipped the photos can read the actual stories or captions that accompanied them.

MARCH 6
activities

▣ Renaissance man

Michelangelo was not only one of the world's greatest artists but also a distinguished architect. In fact, he was chief architect of St. Peter's Church in Rome and designed its famous dome. Have students research other buildings designed by Michelangelo, then list the features that are common to his work and to the Renaissance style. Do any local buildings contain these features? What other architectural styles (classical, Gothic, Art Nouveau, postmodernist) are displayed by buildings in your students' hometown?

⚗ That queasy feeling

None of the astronauts in the Mercury or Gemini programs suffered from the queasy feeling known as space sickness. But Apollo 9 astronaut Russell Schweickart had to contend with it during his mission. Luckily, he started to feel better in time to test a backpack, go on a space walk, and take photographs. Have your students write a humorous poem about Schweickart's predicament or a time when they experienced motion sickness.

✎ Being a borrower

Lead a class discussion about borrowing—from family, friends, and others. What kinds of things can be borrowed? What items have your students borrowed recently? Have they ever broken or lost a borrowed item? What would they do in such a situation? Have your students agree on a class list of rules for borrowers. They may want to take the list home to share with their families.

BIRTHDAYS

1475 • **MICHELANGELO, Italian sculptor** ▣ **and artist**

1806 • **ELIZABETH BARRETT BROWN-ING, English poet**

1877 • **ROSE FYLEMAN, children's author**

1937 • **VALENTINA VLADIMIROVNA TERESHKOVA, Russian cosmonaut and the first woman in space**

EVENTS

1716 • **AN AURORA BOREALIS lit up the skies from western Holland to central Russia.**

1834 • **The city of York, Canada, was incorporated as TORONTO.**

1836 • **THE ALAMO FELL after a 12-day siege by 4,000 Mexican soldiers.**

1930 • **FROZEN FOODS were first sold.**

1969 • **After a good night's sleep,** ⚗ **Apollo 9 astronaut Russell Schweickart recovered from "SPACE SICKNESS."**

1990 • **THE POPULATION OF THE UNITED STATES reached 250 million.**

✎ **RETURN THE BORROWED BOOKS WEEK**

MARCH 7
activities

 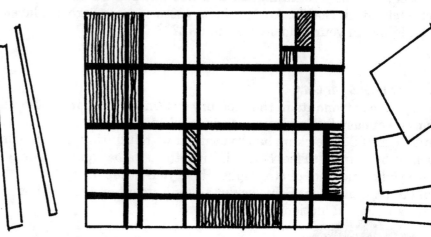
Geometric artwork

Piet Mondrian was a leading abstract artist. Show your class pictures of his distinctive geometric artwork. Next, give each student a large sheet of paper, a glue stick, and a variety of geometric shapes cut from construction paper of many colors. Then have the kids create their own abstract compositions in the style of Mondrian. Display their works on a bulletin board or in the hall.

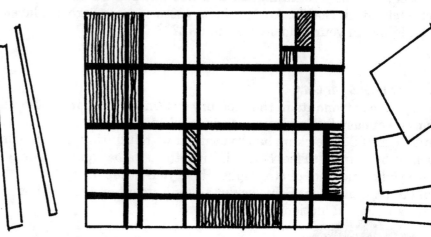

Animal alphabet

To celebrate National Aardvark Week, encourage your class to investigate this unusual animal. Where does it live? What does it eat? What special adaptations does it have?

Alphabetically speaking, the aardvark is first among animals. It would be a good choice to begin a class animal ABC book. So draw a picture of an aardvark on a piece of white construction paper. Write a capital and lowercase *a* at the top of the page and a sentence using the word *aardvark* at the bottom. Show the page to your class. Then assign each student another letter of the alphabet with the instructions to create a similar page for that letter. Bind your class animal alphabet into a book. Present it to a kindergarten or 1st-grade teacher or display it in the library.

MARCH 8
activities

📖 Creative creatures

Tell your students that Kenneth Grahame, who was orphaned at age 5, lived with his grandmother in Berkshire, England. His adventures wandering the riverbanks there provided fodder for the bedtime stories he used to tell his son. Those tales centered on Mole, Rat, and Toad—animals who lived on a riverbank but who thought and acted like people. In 1908, Grahame's bedtime stories were published as *The Wind in the Willows*. Have your students tell a story using animals with human characteristics. They can draw a four-frame cartoon and use dialogue balloons for conversation between the characters.

🐾 Laws for dogs

Ask your students to list reasons for dogs to be licensed. Then have them find out if there's a dog-licensing law in their state. What other animals do they think should be licensed? Younger children can design a fancy pet collar and attach a license, including the pet's name as well as the owner's name and address.

🏴 Family feelings

In the spirit of Aunts' Day, help your students appreciate the importance of extended families. List on the board the kinds of activities students enjoy with members of their extended families. Then have each student make a family mobile. First, the kids should draw and color or cut out pictures of family members—including themselves—and paste the pictures onto squares of oaktag. Next, they should put a small hole in the top of each picture and thread a piece of yarn through the hole. Finally, have them hang the pictures from coat hangers to form mobiles.

BIRTHDAYS

1841 • **OLIVER WENDELL HOLMES, JR.,** U.S. Supreme Court justice

1859 • **KENNETH GRAHAME,** children's 📖 author who wrote the classic *The Wind in the Willows*

1862 • **JOSEPH LEE,** pioneer in the development of children's playgrounds

EVENTS

1834 • **A DOG NAMED HERO SAVED TWO BOYS** from drowning in the Thames River in London.

1849 • President Zachary Taylor appointed Thomas Ewing as the **FIRST SECRETARY OF THE INTERIOR.**

1855 • A train first crossed the **SUSPENSION BRIDGE AT NIAGARA FALLS.**

1894 • New York became the **FIRST STATE TO REQUIRE DOG LICENSES.**

1917 • **THE RUSSIAN REVOLUTION** began.

1968 • A 6-year-old golfer named Tommy Moore, of Hagerstown, Md., made the **FIRST OF TWO HOLES-IN-ONE** he would score on the same hole during the year.

🏴 **AUNTS' DAY**
INTERNATIONAL WOMEN'S DAY

MARCH 9
activities

Armored-ship skirmish

During the Civil War, the crews of the *Monitor* and the *Merrimac* fought for 4 hours off the Virginia coast. Have students work in teams to research this battle. Give each team an oversized sheet of paper. Then have the teams work together to draw and color a wall mural depicting the struggle.

Toss up

For his record-breaking feat, Eric Krenz threw the discus 163 feet $8\frac{3}{4}$ inches. Have your students calculate that distance in meters. Then take the kids outdoors and hold a class "discus" toss, using a Frisbee. Give each student three turns, and have volunteers measure and record all three distances—in meters—for every child. Back in class, have the children calculate their average distances. The winner is the child with the highest average.

Miss Popularity

Since the Mattel Toy Co. first introduced the Barbie doll, over 500 million of the dolls have been sold. Why do your students think the dolls are so popular? Have them conduct a schoolwide survey to determine the total number of dolls owned by schoolmates as well as the average number of Barbie dolls owned per student. They can also ask schoolmates who own Barbie dolls why the dolls are appealing. Encourage your students to use a computer to record their data.

MARCH 10
activities

☎ Famous phone call

Alexander Graham Bell, inventor of the telephone, first used his invention to call his assistant for help. Ask your students to interview their parents and grandparents about the most important telephone call of their lives.

✎ Finding freedom

After escaping from slavery herself, Harriet Tubman repeatedly risked her life by returning to the South and leading other slaves to freedom. She and her followers traveled at night via what became known as the Underground Railroad—a network of hiding places, or "stations," through which the slaves were guided north. Ask students to speculate about the roles of "station masters" (people who provided refuge for the slaves), "conductors" (people who led slaves from one station to another), and "passengers" (runaway slaves). What are some reasons for using such code terms?

✻ Steadfast soldier

Tell your students that Hiroo Onoda, a Japanese soldier, had lived alone in the Philippine jungle for nearly 30 years because no one told him World War II had ended. When asked why he hadn't come out, Onoda said, "I had not received the order." When he finally returned to Japan, Onoda was given a hero's welcome. But he hardly recognized the world. Have students create a time line showing some events and inventions Onoda missed while in hiding between 1944 and 1974. Besides doing library research, students can conduct interviews with parents, grandparents, and senior citizens to gather information.

BIRTHDAYS

1920 • JACK KENT, children's author
1940 • CHUCK NORRIS, American actor

EVENTS

1785 • Thomas Jefferson was named **U.S. MINISTER TO FRANCE**, succeeding Benjamin Franklin.

1848 • The U.S. Senate ratified the **TREATY OF GUADALUPE HIDALGO**, which ended the Mexican-American War.

1849 • Abraham Lincoln became the **FIRST PRESIDENT TO APPLY FOR A PATENT.**

1862 • The U.S. government issued its **FIRST PAPER MONEY.**

1876 • Alexander Graham Bell used the ☎ **TELEPHONE for the first time.**

1913 • American abolitionist **HARRIET** ✎ **TUBMAN died.**

1961 • Wilt Chamberlain became the **FIRST BASKETBALL PLAYER TO SCORE 3,000 POINTS in one** season.

1971 • The U.S. Senate passed a law **LOWERING THE VOTING AGE TO 18.**

1974 • A Japanese soldier who had ✻ spent nearly 30 **YEARS HIDING IN THE PHILIPPINE JUNGLE,** unaware that World War II had ended, was discovered by a Filipino.

10

MARCH 11
activities

BIRTHDAYS

1893 • **WANDA GA'G,** children's author and illustrator

1916 • **EZRA JACK KEATS,** children's author

1934 • **SAM DONALDSON,** American TV journalist

EVENTS

1818 • Mary Shelley's thriller *FRANKENSTEIN* was published.

1850 • Women's Medical College in Philadelphia became the FIRST MEDICAL SCHOOL FOR WOMEN.

1861 • THE CONSTITUTION OF THE CONFEDERACY was adopted in Montgomery, Ala.

1930 • William Howard Taft became the FIRST U.S. PRESIDENT BURIED IN THE NATIONAL CEMETERY at Arlington, Va.

1959 • *A Raisin in the Sun,* by Lorraine Hansberry, became the FIRST PLAY BY AN AFRICAN-AMERICAN WOMAN TO OPEN ON BROADWAY.

BURGSONNDEG (Luxembourg)
HUMAN SERVICES DAY

📖 Good and bad monsters

Have your students ever heard the name "Frankenstein"? Most people think Frankenstein was a monster. Actually, though, Frankenstein was the doctor who created the monster in English author Mary Shelley's book. And the monster never had a name. *Frankenstein* has been adapted in comic books, television shows, plays, and movies. Ask your students if they think monsters really exist. Why or why not? Can a monster be good? If the children met a monster, what would they do or say? Next, ask each child to draw a monster and write about things it does. Afterward, post the drawings and stories.

🇺🇸 Solemn ceremonies

Arlington National Cemetery is located across the Potomac River from Washington, D.C. The cemetery, which covers 612 acres, encircles the home of Confederate general Robert E. Lee. More than 200,000 bright white markers pay tribute to the members of the U.S. armed forces buried there. The most visited place in the cemetery is the Tomb of the Unknown Soldier, which is guarded at all times. The soldier on guard paces off 21 steps in front of the tomb, stops, waits 21 seconds, then retraces his route. He continues this routine until the changing of the guard, when a new soldier takes over. People visiting the tomb are always quiet and respectful. What solemn scenes or events have your students witnessed? Have them share their experiences.

MARCH 12
activities

BIRTHDAYS

1923 • WALTER MARTY SCHIRRA, U.S. astronaut

1936 • VIRGINIA HAMILTON, children's author

1946 • LIZA MINNELLI, American singer and actress

1962 • DARRYL STRAWBERRY, baseball star

EVENTS

1789 • THE U.S. POST OFFICE was established.

1877 • THE FIRST DEPARTMENT STORE, Wanamakers in Philadelphia, opened.

1904 • THE CARNEGIE HERO FUND was established.

1912 • Juliette Gordon Low organized the FIRST U.S. GIRL SCOUT TROOP.

1933 • President Franklin Roosevelt broadcast his FIRST "FIRESIDE CHAT" over the radio.

1954 • At a bridge game in Cranston, R.I., each player was dealt A PERFECT HAND OF 13 CARDS of the same suit.

1969 • The Concorde, the FIRST SUPERSONIC PASSENGER JET, made its maiden flight, reaching speeds of 1,448 mph.

1974 • Atha Mathieu, a 13-year-old from Anselmo, Calif., became the country's YOUNGEST PARK COMMISSIONER.

1989 •  Flag-waving demonstrators marched to the Chicago Art Institute to protest an exhibit they felt desecrated the AMERICAN FLAG.

GIRL SCOUTS DAY

▬ Protected speech?

The exhibit the Chicagoans were protesting required museum-goers to walk on the American flag to view the entire work. The issue of how the flag may be handled has frequently created heated controversy. Some people have maintained that such activities as burning the flag or stitching it onto the seats of pants should be prohibited by law. Other people have vehemently defended these activities as constitutionally protected free speech. Where does your class stand on this issue? Ask for a show of hands. Then ask your students to prepare for a debate about flag desecration. Their preparation might include reading about the First Amendment and pertinent Supreme Court decisions, thinking about what the flag represents, and considering analogous situations. For the actual debate, divide the classroom down the middle, with proponents of each position on opposite sides. Call up one student at a time from each side. Give the first child 30 seconds to state a reason for supporting his position. Give the second child 30 seconds to refute the argument. Then have the students switch roles. After everyone has had a chance to debate in front of the class, find out how many kids have changed their minds about the issue. Ask them to explain why.

✑ Developing leaders

To celebrate Girl Scouts Day, have your students use subject webs as they brainstorm for words associated with Girl Scouts. The kids might also enjoy researching how Girl Scout uniforms have changed since 1912, then designing a new uniform for Girl Scouts of the 21st century.

BIRTHDAYS

1733 • JOSEPH PRIESTLY, English chemist who discovered oxygen

1813 • LORENZO DELMONICO, Swiss-American restaurateur known as "the Father of American Restaurants"

1855 • PERCIVAL LOWELL, American astronomer

1928 • ELLEN RASKIN, children's author

1933 • DIAN DILLON, children's author and illustrator

• THOMAS ROCKWELL, children's author

EVENTS

1779 • African-American pioneer JEAN BAPTISTE POINT DU SABLE founded Chicago.

1781 • English astronomer William Herschel discovered the planet URANUS.

1852 • THE FIRST CARTOON OF UNCLE SAM appeared in the New York *Lantern.*

1877 • Chester Greenwood of Farmington, Me., received a patent for EARMUFFS.

1884 • A WORLD SYSTEM OF STANDARD TIME was established.

1923 • A MOTION PICTURE WITH SOUND was demonstrated in New York City by inventor Lee De Forest.

1982 • John Jaszkowski, age 11, became the YOUNGEST BOWLER TO ROLL A PERFECT GAME.

1989 • The "CHIX IN SPACE" egg experiment began with the launching of the shuttle *Discovery.*

BE KIND TO YOUR AMOEBA DAY!

13

MARCH 13
activities

⚜ National symbols
Ask your students what the symbol Uncle Sam means to them, then discuss the significance of other national symbols, including the Statue of Liberty, the American flag, and the bald eagle.

💡 Funny phrases
Chester Greenwood called his earmuffs "ear mufflers." Younger students will enjoy drawing "literal" pictures of what ear mufflers might look like. Challenge your students to list other terms and phrases that are funny when taken literally—for example, a fork in the road, a frog in your throat, fast food, ants in your pants, rats in your hair, shoe tree, river bed, pajama party, bookworm. Then have the kids illustrate these for a class book or a poster for the library.

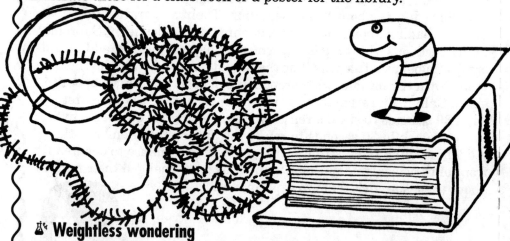

🧪 Weightless wondering
Junior high student John Vellinger hypothesized that weightlessness would aid the development of chicken embryos. To test his theory, he designed an incubator, which eventually was carried aboard the space shuttle *Discovery.* His theory was proved incorrect when many of the embryos died. Discuss the concept of gravity with your students, then have them work in teams to design experiments that could be conducted in space. To get them thinking, pose the following questions: Would a regular soft-drink can work in space? How do you take a bath in space? What games would be impossible to play in space? Will plants grow toward the sun in space?

MARCH 14
activities

✿ Professional skills

When Lucy Hobbs Taylor was born in 1833, dentistry had not yet become a profession. It wasn't until 1840 that the first dental school was established. Besides having top-notch academic skills, a dentist must also possess good manual dexterity. Have students list activities and hobbies that help develop manual skills (sewing, model building, drawing, painting). What other professions require specific physical skills? How can those skills be acquired?

American folk hero

John Luther "Casey" Jones gave his life to save his passengers when the train he was driving, the "Cannonball Express," collided with another train blocking the tracks near Vaughan, Miss. Invite your students to tell about their heroes. Has someone ever helped them in an extraordinary way? How can they help other people?

✾ Peanuts galore

Peanuts have been growing in South America for more than 1,000 years. Indians along the Chicma River in central South America were the first people to realize the plant's food value. But it was George Washington Carver who found the most uses—more than 300—for peanuts. For example, Carver used peanuts to make fuel, medicines, cosmetics, inks, and dyes. Have your students cut out peanut shapes from brown construction paper, then list on them as many uses for peanuts as they can think of. Post the paper peanuts on a bulletin board to mark National Peanut Month.

BIRTHDAYS

1833 • LUCY HOBBS TAYLOR, American ✿ who became the first female dentist
1864 • CASEY JONES, American railroad engineer
1879 • ALBERT EINSTEIN, German-American physicist
1889 • MARGUERITE DeANGELI, children's author
1920 • HANK KETCHAM, American cartoonist who created "Dennis the Menace"
1933 • QUINCY JONES, American composer and musician
1947 • BILLY CRYSTAL, American comedian and actor

EVENTS

1743 • THE FIRST TOWN MEETING IN AMERICA was held at Faneuil Hall in Boston.
1794 • Eli Whitney patented the COTTON GIN.
1900 • Congress voted to adopt the GOLD STANDARD.
1903 • President Theodore Roosevelt established the FIRST NATIONAL WILDLIFE REFUGE at Pelican Island, Fla.
1923 • Warren Harding became the FIRST U.S. PRESIDENT TO SUBMIT AN ACCOUNT OF HIS INCOME and pay tax on it.
1950 • The FBI'S "10 MOST WANTED" LIST was initiated.
      • New York, in the midst of a prolonged drought, hired the director of the Mt. Washington Observatory as its OFFICIAL RAINMAKER.
1987 • Piotr Fijas of Poland made the LONGEST SKI JUMP on record, soaring 636 feet (193.85 meters).

✾ NATIONAL PEANUT MONTH

MARCH 15
activities

A stroll through the country

Have your students use atlases to find the distance of Edward Weston's long walk. Then have them figure out the average distance he covered each day.

Record rains

To help your students visualize how much rain fell on Cilaos, measure 6 feet on the classroom wall. Then challenge the kids to track the amount of rainfall their town receives for the rest of the month. Does it come anywhere close to 6 feet?

Under-the-sea scapes

What would students expect to find at an underwater park? List their responses on the board, then have them research Key Largo Coral Reef. Next, ask the kids to draw pictures of what they might see there. When the pictures are finished, cover them with blue cellophane and display them on a classroom bulletin board.

Birds of a different feather

The annual return of the turkey vultures (often called buzzards) to Hinckley, Ohio, is as dependable as the return of the swallows to the San Juan Capistrano Mission in California. Have your students explore the place of buzzards and swallows in the ecological scheme. Divide the class into small groups, and have each group research the physical appearance, size, habitat, and migratory patterns of these two bird species. Record the information on a wall chart for comparison.

MARCH 16
activities

⚗ The Bard's birds

Eugene Schieffelin was active in the Acclimatization Society—an organization dedicated to establishing nonnative plants and animals in the United States. Because he was an avid reader of William Shakespeare, Schieffelin's personal goal was to import any bird species mentioned in the Bard's works but not found in North America. This included the starling. With few natural predators, the starling quickly multiplied and spread throughout the continent. Today, many communities regard starlings as pests. Have your students research starling behavior and adaptability. Why would some ornithologists say starlings have their own kind of "Yankee ingenuity"?

📖 Telling tall tales

Children's author Sid Fleischman's first love was magic. He spent his first few years after high school traveling the country in vaudeville shows and creating sleight-of-hand tricks for magicians. Fleischman published a book of original magic tricks when he was just 17. Later, he wrote mystery and suspense stories and tall tales. Explain to your students that tall tales are a special branch of folklore linked to the American frontier. Share with the class some examples of Fleischman's tall tales, such as *Chancy and the Grand Rascal* and *The Whipping Boy*. Then have each student select an event from American history and fashion a tall tale about it.

BIRTHDAYS

1750 • **CAROLINE LUCRETIA HERSCHEL,** English astronomer
1751 • **JAMES MADISON, fourth president of the United States**
1920 • **SID FLEISCHMAN, children's** 📖 **author**
1927 • **MARY CHALMERS, children's author**

EVENTS

1521 • **THE PHILIPPINE ISLANDS were** sighted by Ferdinand Magellan.
1621 • **CHIEF SAMOSET first visited the** Pilgrims of Plymouth Colony. He taught them how to plant corn and other native crops.
1802 • **THE U.S. MILITARY ACADEMY at** West Point was established.
1827 • *Freedom's Journal,* **THE FIRST NEWSPAPER EDITED FOR AND BY AFRICAN-AMERICANS,** was published in New York City.
1830 • **The record for FEWEST STOCKS TRADED ON THE NEW YORK STOCK EXCHANGE in a single day was established. Just 31 stocks changed hands.**
1890 • Eugene Schieffelin released 60
⚗ **STARLINGS in New York City's Central Park.**
1926 • **THE FIRST LIQUID-PROPELLANT ROCKET was launched by Robert Goddard.**
1966 • **For the first time, TWO U.S. SPACECRAFTS DOCKED DURING ORBIT.**

BLACK PRESS DAY

MARCH 17
activities

📖 Questions in verse

In 1879, Kate Greenaway published a collection of poems and drawings called *Marigold Garden*. Read aloud Greenaway's poem "Susan
Blue," which centers on a few rhyming questions. Then have your
students create their own poems that incorporate questions. Start
the children thinking by asking, "What is something you wonder
about?"

❄ Landmark building

The Empire State Building
in New York City has 102
stories. Tell your students
that the framework rose at
a rate of $4\frac{1}{2}$ stories per
week, and challenge them to
calculate how many weeks
it took for the entire framework to go up.

🎵 Percussion party

Legend has it that St. Patrick
chased the snakes from Ireland
by banging furiously on a
drum. So why not celebrate
this St. Patrick's Day with
some rat-tat-tatting of your
own? Share the verse below
with your students. Then have
them create their own drums
using tabletops, oatmeal boxes,
plastic milk jugs, and so on.
Fingers and knuckles can
serve as drumsticks, but have
your students find creative
alternatives—wooden spoons,
paintbrushes, whisk brooms, or
coat hangers, for example.

Won't you join
Our St. Patrick's Day band?
We play real loud
And sound so grand.

MARCH 18
activities

⚙ Crazy 'bout clocks

When alarm clocks were offered for sale in a Chicago department store on this day in 1944, more than 2,000 customers stampeded security guards and salespeople in a buying frenzy. Ask your students to speculate why the advent of World War II had made these items scarce. What other items might have been in short supply during the war?

⚙ The view from above

As he prepared to step out of his spacecraft, *Voskhod 2,* Aleksei Leonov looked down to see his homeland (the former Soviet Union) 308 miles below. He spotted the Black Sea, the Volga River, and the Ural Mountains. Attached to his spacecraft by a 16-foot cable, Leonov spent 10 minutes somersaulting in space. Have your students draw a picture of what they think they'd see if they took a space walk 308 miles above the United States. Would they see the Great Lakes, the Rockies, the Mississippi River?

⚗ Energy IQ

Find out what your students know about the amount and types of energy being used in the United States each day. For example, can they name at least two fossil fuels? (These include petroleum, natural gas, and coal.) Which energy sources are renewable? (Wind, geothermal, solar, hydro.) What is the most plentiful energy source in the United States? (Coal.) Have students research these and other energy issues, then design a 10-question quiz (with answer key) to distribute schoolwide—and take home for parents.

BIRTHDAYS

1837 • **GROVER CLEVELAND,** 22nd and 24th president of the United States

1858 • **RUDOLF DIESEL,** German inventor

EVENTS

1865 • **THE CONGRESS OF THE CONFEDERATE STATES OF AMERICA** adjourned for the last time.

1900 • **JOHN LUTHER "CASEY" JONES,** Illinois Central engineer on the Chicago-New Orleans run, was killed when his train crashed into another train.

1931 • **ELECTRIC RAZORS** first went on sale in the United States.

1936 • **Ruth Hughes Aarons of New York became the FIRST AMERICAN TO WIN THE WOMEN'S WORLD TABLE TENNIS TITLE.**

1944 • **ALARM CLOCKS**—which had ⚙ been virtually unobtainable in the United States since the outbreak of World War II—were again put on sale in Chicago.

1965 • **Soviet cosmonaut Lieutenant** ⚙ **Colonel Aleksei Leonov became the FIRST PERSON TO WALK IN SPACE.**

1989 • **Archaeologists discovered a 4,400-year-old mummy at the Pyramid of Cheops in Egypt.**

CASEY JONES DAY
IBU AFO FESTIVAL (Nigeria)
⚗ **NATIONAL ENERGY EDUCATION DAY**
SPACE WALK DAY

MARCH 19
activities

 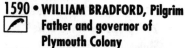

Birthday time line

Make a giant card in the shape of a Pilgrim hat to celebrate William Bradford's birthday. How old would he be today? Have your students work in teams to develop a time line including the birth dates and accomplishments of at least 20 famous people.

Battle of the sexes

Ask your students what they think about Pennsylvania's decision to allow girls to compete with boys in high school sports. Are there any sports your kids feel both sexes should *not* compete in together? Why? Take the children outside for a shuttle race between the girls and the boys. Was the race competitive?

Tracking migration patterns

Since 1776, thousands of swallows have returned to the San Juan Capistrano Mission in California each year on this date. Ornithologists believe that the amount of daylight, not the temperature, triggers the swallows to return from their winter homes in Central and South America. The humpback whale is another species that has a predictable migration. Ask your students to find and compare the distances of these two species' annual migrations.

MARCH 20
activities

✒ Forever free

Harriet Beecher Stowe's antislavery novel, *Uncle Tom's Cabin*, stirred deep discord among Northerners and Southerners before the Civil War. Ask your students to do a time line beginning in 1852 with the publication of Stowe's novel and ending in 1863 with the Emancipation Proclamation.

📖 Round-trip stories

Use Bill Martin's *The Ghost Eye Tree* to introduce children to "round-trip" stories—stories that begin and end in the same place. Provide your students with circles divided into quarters. Then have them retell *The Ghost Eye Tree* by drawing pictures depicting scenes from the book in sequence around the circle. Tell them to begin at the top and go clockwise.

🦢 Animal behavior

Young students will enjoy celebrating National Agriculture Day by taking turns imitating different farm animals while classmates guess what they are. Also have the kids draw and color pictures of their favorite barnyard animals, then bind them together into a book.

BIRTHDAYS

1916 • BILL MARTIN, children's author 📖

1926 • MITSUMASA ANNO, children's author and illustrator

1928 • FRED ROGERS, host of the TV show "Mr. Rogers' Neighborhood"

1937 • LOIS LOWRY, children's author

1945 • PAT RILEY, basketball player and coach

BIG BIRD, "Sesame Street" character

EVENTS

1852 • Harriet Beecher Stowe's anti-slavery novel, *UNCLE TOM'S CABIN*, was published.

1883 • African-American inventor Jan Matzeliger received a patent for his SHOE-MAKING MACHINE.

1914 • THE FIRST INTERNATIONAL FIGURE SKATING CHAMPIONSHIP was held in New Haven, Conn.

1954 • THE FIRST NEWSPAPER VENDING MACHINE was leased.

1966 • Soccer's WORLD CUP was stolen. A dog named Pickles discovered it in a garden a few days later.

1978 • Krystyna Chojnowska-Liskiewicz became the FIRST WOMAN TO SAIL AROUND THE WORLD ALONE.

🦢 NATIONAL AGRICULTURE DAY (first day of spring)

20

MARCH 21
activities

Sounds of Bach
Tell your students that Bach composed music for the harpsichord and clavichord, keyboard instruments predating the piano. Check your local library for Bach recordings. Play a selection performed on one of these early instruments and one performed on the piano. What differences do your students hear?

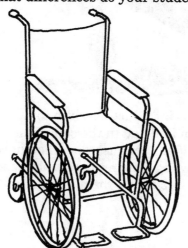

Courageous traveler
It took Rick Hansen over 2 years to push himself around the world in his wheelchair. His trip raised $7.5 million for spinal-cord-injury research and rehabilitation. Hansen averaged 60 miles per day. Make his accomplishment more meaningful by taking a mile-long hike with your students. Ask them to estimate how long it would take to travel 60 miles.

Free-flowing poetry
To celebrate Children's Poetry Day, read aloud poems of various forms, and have each student select one form in which to write a poem. Then have the kids recite their work while you make an audiotape recording. Allow students to borrow the tape to share at home with parents.

Family rituals
No-ruz celebrates the beginning of the Iranian new year and the arrival of spring. Just before the big event, families give their houses a thorough cleaning, and one family member places wheat, celery, or lentil seeds in a clay jug filled with water. The seeds,

which soon sprout, are kept in a place of honor and tended every day. On the 13th day of the new year, the family tosses the sprouts over a garden wall or into running water to symbolically end all family quarrels and begin the new year in peace. Can your students suggest some rituals to celebrate family harmony?

MARCH 22
activities

📖 Artful illustration

Randolph Caldecott was the first to bring an interpretive touch to the art of illustrating. His picture books were imaginative and appealing, adding delightful life to the stories. Today, the literary world honors his contributions by annually bestowing the Caldecott Medal for excellence in a children's picture book. Share some Caldecott Medal books with your students, asking them to concentrate on the illustrations only. Then have them choose one illustration and make up a story based on what they see. How close is their story to the actual one?

🎭 Master mime

Marcel Marceau's body and facial movements entranced millions who watched him mime everyday occurrences using invisible props. Have students take turns miming an everyday activity—for example, brushing teeth, eating a meal, or playing a sport.

🥦 Broccoli bashing

After his mother made him eat broccoli as a child, President Bush never liked the vegetable. What foods would your students like to banish from their diets? Have them create ads or posters expressing their points of view.

BIRTHDAYS

1599 • **ANTHONY VAN DYCK**, Flemish painter
1846 • **RANDOLPH CALDECOTT**, English 📖 illustrator and painter
1923 • **MARCEL MARCEAU**, French mime 🎭
1948 • **ANDREW LLOYD WEBBER**, British composer

EVENTS

1765 • The English Parliament passed **THE STAMP ACT** to raise revenue in the American colonies. It was intended to defray the costs of maintaining royal troops there.
1894 • The first **STANLEY CUP** hockey game was played.
1898 • J.W. Smith patented the **LAWN SPRINKLER**.
1972 • The Senate passed the **EQUAL RIGHTS AMENDMENT**, sending it to the states for ratification.
1980 • **THE GREAT AMERICAN FLAG**— the largest flag ever made— was displayed in Evansville, Ind. It weighed 7.7 tons and measured 411×219 feet.
1982 • The U.S. space shuttle *COLUMBIA* lifted off for its third voyage into space.
1990 • President George Bush publicly 🥦 declared that he **WOULDN'T EAT BROCCOLI.**

NATIONAL GOOF OFF DAY!

MARCH 23
activities

WORLD METEOROLOGICAL DAY

23

▣ Call to action

Patrick Henry's famous call to action was preceded by the question "Is life so dear, or peace so sweet, as to be purchased at the price of chains and slavery?" Ask your students to write short essays that examine three U.S. wars—the American Revolution, the Civil War, and World War II—in light of Henry's question. In what ways were each of these conflicts about "chains and slavery"? Was the tremendous suffering justified by the principles involved? Can your students think of any ways the wars could have been avoided and freedom still defended?

⚗ Moon mythology

Before people traveled to the moon, scientists used photos to learn more about this heavenly body. Before that, various cultures created fanciful stories and myths explaining what the moon was and how it came into existence. Have your students work in teams to create a fanciful story or myth of their own explaining how the moon came to be.

✎ Precise food preparation

Ask your students to imagine following a recipe with these measurements—"butter the size of an egg," "a handful of flour," and a "pinch of sugar." Fannie Farmer, the first cookbook author to use standard measurements, faced this obstacle when she began culling recipes for her book, *The Boston Cooking School Cook Book*. Farmer believed that cooking was a science and that recipes needed to include precise measurements for all ingredients. For homework, have students review recipes for their favorite dishes and list common standard measurements. Then invite the kids to create recipes for fanciful dishes—such as Witch's Brew or Leprechaun Stew. Encourage students to draw pictures of their dishes and write about how the food would taste.

MARCH 24
activities

✿ Car counting

Have students survey the school parking lot to determine whether more staffers drive American-made or foreign-made cars, then calculate the percentage of each.

✎ To the mountaintop

Tell your students that Robert Kennedy was motivated to climb Canada's Mount Kennedy because it had been named for his brother, President John F. Kennedy. When he reached the summit, he buried a U.S. flag bordered in black along with a copy of his brother's inaugural speech. The speech contained these words: "...ask not what your country can do for you—ask what you can do for your country." What do your students think President Kennedy meant? Make a class list of things children can do for their family, school, community, and country.

⚗ Dramatizing pollution

The *Exxon Valdez* oil spill resulted in the deaths of thousands of fish, birds, and animals that lived in or near Prince William Sound. To help your students understand how pollutants affect water purity, conduct a simple experiment: Brush some water-based paint onto a sheet of paper, then place the paper into a basin of water. What do the kids observe?

BIRTHDAYS

1834 • **JOHN WESLEY POWELL,** American geologist, anthropologist, and explorer
1901 • **UB IWERKS,** film animator who drew Mickey Mouse
1920 • **MARY STOLZ,** children's author
• **BILL CLEAVER,** children's author

EVENTS

1644 • A charter was granted to Roger Williams for the COLONY OF RHODE ISLAND.
1898 • THE FIRST AMERICAN-MADE CAR was sold.
1900 • Ground was broken for the NEW YORK CITY SUBWAY SYSTEM.
1945 • SYLVESTER THE CAT first appeared in a cartoon.
1964 • The JOHN F. KENNEDY HALF-DOLLAR was issued.
1965 • Martin Luther King, Jr., and 25,000 civil rights supporters finished a "FREEDOM MARCH" from Selma to Montgomery, Ala.
• Senator ROBERT F. KENNEDY reached the summit of the highest unclimbed mountain in North America, Mount Kennedy in the Yukon Territory.
1988 • Pole-sitter Mellissa Sanders established a WORLD RECORD FOR POLE-SITTING. She had begun her quest on Oct. 26, 1986.
1989 • The tanker *EXXON VALDEZ* spilled 10 million gallons of oil into Prince William Sound, Alaska.

MARCH 25
activities

BIRTHDAYS

1867 • **ARTURO TOSCANINI, Italian conductor**

1871 • **GUTZON BORGLUM, American sculptor known for his Mount Rushmore project**

1881 • **BELA BARTOK, Hungarian composer**

1947 • **ELTON JOHN, English singer and songwriter**

1967 • **DEBI THOMAS, American figure skater**

EVENTS

1634 • **ENGLISH COLONISTS first arrived in Maryland.**

1665 • **THE FIRST RECORDED HORSE RACE IN AMERICA took place in Hempstead, N.Y.**

1775 • **GEORGE WASHINGTON PLANTED PECAN TREES—gifts from Thomas Jefferson—at Mount Vernon.**

1776 • **The Continental Congress gave its FIRST MEDAL to George Washington.**

1882 • **PANCAKES were first made in New York City.**

1954 • **RCA began production of COLOR TV SETS, which sold for $1,000 each.**

GLOBAL UNDERSTANDING DAY
GREEK INDEPENDENCE DAY
PECAN DAY
WAFFLE DAY (Sweden)
LET'S GO FLY A KITE MONTH

Massive monuments

Tell your students that Gutzon Borglum and 36 hard-rock miners began work on Mount Rushmore in 1927. The project, a memorial to four presidents—Washington, Jefferson, Lincoln, and Theodore Roosevelt—was finally finished in 1941. The faces of the presidents are about 60 feet high. Challenge your students to come up with a method for figuring out approximately how many times larger than life the faces are. Then have the kids try their methods and do the computations.

Pancake party

Do your students like pancakes? Pass out copies of your favorite pancake recipe, then challenge the kids to convert the measurements to metric. Can they also calculate how much of each ingredient they'd need to double or triple the batch? If possible, allow your students to make a batch for a class pancake party.

High-flying heroes

To celebrate Let's Go Fly a Kite Month, have each student create a cartoon superhero who uses a kite to perform daring deeds, dangerous rescues, and fabulous feats. The children can draw cartoon strips of the character's adventures. They can also make a list of kite-flying safety rules—for example, *Keep kites away from electric lines; Don't climb trees, buildings, or poles to retrieve a kite; Never fly kites near roadways.* Have them write each rule on a sheet of paper and illustrate it, then bind their work into a book to keep in the school library.

MARCH 26
activities

📖 Messages for daily living

Help your students see how Robert Frost's poems are still relevant today. Share with them such poems as "The Road Not Taken," "Mending Wall," and "Fire and Ice." Then challenge the kids to cut out newspaper stories or photos that remind them of the theme of one of these poems. For example, photos depicting local or international conflict might bring to mind "Mending Wall." Or stories of people who made fateful romantic, financial, or political decisions could aptly illustrate "The Road Not Taken." Not only will your students be reading Frost's poetry, but they'll also come to appreciate its enduring relevance.

🌿 Happy holidays

Your students can give their imaginations free rein as they create their own holidays. Have the children name their holidays, select dates on which to observe them, and describe the kinds of activities that would occur.

🍔 Hamburger survey

National Hamburger Month is a great time for students to do a taste and price survey of the hamburger chains in their area. Have the kids design a questionnaire, then distribute it schoolwide. Encourage your students to record their data on a computer, then graph the results.

BIRTHDAYS

1874 • **ROBERT FROST**, American poet 📖

1930 • **SANDRA DAY O'CONNOR**, U.S. Supreme Court justice

1931 • **LEONARD NIMOY**, American actor

1943 • **BOB WOODWARD**, American journalist

1950 • **MARTIN SHORT**, Canadian actor and comedian

EVENTS

1827 • Shortly before he died, deaf composer **LUDWIG VAN BEETHOVEN** said, "I shall hear in heaven."

1872 • Thomas Martin received a patent for the **FIRE EXTINGUISHER**.

1937 • Residents of Crystal City, Tex., dedicated a **STATUE OF POPEYE** during their spinach festival.

1953 • **THE POLIO VACCINE** was made available for public use.

1982 • Ground-breaking ceremonies took place for the **VIETNAM VETERANS MEMORIAL** in Washington, D.C.

1989 • Soviets voted in their country's first contested elections since 1917. Among the winners was **BORIS YELTSIN**, who was elected president of the Russian Republic.

🌿 **MAKE UP YOUR OWN HOLIDAY DAY**

🍔 **NATIONAL HAMBURGER MONTH**

26

MARCH 27
activities

Fantastic photographs

Show your students some of Edward Steichen's photographs. His book, *A Life in Photography,* is a rich source. Then choose some outstanding photographs from books or magazines to discuss as a class. Have your students each choose one photo to write about. They should explain what may have happened just before or after the picture was taken.

Long-distance callers

Ask your students to name the farthest place they've called on the telephone, then chart the locations on a map. Which location is farthest from the kids' hometown?

Signs of spring

Knowing that first lady Helen Taft wanted to brighten and beautify Washington, the Japanese government sent her 3,000 cherry trees as a symbol of friendship. Today, more than 3,000 cherry trees (including 60 of the original ones) grow around the Tidal Basin, on the Washington Monument Grounds, and in East Potomac Park. Washington residents and tourists look forward to their pink and white blossoms, which appear in late March or early April each year. Have your students keep their eyes open for signs of spring in your community. Keep a class record of spring "firsts," such as the first butterfly, the first dandelion, and the first robin.

MARCH 28
activities

📖 Rock-y writing

Author Byrd Baylor explains how to choose a rock in her book *Everybody Needs a Rock*. After reading her story aloud, ask each of your students to bring in a stone small enough to fit in their hands. Have the children close their eyes as they hold their rocks, then complete the sentence: "My stone feels like _____." Children can also write poems about the creation of their rocks. For example:

> *Maybe my rock*
> *Rolled down the road for me*
> *Or tumbled in a stream*
> *To the sea.*

⚗ Energy safety

The accident at the Three Mile Island nuclear power plant near Harrisburg, Pa., released low levels of radiation into the environment. But had there been a meltdown of the reactor's core—as some investigators believe nearly occurred—the results would have been catastrophic. After the accident, safety standards for the construction and operation of U.S. nuclear power plants were reassessed. Have your students work in teams to research nuclear energy. Then have each team prepare a 3-minute presentation on either the benefits or the drawbacks of nuclear power.

🌐 Honoring teachers

In 1658, Jan Amos Komensky's *Visible World of Pictures* —the first book just for children—was published. This pocket-sized book, filled with woodcut illustrations, helped young readers remember words by looking at pictures. Czech children honor Komensky's birthday by giving their teachers flowers and gifts. What U.S.-born author would your students select for a class Teacher's Day?

BIRTHDAYS
1592 • **JAN AMOS KOMENSKY, Czech educational reformer**
1924 • **BYRD BAYLOR, children's author**
📖

EVENTS
1787 • **Pennsylvania elected BEN FRANKLIN as a delegate to the Constitutional Convention in Philadelphia.**
1797 • **Nathanial Briggs was granted a patent for a WASHING MACHINE.**
1895 • **Construction of AMERICA'S FIRST SUBWAY SYSTEM began in Boston, Mass.**
1922 • **THE MICROFILM READING MACHINE was patented.**
1979 • **A series of equipment malfunc-**
⚗ **tions caused radiation to be released from Pennsylvania's THREE MILE ISLAND nuclear power plant.**

🌐 **TEACHER'S DAY**
     (Czechoslovakia)

MARCH 29
activities

BIRTHDAYS

1790 • JOHN TYLER, 10th president of the United States

1956 • KURT THOMAS, American gymnast

EVENTS

1848 • Ice jams on Lake Erie STOPPED NIAGARA FALLS for 30 hours.

1858 • Hyman W. Lipman patented THE PENCIL WITH AN ATTACHED ERASER.

1867 • THE DOMINION OF CANADA was created.

1886 • COCA-COLA WAS INVENTED by druggist John S. Pemberton.

1958 • The St. Louis Hawks won the FIRST NBA CHAMPIONSHIP CROWN.

1961 • THE TWENTY-THIRD AMENDMENT, which allowed citizens of the District of Columbia to vote for president, was ratified.

1973 • THE LAST U.S. COMBAT TROOPS IN VIETNAM were withdrawn.

1974 • The U.S. spacecraft *Mariner 10* transmitted the FIRST CLOSE-UP PICTURES OF MERCURY.

• The New Jersey State Appellate Court ruled that the state's LITTLE LEAGUE TEAMS HAD TO ACCEPT GIRLS AS WELL AS BOYS.

1989 • THE PEI PYRAMID, a 70-foot-high glass structure, was opened as the new entrance to the Louvre Museum in Paris.

VIETNAM VETERANS DAY

29

Coming to power

Tell your students that John Tyler was the first vice president to assume the presidency because of the death of the president. He took over the office from Benjamin Harrison, who died just 1 month after being inaugurated. Under what circumstances have other vice presidents assumed the duties of the highest office in the land?

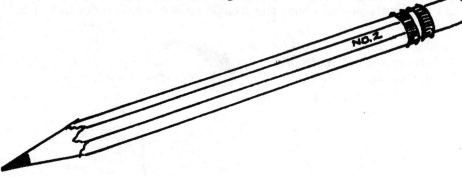

Quick fixes

How important is an eraser? Have your students keep track of how many times in a day they use one. They can also write silly poems honoring this handy invention.

Popular pop

When John S. Pemberton concocted a syrup of coca leaves and kola nut extract, he thought he was inventing a medicine. He added other ingredients—sugar, caramel, lime juice, nutmeg, cinnamon, and vanilla—to cover up the bitter taste. A teaspoon of this "Nerve and Tonic Stimulant" was supposed to cure headaches and stomachaches. Can your students think of other products or inventions whose primary uses were unintended?

MARCH 30
activities

The value of art

Artist Vincent van Gogh never knew wealth or fame. Although he produced about 800 paintings and hundreds of drawings, he sold only one during his lifetime. But van Gogh later came to be regarded as an artistic genius. On March 30, 1987—the 135th anniversary of his birth—his painting *Sunflowers* was sold at a record-breaking price of $39.9 million. Allow your students to look at a picture of *Sunflowers* or another van Gogh painting for 1 minute. Then see how observant the kids are by asking them questions about it—for example: How many flowers are there? What color is the vase? What's in the background? Finally, ask your students if they can name other people whose work went unappreciated during their lifetime but later was recognized as important.

Wise buys

Tell your students that Secretary of State William Seward spent $7,200,000 in gold to buy Alaska. Many Americans believed the purchase was ill-advised, calling it "Seward's folly." Today, of course, we have a different perspective. Have your students write short stories about other purchases that seem foolish but that later turn out to be "great buys." If they're having trouble getting started, suggest they consider the bottom of the ocean, an iceberg, or a plot of territory on the moon. Why might these places become valuable in the future?

BIRTHDAYS

1746 • FRANCISCO JOSE DE GOYA, Spanish painter
1820 • ANNA SEWELL, English author
1853 • VINCENT VAN GOGH, Dutch painter
1945 • ERIC CLAPTON, English singer, songwriter, and guitarist

EVENTS

1842 • Dr. Crawford W. Long performed the FIRST RECORDED OPERATION USING A GENERAL ANESTHETIC.
1843 • THE EGG INCUBATOR was patented.
1867 • Secretary of State William Seward negotiated the PURCHASE OF ALASKA from Russia.
1870 • TEXAS WAS READMITTED TO THE UNION after the Civil War.
• THE FIFTEENTH AMENDMENT TO THE CONSTITUTION, guaranteeing the right to vote regardless of race, took effect.
1886 • J. Ricks patented THE HORSESHOE.
1942 • A LAW WAS PASSED TO CONSERVE CLOTH during World War II. Men's suits were then made without cuffs and pleats.
1981 • PRESIDENT RONALD REAGAN WAS SHOT by John Hinckley outside a Washington hotel.

DOCTORS' DAY
SEWARD'S DAY

30

MARCH 31
activities

BIRTHDAYS

1596 • **RENE DESCARTES, French philosopher**

1811 • **ROBERT WILHELM BUNSEN, German chemist and inventor of the Bunsen burner**

EVENTS

1870 • **Thomas Peterson Mundy became the FIRST BLACK TO VOTE following ratification of the Fifteenth Amendment.**

1889 • **THE EIFFEL TOWER was officially opened to the public in Paris.**

1893 • **Whitcomb Judson patented the "hookless fastener"—an early form of the ZIPPER.**

1918 • **DAYLIGHT SAVING TIME WAS FIRST INSTITUTED as a wartime fuel-saving measure.**

1923 • **Alma Cummings won the FIRST AMERICAN DANCE MARATHON in New York City. She danced 27 hours straight.**

1925 • **Congress authorized the MOUNT RUSHMORE MEMORIAL in the Black Hills of southwestern South Dakota.**

1963 • **Edward J. Dwight, Jr., became the FIRST AFRICAN-AMERICAN SELECTED FOR ASTRONAUT TRAINING.**

1985 • **Harry Lee Welch did a RECORD-SETTING 100 CONSECUTIVE ONE-FINGER PUSH-UPS.**

● Tall towers

The Eiffel Tower was built for the Paris Exhibition of 1889, which celebrated the 100th anniversary of the French Revolution. At 300 meters high, it remained the tallest structure in the world for several years. Have your students convert this height to feet, then mark it on graph paper. Next, ask the kids to find and graph the heights of current tall structures, such as the Sears Tower, the Empire State Building, the World Trade Center, the St. Louis Arch, and the tallest building in their community.

⌁ Fascinating fasteners

Conduct a quick survey of your students' clothing to see how many children are wearing garments fastened with zippers, buttons, snaps, Velcro, and so on. Have students tabulate the results, then make a bar graph. Which fastener was most common? Which do the kids think is easiest to use?

❋ Extra hours

To get an extra hour of daylight in the evening, people in the United States set their clocks ahead 1 hour on the first Sunday in April. Daylight saving time then remains in effect until the last Sunday in October. Have your students write and illustrate stories about what they plan to do with that extra hour of sunlight. Have the kids share their stories with the class.

✿ Movers and shakers

During recess, invite students to stay indoors and hold a class dance marathon. Can they last the entire period?

APRIL

MONTHLONG OBSERVANCES

Boost Your Home Team Month
Keep America Beautiful Month
Math Education Month
Month of the Young Child
National Garden Month
National Humor Month
National Library Month

WEEKLONG EVENTS

National Laugh Week (first week)
National Library Week
  (week of the first Sunday)
Pan American Week
  (week of April 14)
Gardening Week (second full week)
National Bike Safety Week
  (third week)
National Coin Week (third week)
Reading Is Fun Week (third week)
Professional Secretaries Week
  (third or fourth week)
Earth Week (week of April 22)
Big Brothers/Big Sisters Appreciation
  Week (last week)
National Science and Technology
  Week (last full week)

SPECIAL DAYS AND CELEBRATIONS

Daylight saving time returns
  (first Sunday)
The Boston Marathon (third Monday)
Look-Alike Day (third Tuesday)
National Arbor Day (last Friday)
Easter (first Sunday after the first
  full moon following the vernal
  equinox)
Passover (in March or April)
Holocaust Memorial Day
  (in April or May)

☆ Project of the Month: Beyond Book Talks

During National Library Month, collect information on your students' library usage and areas of interest. Start by creating two posterboard lists. List 1 should have two categories: "I own a library card" and "I don't own a library card." List 2 should have five categories of favorite books: animals, families, famous people, adventure, and other. Invite the kids to write their names in the appropriate places on the lists, then have student volunteers tabulate the results. Use the information to create bar graphs, and post them on a bulletin board.

Next, divide the class into four groups, and assign each group a genre—for example, poetry, general nonfiction, chapter books, and picture books. Then explain that each group will be responsible for preparing book talks on the assigned genre for 1 week. For instance, during each day of the first week, have one or two students from the poetry group do a book talk. If they like, the students can choose books from their preferred categories on the second posterboard list. By month's end, each child will have had a turn making a presentation—and all of your students will have been introduced to 20 new books.

EXTENDER: Invite your students to write mini book reviews or advertisements for the new books they've discovered this month, then post them on the library bulletin board.

APRIL 1
activities

APRIL FOOLS' DAY

☞ Silly illustrations

Norman Rockwell is best known for his more than 300 *Saturday Evening Post* covers. Even though Rockwell went to great pains to make these illustrations authentic to the last detail, readers sometimes wrote to him about errors they had spotted. And that gave him the idea for his first April Fools' cover, which he purposely packed with over 40 errors. Share copies of some of Rockwell's April Fools' covers with your students. Then have them make their own hidden-error pictures. Older students can create some sly errors by doing research. For example, they might slip in an anachronism when depicting a scene from the past, show an animal in the wrong habitat, or place shadows in the wrong positions.

📖 Bear-y funny books

Stan and Jan Berenstain have two sons. When the boys were young, they asked their parents to buy them funny books. The Berenstains eventually ran out of books to buy, so they created their own. Read several of the Berenstains' books to the class, discussing how humor makes the stories appealing. Then choose one story and ask the students to write and illustrate another episode or a different ending for it.

✎ Foolish news

Have your students use the *Guinness Book of World Records* or a similar collection of facts to write strange-but-true headlines for an April Fools' Day newspaper edition.

THE STRANGE-FACTS GAZETTE
★★★ LOUDEST SCREAMER
SIMON ROBINSON OF McLAREN VALE, SOUTH AUSTRALIA SCREAM MEASURED AT 120 dB.

APRIL 2
activities

▰ How to make money

When Congress first authorized the creation of a mint, it decided that the coins made there should contain a certain amount of silver. But America was a new country and didn't have enough silver for the task. So George Washington donated some of his own household silver.

Without looking, can your students describe the front and back of a penny, nickel, dime, and quarter? Have them share their descriptions with one another, then check their accuracy with some coins. Next, ask the kids to imagine that they're archaeologists carefully examining U.S. coins. What do the various designs, symbols, buildings, and people pictured on the coins tell about American culture?

📖 Famous fairy tales

Tell your students that Hans Christian Andersen once said that fairy tales must contain the elements of tragedy, comedy, irony, and humor. Share with your students some of Andersen's most famous tales—"The Ugly Duckling," "The Emperor's New Clothes," "The Red Shoes," and so on. Then ask the children to note how Andersen wove in the elements he cited.

✍ Laugh it up

During National Humor Month, poll your students to find out what makes them laugh. Then have them each write a story or draw a picture of a time when they laughed because they saw or heard something funny. Invite the kids to share their work with the class.

BIRTHDAYS

- 742 • **CHARLEMAGNE (Charles the Great)**, Frankish king
- 1805 • **HANS CHRISTIAN ANDERSEN,** 📖 Danish author of fairy tales
- 1834 • **FREDERIC AUGUSTE BARTHOLDI,** French sculptor who created the Statue of Liberty

EVENTS

- 1792 • Congress authorized the establishment of the **FIRST U.S. MINT.**
- 1865 • **CONFEDERATE PRESIDENT JEFFERSON DAVIS** and most of his Cabinet fled the Confederate capital of Richmond, Va.
- 1871 • **THE FIRST CANADIAN CENSUS** recorded 3,689,257 persons.
- 1902 • **THE FIRST MOTION-PICTURE THEATER IN THE UNITED STATES** opened in Los Angeles.
- 1917 • President Woodrow Wilson asked Congress to declare war on Germany so that America could help **MAKE THE WORLD SAFE FOR DEMOCRACY.**
- 1980 • **THE U.S. PRIME INTEREST RATE** hit a record 20%.
- 1989 • In an editorial, *The New York Times* **DECLARED THAT THE COLD WAR WAS OVER.**

  INTERNATIONAL CHILDREN'S BOOK DAY
- ✍ **NATIONAL HUMOR MONTH**

APRIL 3
activities

BIRTHDAYS

1783 • **WASHINGTON IRVING,** American author

1934 • **JANE GOODALL,** ethologist and chimpanzee expert

1961 • **EDDIE MURPHY,** American actor and comedian

EVENTS

1776 • Harvard College conferred an **HONORARY DEGREE OF DOCTOR OF LAWS** on General George Washington.

1793 • **THE FIRST AMERICAN CIRCUS** opened in Philadelphia.

1800 • Congress authorized the widowed Martha Washington to send all her mail **POSTAGE-FREE.**

1805 • Ten members of the **LEWIS AND CLARK EXPEDITION** returned to Washington to show President Jefferson animal and plant specimens they'd collected.

1837 • The Ohio Institution for the Blind, the **FIRST STATE-SUPPORTED SCHOOL FOR THE BLIND,** was authorized.

1860 • **THE PONY EXPRESS** began service between St. Joseph, Mo., and Sacramento, Calif.

1933 • An airplane first **FLEW OVER MT. EVEREST.**

1944 • **ANNE FRANK,** age 14, described her family's eating habits in her diary.

1971 • **GORDIE HOWE** retired from professional hockey after 25 years.

▆ Let's explore

Commissioned by President Jefferson to find a land route to the Pacific Ocean, expedition leaders Meriwether Lewis and William Clark set out in 1804 from St. Louis, Mo., with 45 men. In a keelboat and two dugouts, they traveled up the Missouri River to the mouth of the Platte, reaching the site of present-day Bismarck. From there they traveled to the mouth of the Yellowstone River, sighted the Rocky Mountains, and followed the Jefferson branch of the Missouri through the Rockies. Then they followed the Columbia River to the Pacific. Have your students trace the route on your class map. Throughout their journey, Lewis and Clark collected plant and animal specimens and kept detailed journals of their travels. Have your students sketch and describe a plant or animal native to your region.

⚗ Realizing early dreams

When she was 7 years old, Jane Goodall read *The Story of Dr. Dolittle* by Hugh Lofting. The book started her dreaming of going to Africa to study animals. In 1960, at age 26, she traveled to East Africa to live in the wild and study chimpanzees. Have any books inspired your students to set career goals? Ask them to list three major goals they'd like to attain after they finish school.

✒ Food for thought

Through her diary, Anne Frank gave the world an account of her feelings and experiences as she and her family hid from the Nazis during World War II. After 21 months in hiding, she wrote about "food cycles"—times when she and her family ate only one food, prepared in various ways. For example, "We had nothing but endive for a long time, day in, day out, endive with sand, endive without sand, stew with endive, boiled or *en casserole*...." Ask your students to keep a diary recording what their family eats for 1 week. Compare their diet with that of Anne Frank.

APRIL 4
activities

🇺🇸 Striving for social reform

Tell your students that a Sunday school teaching assignment at a Massachusetts jail changed Dorothea Dix's life—and the lives of many of the state's mentally ill. During her assignment, Dix noticed that mentally ill prisoners received poor care. This discovery spurred her to investigate other places across Massachusetts where the mentally ill were kept. When she presented her findings to the state legislature, reforms were enacted. Ask your students to identify living conditions in their area that require reform. If possible, have the kids go on fact-finding missions with cameras and notebooks in hand. Then have them present their findings to local government officials.

✒️ Remembering Dr. King

Have your students develop questionnaires and interview their parents about the day Dr. King died. How old were their parents then? What was their immediate reaction to the tragedy? Afterward, students can read parts of the interviews at a class memorial service for Dr. King, which could also include readings from some of his speeches.

🐚 Map mania

To celebrate National Reading a Road Map Day, ask your students to bring in as many road maps as they can. Then divide the class into groups of three or four, and give each group at least two maps. Next, challenge the kids to devise five questions that can be answered by studying their maps. Afterward, have the groups switch maps and try to answer the questions. To culminate the celebration, students can use mural paper to draw and color a road map of their school neighborhood.

BIRTHDAYS

1802 • **DOROTHEA DIX,** American social 🇺🇸 reformer
1928 • **MAYA ANGELOU,** American poet

EVENTS

1841 • **PRESIDENT WILLIAM HENRY HARRISON DIED** a month after his inauguration.

1850 • The city of **LOS ANGELES** was incorporated.

1877 • **A TELEPHONE** was first installed in a private home.

1887 • Susanna Medora Salter was elected mayor of Argonia, Kan., thus becoming the **FIRST WOMAN MAYOR IN THE UNITED STATES.** She served for 1 year at a salary of $1.

1949 • **THE NORTH ATLANTIC TREATY ORGANIZATION (NATO)** was formed.

1968 • Civil rights leader **MARTIN ✒️ LUTHER KING, JR., WAS ASSAS-SINATED** in Memphis, Tenn.

1969 • Doctors in Houston implanted the **FIRST ARTIFICIAL HEART** in Haskell Karp of Skokie, Ill.

1974 • **HANK AARON** of the Atlanta Braves tied Babe Ruth's record of 714 career home runs.

1976 • Kazukiki Asaba **FLEW 1,050 KITES** at one time.

🐚 **NATIONAL READING A ROAD MAP DAY**

BIRTHDAYS

1827 • SIR JOSEPH LISTER, English physician and pioneer in antiseptic surgery

1856 • BOOKER T. WASHINGTON, African-American educator

1858 • W. ATLEE BURPEE, Canadian-American seed merchant

1934 • RICHARD PECK, children's author

1937 • COLIN POWELL, first African-American chairman of the Joint Chiefs of Staff

EVENTS

1614 • POCAHONTAS, daughter of the Indian chieftain Powhatan, married English colonist John Rolfe in Virginia.

1792 • GEORGE WASHINGTON ISSUED THE FIRST PRESIDENTIAL VETO, rejecting a bill affecting state representation.

1793 • PLANS FOR THE U.S. CAPITOL were accepted.

1963 • The Soviet Union and the United States established a TELEPHONE "HOT LINE" linking their two leaders. The need for a direct channel of communication was demonstrated during the Cuban Missile Crisis.

1984 • Kareem Abdul-Jabbar scored his 31,421st point, becoming the HIGHEST-SCORING BASKETBALL PLAYER IN NBA HISTORY.

1986 • A British Guiana 1-CENT STAMP SOLD FOR $850,000, the highest price ever paid for a stamp at an auction.

🔅 NATIONAL LAUGH WEEK

📖 NATIONAL LIBRARY MONTH

APRIL 5
activities

🔖 Stamp stories

To mark the anniversary of the record-setting postage stamp auction, have your students design their own stamps commemorating a historic event or person.

🔅 A laughing matter

During National Laugh Week, read aloud each day from joke or riddle books. At the end of the week, invite each student to tell a favorite joke to the class.

📖 Booking it

For each week of National Library Month, give your students book-related goals. For example:

Week 1: Read as many animal books as you can, then write a paragraph on the most unusual animal you learned about.

Week 2: Design bookmarks or organize storytelling sessions for kindergartners.

Week 3: Read a book in a genre you've never read before.

Week 4: Read a fiction book, then draw and color a picture of your favorite scene.

APRIL 6
activities

📖 Alphabet alliteration

Graeme Base is the author and illustrator of *Animalia* and *The Eleventh Hour,* two books that enchant children with their intricate designs. Share *Animalia* with your students. They'll soon discover that the illustration for each letter of the alphabet contains pictures of objects that begin with that letter. Plus, the text for each page is an alliterative sentence. Invite your students to work in pairs to create a class "Alphabet Alliteration Anthology" patterned after *Animalia*. Then bind the anthology and add it to your class library.

🇺🇸 Cleaning up the country

During Keep America Beautiful Month, have your students brainstorm for tasks they can do to help protect the nation's environment. Then have them each pick one task to do after school. The next day, ask the kids to share stories of their good work. Afterward, give each student a piece of posterboard on which to create an illustrated sign detailing the task performed "to Keep America Beautiful." For example: "I picked up trash in the schoolyard to Keep America Beautiful" or "I recycled glass bottles to Keep America Beautiful." At the bottom of their signs the kids can write this challenge: "What will *you* do to help today?" Post the signs around the school and throughout the community to promote awareness of Keep America Beautiful Month.

BIRTHDAYS
1483 • RAPHAEL, Italian painter
1928 • JAMES WATSON, American biochemist who was one of the discoverers of the molecular structure of DNA
1958 • GRAEME BASE, children's author 📖

EVENTS
1748 • THE BURIED CITY OF POMPEII was discovered by an Italian peasant digging in a vineyard.
1869 • CELLULOID, the first plastic, was patented.
1896 • THE FIRST MODERN OLYMPIC GAMES opened in Athens, Greece.
1909 • American explorers Robert Peary and Matthew Henson reached the NORTH POLE.
1927 • THE FIRST PILOT'S LICENSE was issued by the U.S. Department of Commerce.
1965 • Early Bird, the FIRST COMMERCIAL COMMUNICATIONS SATELLITE, went into orbit.
1978 • President Jimmy Carter signed into law legislation RAISING THE MANDATORY RETIREMENT AGE for government workers from 65 to 70.
1985 • William J. Schroeder became the FIRST ARTIFICIAL HEART RECIPIENT TO BE DISCHARGED from a hospital.

NORTH POLE DAY
🇺🇸 KEEP AMERICA BEAUTIFUL MONTH

APRIL 7
activities

Cereal-box bonanza

Will Keith Kellogg founded the Toasted Corn Flakes Co., which later became Kellogg's, in 1906. By 1909, he'd sold more than 1 million cases of cornflakes. Gather five different cereals, then ask your students to vote for the one they'd most likely buy—based solely on their first impression of the box. Next, discuss the techniques that companies use to get people to buy their cereals—for example, colorful packaging, enticing pictures, appealing brand names, and bold print. Then challenge the children to use those techniques to design their own cereal boxes. Have the class vote for the most appealing design.

One hump or two?

The camel played a vital role in the desert cultures of North Africa, Arabia, and Asia. Its unique adaptations—including its capacity to store 1½ gallons of water in one of its three stomachs—made it the ideal mode of transportation in the desert. Tell your students that there are two kinds of camels: the one-humped camel, or dromedary; and the two-humped, or Bactrian, camel. The dromedary, the swifter of the two, can cover 100 miles in a single day and is used primarily for riding. The Bactrian camel can cover only 30 miles per day but can carry loads of up to 1,000 pounds. Pose this story problem to your students: You live in a desert town and own two dromedaries and a Bactrian camel. A merchant offers you money to transport 1,000 pounds of pots to a town that is 75 miles to the south of your town, pick up a load of cloth, and return. While you're considering this offer, another man approaches. He'll pay you the same amount of money to deliver a letter to his sister and one to his mother, then return with any letters they might have for him. His sister's town is 135 miles east of yours, and his mother's town is 90 miles west of yours. Which job would require less of your time?

APRIL 8
activities

📖 Fairy tales come true?

Trina Schart Hyman has illustrated several Grimm's fairy tales, including *Sleeping Beauty* and *Snow White*. As a child, Hyman liked to pretend she was Red Riding Hood. Which famous fairy-tale characters would your students like to be? Have each student select one and write a story describing what happened to the character the day after the fairy tale ended.

🌐 Frosty festival

The Cuchumatan Indians of Santa Eulalia in Guatemala believe that frost dwells in cliffs. Once a year, a prayer-maker treks up a cliff and locates a crack in the rock. He then seals it with cement to trap the frost inside and keep the villagers' corn plants safe. What other places besides rocks might frost choose for a home? Encourage your students to write poems titled "Sealing the Frost."

📣 Go, team, go!

To celebrate Boost Your Home Team Month, have your students work in groups to create cheers for local professional or school sports teams. Ask the groups to perform their cheers, then hold a class vote to choose the best one.

BIRTHDAYS

1912 • **SONJA HENIE**, Norwegian figure skater

1939 • **TRINA SCHART HYMAN**, children's author and illustrator 📖

EVENTS

1730 • **THE FIRST JEWISH CONGREGATION IN THE UNITED STATES**, Shaarit Israel, consecrated its synagogue in New York City.

1858 • **BIG BEN**, the bell on the famous London Clock Tower at the Houses of Parliament, was cast.

1895 • **THE 1894 INCOME TAX was declared unconstitutional.** All the money collected was eventually returned.

1904 • Longacre Square in New York City was renamed **TIMES SQUARE**.

1939 • **THE FIRST TELEPHONE WEATHER FORECASTING SERVICE** began in New York City.

1974 • Hank Aaron hit his **715TH CAREER HOME RUN**, breaking Babe Ruth's long-standing major-league record.

1990 • **RYAN WHITE DIED** at age 18. A hemophiliac who had contracted AIDS through a blood transfusion 5½ years earlier, White had promoted a greater understanding of the disease.

🌐 **SEALING THE FROST** (Guatemala)

📣 **BOOST YOUR HOME TEAM MONTH**

APRIL 9
activities

APPOMATTOX DAY

9

Space-y adventures

The first seven astronauts selected by NASA were Scott Carpenter, Gordon Cooper, John Glenn, Gus Grissom, Wally Schirra, Alan Shepard, and Donald Slayton. When astronauts fly a mission, they're allowed to bring several small items in a sealed container. Later, these items are designated as having officially flown in space. What items would your students want to take on a space mission? Why? To begin a class "Mission to the Future," use a Polaroid camera to snap pictures of your students. (If a camera is not available, have the kids draw self-portraits.) Then have the students glue their pictures onto their own drawings of the future or of space. For example, they might put themselves in the cockpit of a special vehicle that tours Mars. Post the completed designs in the hallway.

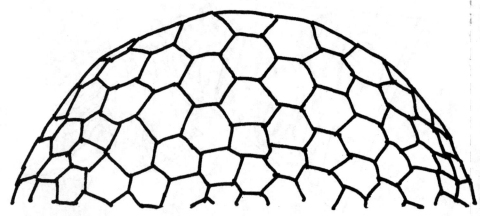

Dome designs

The Houston Astrodome, which cost $20 million to build, has a plastic dome that's 208 feet above the stadium floor at its highest point. Challenge your students to work in teams to create freestanding domes using only plastic wrap and straws for support.

APRIL 10
activities

✸ Pet projects

Henry Bergh, founder of the ASPCA, devised many ways to protect animals. Challenge your students to find ways to make their community a pet haven. For example, they can:
• Contact the local animal shelter to find out about stray cats or dogs needing a home. Students can then raise money to place an adopt-a-pet advertisement in a local newspaper.
• Make posters describing an animal that's ready for adoption, then place the posters in the cafeteria or in hallways. A group of students could also work together to write an article for the school paper describing the animal and including, if possible, a photo.

✿ Growing green

If possible, commemorate the anniversary of the first Arbor Day by having your class plant trees on the school grounds. Also mark the occasion by helping your students learn all about trees. First, have the kids survey the school grounds and draw a map that shows the location of each tree. Then have them collect a leaf from each different kind of tree, check a field guide to find out the trees' common and scientific names, and mark their maps accordingly. Finally, have the kids make a neat copy of the tree map and photocopy it along with pages on which they've glued and labeled each type of leaf they collected. Bind the pages into a "tree guide" for your school. Update the guide on future Arbor Days if new trees are planted. If there's no room outside your school for trees, ask a local nursery or garden club for donations of bonsai trees for your classroom.

BIRTHDAYS

1880 • FRANCES PERKINS, first woman to serve in a U.S. cabinet post (secretary of labor under Franklin D. Roosevelt)
1897 • ERIC MOWBRAY KNIGHT, English author who wrote *Lassie Come Home*
1947 • DAVID ADLER, children's author

EVENTS

1790 • THE U.S. PATENT SYSTEM was established.
1849 • Walter Hunt invented the SAFETY PIN.
1866 • Henry Bergh founded the AMERICAN SOCIETY FOR THE PREVENTION OF CRUELTY TO ANIMALS (ASPCA).
1872 • Nebraska celebrated the FIRST ARBOR DAY by planting more than a million trees.
1892 • THE TUBERCULOSIS SOCIETY was founded in Philadelphia.
1912 • The luxury liner *TITANIC* set sail from Southampton, England, on its ill-fated maiden voyage.
1924 • Simon and Schuster published the FIRST CROSSWORD PUZZLE BOOK.
1946 • JAPANESE WOMEN VOTED for the first time.
1953 • *The House of Wax*, the FIRST FEATURE-LENGTH 3-D MOVIE IN COLOR, premiered in New York City.

HUMANE DAY

10

APRIL 11
activities

Submarine science

To help your students understand how a submarine can dive beneath the surface of the water and then rise again, have them make Cartesian divers. Give pairs of students an empty 2-liter plastic bottle and an eyedropper. Then give the kids the following directions: Fill your bottle with tap water until it's almost overflowing. Then place the eyedropper in the bottle and screw the cap on securely. Now, squeeze the sides of the bottle, let go, and observe what happens inside the eyedropper.

The children will notice that water enters the eyedropper as it sinks and leaves it as it rises. Discuss sinking, floating, buoyancy, and density. Then ask your students to compare the Cartesian diver to a submarine.

A taxing matter

Do your students know how states use money raised by taxes? Make a class list of services provided by your state.

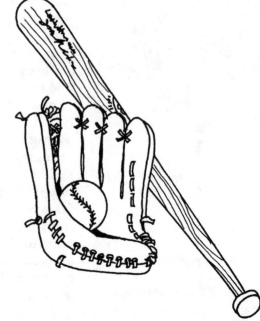

Legendary major leaguer

Jackie Robinson's illustrious career was filled with honors: Rookie of the Year (1947); National League Most Valuable Player (1949); Hall of Fame election (1962). Before joining the majors, Robinson played in the "Negro leagues." Have your students research these leagues and one of the men who played in them—such as Satchel Paige or Cool Papa Bell—then write a brief biography.

APRIL 12
activities

✒ Clever compromises

In honor of Henry Clay, have your students look up and discuss the term *compromise*. Then ask them to work in small groups to brainstorm for problems at home or at school that were solved by compromise—or that *could have been solved* by compromise. Each group can then role-play a particular situation. Older students can read about Clay's role in the Missouri Compromise of 1820 (in which Congress simultaneously admitted one slave state and one non-slave state to the Union to maintain a balance) and tell how each side gave up something to gain something.

📖 Bev's birthday bash

To celebrate Beverly Cleary's birthday, invite your students to make a class card depicting scenes from her books. Or have the kids write individual letters to her telling why certain characters and events from her books rang true and recounting similar events in the students' lives.

✿ Record-breaking winds

Using wind tunnels, people can simulate the high winds found in nature. Tell your students that wind tunnels are tubelike passages often used for testing aircraft on the ground. Large fans create a wind that flows over whatever is being tested—full-sized aircraft or rockets, component parts (wings, tails, landing gear), or models. The speed of the air flowing through a wind tunnel is expressed as a Mach number, which relates it to the speed of sound at sea level—760 mph. At Mach 0.5, for example, the air speed is 380 mph. Ask your students to compute the air speed generated in the Mach 50 tunnel at NASA's Ames Research Center in California—the fastest wind tunnel in the world (38,000 mph).

BIRTHDAYS

1777 • **HENRY CLAY**, American statesman known as "the Great Compromiser"

1879 • **FREDERICK G. MELCHER**, founder of Children's Book Week

1907 • **HARDIE GRAMATKY**, children's author

1911 • **BARBARA CORCORAN**, children's author

1916 • **BEVERLY CLEARY**, children's author

EVENTS

1859 • Michael Phelan won the **FIRST U.S. BILLIARDS CHAMPIONSHIP.**

1861 • **THE CIVIL WAR BEGAN** as Confederate forces fired on Fort Sumter at Charleston, S.C.

1877 • **A CATCHER'S MASK** was first used in a baseball game.

1934 • **THE HIGHEST-VELOCITY NATURAL WIND** ever recorded—231 mph—occurred at Mt. Washington, N.H.

1955 • **THE POLIO VACCINE**, developed by Jonas Salk, was pronounced safe and effective.

1961 • The Soviet cosmonaut Yuri Gagarin became the **FIRST MAN IN SPACE.**

1981 • **THE FIRST SPACE SHUTTLE**, *Columbia*, was launched.

1984 • **THE CREW OF THE SPACE SHUTTLE *CHALLENGER*** placed a satellite it had retrieved and repaired back into orbit.

1988 • The U.S. Patent Office issued a **PATENT FOR A LIVE MOUSE**, a new breed genetically altered to aid in the study and treatment of cancer.

COSMONAUT DAY
SPACE SHUTTLE DAY

APRIL 13
activities

A most gifted American

Do your students know that Thomas Jefferson wrote the Declaration of Independence; designed his beautiful home, Monticello; and founded the University of Virginia? Divide the class into groups, and ask each group to research some of Jefferson's other accomplishments. Then have each group use its information to design a poster titled "The Thomas Jefferson Most People Don't Know."

Elephantine math

Visitors to America's first elephant exhibition must have been astonished—as many of your students no doubt were—at their first sight of one of these gigantic and wondrous creatures. Use pachyderm stats to get your students working with ratios. Tell the kids that at birth, an African elephant is typically about 3 feet tall at the shoulders and weighs about 200 pounds. Have your students find out their measurements at birth and compare them with the elephant's. Next, have your students estimate how many pounds of food they eat (use the size of an average hamburger, $1/4$ pound, as a point of reference) and how much they drink (a can of soda contains 12 ounces) each day. Then give them the figures for an elephant—1,000 pounds of food and 40 gallons of water—and have them work out the ratios. Finally, go around the room asking for each child's weight, and use a calculator to get a class total. Then ask the kids to compare this figure with the weight of the heaviest elephant on record—14,641 pounds. How many more classes the size of yours would it take to equal the weight of this animal?

Welcoming baby tiger

Tell your students that the white tiger is one of the world's rarest tigers. So when a white tiger cub was born at the National Zoo, there was much rejoicing. To commemorate this event, have your students draw and color a "birth announcement" for the baby tiger.

APRIL 14
activities

✿ Word game

To celebrate the publication of the first Webster's dictionary, divide the class into groups to play the dictionary game. Give each group a dictionary, and have group members take turns finding a word they think no one else will know and reading and spelling the word aloud. All the other kids in the group write the word and what they think it means on a slip of paper, while the reader writes the word and what it really means. The papers are collected, and the student with the dictionary reads the definitions (including the real one). Students then vote for the definition they think is correct. For each incorrect vote, the reader gets one point. Each group member to identify the correct definition gets two points.

✎ In the president's pockets

At the time of his death, everything in President Lincoln's pockets was placed in a box wrapped in brown paper and tied with string. The box remained unopened until 1976. Inside was a linen handkerchief, an ivory pocketknife, eyeglasses mended with string, and eight newspaper clippings praising Lincoln. Lincoln had been criticized frequently, but he'd appeared unaffected. Perhaps his possession of these clippings demonstrates that even self-confident people like him need encouragement. Have each of your students write a newspaper article praising something one of their classmates said or did.

🌐 Celebrating spring

The people of Thailand celebrate the Buddhist New Year with a Water Festival, called Sogran. During the celebration, children play water games and families feast on *kanoms*—desserts made with coconut, rice, and tropical fruits. Ask your students why spring can be considered the beginning of a new year. Then have them talk about what they do to celebrate the arrival of spring.

BIRTHDAYS

1527 • **ABRAHAM ORTELIUS,** Flemish geographer who published the first modern atlas

1927 • **ROBERT LOPSHIRE,** children's author

1941 • **PETE ROSE,** baseball great who set the all-time career record for hits

EVENTS

1755 • Benjamin Franklin and Philadelphia Quakers organized the FIRST AMERICAN SOCIETY FOR THE ABOLITION OF SLAVERY.

1828 • The first edition of Noah ✿ Webster's *AN AMERICAN DICTIONARY OF THE ENGLISH LANGUAGE* was published.

1865 • **PRESIDENT ABRAHAM LINCOLN** ✎ **WAS SHOT** and fatally wounded by John Wilkes Booth at Ford's Theater in Washington, D.C.

1912 • The luxury liner *TITANIC* HIT AN ICEBERG just before midnight.

1956 • **VIDEOTAPE WAS FIRST DEMONSTRATED** to the public.

1981 • The SPACE SHUTTLE *COLUMBIA* ENDED ITS FIRST TEST FLIGHT with a smooth landing in California.

1990 • THE SPACE SHUTTLE *DISCOVERY* was launched with a copy of the U.S. Constitution on board.

PAN AMERICAN DAY
🌐 **SOGRAN** (Thailand)

BIRTHDAYS

1452 • LEONARDO DA VINCI, Italian artist, scientist, and inventor

1832 • WILHELM BUSCH, German caricaturist considered the father of the modern comic strip

EVENTS

1621 • THE *MAYFLOWER* SAILED FROM PLYMOUTH, MASS., on its first return voyage to England.

1817 • THE FIRST AMERICAN SCHOOL FOR THE DEAF was opened in Hartford, Conn., by Thomas Gallaudet.

1870 • THE METROPOLITAN MUSEUM OF ART was founded in New York City.

1895 • JOSEPHINE BLATT LIFTED 3,564 POUNDS, a record that still stands.

1912 • Albert Einstein first spoke of TIME AS THE FOURTH DIMENSION.

• THE OCEAN LINER *TITANIC* SANK in the North Atlantic.

1952 • The Franklin National Bank of New York issued the FIRST BANK CREDIT CARD.

1955 • THE FIRST McDONALD'S RESTAURANT OPENED in Des Plaines, Ill.

1985 • THE WORLD'S LARGEST MARCHING BAND, 4,524 students, performed at Dodger Stadium in Los Angeles.

1989 • THE HIGHEST AND FASTEST STEEL ROLLER COASTER—the "Great American Scream Machine"—opened at Great Adventure in Jackson, N.J.

FESTIVAL OF THE SARDINE (Spain)

INCOME TAX DAY

NATIONAL GRIPER'S DAY

APRIL 15 activities

At arms' length

Tell your students that Leonardo da Vinci—inventor, painter, sculptor, and scientist—is considered one of the most intelligent people in history. But do the kids think da Vinci was right when he said that a person's arm span and height are approximately equal? Have your students write down their opinions, then conduct a simple experiment to find the answer. Ask the kids to measure one another's arm span (from tip to tip of the middle fingers on outstretched arms) and height (standing against a wall). Chart the data, then tally the number of students whose arm span and height measurements are 1 inch or less apart. Also calculate the average arm span and average height. Was da Vinci right?

Infamous shipwreck

Did your students know that the captain of the *Titanic* had received several wireless warnings about icebergs in the area but had ignored them? Share some more fascinating facts about this ill-fated ship. For example, the *Titanic*:

• weighed 46,328 gross tons and was 882.5 feet long

• carried 2,200 passengers

• included among its cargo 75,000 pounds of fresh meat, 35,000 fresh eggs, 20,000 bottles of beer, 1,500 bottles of wine, and 40 tons of potatoes.

Divide your class into teams, and challenge them to uncover more interesting bits of information about the *Titanic*. Have the teams share their research with the class.

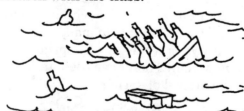

Complaints, complaints

To mark National Griper's Day, ask your students to look up the definition of "gripe," then make a list of 5 to 10 things that irritate them. Challenge the kids to fix at least one of these things.

APRIL 16
activities

📖 Illustrated verse

Garth Williams illustrated several stories by Margaret Wise Brown. In *Wait Till the Moon Is Full*, Brown writes about a little raccoon who asks a lot of questions about the dark. His mother makes him wait until the moon is full to find the answers. Have your students brainstorm for things they see at night—babies being bathed, airplane lights in the sky, families watching television, and so on. Share the poem below with your students, then have them turn their nighttime images into verse. Of course, invite the children to illustrate their poems.

> *When the moon is full*
> *I hear geese*
> *Cry ow ow*
> *Like a hurt child.*
> *I see deer eyes*
> *Shine like*
> *Candles.*

🌼 Penny-pinchers

The residents of Fort Madison, Iowa, housed their 1,238,306 pennies in the high school gymnasium. To give your students a sense of Fort Madison's accomplishment, cover a dollar bill with 100 pennies. Then ask the kids to estimate how many dollar bills would be needed to cover a desk top. Next, trace a dollar bill on drawing paper and have your students cut out enough to cover one desk top. (A 24×18-inch desk would require 26 dollars.) Now, ask your students to calculate how many desk tops could be covered by $12,383.06. How many classrooms' worth would that be?

BIRTHDAYS

1867 • **WILBUR WRIGHT**, American inventor and aviator

1889 • **CHARLIE CHAPLIN**, English silent film star and comedian

1912 • **GARTH WILLIAMS**, children's 📖 book illustrator

1922 • **JOHN CHRISTOPHER**, children's author

1947 • **KAREEM ABDUL-JABBAR**, basketball center who set the NBA career scoring record

EVENTS

1789 • **PRESIDENT-ELECT GEORGE WASHINGTON left Mount Vernon** for New York City for his inauguration.

1862 • **CONGRESS ABOLISHED SLAVERY** in the District of Columbia.

1926 • **THE BOOK-OF-THE-MONTH CLUB** was founded in New York City.

1940 • Bob Feller of the Cleveland Indians pitched an **OPENING-DAY NO-HITTER** against the White Sox in Chicago.

1972 • **CHINESE GIANT PANDAS** arrived at the U.S. National Zoo.

1988 • Residents of Fort Madison, 🌼 Iowa, **RAISED $12,383.06 IN PENNIES** for a playground.

APRIL 17
activities

BIRTHDAYS
1961 • **BOOMER ESIASON, professional football quarterback**

SHERLOCK HEMLOCK, "Sesame Street" character

EVENTS
1492 • **King Ferdinand of Spain AGREED TO FINANCE CHRISTOPHER COLUMBUS'S VOYAGE seeking a westerly route to the Orient.**

1524 • **Giovanni Verrazano, a Florentine navigator, discovered NEW YORK BAY.**

1629 • **THE FIRST COMMERCIAL FISHERY was established.**

1704 • **THE FIRST SUCCESSFUL NEWSPAPER in America, *The News-Letter*, was published in Boston by John Campbell.**

1953 • **Yankee slugger Mickey Mantle hit a 565-FOOT HOME RUN, the longest ever measured.**

1964 • **Jerrie Mock of Columbus, Ohio, became the FIRST WOMAN TO COMPLETE A SOLO FLIGHT around the world.**

1982 • **Queen Elizabeth II GAVE CANADA THE RIGHT TO AMEND ITS CONSTITUTION, thus severing its last legislative link with Britain.**

ALP AUFZUG (Switzerland) PROFESSIONAL SECRETARIES WEEK (third or fourth week in April)

17

Setting sail with Columbus
Tell your students that Christopher Columbus made four voyages to the New World. Then divide the class into four teams, and have each team research one of the voyages. Have the kids label on a world map the places Columbus traveled and list two important facts about each of his trips.

Fish for dinner?
Survey your students to find out how many of them eat fish regularly. Make a class chart listing "fish favorites," then have students determine the percentage of kids in their class who like the different kinds of fish listed.

World travelers
Jerrie Mock traveled nearly 23,000 miles during her around-the-world flight. Ask your students to imagine that they could fly around the world. Then, using a world map, have them each chart an imaginary flight plan, including stopovers in at least five cities. The kids should note the countries and continents where their stopover cities are located.

Professional Secretaries Week

Saying thanks to school secretaries
During Professional Secretaries Week, invite your class to design a banner honoring the school secretary.

APRIL 18
activities

Ride of a lifetime
Paul Revere's patriotic action was commemorated by Henry Wadsworth Longfellow in the poem "The Midnight Ride of Paul Revere." Read this poem aloud to your students. What images are most vivid to them?

Natural disasters
The earthquake that left more than 250,000 San Franciscans homeless began at 5:12 a.m. on this date in 1906. In 1989, San Francisco was again hit by a destructive quake. Have your students work in teams to investigate other major earthquakes. Tell them to use pushpins to mark the locations of these quakes on a large wall map of the world. Are the major quakes clustered in certain areas? Have the kids try to find out why.

Strikeout stars
Tom Seaver went on to strike out 640 more batters after achieving his 3,000-strikeout milestone in 1981. He retired in 1986. Ask your students to figure out how many strikeouts Seaver averaged per year over his 20-year career. Tell the kids that through the 1992 season, Nolan Ryan, baseball's all-time strikeout leader, had fanned 5,668 batters over the course of a 26-year career. How many strikeouts had Ryan averaged per year?

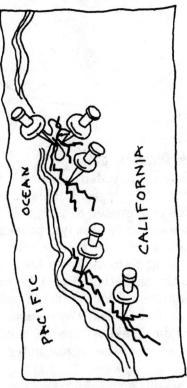

BIRTHDAYS
1857 • CLARENCE DARROW, American lawyer
1962 • WILBUR MARSHALL, professional football player

EVENTS
1775 • PAUL REVERE BEGAN HIS FAMOUS RIDE from Boston to Lexington, Mass., warning the colonists that the British were coming.
1818 • President James Monroe signed a bill creating the state of ILLINOIS.
1906 • A devastating EARTHQUAKE STRUCK SAN FRANCISCO, destroying 3,000 acres of the city.
1923 • YANKEE STADIUM opened in New York City.
1934 • THE FIRST LAUNDROMAT— called a "Washateria"— opened.
1946 • THE LEAGUE OF NATIONS officially went out of existence.
1981 • PITCHER TOM SEAVER struck out his 3,000th batter.
1988 • Kenya's Ibrahim Hussein became the FIRST AFRICAN TO WIN THE BOSTON MARATHON.

APRIL 19
activities

BIRTHDAYS
1721 • ROGER SHERMAN, American political leader who was the only person to sign all four of the following documents: the Continental Association of 1774, the Declaration of Independence, the Articles of Confederation, and the Constitution

1883 • RICHARD VON MISES, German mathematician

1903 • ELIOT NESS, American crime fighter

EVENTS
1739 • John Winthrop, the FIRST COLONIAL ASTRONOMER, made observations of sunspots.

1775 • THE AMERICAN REVOLUTION BEGAN with battles at Lexington and Concord, Mass.

1865 • ABRAHAM LINCOLN'S FUNERAL SERVICE was held in the Capitol.

1950 • Ham Kee Young, a 19-year-old from South Korea, became the YOUNGEST RUNNER TO WIN THE BOSTON MARATHON.

1985 • Susan Montgomery Williams of Fresno, Calif., blew the BIGGEST BUBBLE GUM BUBBLE ON RECORD. It was 22 inches in diameter.

SECHSELAUTEN (Switzerland)

Taking chances
Mathematician Richard von Mises did significant work in the area of probability. Introduce even young children to probability with this simple activity. Fill a bowl with green and red grapes the total number of which equals the number of children in your class, but include fewer of one color. Ask the children to predict their chances of getting a green (or red) grape if they pick one grape while blindfolded. Record the predictions, then blindfold each child and have him pick a grape. As the kids eat their grapes, discuss the concepts of "probability" and "hypotheses" to help them understand what their predictions involved. Encourage students to bring in their own multicolor mixes of candies or other foods so they can develop more probability games.

Diameter day
Have your students draw a circle with a 22-inch diameter, the diameter of the biggest bubble gum bubble ever recorded. To reinforce the idea of diameter, declare this "Diameter Day." Arm the kids with measuring devices (yardsticks, metersticks, tape measures) and ask them to see how many circles they can find and measure in the classroom and around the school (for example, clocks, buttons, the circles on the basketball court). Have the kids keep a list of the objects and diameters. Older students can figure out diameters of spheres such as balls and beads by measuring their circumferences. At the end of the day, make a class list of diameters—from largest to smallest. Where does the largest bubble gum bubble fit on the list?

APRIL 20
activities

✒ Looking at Lincoln

Tell your students that Daniel French first fell in love with sculpting at age 13, after building a lifelike snow sculpture of a lioness and her cub. French's parents encouraged his natural talent. And at age 23, French was chosen to create a statue commemorating the Revolutionary War battle at Concord, Mass. That statue, *The Minuteman,* brought French immediate renown. At age 72, French crafted one of his most famous works, the stately, seated *Abraham Lincoln.* Share photographs of the Lincoln Memorial statue with your students, and invite kids who've visited the memorial to describe it to the class. Which design elements make Lincoln seem powerful and majestic? Does Lincoln also seem tranquil? Have students write letters to Lincoln asking him specific questions about his life. Collect the letters, then distribute them randomly among your students. Finally, have the kids conduct research to answer one another's questions—and letters.

🏴 Recycling awareness

Conduct a class survey about recycling. How many of your students' families recycle newspapers, plastic, glass, tin, or aluminum? Graph the results.

※ A lifesaving lesson

Teacher Alice Meyer relied on her childhood experience reviving farm animals to save a puppy that had nearly suffocated. Discuss proper care of pets with your students, then have them develop a list of dos and don'ts.

BIRTHDAYS
1850 • **DANIEL CHESTER FRENCH,** American sculptor whose work includes the statue of Abraham Lincoln at the Lincoln Memorial
1889 • **ADOLF HITLER,** Nazi dictator of Germany
1893 • **JOAN MIRO,** Spanish surrealist painter
1962 • **DON MATTINGLY,** professional baseball player

EVENTS
1832 • **THE HOT SPRINGS NATIONAL RESERVATION,** in Hot Springs, Ark., became the first area set aside for public recreation by federal action.
1836 • Congress established the **TERRITORY OF WISCONSIN.**
1902 • French scientists Marie and Pierre Curie discovered **RADIUM.**
1940 • **THE ELECTRON MICROSCOPE** was demonstrated for the first time.
1971 • The Supreme Court upheld **BUSING AS THE PRIMARY MEANS TO ACHIEVE RACIAL BALANCE** in the public schools.
1979 • Thirty-five riders pedaled the **LONGEST TRUE TANDEM BICYCLE** ever built. It was almost 67 feet long.
1987 • New Jersey became the third state (after Rhode Island and Oregon) to pass a **STATEWIDE RECYCLING LAW.**
1988 • Teacher Alice Meyer performed **MOUTH-TO-MOUTH RESUSCITATION ON A PUPPY** that had been stuffed into a student's book bag.

CUCKOO DAY (Europe)
PARO TSECHU (Bhutan)

20

APRIL 21
activities

BIRTHDAYS
1782 • FRIEDRICH FROEBEL, German educator and founder of the first kindergarten
1816 • CHARLOTTE BRONTE, English novelist
1838 • JOHN MUIR, American naturalist
1926 • QUEEN ELIZABETH II, British monarch

EVENTS
753 B.C. • According to legend, ROME was founded by Romulus and Remus.
1789 • John Adams was sworn in as the FIRST U.S. VICE PRESIDENT.
1790 • Twenty-thousand people—the largest public gathering America had seen—attended BENJAMIN FRANKLIN'S FUNERAL in Philadelphia.
1843 • HOGS were prohibited from running wild in Chicago.
1898 • THE SPANISH-AMERICAN WAR began.
   • Billy Duggleby became the only major league baseball player to HIT A GRAND SLAM HOME RUN HIS FIRST TIME AT BAT.
1908 • According to Dr. Frederick Cook, he reached the NORTH POLE on this date.
1959 • Alf Dean caught a 2,664-pound GREAT WHITE SHARK.
1977 • The musical Annie opened on Broadway.

KARTINI DAY (Indonesia)
KINDERGARTEN DAY

21

✐ Environmental pioneer
At the age of 28, John Muir was blinded in a factory accident. He vowed to devote himself to nature if he ever recovered his sight. Weeks later his sight returned, and Muir spent the rest of his life keeping his promise. He hiked thousands of miles across the United States and kept detailed drawings and journal accounts of his observations. Believing that human greed was destroying the environment, he wrote articles and gave speeches encouraging the government to establish national parks. Ask your students what they think Muir meant when he said, "The clearest way into the universe is through a forest wilderness."

⁂ Disputed discovery
Although Frederick Cook kept a journal purportedly proving he'd discovered the North Pole, another man has been given credit for the discovery. Challenge your students to find out who that man was.

⚗ A real whopper
The great white shark is known as a man-eater. Ask your students to find out more about sharks. What other kinds of sharks prey on humans? Where are these sharks mostly found? How do they compare in size with the great white?

✑ In the children's garden
To celebrate Kindergarten Day, have your students create a list of favorite toys and games, activities, foods, routines, and events they enjoyed in kindergarten. Then have the kids interview children currently attending kindergarten and make a list of *their* favorite activities. Finally, ask your students to compare the two lists.

APRIL 22
activities

✒ Important treaties

After discussing the treaty to rescue astronauts, talk about treaties and their significance in history. Then ask each student to research an important treaty and report to the class. As each treaty is discussed, note its place in history on a class time line.

🐊 Going green

The first Earth Day was celebrated on April 22, 1970, with the motto "Give Earth a Chance." Observances focused on the need to reclaim the purity of the air, water, and living environment. Take a walking trip around your school neighborhood and ask the children to look for ways in which homeowners, businesses, and municipal officials are supporting the environment.

Afterward, have the students create a certificate for commendable environmental practices. The certificate might read: "You have chosen to give the earth a chance, and our class commends you." Have the kids decorate the awards, then deliver them.

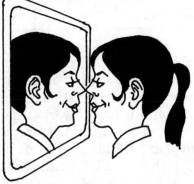

⁂ Seeing double

As homework for Look-alike Day, ask your students to stand in front of a mirror and draw a look-alike picture of themselves.

BIRTHDAYS

1451 • ISABELLA I, queen of Spain and Columbus's sponsor
1923 • HOMAS BAIRD, children's author
    • PAULA FOX, children's author

EVENTS

1500 • Pedro Alvares Cabral landed in BRAZIL, which he claimed for King Manuel I of Portugal.
1715 • The greatest ECLIPSE OF THE SUN seen in 500 years occurred.
1864 • Congress authorized the use of the motto "IN GOD WE TRUST" on U.S. coins.
1876 • THE FIRST NATIONAL LEAGUE BASEBALL GAME—between Philadelphia and Boston—took place.
1884 • Thomas Stevens began a BICYCLE TRIP AROUND THE WORLD.
1889 • OKLAHOMA was opened to homesteaders.
1968 • Forty-four countries signed a ✒ TREATY PLEDGING COOPERATION IN RESCUING ASTRONAUTS in trouble.
1970 • THE FIRST EARTH DAY was observed.
1990 • Millions of Americans celebrated the 20TH ANNIVERSARY OF EARTH DAY.

🐊 EARTH DAY
⁂ LOOK-ALIKE DAY (third Tuesday in April)

APRIL 23
activities

BIRTHDAYS
1791 • JAMES BUCHANAN, 15th president of the United States
1856 • GRANVILLE WOODS, African-American inventor who obtained 50 patents
1891 • SERGEI PROKOFIEV, Russian composer

EVENTS
1635 • Boston Latin School, the OLDEST PUBLIC SCHOOL IN THE UNITED STATES, was established.
1789 • President-elect and Mrs. George Washington moved into the FIRST PRESIDENTIAL MANSION, the Franklin House in New York.
1949 • Governor Adlai E. Stevenson of Illinois vetoed A BILL REQUIRING CATS TO BE LEASHED.
1954 • Home run king HANK AARON HIT HIS FIRST HOMER in the major leagues.
1969 • Robin Knox-Johnston completed the FIRST NONSTOP, AROUND-THE-WORLD SOLO SAILING TRIP.
1989 • KAREEM-ABDUL JABBAR, professional basketball's all-time leading scorer, played his last regular-season game.

CHILDREN'S DAY (Turkey)

Unleashing cats
In refusing to sign the bill requiring cats to be leashed, Governor Stevenson noted, "It is in the nature of cats to do a certain amount of unescorted roaming." Do your students agree? Ask them to make a class list of things pet owners can do to ensure their pets aren't a nuisance to other people.

Solitary journey
Tell your students that Robin Knox-Johnston was at sea for 312 days and covered 29,500 miles. Then ask the kids if they'd ever want to go on an adventure alone. Why or why not? Have a class discussion about being alone. What's it like? Can being alone feel good sometimes? Can it also be frightening? Ask students to imagine that they were going to duplicate Robin Knox-Johnston's journey. What kinds of skills would they need?

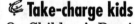

ASSISTANT   MAYOR   POLICE CHIEF

Take-charge kids
On Children's Day in Turkey, kids take over the government. Four hundred students (elected by their classmates) travel to the national capital at Ankara, where they take seats in the national government and spend the day observing and learning how it works. And all Turkish children can get free ice cream, movies, and transportation on this day. Ask your students to plan a Children's Day during which they take over your classroom. Tell them you'll be willing to entertain any *reasonable* suggestions for food, privileges, and activities.

APRIL 24
activities

▤ The nation's library

In 1800, when President John Adams signed the bill moving the nation's capital from Philadelphia to Washington, D.C., he also approved funding for a reference library for Congress. Today, the Library of Congress has more than 81 million items. One of its most precious items is a copy of the Gutenberg Bible. How many items does your school library have? Challenge students to find the most unusual or valuable item in the collection.

✐ Secret strengths

Sir Winston Churchill is noted for his outstanding military and political leadership during World War II. When Britain seemed on the verge of collapse, he rallied the nation with magnificent speeches and directed the war effort with unflagging nerve. Churchill was also a fine writer—he won the Nobel Prize in literature in 1953—the same year he was knighted by Queen Elizabeth II. As a child, Churchill had been considered a poor student. His mother felt a military career would suit him because he liked playing with toy soldiers. After taking the entrance exams for the Royal Military College three times, Churchill was finally admitted. There he excelled. His great interest in the military had sparked his hidden abilities. Ask your students if they think they have hidden abilities. Can they identify the hidden abilities in others? Have partners interview each other in an attempt to find out. Then have each child write a paragraph of praise about his partner. Post the paragraphs.

BIRTHDAYS

1822 • JAMES PIERPONT, American composer noted for "Jingle Bells"

1911 • EVALINE NESS, children's author

EVENTS

1800 • THE LIBRARY OF CONGRESS was established with a fund of $5,000.

1833 • THE SODA FOUNTAIN was patented.

1913 • The Woolworth building opened in New York City. At 792 feet, it was THE TALLEST BUILDING IN THE WORLD.

1951 • The Soviet Union applied to PARTICIPATE IN THE OLYMPIC GAMES for the first time since 1912.

1953 • WINSTON CHURCHILL WAS KNIGHTED by Queen Elizabeth II.

1956 • Willard Cravens caught a 360-pound, 9-foot-long white sturgeon in Idaho's Snake River. It was the LARGEST FRESHWATER FISH EVER CAUGHT WITH ROD AND REEL.

1967 • SOVIET COSMONAUT VLADIMIR KOMAROV WAS KILLED when the parachute straps of his spacecraft got tangled during a landing attempt.

CHILDREN'S DAY (Iceland)
WORLD DAY FOR LABORATORY ANIMALS

APRIL 25
activities

BIRTHDAYS

1874 • **GUGLIELMO MARCONI, Italian inventor of wireless telegraphy**

1927 • **ALVIN SCHWARTZ, children's author**

EVENTS

1507 • **The German geographer Martin Waldseemuller published the FIRST MAP OF THE NEW WORLD, which he named "America" in the mistaken belief that it had been discovered by Amerigo Vespucci.**

1719 • **The first edition of *ROBINSON CRUSOE* was published.**

1805 • **LEWIS AND CLARK reached the junction of the Missouri and Yellowstone rivers.**

1859 • **Construction began on the SUEZ CANAL.**

1901 • **New York became the FIRST STATE TO REQUIRE AUTOMOBILE LICENSE PLATES.**

1928 • **Buddy, THE FIRST SEEING EYE DOG, was presented to its blind owner.**

1945 • **Delegates from 45 nations convened in San Francisco to organize the UNITED NATIONS.**

1980 • **A MISSION TO RESCUE AMERICAN HOSTAGES being held in Iran had to be aborted because of equipment failures.**

Out for a drive

New York State charged a dollar apiece for license plates, which had to be over 3 inches high and include the owner's initials. Ask your students what they think it was like before there were driver's licenses, and people of any age could drive. For homework, have students interview older family members about their memories of their first driving experiences.

A matter of trust

It takes 3 to 5 months of training before a Seeing Eye dog is ready to serve its blind owner. Then the owner must spend another month learning signals, commands, and how to work in partnership with the dog. Have any of your students seen a Seeing Eye dog with its blind master? Ask them to describe the relationship they observed. Afterward, your students might enjoy taking a "trust walk" around the playground. Divide the class into pairs, then blindfold one member of each pair. Next, lead the pairs around swings, slides, trees, and other obstacles, cautioning the seeing students to hold onto their partners and give clear directions. After 5 minutes, have the students trade roles.

International symbols

The flag of the United Nations includes a world map surrounded by olive branches. Why is this an appropriate symbol for the U.N.? Divide the class into teams, then have each team research the flag of a different U.N. member nation. What do *these* flags symbolize?

APRIL 26
activities

Revolutionary heroine

After the British raided nearby Danbury, Conn., Sybil Ludington rode her horse through the night to muster volunteers to meet the Redcoat threat. Have your students write a story detailing a similar act of heroism with a modern-day setting.

Bird-watcher

John James Audubon used watercolors to paint wild birds of 19th-century America. His *Birds of America* contained 435 colored engravings. Challenge your students to look through a copy of this volume and find a bird that no longer exists. Then have the kids investigate why the species disappeared.

A list of laughs

Author Patricia Reilly Giff taught school for nearly 20 years before writing her first story. One of her motivations for becoming a writer was to make children laugh. Why is it important to laugh? Have your students make a class list of authors and books that make them laugh.

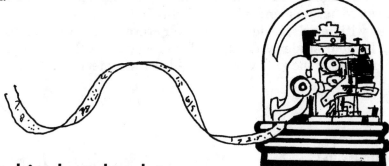

Studying the stock market

Have your students note the level at which the Dow Jones industrial average closes today. Then have them monitor it for the next 2 weeks, also following the national news closely during this period. Can they speculate on which events (if any) affected the Dow's performance?

BIRTHDAYS

1785 • **JOHN JAMES AUDUBON,** American ornithologist and artist

1900 • **CHARLES RICHTER,** American seismologist who developed a 10-point scale for measuring earthquake intensity

1935 • **PATRICIA REILLY GIFF,** children's author

EVENTS

1607 • **CAPTAIN JOHN SMITH** and 150 colonists aboard three vessels arrived at Cape Henry, Va., from Portsmouth, England.

1777 • **SYBIL LUDINGTON,** 16, rode horseback 40 miles to inform patriot militias of the British attack on Danbury, Conn.

1865 • Lincoln assassin **JOHN WILKES BOOTH** was cornered in a barn near Bowling Green, Va., and shot.

1962 • **THE FIRST INTERNATIONAL SATELLITE,** a U.S.-British venture, was launched from Cape Canaveral.

1983 • **THE DOW JONES INDUSTRIAL AVERAGE** closed above 1,200 for the first time in history.

1986 • **THE WORLD'S WORST NUCLEAR ACCIDENT** began when a reactor exploded at the Chernobyl power plant in the Soviet Union.

• Kip Grangier, age 7, became the **YOUNGEST FIRST-PRIZE WINNER AT THE WORLD CHAMPION WILDFOWL WOOD CARVING COMPETITION.**

26

APRIL 27
activities

⚾ Bidding good-bye to the Babe

To commemorate Babe Ruth's farewell to baseball, share some details about his legendary career with your students. Tell them that he:

• began his career as a pitcher
• played in 10 World Series
• set or tied 76 batting and pitching records during his career
• hit 714 home runs (a record that lasted until 1974)
• had a lifetime batting average of .342
• played in over 2,500 games.

Have teams of students use these facts and other information they research to design posters announcing Babe Ruth's last day at Yankee Stadium.

🥚 Eggs-traordinary!

The expensive egg auctioned on this day in 1977 was made by the jeweler Faberge in 1913. The egg was a gift from Czarina Alexandra of Russia to her husband, Czar Nicholas II. The egg's outside was covered with jewels; inside was a silver statue of the czar riding a horse. Do your students decorate Easter eggs? Ask the school art teacher to show the kids various egg-decorating techniques.

🎈 Spring-y lists

Sham El-Mesim, an Egyptian holiday, is also known as "Smell the Spring Day." Ask your students to list some things they can smell—as well as see, hear, taste, and touch—in the springtime.

APRIL 28
activities

✿ Cartoon characters

For this fun activity, collect five or six ink pads and place them around the room. Give each student a large sheet of white paper to be divided into six to eight squares. Then challenge the kids to each create a thumbprint cartoon strip. (Their inked thumbprint can serve as the "body" for the main character.) Be sure that students include a title square and write large enough for others to read the strip easily.

✒ Amazing adventure

Thor Heyerdahl set out to prove that prehistoric man could have navigated the ocean between the islands of the South Pacific and the Americas. He and his crew drifted for 101 days, covering some 4,300 miles. Heyerdahl described the journey in his book *Kon-Tiki*. Ask your students to imagine an adventure journey they'd like to take. Then have them write about it and create accompanying illustrations. Compile the "fantasy adventures" into a class book.

❦ Read-aloud poetry

Begin class today by reading your favorite poem aloud. Have the children draw or paint a picture reacting to the poem. It might be a representational rendition or an abstract creation, depending on the poem. Next, invite the kids to brainstorm for a list of 10 nature words (for example, rain, grass, mountain). Then have them write free-form poems on one of these topics. Have the kids take turns reading their work aloud.

BIRTHDAYS

1758 • **JAMES MONROE, fifth president** of the United States

1934 • **LOIS DUNCAN, children's author**

1950 • **JAY LENO, American comedian** and talk-show host

EVENTS

1788 • **MARYLAND became the seventh** state.

1855 • **THE FIRST VETERINARY COLLEGE** was incorporated in Boston.

1919 • **The army Model A PARACHUTE** was successfully tested at McCook Field in Dayton, Ohio.

1925 • **A WIND TUNNEL was first used,** at Langley Field, Va.

1932 • **THE FIRST YELLOW FEVER VACCINE was used.**

1937 • **AN ELECTRICAL ANIMATED CARTOON WAS FIRST DISPLAYED,** on the front of a building in Times Square.

1942 • **WARTIME COFFEE RATIONING** began in the United States.

1947 • **The Norwegian anthropologist** Thor Heyerdahl and his crew set sail from Peru on a raft named *KON-TIKI*.

1969 • **Dorothy Fields became the FIRST WOMAN ELECTED TO THE SONGWRITERS HALL OF FAME.**

❦ **GREAT POETRY READING DAY**

28

APRIL 29
activities

Jazz it up

In honor of Duke Ellington's birthday, play some of his most popular works, including "Mood Indigo" and "Sophisticated Lady." Challenge your students to use just one word to describe how Ellington's music makes them feel.

Learning about endangered species

Tell your students that the California condor is nearly extinct, in large part because of destruction of its habitat. Then have small groups research another animal listed as an endangered species (for example, the gray wolf, the humpback whale, the cheetah, the ivory-billed woodpecker). Ask the groups to find out some general information on their species as well as why it's endangered and what can be done to save it. Have the kids incorporate their findings in large posters.

The big board

Younger children will enjoy setting up a big board game on the school playground or parking lot. Select a simple game, such as checkers or Chutes and Ladders. Then use chalk or rocks to mark the boundaries, and let the students be the game pieces. Challenge another class to a game.

Here's to the losers

Many students probably remember the teams and players who've won contests, but how many can remember those who've lost? Have a class contest to see how many students recall last year's losers. For example, you might ask:

• What NBA and NCAA teams came in second place?
• What team lost the Super Bowl?
• Who came in second in the Indianapolis 500?
• Who lost the women's and men's finals at the U.S. Open tennis tournament?

Have students check their answers in a sports almanac.

APRIL 30
activities

📝 Presidential emotions

George Washington was notified of his presidential election victory by the secretary of Congress, who rode out to Mount Vernon. Ten days after the votes were counted, Washington began his journey to New York City for his inauguration. Share with your students this entry from Washington's diary: "I bid adieu to Mount Vernon, to private life, and to domestic felicity; and with a mind oppressed with more anxious and painful sensations than I have words to express, set out for New York." Discuss this quote with your class. What would Washington lose by becoming president? What would he gain? Can your students imagine what it would be like to be president today?

📺 Too much TV?

Do your students watch a lot of TV? On slips of paper, have them list the shows they usually watch each weekday. They can then add up the half hours and hours for their weekly totals. Next, create a graph showing ranges of hours spent watching TV, and have students place their names on the appropriate spots on the graph. Discuss the results. What do your students think about the amount of TV they watch? What might their parents say?

🐊 To tell the truth

Have an honest discussion with your class in honor of National Honesty Day. Ask your students what it means to be honest. Do they agree that "honesty is the best policy"?

BIRTHDAYS

1777 • **KARL FRIEDRICH GAUSS,** German mathematician and scientist

1933 • **WILLIE NELSON, American country singer**

1961 • **ISAIAH THOMAS, basketball star**

EVENTS

1789 • **GEORGE WASHINGTON WAS INAUGURATED as the first president of the United States.**

1798 • Congress established the **NAVY DEPARTMENT.**

1803 • **THE UNITED STATES PURCHASED THE LOUISIANA TERRITORY** from France for $15 million, about 4¢ an acre.

1812 • **LOUISIANA** became the 18th state.

1904 • **HAMBURGERS WERE INTRODUCED** at the Louisiana Purchase Exposition.

1939 • **REGULAR TV BROADCASTING BEGAN** with a live show about the opening of the World's Fair in New York.

1961 • Willie Mays hit **FOUR HOME RUNS IN A SINGLE BASEBALL GAME.**

1985 • Richard Bass became the **OLDEST PERSON TO REACH THE SUMMIT OF MT. EVEREST.** He was 55 years and 130 days old.

1986 • Ashrita Furman, age 31, did **8,341 SOMERSAULTS** in 10 hours and 40 minutes.

🐊 **NATIONAL HONESTY DAY**

30

MAY

☆ Project of the Month: Intergenerational Connections

To celebrate Older Americans Month, contact local nursing homes, senior citizens' centers, religious groups, or your students' own grandparents to find older Americans who'd like to spend time with your class. Then try some of these activities during the month:

• Each week, invite an older American to class to be interviewed about life 50-plus years ago. Have each student write questions for the interviews, then choose one or two children to ask the questions the day of the interview. Be sure to allow extra time for spontaneous questions. After each interview, students can write an article for the class or school newsletter.

• Have students create an "About Our Class" booklet to share with seniors from a local community organization. The booklet can include photos or drawings of each child with one-paragraph autobiographies, as well as a description of daily classroom activities.

• Hold a classroom open house for local seniors, giving them a chance to share their talents and hobbies with your students.

• Invite students' grandparents to class to read aloud their favorite childhood stories.

At the end of the month, make a class list of ways that students are similar to and different from the seniors they've gotten to meet. Then invite them to write stories about what they think life will be like when they, too, become older Americans.

MONTHLONG OBSERVANCES

American Bike Month
Asian-American Heritage Month
Better Sleep Month
National Barbecue Month
National Egg Month
Older Americans Month

WEEKLONG EVENTS

International Music Week
  (first week)
National Letter Writing Week
  (first week)
National Nurses Week (first week)
National Pet Week (first week)
Asian American Week
  (first full week)
Be Kind to Animals Week
  (first full week)
National Family Week
  (first full week)
National Postcard Week
  (first full week)
Teacher Appreciation Week
  (first full week)
Metric Week (second week)
National Be Silly Week
  (second or third week)
Police Week (week including May 15)
National Transportation Week
  (week including the third Friday)
National Science Week (third week)
All-American Buckle-Up Week
  (third full week)
Clean Air Week (last full week)

SPECIAL DAYS AND CELEBRATIONS

Kentucky Derby Day (first Saturday)
Mother's Day (second Sunday)
Native American Day (second Saturday)
Memorial Day (last Monday)

MAY 1
activities

✏️ High risers
Tell your students that when the 102-story, 1,250-foot-tall Empire State Building opened, its closest rival in height was New York's 77-story Chrysler Building, which was 1,046 feet tall. Have your students calculate, as a percentage, how much taller the Empire State Building is in feet and in number of stories.

🐊 Legal eagles
Law Day was established by presidential proclamation in 1958. Ask your students what they think a law is. Then have them list five laws, school rules, or home rules they follow every day. How do these laws and rules protect them? Tell your students that an Illinois congressman once asked the people in his district for ideas for new laws. He got some interesting responses from schoolchildren. For instance, certain 2nd graders wanted to outlaw kissing in moving vehicles, whereas a group of 3rd graders suggested closing schools for 300 years. And other students wanted police officers in schools to ward off drug dealers. What new laws would your students want on the books? Why?

🦢 Mother Goose solutions
On Mother Goose Day, ask your students to help some nursery characters solve their problems. For example, how might Bo Peep find her sheep? How could Miss Muffet get rid of her spider? What could Little Boy Blue do to keep from falling asleep? How might Jill help Jack's injured head? Where are the mittens that belong to the three kittens? Have students write their solutions on goose-shaped sheets of construction paper.

BIRTHDAYS
1764 • BENJAMIN LATROBE, American architect who designed the south wing of the U.S. Capitol
1825 • GEORGE INNESS, American landscape painter
1925 • SCOTT CARPENTER, American astronaut

EVENTS
1704 • The Boston *News-Letter* published the FIRST NEWSPAPER ADVERTISEMENT IN AMERICA.
1707 • England and Scotland formally adopted THE NAME "GREAT BRITAIN" when the two kingdoms were constitutionally united.
1847 • The cornerstone was laid for the SMITHSONIAN INSTITUTION in Washington, D.C.
1931 • ✏️ THE EMPIRE STATE BUILDING in New York City opened.
1950 • Gwendolyn Brooks became the FIRST BLACK WOMAN TO BE AWARDED A PULITZER PRIZE IN POETRY.
1963 • James W. Whittaker became the FIRST AMERICAN TO REACH THE TOP OF MT. EVEREST.
1983 • More than TWO DOZEN TORNADOES HIT THE MIDWEST.

🐊 LAW DAY
LOYALTY DAY
🦢 MOTHER GOOSE DAY
SAVE THE RHINO DAY

MAY 2
activities

BIRTHDAYS
1892 • STEPHEN MEADER, children's author
1903 • BENJAMIN SPOCK, American pediatrician and author
1904 • BING CROSBY, American singer and actor

EVENTS
1853 • A CHARIOT AND OSTRICH RACE highlighted the opening of Franconi's Hippodrome in New York City.
1887 • THE FIRST KINDERGARTEN FOR THE BLIND opened.
1917 • In a baseball game between the Cincinnati Reds and the Chicago Cubs, BOTH PITCHERS HURLED NINE NO-HIT INNINGS. The Reds finally got two hits and a run in the 10th inning and won, 1-0.
1927 • ALASKA'S FLAG was adopted. It had been designed by 7th grader Benny Benson.
1936 • Sergei Prokofiev's *PETER AND THE WOLF* premiered in Moscow.
1954 • Stan Musial of the St. Louis Cardinals hit a record FIVE HOME RUNS IN A DOUBLE-HEADER.
1972 • J. EDGAR HOOVER, director of the FBI for 48 years, died at age 77.

 BACKWARDS DAY

✒ Dr. Spock's next generation
Invite students—and their parents—to evaluate Dr. Spock's contributions to their lives. Read aloud selected excerpts from one of his books. Then ask the kids to respond to Spock's ideas on a given topic. Next, have a parent or two share their feelings. Afterward, have the students develop their own guidelines for good parenting, based on their own and their siblings' experiences. Compile these guidelines into a class booklet, then send copies home for parents to critique.

▬ Flag festival
Have your students design a flag for their own state or for any other state they choose. When they've finished their designs, ask them to write two or three sentences explaining why they used certain colors and symbols. Next, have the kids compare their flags with the official state flags. Display the flags—along with the explanations—in the hallway.

✎ From end to beginning
In honor of Backwards Day, invite your students to try these activities:
• List daily classroom routines in reverse order.
• Take a backward walk outdoors or in the hallway.
• Read Shel Silverstein's poem "Backwards Billy," then create stories, poems, or cartoons featuring a character who does everything backward.
• Make a videotape of selected segments of the school day, then view the tape in reverse.
• Recite songs, poetry, or tongue twisters backward.

MAY 3
activities

✍ Women in power

Tell your students that before becoming prime minister of Israel, Golda Meir served as the first woman foreign minister. Have older students work in teams to research Meir's accomplishments in office. Afterward, ask the kids to name other women who have held—or currently hold—important leadership positions in countries around the world, then locate the countries on a map.

✿ Toll-bridge math

When the first toll bridge opened, people could cross for free but had to pay when their livestock crossed. Younger children can decide on tolls for different animals, such as pigs, cows, horses, and chickens. They can then use their invented fees to develop toll-bridge math problems. For example: How much money would Farmer Smith owe if he took three chickens, eight cows, 10 horses, and two pigs across the bridge?

⁂ Comparing areas

The Sears Tower is 1,454 feet (110 stories) high and has 4,500,000 square feet of floor space. To help older students understand area, take them to the gym, cafeteria, or playground and have them estimate, then measure, the area in square feet. Compare this with the floor space of the Sears Tower. Students studying ratio and proportion can select a familiar local landmark and draw it to scale next to the Sears Tower.

✑ Teacher talk

To mark National Teacher Appreciation Week, share with your students recollections of *your* favorite teacher. Then invite the children to write whimsical stories about what their "ideal" teacher would be like.

BIRTHDAYS

1849 • JACOB RIIS, photographer considered the first American photojournalist

1898 • GOLDA MEIR, prime minister of ✍ Israel

1934 • JAMES BROWN, American singer

EVENTS

1654 • THE FIRST TOLL BRIDGE opened ✿ over the Newbury River in Rowley, Mass.

1715 • A TOTAL ECLIPSE OF THE SUN was observed and documented.

1765 • THE FIRST U.S. MEDICAL SCHOOL was established at the University of Pennsylvania.

1904 • New York became the FIRST STATE TO PASS A SPEED LAW FOR AUTOS (suggested maximum speeds: city, 10 mph; small town, 15 mph; country, 20 mph).

1921 • West Virginia imposed the FIRST STATE SALES TAX.

1937 • Margaret Mitchell won a Pulitzer Prize for *GONE WITH THE WIND*.

1943 • ROBERT FROST won his fourth Pulitzer Prize in poetry.

1971 • NATIONAL PUBLIC RADIO began broadcasting.

1973 • Chicago's SEARS TOWER became ⁂ the world's tallest building.

INTERNATIONAL TUBA DAY ✑ NATIONAL TEACHER APPRECIATION WEEK

BIRTHDAYS

1796 • **HORACE MANN,** American educator and author considered a pioneer in the development of public education in the United States

1959 • **RANDY TRAVIS,** country singer

SUSAN, "Sesame Street" character

EVENTS

1494 • **CHRISTOPHER COLUMBUS** landed on the island of Jamaica.

1626 • The Dutch colonial administrator Peter Minuit landed on **MANHATTAN ISLAND.** He later bought the island from its Indian inhabitants for beads and trinkets worth about $24.

1776 • Rhode Island became the **FIRST AMERICAN COLONY TO DECLARE ITS INDEPENDENCE** from Great Britain.

1884 • **THE FIRST PHOTOGRAPH OF A LIGHTNING FLASH** was taken.

1897 • J. H. Smith patented the **LAWN SPRINKLER.**

1927 • **THE ACADEMY OF MOTION PICTURE ARTS AND SCIENCES,** which annually awards Oscars, was formed.

1975 • **MAJOR LEAGUE BASEBALL'S MILLIONTH RUN** was scored by Bob Watson of the Houston Astros.

1989 • *MAGELLAN,* a U.S. space probe destined for Venus, was launched from the space shuttle *Atlantis.*

CHILDREN'S DAY (China)
NATIONAL WEATHER OBSERVER'S DAY
THANK YOUR SCHOOL LIBRARIAN DAY

MAY 4
activities

⚗ Lightning lookout

Tell your students that lightning is a visible flash of electrical charges between two clouds or between clouds and the ground. There are several different forms of lightning. Forked lightning branches out like the forks of a tree limb. Streak lightning is a single line. Ribbon lightning consists of two or more parallel streaks. Beaded lightning appears as a broken line. A special kind of ball lightning, called St. Elmo's fire, looks like a ball and is seen near airplanes and ships. Discuss the dangers of lightning. Then have your students each prepare a poster that depicts a type of lightning and includes a safety rule beneath the illustration.

✎ A book of thanks

Invite your students to write notes of appreciation to the school librarian, then compile the notes into a class booklet for presentation.

MAY 5
activities

✏ Mile math

On the anniversary of the first sub-4-minute mile by an American runner, give your students this math problem to do in their heads: What is the average speed (in mph) of a runner who finishes a mile in 4 minutes?

✤ Helpful letters

In honor of National Letter Writing Week, have your students write letters to next year's class describing the learning experiences that await and providing some helpful hints for success.

ℰ Patriotic celebrations

Tell your students that Cinco de Mayo (the fifth of May) honors the Mexican military victory over French troops at the town of Puebla, Mexico, in 1862. The Mexicans, commanded by Ignacio Zaragoza, were outnumbered three to one. May 5 is a national holiday in Mexico, and people of Mexican descent everywhere celebrate the victory with bands, fireworks, and reenactments of the battle. Have students compare the origin of this patriotic celebration with that of Bastille Day (France) and Independence Day (United States).

BIRTHDAYS
1818 • KARL MARX, German political philosopher who laid the theoretical foundations of modern communism
1867 • NELLIE BLY (real name: Elizabeth Cochrane), American journalist
1910 • LEO LIONNI, children's book author and illustrator

EVENTS
1809 • Mary Kies of Connecticut became the FIRST WOMAN TO RECEIVE A PATENT IN THE UNITED STATES, for a process for weaving silk and straw.
1847 • THE AMERICAN MEDICAL ASSOCIATION was formed in Philadelphia.
1904 • Cy Young of the Boston Americans pitched MAJOR LEAGUE BASEBALL'S FIRST PERFECT GAME.
1925 • John T. Scopes, a biology teacher in Dayton, Tenn., was ARRESTED FOR TEACHING THE THEORY OF EVOLUTION.
1956 • Jim Bailey became the FIRST ✏ AMERICAN RUNNER TO RUN A MILE IN UNDER 4 MINUTES.
1961 • Alan B. Shepard became the FIRST AMERICAN IN SPACE.

CHILDREN'S DAY (Japan and Korea)
ℰ CINCO DE MAYO (Mexico)
✤ NATIONAL LETTER WRITING WEEK (first week)

MAY 6
activities

BIRTHDAYS

1856 • **ROBERT EDWIN PEARY,** American Arctic explorer credited with being the first person to reach the North Pole

• **SIGMUND FREUD,** Austrian neurologist and founder of psychoanalysis

1931 • **WILLIE MAYS,** American baseball superstar

1948 • **SHASTA THE LIGER** (half lion, half tiger)

EVENTS

1840 • **"Penny Blacks"—THE FIRST ADHESIVE POSTAGE STAMPS—** went on sale in England.

1889 • The **EIFFEL TOWER** in Paris was completed.

1915 • **BABE RUTH** hit his first home run.

1933 • Richard Hollingshead was issued a patent for an **OUTDOOR DRIVE-IN MOVIE THEATER.**

1937 • **THE AIRSHIP *HINDENBURG* EXPLODED** at Lakehurst, N.J.

1954 • Roger Bannister of England became the **FIRST PERSON TO RUN THE MILE IN LESS THAN 4 MINUTES.** His official time was 3:59.4.

1960 • President Dwight Eisenhower signed the **CIVIL RIGHTS ACT,** aimed at making voter registration fair.

1976 • An earthquake measuring up to 8.9 **ON THE RICHTER SCALE** devastated towns in northeastern Italy.

🌐 **TINJAUA** (Romania)

🔆 At the movies

In celebration of Richard Hollingshead's patent for an outdoor drive-in movie theater, help your students hold their own one-night outdoor movie festival in the school parking lot or playground. Divide the class into groups, and assign each group a task—for example, making posters to advertise the event, choosing the movies, designing tickets, preparing refreshments, operating the projector and sound system, selecting a charity to receive the proceeds. The kids could also make souvenir programs with background information on the original "Automobile Movie Theatre" created by Hollingshead in Camden, N.J.

Rhions and ligers and zears, oh my!

On the anniversary of the birth of Shasta the liger, ask younger students to combine two animals and name and draw the result. How about a rhinoceros and a lion, a zebra and a bear, or a giraffe and an elephant?

🌐 Planting festival

Tell your students that Tinjaua is an ancient planting festival held in villages throughout Maramures, a mountainous area in northern Romania. Village elders select one farmer to be the first to plow the fields. The farmer then sits on a plow covered with flowers and is paraded through the village. Ask your students to make miniature plows from toothpicks or craft sticks and to decorate them with real or paper flowers. They can then present these plows to farmers or gardeners they know.

MAY 7
activities

Special symphony

Do your students know what's unusual about Beethoven's Ninth Symphony? It ends with lyrics. Beethoven was the first major composer to write a symphony that included lyrics. The words he selected for the finale were taken from Johann von Schiller's poem "Ode to Joy." Beethoven had always loved the poem and had long thought of setting it to music. Tell your students that Beethoven "heard" his Ninth Symphony only in his head, because he was completely deaf when he composed it. Play part of the symphony for your class, and ask your students for their reactions.

Award-winning artwork

Tell your students that Noony Hogrogian received the Caldecott Medal in recognition of her outstanding illustrations for the picture book *Always Room for One More,* which was written by Sorche Nic Leodhas. Then challenge the children to find a favorite picture book and create a new illustration or cover for it. Next, tell them that they've each been awarded the Caldecott Medal for their creations, and have them write speeches accepting their awards. Finally, ask the kids to show their artwork and read their speeches to small groups of classmates.

Peak performance

Challenge your students to name the highest mountain on each continent. If they get stumped, have them check an atlas or almanac. Then have volunteers point out the mountains' locations on a wall map.

BIRTHDAYS

1774 • **SIR FRANCIS BEAUFORT, British naval officer who developed a scale to measure wind force**

1812 • **ROBERT BROWNING, English poet**

1833 • **JOHANNES BRAHMS, German composer**

1840 • **PETER ILICH TCHAIKOVSKY, Russian composer**

1909 • **EDWIN H. LAND, American inventor**

1932 • **NOONY HOGROGIAN, children's author and illustrator**

EVENTS

1789 • **THE FIRST PRESIDENTIAL INAUGURAL BALL was held in honor of George Washington.**

1824 • **BEETHOVEN'S NINTH SYMPHONY was performed for the first time.**

1915 • **The British liner *LUSITANIA* was attacked and sunk by a German submarine.**

1934 • **Fishermen removed a 14-POUND PEARL from a giant clam in the Philippines.**

1962 • **THE TELSTAR COMMUNICATIONS SATELLITE was launched.**

1986 • **Patrick Morrow became the FIRST PERSON TO CLIMB THE HIGHEST MOUNTAIN on each of the seven continents.**

MAY 8
activities

BIRTHDAYS

1753 • MIGUEL HIDALGO, Mexican priest known as "the Father of Mexican Independence"

1884 • HARRY S. TRUMAN, 33rd president of the United States

EVENTS

1541 • The Spanish explorer HERNANDO DE SOTO sighted the Mississippi River.

1864 • The Geneva Convention established the INTERNATIONAL COMMITTEE OF THE RED CROSS.

1877 • THE FIRST DOG SHOW was held at the Hippodrome in New York.

1879 • George Selden filed for the FIRST PATENT FOR AN AUTOMOBILE.

1886 • COCA-COLA WAS SOLD for the first time.

1915 • Regret became the FIRST FILLY TO WIN A KENTUCKY DERBY.

1945 • The Allies celebrated V-E DAY (Victory in Europe Day) as Germany surrendered.

1961 • THE FIRST SEAWATER CONVERSION PLANT opened.

1978 • Reinhold Messner completed the FIRST ASCENT OF MT. EVEREST WITH NO SUPPLEMENTAL OXYGEN.

⚙ FESTIVAL OF CATS (Belgium; second Sunday in May)

🐱 MOTHER'S DAY (second Sunday in May)

NO SOCKS DAY

STORK DAY (Denmark)

8

⚙ Fizzy science

Explain to your students that the fizz in Coca-Cola and other soft drinks results when carbon dioxide is released and forms bubbles (the gas is put into the liquid ahead of time). Then let the children make their own soft drinks by stirring 1 teaspoon of baking soda into a glass of lemonade or fruit juice.

🐱 Cat parade

Since 1938, Belgians have celebrated the Festival of Cats by dressing up as cats and marching in a parade. Have your students name well-known cats from literature—for example, the Cheshire cat, Puss in Boots, and the three little kittens. Encourage them to read the stories or poems involving these famous felines. Then invite students to dress up as their favorite cat for a classroom parade.

🐱 Honors for moms

Mother's Day was started by a Philadelphian named Anna Jarvis. After the death of her mother in 1905, Jarvis wanted to find a way to honor not only her own mother, but all mothers everywhere. Ask your students to think of other ways mothers could be honored. Encourage them to use the ideas to honor their mothers.

MAY 9
activities

🐾 Ducklings in distress

To rescue the trapped ducklings, four fire fighters removed the heavy sewer grate, then one of them climbed down and got the 14 babies. Have older students each find the name of another animal's babies, such as the oyster (spat), swan (cygnet), turkey (poult), eel (elver), pigeon (squab), or kangaroo (joey). Then let the kids try to stump their teacher: They tell you the name of the offspring, and you try to identify the parent. Younger children might enjoy reading *Make Way For Ducklings* by Robert McCloskey.

⚗ No-mess dessert

Tell your students that the 6th graders who invented a dripless ice cream cone created their own recipe and made a traditional cone topped with a saucer-sized rim. (They used confectioners' sugar to seal the seams.) Challenge your students to think of ways to improve a commonly used item.

⚞ Windmill wizards

To celebrate Holland's Windmill Day, ask older students what windmills are used for (to pump water and drive machinery). Then challenge teams of students to create working miniature windmills using any or all of the following materials: milk cartons (for the base), pencils or drinking straws (for the shaft), string (to attach to the shaft), cardboard, paper, craft sticks, toothpicks, fabric scraps, paper clips, push-pins or thumbtacks, and glue. Tell the teams that their wind-mills will have to be able to lift a paper clip. Test the finished wind-mills outdoors if it's windy enough or indoors with your stu-dents' lungs providing the wind. Which designs were most effec-tive in lifting the paper clip? Why?

BIRTHDAYS

1800 • JOHN BROWN, American aboli-tionist
1860 • SIR J.M. BARRIE, Scottish novel-ist and creator of Peter Pan
1873 • HOWARD CARTER, English Egyptologist who discovered the tomb of King Tutankhamen
1916 • WILLIAM PENE DU BOIS, chil-dren's author

EVENTS

1502 • CHRISTOPHER COLUMBUS began his fourth and final voy-age to the New World.
1754 • THE FIRST POLITICAL CARTOON PUBLISHED IN AN AMERICAN NEWSPAPER, titled "Join or Die," appeared in Benjamin Franklin's *Pennsylvania Gazette*.
1899 • John Burr of Agawam, Mass., patented the LAWN MOWER.
1927 • Days before Charles Lindbergh's historic transatlantic flight, two French airmen, Charles Nungesser and Francois Coli, DISAPPEARED DURING AN ATTEMPTED TRANSATLANTIC FLIGHT from France to New York.
1988 • Fire fighters in Warren, Mich.,
🐾 RESCUED 14 DUCKLINGS TRAPPED IN A SEWER.
1990 • A group of 6th graders won an
⚗ invention contest with a NO-DRIP ICE CREAM CONE.

⚞ WINDMILL DAY (Holland)

MAY 10
activities

BIRTHDAYS

1775 • **ROBERT GRAY, American sea captain who was the first seaman to carry the flag of the new United States around the world**

EVENTS

1620 • 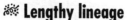 **MARY HONEYWOOD of Kent, England, died at the age of 93. She had 16 children, 114 grandchildren, 228 great-grandchildren, and 9 great-great-grandchildren.**

1869 • **THE FIRST TRANSCONTINENTAL RAILROAD was completed as a golden spike connecting the Union Pacific and the Central Pacific railroads was driven at Promontory, Utah.**

1872 • **Victoria Woodhull became the FIRST FEMALE PRESIDENTIAL CANDIDATE, receiving the nomination of the National Radical Reformers.**

1876 • **THE CENTENNIAL EXPOSITION opened in Philadelphia. Nine million visitors attended, each paying 50¢ admission.**

1924 • **J. Edgar Hoover was named the FIRST DIRECTOR OF THE FBI.**

1930 • **Chicago's Adler Planetarium became the FIRST PLANETARIUM IN THE UNITED STATES.**

1981 • **Francois Mitterrand was elected**

Lengthy lineage

In honor of Mary Honeywood of Kent—who had so many descendants—have your students visit a local senior citizens' center and offer to create family trees for the members. Or have the kids each do a family tree for an older member of their own family or for a royal, political, or fictional family.

Railroad connections

Tell your students that during the Civil War, two construction companies were chartered to complete a transcontinental railway. One track headed east from Sacramento, Calif., while the other headed west from Omaha, Neb. When the tracks met, a golden spike was hammered into place. Telegraphs clicked a short message from coast to coast: "Done." Have your students locate Omaha and Sacramento on a map and use the map scale to estimate the distance between them.

Women's rights

Help your students explore the evolution of the women's rights movement. To begin, have them write down questions they'd want to ask Victoria Woodhull about the status of the women's movement in 1872. Then have the kids work in groups to research her life. Next, ask one child to portray Victoria Woodhull while other students portray contemporary women's rights leaders. Hold a forum in which these leaders react to contemporary women's issues.

MAY 11
activities

America's songwriter

Irving Berlin wrote more than 1,500 songs during his distinguished career. He also wrote the scores for 16 Broadway shows. These achievements are especially astounding in light of the fact that Berlin never received any formal musical training and couldn't read or write musical notation. He needed special pianos and musical secretaries to transcribe his ideas into notes on a scale. Though he was born in Russia, he became one of America's most popular songwriters with such quintessentially American songs as "God Bless America," "White Christmas," "Alexander's Ragtime Band," "Easter Parade," and "There's No Business Like Show Business." Play some of Berlin's music for your students. Then play some songs by composer Jerome Kern, one of his contemporaries. In what ways is their music similar? In what ways does it differ?

Master of the surreal

Salvador Dali was born in the town of Figueras, Spain, near Barcelona. Have students locate his birthplace on a world map. Then tell them that Dali's artistic talents emerged early: Before turning 10, he'd painted two outstanding works. Dali is best remembered, though, for his contributions to the surrealist movement. In an attempt to express a different reality, surrealist painters juxtaposed and combined images that normally wouldn't go together. Share photographs of Dali's work with your class. Point out the meticulous detail and sharp clarity of the paintings. Then challenge the kids to create a surrealistic drawing or painting of their own.

BIRTHDAYS

1888 • IRVING BERLIN, American composer
1894 • MARTHA GRAHAM, American modern dancer
1904 • SALVADOR DALI, Spanish artist

EVENTS

1858 • MINNESOTA became the 32nd state.
1911 • GLACIER NATIONAL PARK in northwestern Montana was created.
1949 • ISRAEL became a member of the United Nations.
1950 • President Harry Truman dedicated the GRAND COULEE DAM in Washington State.
1986 • Fred Markham set a WORLD SPEED RECORD FOR A HUMAN-POWERED VEHICLE. He pedaled a streamlined, enclosed bicycle 65.484 mph.

MAY 12
activities

Lots of limericks

Tell your students that Edward Lear has been called "the poet laure-ate of the limerick." Read aloud several limericks from his *Book of Nonsense,* and invite the children to illustrate them. Next, go over the meter and rhyme scheme of limericks. Then have the kids work in groups to write and illustrate silly limericks of their own. Compile their work into a class limerick book. The groups can go on to illus-trate their favorite limericks on posterboard for display in the library.

Nursing then and now

In honor of Florence Nightingale's birthday—and to commemorate International Nurses Day—invite nurses from a local hospital to visit your class. Students can conduct background research about Nightingale's public service, then prepare interview questions about the impact of her ideas on today's nurses.

Food fantasies

For Eat What You Want Day, have your students create fantasy recipes and menus. Younger children might also have fun transform-ing the classroom into a restaurant to serve their fantasy meals. Have the children work in groups to develop the restaurant's name, decor, menu design, and so on. Then open the restaurant for this spe-cial day. You may want to videotape or photograph the children enjoying their food fantasies.

MAY 13
activities

✦ Jumping for joy

Commemorate Robert Commers's record-setting jump-rope feat by challenging your students to set some records of their own. You'll need jump ropes and stopwatches. Have pairs of students count the number of jumps completed by a partner in 1 minute. Can the kids figure out how many jumps they'd make in an hour at the same pace? How would that stack up against Commers's record? How many jumps did Commers average per minute?

✳ Sporty shoes

Ask your students to bring to class as many different kinds of sport shoes (tennis, running, walking, golf, bowling, football, basketball, soccer, and so on) as they can. Then have them identify the special features each kind of shoe has to enhance an athlete's performance in the particular sport.

✐ Bike tales

Young children will enjoy rolling into American Bike Month by reading *Bicycle Race,* a picture book by Donald Crews. When they've finished the book, have a class discussion about bicycles. Have your students ever had a bicycle—or tricycle—race? Ask the kids to write a true or fictional story about their bike.

BIRTHDAYS

1914 • JOE LOUIS, American boxer who held the world heavyweight title from 1937 to 1949

1938 • NORMA KLEIN, children's author

1950 • STEVIE WONDER, American singer and songwriter

EVENTS

1607 • Jamestown, THE FIRST PERMANENT ENGLISH SETTLEMENT IN AMERICA, was established in Virginia by Captain John Smith and 105 colonists.

1918 • THE FIRST U.S. AIRMAIL POSTAGE STAMPS were issued.

1942 • THE FIRST CROSS-COUNTRY HELICOPTER flight began in Stratford, Conn.

1980 • Henrick Doornekamp, a Dutch farmer, RAN THE NEW YORK CITY MARATHON WEARING WOODEN SHOES.

1981 • POPE JOHN PAUL II was seriously wounded by a Turkish gunman in St. Peter's Square. The pontiff later recovered from his wounds.

1989 • Robert Commers set a world record when he JUMPED ROPE 13,783 TIMES IN 1 HOUR.

✐ AMERICAN BIKE MONTH

MAY 14
activities

"THE STARS AND STRIPES FOREVER" DAY

14

Movie monsters

To celebrate the birthday of George Lucas—a master of science fiction and special effects—have your students discuss movie monsters. Begin by making a monster chart, with the headings "Past," "Present," and "Future." List the monsters your students name under the appropriate headings. (For example, the creatures in Lucas's three Star Wars movies belong under "Future.") Ask your students to bring in any action figures that represent monsters on the list. Now that your class is thinking about past, present, and future, it may be a good time to review verb tenses.

Stars and stripes parade

Younger students can "perform" John Philip Sousa's "Stars and Stripes Forever" with construction-paper instruments and flags. Have the children draw various marching band instruments on construction paper, then cut them out. Next, have them draw and color the American flag on one side of a piece of large, white construction paper. On the other side, have them glue their construction-paper instruments. Now that they've made their "instrumental flags," play a recording of Sousa's famous march and let them parade around the classroom or playground.

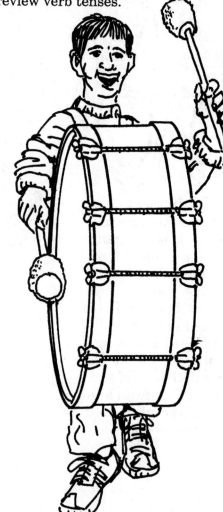

Cold war milestone

Ask your students to consult encyclopedias or other reference books to find out which eight nations originally formed the Warsaw Pact. Then have the kids locate these nations on a world map. Do all of them still exist? Have their forms of government changed since 1955? How? Do your students know which organization (NATO) the Warsaw Pact was intended to counterbalance?

MAY 15
activities

⟦⟧ Paint by numbers

Tell your students that Jasper Johns often incorporated numbers into his works. Share some photographs of Johns's paintings, including *Zero Through Nine*. How many numbers can the kids find?

✿ Friendly skies

Ellen Church, a registered nurse, was the world's first airline stewardess. She and seven other nurses were hired by United Airlines to serve food, allay passengers' fears, and help with the upkeep of the plane. Ask your students why they think nurses were hired for this job. What skills do today's flight attendants need?

◎ Hitting streak

For 56 consecutive games, New York Yankee star Joe DiMaggio managed to get one or more hits, a streak many believe will never be matched. Ask your students to estimate what percentage of the 154-game season DiMaggio's hitting streak covered. Then have them check their estimates using calculators. Whose estimate came closest?

✄ Hats off

Celebrate Straw Hat Day by asking your students to wear their favorite hats to school. Invite each child to share a story about the hat, telling where it came from, how old it is, when it's usually worn, why it's special, and so on. Students who don't have favorite hats can use paper plates to create their own, then decorate them to show their favorite sports or hobbies.

BIRTHDAYS

1856 • **L. FRANK BAUM,** children's author who wrote *The Wonderful Wizard of Oz*

1859 • **PIERRE CURIE,** French physicist and codiscoverer of the element radium

1930 • **JASPER JOHNS,** American artist ⟦⟧

EVENTS

1602 • English explorer **BARTHOLOMEW GOSNOLD** discovered Cape Cod.

1862 • **THE U.S. DEPARTMENT OF AGRICULTURE** was established.
 • **THE FIRST BASEBALL STADIUM** opened in Brooklyn, N.Y.

1930 • **THE FIRST AIRLINE STEW-**
✿ **ARDESSES** started work.

1941 • Baseball player Joe DiMaggio
◎ began his record-breaking 56-**GAME HITTING STREAK.**

1942 • **WARTIME GASOLINE RATIONING BEGAN,** with most people limited to 3 gallons a week.

1989 • The apple industry **AGREED TO STOP USING THE CHEMICAL ALAR,** a ripening and preserving agent, because of its suspected carcinogenic effects.

PEACE OFFICERS MEMORIAL DAY
POLICE MEMORIAL DAY
STRAW HAT DAY

MAY 16
activities

BIRTHDAYS

1801 • WILLIAM SEWARD, U.S. secretary of state who promoted the purchase of Alaska from Russia

1804 • ELIZABETH PALMER PEABODY, American educator and founder of the first English-speaking kindergarten in America

1928 • BETTY MILES, children's author

1955 • OLGA KORBUT, Russian gymnast

1964 • JOHN SALLEY, basketball star

EVENTS

1866 • A U.S. FIVE-CENT PIECE was authorized.

1875 • THE FIRST KENTUCKY DERBY took place.

1903 • George Wyman left San Francisco on the FIRST TRANSCONTINENTAL MOTORCYCLE TRIP.

1929 • THE FIRST ACADEMY AWARDS (Oscars) were presented.

1939 • Rochester, N.Y., introduced the FIRST FOOD STAMP PROGRAM.

1973 • THE FIRST FLIGHT OF A SOLAR-POWERED BALLOON took place.

1975 • Junko Tabei of Japan became the FIRST WOMAN TO REACH THE TOP OF MT. EVEREST.

1988 • Richard Stokes became the FIRST BLACK TO JOIN THE BUCKINGHAM PALACE GUARD.

1990 • Muppet master JIM HENSON died.

 BIOGRAPHERS DAY
NATIONAL EGG MONTH

🇺🇸 Noticing nickels

Have younger students calculate the number of years nickels have been in circulation. Then have the children collect 10 to 20 nickels. Arrange them in order from the oldest to the newest. How old is the oldest? Compare the head and tail impressions. Are they all alike? Have the children speculate about how the terms *heads* and *tails* might have originated.

🎟️ Oscar excitement

Ask your class to list eight Oscar categories, real or made up. Then divide the class into eight teams, assigning each team one of the categories. Have team members create brief written nominations in their category, then read them to the whole class. Hold a class vote to determine the winners.

🌸 Brief biographies

To mark Biographers Day—and in memory of Muppeteer Jim Henson—have your students each select a favorite Muppet character, then write a short biography of that character.

🐔 Eggs-asperating question

Ask your students: Which came first, the chicken or the egg? Tally the responses, then encourage the kids to conduct some background research. Afterward, have them each write a persuasive paragraph supporting their position.

MAY 17
activities

⚜ Discovering Jupiter

No one has ever seen the surface of Jupiter—the largest planet in the solar system—because the gases in its atmosphere shroud the planet from full view. These gases also form the bands around the planet known as belts. Jupiter is the fastest-rotating planet, completing one rotation every 10 hours. But it takes nearly 12 years to orbit the Sun. Jupiter's surface gravity is 2.65 times greater than Earth's. That means a person weighing 100 pounds on Earth would weight 265 pounds on Jupiter. Challenge your students to calculate how much they'd weigh on Jupiter.

✒ Wanted: Fearless explorers

Have students work in groups to conduct background research about Marquette and Jolliet's famous expedition. Then ask the kids to imagine that they're interviewing candidates to accompany Marquette and Jolliet on their journey. What personal qualities or special skills would be required? Have each group create a list of interview questions, then hold mock interviews to select appropriate candidates.

☙ Getting from here to there

Mark Transportation Week by taking a closer look at how we get places. Explain to your students that transportation can be as simple as walking across a room or as exotic as rocketing into space. Then challenge them to list different kinds of transportation for each of these categories: air (airplane, balloon, blimp, glider, helicopter); land (bicycle, bus, car, feet, horse, subway); water (barge, submarine, water skis); and space (rocket, space shuttle).

BIRTHDAYS

1749 • EDWARD JENNER, English physician who discovered vaccination

1929 • ELOISE GREENFIELD, children's author

1956 • SUGAR RAY LEONARD, American boxer

EVENTS

872 • THE KINGDOM OF NORWAY was founded.

1503 • Columbus discovered the CAYMAN ISLANDS.

1630 • THE BELTS OF JUPITER were first recognized.

1673 • FATHER JACQUES MARQUETTE AND LOUIS JOLLIET began exploring the Mississippi River.

1792 • THE NEW YORK STOCK EXCHANGE was founded.

1954 • In its landmark ruling in the case of Brown vs. the Board of Education of Topeka, Kan., THE SUPREME COURT DECLARED RACIAL SEGREGATION IN SCHOOLS UNCONSTITUTIONAL.

1955 • Physicists Enrico Fermi and Leo Szilard obtained a patent for the FIRST ATOMIC REACTOR.

1972 • The Boston terrier became the STATE DOG OF MASSACHUSETTS.

FUTURE NURSES' DAY
INTERNATIONAL MUSEUM DAY
NATIONAL TRANSPORTATION WEEK (week including the third Friday in May)

17

MAY 18
activities

📖 Special time alone

Lillian Hoban has illustrated numerous books written by her husband, Russell Hoban. Her love of books began during her childhood, when she spent many hours in the libraries of Philadelphia, her hometown. She called these hours "the coziest kind of private time...." Ask your students where their favorite private place is. What do they like to do best there?

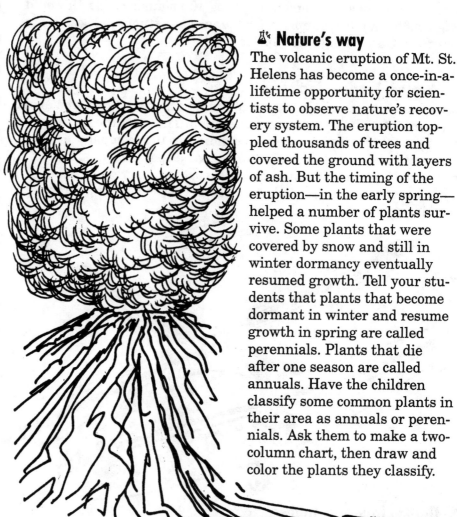

⚗ Nature's way

The volcanic eruption of Mt. St. Helens has become a once-in-a-lifetime opportunity for scientists to observe nature's recovery system. The eruption toppled thousands of trees and covered the ground with layers of ash. But the timing of the eruption—in the early spring—helped a number of plants survive. Some plants that were covered by snow and still in winter dormancy eventually resumed growth. Tell your students that plants that become dormant in winter and resume growth in spring are called perennials. Plants that die after one season are called annuals. Have the children classify some common plants in their area as annuals or perennials. Ask them to make a two-column chart, then draw and color the plants they classify.

📚 Museum day

Use the theme "My Favorite Things" for a class museum day. Ask your students to bring in one of their favorite objects, then write a descriptive paragraph about it. The kids can then create a display of the items and invite other classes to view the "exhibit."

MAY 19
activities

❋ Fingerprint sleuths

Tell your students that the FBI has the largest collection of finger-prints in the world—over 170 million are on file. There are eight basic fingerprint patterns, which are divided into loops, arches, and whorls. No two people have the same fingerprints. As people grow older, their fingerprints become larger but do not change. When fin-gerprints are taken, each finger is first covered with a thin film of ink, then gently rolled from one side to the other onto a sheet of paper. Divide the class into five groups. Give each group a sheet of white paper, one index card for each group member, and an ink pad. Have the group members each print their little finger twice, once on the white paper and once on their individual index card. Then collect each group's index cards, pick one at random, and return it to the group. Challenge the group members to match the print on the card with the right print on the group sheet. (If available, a magnifying glass would help.) What characteristics led to the identification?

⚑ Encouraging geo-literacy

More than a million students in grades 4 to 8 took part in National Geographic's First Annual National Geography Bee. Jack Staddon, of Great Bend, Kan., won first prize when he answered, "Gondwanaland." Ask your students to figure out the question. ("After the breakup of Pangaea, what supercontinent included only Africa, South America, Australia, Antarctica, and India?") Divide your class into groups of three or four, and have each group develop 10 to 15 questions—and answers—about geography. Have the groups write their questions and answers on individual 3×5-inch cards and label them with a group symbol. Then hold your own class geography bee, making sure that group members aren't asked their own questions.

BIRTHDAYS

1879 • **NANCY LANGHORNE (Lady Astor)**, American-born British political leader who became the first woman to sit in the British Parliament

1925 • **MALCOLM X**, African-American leader

1930 • **LORRAINE HANSBERRY**, play-wright whose play *A Raisin in the Sun* was the first by an African-American woman to be produced on Broadway

1939 • **FRANCIS (DICK) SCOBEE**, American astronaut and com-mander of the space shuttle *Challenger* on its final, ill-fated mission

EVENTS

1849 • In a letter to a friend, **ABRAHAM LINCOLN** wrote, "The better part of one's life consists of...friendships."

1884 • **THE FIRST RINGLING BROTHERS CIRCUS** opened in Baraboo, Wis.

1911 • Caesar Cella became the FIRST
❋ **PERSON CONVICTED OF A CRIME ON THE BASIS OF FIN-GERPRINTS.**

1965 • Patricia Roberts Harris became the **FIRST AFRICAN-AMERICAN WOMAN TO SERVE AS A U.S. AMBASSADOR.**

1989 • Jack Staddon, age 15, won the
⚑ **FIRST ANNUAL NATIONAL GEOGRAPHY BEE.**

MAY 20 activities

Everyday inventions

In honor of American inventor Emile Berliner, have a contest to tap the ingenuity of the "inventors" in your classroom. Ask your school librarian to collect books on inventors and inventions. Good prospects include *The World Almanac Book of Inventions* by Valerie-Anne Giscard d'Estaing and *Steve Caney's Invention Book*. Have the kids review the books for insights into how inventors came up with their ideas and produced their products. Then challenge students to design and name an invention that would solve an everyday problem. Award small prizes in several categories—for example, wackiest, most futuristic, most sensible.

Feat of flight

It took Charles Lindbergh 33½ hours to fly from Long Island, N.Y., to Paris, France. Have your students mark his route on a world map, then calculate the number of miles he flew. Next, have the kids find out how long it takes a commercial airliner to make a transatlantic flight today.

Weighing in

On Weights and Measures Day, use a balance scale to weigh a notebook. Record the weight on the chalkboard, then divide the class into teams. Challenge each team to find a combination of classroom objects—pencils, erasers, thumbtacks, and so on—that they think will equal the weight of the notebook. Which team can come closest? Weigh the collections to find out.

MAY 21
activities

 Observing animals

Students can celebrate the birthday of Albrecht Durer by doing their own animal observation sketches. To begin, show students examples of Durer's works, such as *The Hare*. Tell the children that Durer felt a true artist had only to observe nature carefully in order to capture it in art. Next, ask a volunteer to bring a pet to class for a week. Each day, set aside a 20-minute period during which students can sketch the pet, preferably using black crayon or pencil. Display the students' finished artwork next to a photo of the pet.

Celebrating important firsts

Tell your students that Amelia Earhart achieved a number of aviation firsts in her lifetime. Before flying solo across the Atlantic, she had been the first female passenger on a transatlantic flight. She was also the first woman to fly from Honolulu to the U.S. mainland and the first woman to receive the Distinguished Flying Cross. Have your students each name another person—family member, friend, community member, celebrity, or sports star—who achieved an important first. Then have the kids design a medallion for that person.

Safety stickers

During All-American Buckle-Up Week, have your students create buckle-up slogans and write these on plain mailing labels. With their parents' permission, the kids can display their important messages on the glove compartment or dashboard of the family car.

BIRTHDAYS
1471 • **ALBRECHT DURER, German artist**
1688 • **ALEXANDER POPE, British poet**
1878 • **GLENN CURTISS, American inventor of the seaplane**

EVENTS
1881 • Clara Barton founded the **AMERICAN RED CROSS Society.**
1927 • Charles Lindbergh landed at Le Bourget Airport in Paris, thus completing the **FIRST NONSTOP SOLO TRANSATLANTIC FLIGHT.**
1932 • Amelia Earhart became the **FIRST WOMAN TO COMPLETE A SOLO TRANSATLANTIC FLIGHT,** from Newfoundland to Ireland.
1972 • Jane Dorst of Atherton, Calif., released a **HELIUM BALLOON** with her name and address inside. It was found 200 days later in Pietermaritzburg, South Africa.
1974 • **THE FIRST NUCLEAR-POWERED LIGHTHOUSE** began operating.
1980 • *THE EMPIRE STRIKES BACK,* the sequel to *Star Wars,* opened.

• **ALL-AMERICAN BUCKLE-UP WEEK** (third full week in May)

MAY 22
activities

🎨 Impressions of family life

Impressionist artist Mary Cassatt is best known for her paintings of family life. Show students reproductions of her artwork. Then ask them to design and color updates of these pictures, using today's fashions and their own family activities.

🔍 Detectives afoot

Celebrate the birthday of Sir Arthur Conan Doyle by having teams of students conduct a weeklong search for traces of Doyle's most famous character—Sherlock Holmes—in books, newspapers, television programs, films, magazines, and so on. At the end of the week, the teams can share their evidence of Holmes's pervasive influence in daily life.

📖 Two famous friends

In honor of Arnold Lobel's birthday, read aloud a story about two of his well-known characters, Frog and Toad. Afterward, pass around the book so students can become familiar with these characters. Then encourage the children to generate questions about the lives of Frog and Toad. For example: What happened before the story began? What will happen after the story ends? Do Frog and Toad have brothers or sisters? Do they have other friends? After the children have developed a list, ask them each to select a question they'd like to answer. Then have them create stories that answer the questions. Encourage the students to role-play their stories or to write and illustrate them.

🥒 In a pickle

On International Pickle Day, tell your students that the word *pickle* can be used as a noun or a verb. Together, come up with example sentences. Then challenge the kids to list other words that can be used as either nouns or verbs.

MAY 23
activities

🧪 Plant classifications

Have your students look up the word *taxonomy* in the dictionary. Then encourage them to walk through their neighborhoods to observe flowering plants, writing careful notes and making detailed drawings of the specimens they find. Have them use these observational records and their research skills to find the scientific names of their plants.

🇺🇸 A state by any other name

South Carolina is nicknamed the Palmetto State. Have your students investigate their state's nickname. How did the nickname originate? Invite the kids to create a nickname for their hometown, then write a silly story explaining how the name came to be.

📖 Selecting pseudonyms

Margaret Wise Brown wrote stories about feeling lonesome, getting lost, and acting naughty or silly. She wrote more than 100 books in her career, some published under the pen names Golden MacDonald, Timothy Hay, and Juniper Sage. Have your students each write a story using one of the topics Brown often wrote about. Then have them choose their own pen names. Why did they select a particular name?

BIRTHDAYS

1707 • **CAROLUS LINNAEUS**, Swedish 🧪 botanist and founder of taxonomy

1734 • **DR. FRANZ MESMER**, German physician who developed a treatment called mesmerism, which is the basis of the word *mesmerize*

1824 • **AMBROSE EVERETT BURNSIDE**, American Civil War general whose whiskers on the side of his face were called Burnsides and later sideburns

1910 • **MARGARET WISE BROWN**, children's author

EVENTS

1785 • In a letter, Benjamin Franklin wrote about his new invention, **BIFOCAL EYEGLASSES.**

1788 • **SOUTH CAROLINA** became the 🇺🇸 eighth state.

1873 • Canada established the **NORTH-WEST MOUNTED POLICE.**

1903 • Eleven-year-old William Frederick Price became the **YOUNGEST SOLDIER TO ENLIST IN THE BRITISH ARMY** in this century.

1984 • C. Everett Koop, the U.S. surgeon general, said there was solid evidence that **NONSMOKERS CAN SUFFER LUNG DAMAGE FROM INHALING OTHER PEOPLE'S CIGARETTE SMOKE.**

1989 • An Italian interior designer named Stefania Follini **CLIMBED OUT OF THE CAVE IN CARLSBAD, N.M.,** in which she had spent the previous 130 days.

MAY 24
activi...

BIRTHDAYS

1816 • **EMANUEL LEUTZE**, German-born American painter

1941 • **BOB DYLAN** (real name: Robert Zimmerman), American singer and songwriter

1944 • **FRANK OZ**, puppeteer

EVENTS

1775 • **JOHN HANCOCK** was elected president of the Continental Congress.

1844 • Samuel F.B. Morse transmitted the **FIRST TELEGRAPH MESSAGE**, "What hath God wrought?"

1869 • John Wesley Powell led the **FIRST EXPEDITION DOWN THE GRAND CANYON.**

1883 • **THE BROOKLYN BRIDGE** opened. At 1,595 feet, it was the longest single-span suspension bridge in the world.

1935 • **MAJOR LEAGUE BASEBALL'S FIRST NIGHT GAME** took place in Cincinnati, with the Reds hosting the Philadelphia Phillies.

1968 • Chief, the **LAST HORSE OF THE U.S. CAVALRY**, died.

1976 • **THE CONCORDE SUPERSONIC JET** began regular 4-hour flights between Paris and Washington, D.C.

Historical painting?

Your students might not have heard of Emanuel Leutze, but many have probably seen his most famous painting, *Washington Crossing the Delaware.* The painting depicts George Washington's Christmas Eve, 1776, crossing of the Delaware River to surprise the Hessians at Trenton, N.J. Show your students a reproduction of the painting, which Leutze finished in 1850, and ask whether they think it represents a historically accurate view. For instance, is it likely that Washington would have been standing in the boat? Why not? Why then, would Leutze choose to paint him in this posture? Why aren't contemporary leaders painted in a similar fashion?

Grand Canyon travelers

Ask your students to imagine they'll be traveling to the Grand Canyon. What kinds of items (supplies, recreational materials) will they need to pack? What is the weather like this time of year? How much will the trip cost? Encourage the kids to conduct research so they can actually plan an itinerary. Perhaps they might even call travel agents for brochures and trip prices. On the day of the "trip," decorate the classroom with appropriate materials. Then show the students a film about the Grand Canyon.

Puppet plays

To mark the birthday of puppeteer Frank Oz, ask students to bring in puppets or stuffed animals from home. Divide the class into small groups, and have the groups create stories involving their puppets. Then have them present their "puppet plays" to the class. Videotape the presentations so the children can share their creativity with parents at home.

MAY 25
activities

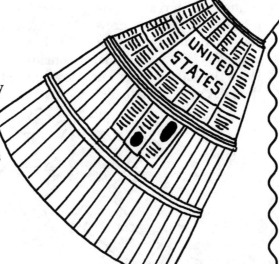Good advice

Ralph Waldo Emerson was a philosopher as well as a poet and essayist. Ask your students what they think Emerson meant when he said:

- "Write it on your heart that every day is the best day in the year."
- "Finish every day and be done with it."
- "You have done what you could."

What advice for daily living would your students give? Compile their thoughts into a class booklet.

⊘ Banner days

Tell your students that Jesse Owens had a banner day while competing in the Big 10 Championships at Ann Arbor, Mich. Between 3:15 and 4:00 p.m., he tied one world record (for the 100-yard dash) and broke five others: for the long jump, the 200-meter and 220-yard dashes, and the 200-meter and 220-yard low hurdles. (He ran only the 220-yard events, but his times were faster than the world records for the longer 200-meter distance, so he got credit for those records too.) The next time your students read a biography, ask them to find a banner day in the subject's life and report on it to the class.

▤ Calls for action

In response to President Kennedy's call for action, the United States succeeded in landing a man on the moon by the end of the 1960s. If your students were president, what would they ask the nation to do by the end of this decade? Make a list of their suggestions, then have the kids send their list (along with a class letter) to the editor of a local newspaper.

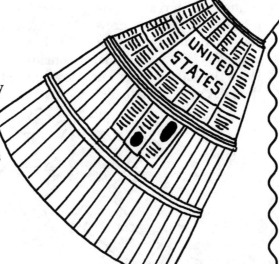

BIRTHDAYS

1803 • **RALPH WALDO EMERSON,** American poet and essayist

1878 • **BILL "BOJANGLES" ROBINSON,** American tap dancer

1920 • **MARTHA ALEXANDER,** children's author

1929 • **BEVERLY SILLS,** American opera singer

EVENTS

1539 • Francisca Hinestrosa arrived at Tampa Bay and became the **FIRST WOMAN COLONIST IN THE NEW WORLD.**

1787 • **THE FIRST REGULAR SESSION OF THE AMERICAN CONSTITUTIONAL CONVENTION** was held in Independence Hall in Philadelphia, Pa.

1935 • **JESSE OWENS BROKE FIVE WORLD RECORDS** and tied a sixth—in only 45 minutes.

1935 • **BABE RUTH** hit his 714th and final home run.

1961 • President John F. Kennedy called for the nation to **PUT A MAN ON THE MOON** by the end of the 1960s.

1976 • White Cascade, the **WORLD'S LARGEST MOBILE,** was installed at the Federal Reserve Bank in Philadelphia.

1986 • More than 5 million Americans formed a **HUMAN CHAIN ACROSS THE COUNTRY.** Proceeds from Hands Across America ($10 per person) went to the homeless.

AFRICAN LIBERATION DAY
NATIONAL MISSING CHILDREN'S DAY
NATIONAL TAP DANCE DAY

25

MAY 26
activities

BIRTHDAYS

1837 • **WASHINGTON A. ROEBLING,** American army officer and chief engineer of the Brooklyn Bridge

1886 • **AL JOLSON,** Russian-born American actor and singer

1934 • **SHEILA GREENWALD,** children's author

1951 • **SALLY RIDE,** U.S. astronaut who became the first American woman in space

EVENTS

585 B.C. • **AN ECLIPSE OF THE SUN STOPPED A BATTLE** between two warring tribes, the Lydians and the Medes, in the Middle East.

1865 • **THE LAST CONFEDERATE TROOPS SURRENDERED** at Shreveport, La.

1868 • By one vote, the U.S. Senate **ACQUITTED PRESIDENT ANDREW JOHNSON OF IMPEACHMENT CHARGES.**

1941 • **THE AMERICAN FLAG HOUSE,** Betsy Ross's home, was donated to the city of Philadelphia.

1969 • **THE** *APOLLO 10* **CREW LOGGED THE FASTEST SPEED—24,791 mph—**in the history of human travel.

1978 • **LEGALIZED CASINO GAMBLING** began in Atlantic City, N.J.

War between the states

Tell your students that the Civil War was the most destructive war in U.S. history. Both sides suffered appalling casualties, and much of the countryside was destroyed. The war caused economic disaster for the South, and relations between the North and South remained strained for more than a century. Quiz your students on what they know about this part of our nation's history. When did the war start? Who was president? What major issues were the North and South fighting over? Have the kids work in teams to prepare a chronology of events, listing three major events for each year from 1861 through 1865.

What a Ride!

Sally Ride was the first American woman in space as well as the youngest American astronaut ever to orbit the earth. Ride's many interests as she was growing up included playing team sports. Ask your students if they think shuttle astronauts need to be "team players." Why? Do your students consider themselves team players? Have the kids suggest qualities that make a team player successful, then list adjectives to describe those qualities.

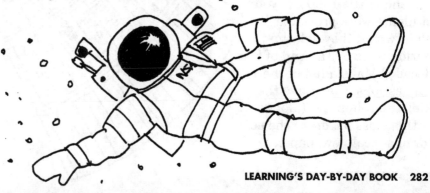

MAY 27
activities

🌐 So many names

Tell your students that in 1914, the city of St. Petersburg was renamed Petrograd. In 1924, its name was changed again—to Leningrad. Then in 1991, its original name was restored. Ask your students to locate this city on a map. Then challenge them to discover why it has had so many different names.

✿ Up, up, and away!

Your students will enjoy learning about ballooning by making models of balloons. Contact a local florist for free or inexpensive helium balloons. Then have teams of students design a gondola to carry a small object into the air. Remind the children that the more weight they conserve, the more altitude their balloon will gain. Conduct the flights inside the school, using thin sewing thread to secure the balloons to the ground.

✒ Building bridges

Tell your students that the Golden Gate Bridge took 4 years to build and cost just under $35 million. Since it opened, more than 1 billion cars have crossed it. Challenge your students to find out more about the Golden Gate Bridge, then build their own suspension bridge. Divide the class into cooperative groups, and assign each group a task—attaching the cables, building the roadway, and so on. For the bridge materials, students can use drinking straws and yarn. Straight pins or staples can hold the straws together. Craft sticks or folded construction paper can serve as the roadway. Invite parents or the principal to attend the grand opening of the bridge.

BIRTHDAYS

1818 • **AMELIA BLOOMER,** American women's rights crusader after whom "bloomers" were named

1819 • **JULIA WARD HOWE,** American reformer who wrote the words to "The Battle Hymn of the Republic"

1837 • **JAMES "WILD BILL" HICKOK,** American scout and frontier marshall

1894 • **DASHIELL HAMMETT,** American detective author

1907 • **RACHEL CARSON,** American biologist and writer

EVENTS

1703 • 🌐 Czar Peter the Great of Russia founded **ST. PETERSBURG,** which became the new capital of Russia.

1919 • Lt. Commander Albert C. Read and his five-member crew completed the **FIRST TRANSATLANTIC FLIGHT IN A NAVY SEAPLANE.**

1921 • **AFGHANISTAN** celebrated its independence from Great Britain.

1931 • ✿ Auguste Piccard became the **FIRST MAN TO REACH THE STRATOSPHERE IN A BALLOON.**

1937 • ✒ **THE GOLDEN GATE BRIDGE,** which spans San Francisco Bay, opened.

1977 • Gerhards Knoll SWAM FOR 7 HOURS AND 53 MINUTES, the longest nonstop crawl.

CHILDREN'S DAY (Nigeria)

MAY 28
activities

✐ World's greatest athlete

Jim Thorpe—best known for winning the decathlon and pentathlon at the 1912 Olympics in Stockholm—was of Native American ancestry. Tell your students that his tribal name, Wa Tho Huck, means Bright Path. From a young age, Thorpe loved and excelled at sports. After his triumphant Olympic performance, the king of Sweden called him "the greatest athlete in the world." Who do your students feel is the world's best living athlete? Have the kids write letters nominating their chosen athlete for a classroom Hall of Fame. Post the letters on a bulletin board, then hold a class vote for the top five.

Movie mania

Have your class conduct a schoolwide poll to determine students' favorite movie of all time. Encourage the children to use computers to record their data and graph the results. Were all the movies named filmed in color?

Saving the species

Invite your students to research the whooping crane and other endangered animals. Then have them use their data to create posters building awareness about animals facing extinction. Display the posters in the hallway or school library. Students can also locate information about organizations that protect certain species, then spearhead a schoolwide campaign to help save one of these animals.

MAY 29
activities

☞ Bob Hope-fuls
To celebrate the birthday of comedian Bob Hope, show your students highlights from his many television shows, making sure to include some of his opening monologues. These monologues usually included topical jokes aimed at the president and other people in the news. Next, give the children a chance to review the current day's headlines. Then have your 21st-century Hope-fuls prepare and deliver their own 90-second "opening monologues" for the class.

✿ Flags at the summit
Tell your students that during the ascent of Mt. Everest, Tenzing Norkay had four flags—representing Nepal, Great Britain, India, and the United Nations—wrapped around the handle of his ice ax. Those flags were significant because Tenzing was born in Nepal; Hillary, in New Zealand, a part of the British Commonwealth; and Colonel John Hunt, the leader of the expedition, in India. Ask your students what they think the U.N. flag signified. (It symbolized international peace.) Then have them look up the word *vexillology* (the study of flags) in the dictionary.

⚗ Rescuing the peregrine
Peregrine falcons almost disappeared from the United States. In one of a number of efforts to reintroduce the birds, the U.S. Forest Service carried a ton of lumber—via helicopter—to a remote location outside Bergland, Mich. Workers then scaled a 300-foot cliff and built a 10-foot-high platform for six peregrine falcons that had been hatched and raised at the University of Minnesota. Have your students draw a food web that includes the peregrine. Can they discover why these falcons almost died out?

BIRTHDAYS
1736 • **PATRICK HENRY, American orator and patriot**
1903 • **BOB HOPE, American comedian** ☞
1917 • **JOHN F. KENNEDY, 35th president of the United States**
1939 • **AL UNSER, American auto racer**

EVENTS
1790 • **RHODE ISLAND became the 13th state.**
1848 • **WISCONSIN became the 30th state.**
1916 • **THE OFFICIAL FLAG OF THE PRESIDENT OF THE UNITED STATES was adopted.**
1953 • Sir Edmund Hillary and Tenzing ✿ Norkay became the **FIRST PEOPLE TO REACH THE SUMMIT OF MT. EVEREST.**
1988 • Members of the U.S. Forest ⚗ Service built a **10-FOOT-HIGH PLATFORM FOR NESTING PEREGRINE FALCONS** on top of a cliff near Bergland, Mich.

MAY 30
activities

Frozen treats
In recognition of William G. Young's patent for the ice cream freezer, invite your students to create their own ice cream. They'll need 1 cup cold milk or cream, ¼ cup sugar, ¼ tsp. flavoring (vanilla, peppermint, or maple), a clean soup can, an empty cottage cheese container, ice, ¼ cup salt, and a metal spoon. Have the kids place all the ingredients—except the salt—into the soup can. Then have them fill the cottage cheese container with ice, add the salt to the ice, and set the soup can inside the container. Next, tell the children to stir the mixture with the metal spoon, making sure to regularly scrape down the sides. After 15 to 20 minutes, they should have ice cream. Ask your students: How long does it take before the milk mixture begins to change? What changes occur? What are the advantages of an ice cream maker?

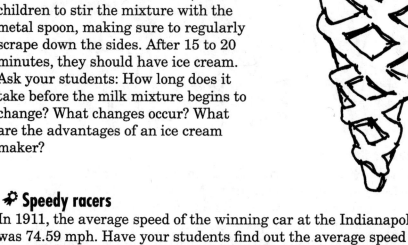

Speedy racers
In 1911, the average speed of the winning car at the Indianapolis 500 was 74.59 mph. Have your students find out the average speed of this year's winner. Then have them use an almanac to find the average speeds of previous Indianapolis 500 winners. Have the kids show the results on a graph.

Comparing states
Ask your students to locate Kansas and Nebraska on a U.S. map, then find each state's capital city. Next, challenge the kids to discover what is unique about Nebraska's legislature. (It is the nation's only unicameral, or one-house, legislature.)

MAY 31
activities

✎ Picturing poetry

To celebrate Walt Whitman's birthday, read some of his poems out loud while your students try to visualize the scene being described. Afterward, ask each student to select and illustrate a favorite poem. Then have each child pass his drawing to a classmate, who will add to the illustration. Repeat the procedure once more, then pass the drawing back to the original artist. What elements did the classmates add?

⬭ Baseball marathon

Here's a math problem for your students: On this day in 1964, the Giants and the Mets played a doubleheader that lasted a total of 9 hours and 52 minutes. The Giants won the second game in the 23rd inning after a record 7 hours and 23 minutes. How long did the first game take?

⚗ Terrible twisters

Tell your students that the United States experiences more tornadoes that any other country. But most aren't as violent as the ones that hit Ohio and Pennsylvania in 1985. Give each of your students a map of the United States, then have them color in "Tornado Alley"—a section running from Texas to Nebraska—where almost one-third of all the tornadoes in this country occur. Can your students figure out why this area is so prone to twisters?

BIRTHDAYS
1819 • **WALT WHITMAN, American poet**
✎
1893 • **ELIZABETH COATSWORTH, children's author**
1930 • **CLINT EASTWOOD, American actor**

EVENTS
1853 • **An expedition led by Elisha Kane became the FIRST AMERICAN EXPEDITION TO REACH THE ARCTIC CIRCLE.**
1868 • **James Moore won the EARLIEST RECORDED BICYCLE RACE.**
1880 • **THE FIRST BICYCLE SOCIETY, the League of American Wheelmen, was formed.**
1889 • **THE JOHNSTOWN FLOOD occurred when a dam above the Pennsylvania town broke, submerging the town under 30 feet of water. Nearly 2,300 people were killed in the disaster.**
1913 • **THE SEVENTEENTH AMENDMENT, providing for the direct election of U.S. senators, was ratified.**
1919 • **THE FIRST WEDDING IN AN AIRPLANE took place.**
1964 • **The San Francisco Giants and the**
⬭ **New York Mets played the LONGEST BASEBALL GAME IN THE HISTORY OF THE NATIONAL LEAGUE (7 hours, 23 minutes).**
1985 • **TORNADOES WITH WINDS esti-**
⚗ **mated at 260 mph ripped through parts of Ohio and Pennsylvania.**

JUNE

☆ Project of the Month: Fresh Fruits and Vegetables Chart

Celebrate June's bounty of fresh fruits and vegetables by helping your students take a closer look at these essential components of a balanced diet. To begin, have the kids name as many fruits and vegetables as they can. Write the responses on a class chart. Then ask each student to name one favorite fruit and one favorite vegetable, and record the results in a table. For each item on the table, ask your students which part of the plant is eaten (root, stem, leaf, fruit, or seed).

For the rest of the month, have each student keep track of the fruits and vegetables he eats daily for lunch. At the end of the month, use the class data to create a table. Which foods were the most popular? Which were the least popular? What was the most unusual fruit or vegetable? Post the results in the school cafeteria, and send home a report to your students' families.

EXTENDER: Do your students think they eat enough fruits and vegetables? Have them list all the produce they eat in 1 day, then compare their list with the FDA guidelines. Could they do better? How?

MONTHLONG OBSERVANCES

Accordion Awareness Month
American Rivers Month
Arts and Crafts Month
Carnival and Circus Month
Fresh Fruit and Vegetable Month
National Adopt-a-Cat Month
National Cheeseburger Month
National Dairy Month
National Recycling Month
National Rose Month
National Theater Month
Papaya Month
Tennis Month
Zoo and Aquarium Month

WEEKLONG EVENTS

International Volunteers Week
(first week)
National Safe Boating Week
(first week)
Teacher Thank You Week (first week)
National Little League Baseball Week
(week beginning with the second Monday)
National Flag Week
(week including June 14)
National Physical Therapy Week
(third week)
Amateur Radio Week
(week ending with the fourth weekend)

SPECIAL DAYS AND CELEBRATIONS

Flag Day (June 14)
Father's Day (third Sunday)
First day of summer
(on or about June 22)

JUNE 1
activities

✿ Signs of a superhero

In honor of Superman's comic-book debut, ask your students to write a paragraph about where they first discovered this superhero (for example, on TV, in motion pictures, or on videos) and to briefly describe him. Then have the kids interview parents and grandparents about their memories of Superman. How do these views compare with those of your students? Finally, make a class list of a superhero's positive qualities. Can your students name real people who also display these qualities?

▷ Have a grouchy birthday

Young children will enjoy celebrating Oscar the Grouch's birthday by brainstorming for yucky things—for example, muddy shoes, liver and onion sandwiches, or hair tangled with bubble gum. List your students' ideas on the chalkboard, then have the children use the list to create silly birthday poems for Oscar. Ask your students to write their poems on construction-paper trash cans.

⬱ Student volunteers

During International Volunteers Week, challenge your students to name volunteer jobs they could do at home, at school, and in the community. Encourage them to each do at least one volunteer activity this week, then report back to the class.

BIRTHDAYS

1637 • JACQUES MARQUETTE, French Jesuit missionary and explorer

1849 • FRANCIS EDGAR STANLEY, inventor of the first successful steam-driven automobile

▷ OSCAR THE GROUCH, "Sesame Street" character

EVENTS

1792 • KENTUCKY became the 15th state.

1796 • TENNESSEE became the 16th state.

1802 • THE FIRST BOOK FAIR took place in New York City.

1813 • Mortally wounded in a War of 1812 naval engagement, Captain James Lawrence told his crew, "DON'T GIVE UP THE SHIP," which became the motto of the U.S. Navy.

1925 • New York Yankees star Lou Gehrig began his record string of PLAYING IN 2,130 CONSECUTIVE BASEBALL GAMES.

1938 • The first issue of the "SUPER-
✿   MAN" ACTION COMICS appeared.

1990 • Soviet president Mikhail Gorbachev and U.S. president George Bush SIGNED MORE THAN A DOZEN AGREEMENTS at the White House.

CHILDREN'S DAY (Germany)
INTERNATIONAL MOTHER'S PEACE DAY
⬱ INTERNATIONAL VOLUNTEERS WEEK (first week in June)

JUNE 2
activities

📖 Adaptable tales
Tell your students that Paul Galdone drew great satisfaction from adapting favorite old tales to a picture-book format. Invite the kids to name familiar fairy tales, fables, and tall tales they enjoy. Then have them work in pairs to adapt and illustrate one of these stories. Arrange for the pairs to share their work with younger students.

🌐 Forms of government
On the anniversary of Italy's governmental referendum, have your students compare and contrast a republican form of government with a monarchy. What are the strengths and weaknesses of each system? Would any of your students prefer a monarchy under any circumstances? Why or why not?

✎ Time for thank-yous
During Teacher Thank You Week, invite your students to write short notes to their former teachers, thanking them for some special kindness or memorable contribution. Arrange to deliver the notes throughout the week as a special way to celebrate the important role teachers play in children's lives.

JUNE 3
activities

✒ A day for dolls

On Broken Dolls Day in Japan, young girls and their mothers bring broken dolls to Buddhist priests to be enshrined. Ask your students to bring in their broken dolls or action figures. Then set up a classroom repair station where students can apply a little glue and a lot of ingenuity to fix the dolls. Also invite the children to use extra parts to create new dolls. Afterward, have them write stories or poems about the dolls. Finally, ask your students if they'd like to donate the rejuvenated dolls to a local children's charity.

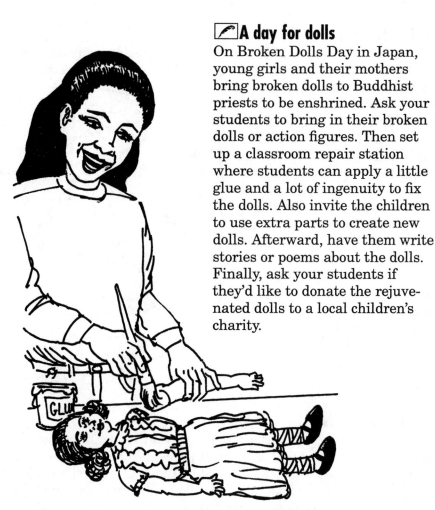

🦐 Spotlight on fruits and vegetables

To celebrate Fresh Fruit and Vegetable Month, challenge your students to create a still-life arrangement out of fruits and vegetables. Then have the kids use watercolors, charcoal, pen and ink, or colored pencils to depict their arrangements. Ask the students to make up fact sheets that list the artwork's title as well as the foods represented and their nutritional benefits. Display the completed works in the school cafeteria under a "Fresh Fruit and Vegetable Month" sign.

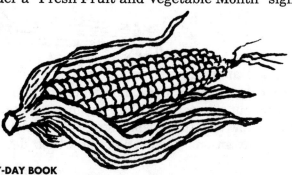

BIRTHDAYS

1808 • JEFFERSON DAVIS, president of the Confederate states

1904 • CHARLES DREW, American surgeon who developed techniques for processing and storing blood plasma for use in transfusions

EVENTS

1851 • The New York Knickerbockers wore THE FIRST BASEBALL UNIFORMS.

1888 • The poem "CASEY AT THE BAT" first appeared in print.

1932 • Lou Gehrig became the FIRST MAJOR LEAGUER TO HIT FOUR CONSECUTIVE HOMERS in one game.

1937 • After renouncing the British throne, the DUKE OF WINDSOR married Mrs. Wallis Simpson.

1948 • THE WORLD'S LARGEST TELESCOPE—a 200-inch reflector—was dedicated at Mount Palomar Observatory in California.

1949 • Wesley A. Brown became the FIRST AFRICAN-AMERICAN TO GRADUATE FROM THE U.S. NAVAL ACADEMY at Annapolis.

1965 • Major Edward H. White took the FIRST SPACE WALK BY AN AMERICAN.
• SILVER WAS ELIMINATED from U.S. dimes and quarters.

✒ BROKEN DOLLS DAY (Japan)
🦐 FRESH FRUIT AND VEGETABLE MONTH

JUNE 4
activities

Moldy meal

According to legend, in 1070 a shepherd boy accidentally left his lunch—bread and sheep's milk cheese—in a cool limestone cave near Roquefort, France. He returned to the cave weeks later and found the lost food covered with black mold. He ate it anyway. The bread had a bad taste. The cheese looked peculiar but tasted good. To this day, cheese made of sheep's milk ages in those same limestone caverns. Bring in some Roquefort cheese and invite your students to sample it. Can they name other foods in which bacteria is an essential ingredient? (Such foods include yogurt, sour cream, and other kinds of cheeses.)

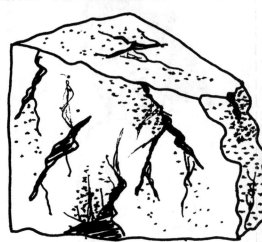

State symbols

Many states have state birds. Challenge your students to find out if their state has one and, if so, what it is. What other things—flowers, insects, trees, songs—are recognized by their state? Invite the kids to select another symbol they think merits recognition, then write a proposal to their state representative.

Checkout challenge

If there were no grocery carts, how would people get their groceries to the checkout counter? Challenge your students to work in groups to invent a new way to transport groceries. Have the groups illustrate their inventions, then explain how their devices would work.

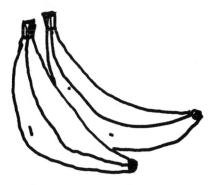

JUNE 5
activities

◌ Awe-inspiring flight

The balloon created by Joseph and Jacques Montgolfier measured over 35 feet in diameter. It was made from paper-lined sections of linen, which were joined together with buttons. Hot air for the balloon came from wood burned in a hole in the ground. The balloon was held over the hole by eight men. When it was released, it rose 6,000 feet and traveled 1½ miles before coming down. Remind your students that this flight took place over 200 years ago. Then ask them to imagine what people viewing this spectacle might have been thinking. Were they afraid? Excited? Have your students write stories about the balloon flight from the perspective of a long-ago spectator.

❀ Banana bonanza

Tell your students that bananas contain important nutrients, such as potassium, carbohydrates, and vitamins A, B, and C. Ask the children to describe the ways they like to eat bananas. Then have them create posters encouraging people to eat more of this healthful fruit.

▀ Honoring a hero

Students, staff, and parents in University City, Mo., decided to rename their school after Dr. Ronald E. McNair because they thought his adventuresome spirit and diversified interests—including scuba diving, karate, gourmet cooking, and jazz—would inspire students to take risks and explore untapped talents. What people would your students consider honoring if their school needed a new name? What special qualities would they look for in an honoree? Have students work in small groups to discuss these questions, then present their ideas to the class.

BIRTHDAYS

1718 • THOMAS CHIPPENDALE, English cabinetmaker
1723 • ADAM SMITH, Scottish political philosopher who helped lay the intellectual foundations of capitalism
1919 • RICHARD SCARRY, children's author and illustrator

EVENTS

1783 • Joseph and Jacques Montgolfier first demonstrated their HOT-AIR BALLOON in a 10-minute, unmanned flight over Annonay, France.
1876 • BANANAS were sold for 10¢ each at the Philadelphia Centennial Exposition. Before then, the fruit had rarely been seen in the United States.
1910 • THE FIRST HOT-AIR BALLOON RACE was held in Indianapolis, Ind.
1917 • More than 9 MILLION AMERICAN MEN began registering for the draft during World War I.
1968 • Moments after addressing supporters celebrating his victory in the California Democratic presidential primary, SENATOR ROBERT F. KENNEDY WAS SHOT in a Los Angeles hotel. He died the next day.
1988 • The Sixth Grade Center in University City, Mo., was renamed THE RONALD E. McNAIR SCHOOL in honor of one of the astronauts killed in the *Challenger* explosion.
1989 • In Poland's first free elections since World War II, the SOLIDARITY PARTY won a decisive majority.

WORLD ENVIRONMENT DAY

JUNE 6
activities

❄ Spring snowstorms
Ask your students to imagine how New Englanders might have felt when they received 10 inches of snow on this date in 1822. Then have the kids create "what's wrong with this picture?" illustrations depicting a snowy summer day. For example, they might draw a beach scene depicting people in swimsuits along with hats, mittens, and boots.

📖 Animal ways
Celebrate Verna Aardema's birthday by reading aloud *Why Mosquitoes Buzz in People's Ears*. Then invite the children to create their own stories explaining why other kinds of animals behave the way they do. Have them illustrate their work.

🪀 Yo-yo tricks
In honor of National Yo-Yo Day, invite your students to bring in their yo-yos and demonstrate tricks they can do. For an extra challenge, have the children write and illustrate the different steps involved.

✎ Rules for safe sports
Tell your students that National Safe Boating Week is a reminder for them to follow safety precautions when they're in boats. Then ask the kids to list other summer activities they plan to enjoy—for example, swimming, tennis, baseball, biking, horseback riding. Have the students brainstorm for safety rules that are important for each of the activities on the list. Then have them create posters showing their safe-sports rules. Display the posters in the hallway.

JUNE 7
activities

☼ Futuristic clothes dryers

Before the clothes dryer was invented, people hung their clothes outside to dry in the air. Ask your students to list the benefits of this method—for example, it uses renewable solar energy and costs nothing. How do students think people of the future will dry their clothes? Have them work in groups to design a clothes dryer for the year 2020.

⚾ Pinch hitting for others

Discuss the term *pinch hitter* with your students. Then challenge them to think of ways the term can be applied to situations outside of baseball. For example, does a substitute teacher "pinch-hit" for a classroom teacher who's ill? Ask your students to recall times when they've pinch-hit for a family member or friend. Have them write about these experiences.

🌐 Rice recipes

Tell your students that about two-thirds of the world's population relies on rice as a staple food. A grain of rice has an outer hull, or shell, which is not eaten. Inside the hull is the kernel, which is covered by thin layers of skin called bran coats. Most of the vitamins and minerals in rice are found in the bran coats. To have your own classroom rice festival, bring in some cooked brown, wild, and white rice for your students to taste. Which kind do they like best? Why? Invite the children to bring in their favorite rice recipes to share with one another.

BIRTHDAYS

1848 • PAUL GAUGUIN, French painter
1917 • GWENDOLYN BROOKS, American poet

EVENTS

1776 • Richard Henry Lee of Virginia proposed to the Continental Congress a RESOLUTION CALLING FOR INDEPENDENCE OF THE AMERICAN COLONIES from Britain.

1862 • The United States and Britain signed A TREATY FOR THE SUPPRESSION OF THE SLAVE TRADE.

1864 • ABRAHAM LINCOLN was renominated for the presidency in Baltimore.

1892 • George T. Sampson invented the CLOTHES DRYER.
• J.J. Doyle of the Cleveland Spiders became BASEBALL'S FIRST PINCH HITTER.

1893 • George Harbo and Frank Samuelson started a ROWBOAT TRIP FROM NEW YORK CITY TO ENGLAND, arriving on Aug. 3.

1948 • DWIGHT EISENHOWER became president of Columbia University.

1984 • A TORNADO leveled the town of Barneveld, Wis.

🌐 RICE FESTIVAL (Japan)

BIRTHDAYS

1867 • FRANK LLOYD WRIGHT, American architect

EVENTS

1504 • Michelangelo's statue *DAVID* was installed in front of the Palazzo della Signoria in Florence.

1783 • Laki, a volcano in southern Iceland, began erupting. The ERUPTION LASTED 8 MONTHS.

1786 • ICE CREAM was first sold in the United States, in New York City.

1789 • THE BILL OF RIGHTS was first proposed by James Madison.

1835 • THE LARGEST FLOWER on record, a calla lily, bloomed at the New York Botanical Gardens. It was 8½ feet tall, 4 feet in diameter, and 12 feet in circumference.

1869 • Ives W. McGaffey received a patent for the VACUUM CLEANER.

1939 • George VI became the FIRST BRITISH MONARCH TO VISIT THE UNITED STATES.

1963 • The American Heart Association began its CAMPAIGN AGAINST CIGARETTE SMOKING.

1982 • Ronald Reagan became the FIRST U.S. PRESIDENT TO ADDRESS THE BRITISH PARLIAMENT.

JUNE 8
activities

Bold architecture

Frank Lloyd Wright, considered one of the world's greatest architects, designed homes and commercial buildings for more than 70 years. Among his most daring designs was "Fallingwater," a house in Pennsylvania that projects out over a waterfall. Show your students pictures of "Fallingwater" and other houses designed by Wright. Discuss how his buildings blend into the surrounding environment. Then ask the kids to describe and illustrate their dream houses, focusing in particular on the relationship of the house to surrounding natural features.

Climatic catastrophe

The Laki volcanic eruption of 1783 created the largest lava flow—about 220 square miles—in recorded history. In addition, it spewed enormous volumes of ash and sulfurous gas into the atmosphere, producing a bluish haze that shrouded Iceland and most of northern Europe for months. Livestock deaths led to a famine that killed 10,000 Icelanders, and climatic changes were worldwide. Several years of poor harvests followed, which may or may not have resulted from the eruption. Some environmentalists believe the Laki eruption should serve as a warning to industrialized societies about the dangers of global climate change. Ask your students to list documented or suspected *man-made* changes to the world's environment (for example, ozone depletion, global warming), their causes (use of certain chemical refrigerants and aerosols; increased carbon dioxide resulting from the burning of fossil fuels), and possible remedies.

Hazards of smoking

In recognition of the American Heart Association's fight against smoking, have your students make a class list of health hazards associated with cigarettes. Post the list in the hallway for other classes to see.

JUNE 9
activities

☞ This duck's not daffy

Donald Duck was created as a foil for Mickey Mouse and made his screen debut in Walt Disney's *The Wise Hen* 6 years after Disney had introduced the world-famous rodent. Ask your students to imagine they're newspaper reporters interviewing Donald Duck. Then provide them with a list of interview questions, such as: *How did you get custody of your nephews Huey, Louie, and Dewey? Who were their parents? What happened to them? Will you and Daisy ever get married? Why do you both have the same last name? What do you do for a living? Does Daisy work? What do you think about Daffy Duck?* Have the students create answers to these questions, then incorporate them into a newspaper article.

※ Dream toys

Three million Cabbage Patch Kids dolls were sold in the first year after their introduction, making them the most successful new dolls in the history of the toy industry. If possible, have a volunteer bring one of these dolls to class, and ask your students to speculate on why they were so popular. Then invite the children to design their own dream toys. Have each student write a description of the toy, the materials it would be made of, how it would operate, what kind of package it would come in, how much it would cost, and so on. Next, have the children draw and color pictures of their toys, design logos, and create names. As an extra challenge, have them create promotional slogans, jingles, or print ads.

BIRTHDAYS
1812 • **JOHANN GALLE,** German astronomer who first sighted the planet Neptune
1893 • **COLE PORTER,** American composer
1961 • **MICHAEL J. FOX,** Canadian actor

EVENTS
1790 • *The Philadelphia Spelling Book* became the FIRST BOOK REGISTERED FOR A U.S. COPYRIGHT.
1877 • **SAMUEL CLEMENS** explained the meaning of his pen name, Mark Twain.
1893 • Dr. Daniel Hale Williams performed the FIRST SUCCESSFUL OPEN-HEART SURGERY.
1934 • The Disney cartoon character ☞ **DONALD DUCK** debuted in *The Wise Hen.*
1943 • Congress authorized employers to WITHHOLD INCOME TAX PAYMENTS from their workers' paychecks.
1973 • With a win at the Belmont Stakes, Secretariat became HORSE RACING'S FIRST TRIPLE CROWN WINNER IN 25 YEARS.
1983 • **CABBAGE PATCH KIDS** dolls ※ made their debut.

9

JUNE 10
activities

🇺🇸 Group dynamics

Tell your students that the drafting committee for the Declaration of Independence had several members, including Thomas Jefferson, Benjamin Franklin, and John Adams. However, Thomas Jefferson did the lion's share of the work. Ask your students to speculate why. Then have them discuss what they're like in a group. Do they let others do most of the work, or do they like to take charge? Finally, have your students take turns reading aloud passages from the Declaration of Independence.

🐾 Panda predicament

Giant pandas, which are native to China and Tibet, may reach 6 feet in length and weigh 220 pounds. They feed mainly on species of bamboo plants, two of which have unusual life cycles. Every 100 years, these plants produce seeds, then die. It takes several years for new plants to grow from the seeds. In the meantime, the giant pandas are without a major food source. This situation last occurred in the 1970s. And by the 1980s, about one-fourth of the giant panda population had starved to death. Have your students research the current status of the world panda population. How many pandas live in zoos?

🏐 Youthful hurler

During World War II, major league baseball teams scrambled to replace their regular players, many of whom were overseas, with any available talent. So it was that Cincinnati pitcher Joe Nuxhall broke into the league before his 16th birthday. To mark this event, have your students write a fantasy story about their debut—at their current age—in a favorite professional sport or other career.

JUNE 11
activities

🖋 Hawaiian celebration

Tell your students that King Kamehameha I united Hawaii's small, quarreling island kingdoms into one strong and peaceful nation. To honor him, Hawaiians hold parades and luaus. Hold a Hawaiian-style celebration in your own classroom. Ask your students to wear colorful shirts or muumuu-like dresses. Make leis out of tissue paper or cutout flowers. Then, with a tablecloth spread on the floor, feast on assorted luau fruits (coconuts, bananas, pineapples, guavas, papayas), plus macadamia nuts and punch.

⚗ Undersea adventures

As a teenager, Jacques-Yves Cousteau injured his arm in a car accident. To aid his recovery, Cousteau used to swim in the Mediterranean Sea. When he got a pair of goggles, Cousteau was able to see the beautiful world beneath the surface of the water and thus began his lifelong pursuit of undersea adventures. Invite your students to imagine the world Cousteau saw for the first time. Then have them construct a semantic web around the word *sea* and illustrate what they "see."

⟋ Sports role models

When Joe Montana started playing sports in grade school, he'd anxiously wait for his father to return from work so they could practice football drills. To develop his passing accuracy, he practiced throwing a football through a moving tire swing. While practicing, he and his best friend would pretend to be stars on the Notre Dame football team. Ask your students to name the athletes they try to emulate.

BIRTHDAYS

1758 • **KAMEHAMEHA I**, Polynesian 🖋 king who unified the Hawaiian Islands

1864 • **RICHARD STRAUSS**, German composer

1880 • **JEANNETTE RANKIN**, American legislator and the first woman elected to the U.S. Congress

1910 • **JACQUES-YVES COUSTEAU**, ⚗ French oceanographer

1945 • **ROBERT MUNSCH**, storyteller and children's author

1956 • **JOE MONTANA**, professional ⟋ football quarterback

EVENTS

1895 • Frank and Charles Duryea were granted a patent on the **FIRST SUCCESSFUL GASOLINE-POWERED AUTOMOBILE** in the United States.

1912 • Joseph H. Dickinson of Cranford, N.J., patented **THE PLAYER PIANO**.

1919 • Sir Barton became the **FIRST HORSE TO WIN THE TRIPLE CROWN**.

1978 • A dog named Martha Faye set the **CANINE DISTANCE RECORD FOR FRISBEE CATCHING** when she caught a 334.6-foot toss.

1988 • Adragon Eastwood Demello— age 11¾—became the **YOUNGEST COLLEGE GRADUATE** on record.

KING KAMEHAMEHA DAY
(Hawaii)
RACE UNITY DAY

JUNE 12
activities

BIRTHDAYS

1806 • **JOHN AUGUSTUS ROEBLING,** German-born American engineer who designed the Brooklyn Bridge

1817 • **HENRY DAVID THOREAU,** American writer

1827 • **JOHANNA SPYRI,** Swiss author who wrote *Heidi*

1924 • **GEORGE HERBERT WALKER BUSH,** 41st president of the United States

1929 • **ANNE FRANK,** German-Dutch diarist

EVENTS

1913 • **THE FIRST ANIMATED CARTOON,** *The Dachshund,* was released.

1917 • **THE SECRET SERVICE** extended its protection to the president's family.

1922 • **THE FIRST DOCUMENTARY FILM**—Robert Flaherty's *Nanook of the North*—was released.

1939 • **THE BASEBALL HALL OF FAME** opened in Cooperstown, N.Y.

1956 • **THE OFFICIAL FLAG OF THE U.S. ARMY** was adopted.

1974 • **LITTLE LEAGUE** was opened to girls.

1979 • Bryan Allen became the **FIRST PERSON TO FLY A HUMAN-POWERED AIRCRAFT** across the English Channel. He supplied the power by pedaling.

Simplifying one's life

At the age of 28, Henry David Thoreau built and moved into a cabin on Walden Pond near Concord, Mass. He lived there alone for the next 2 years, growing beans, observing nature, and writing. In large part, Thoreau retreated to Walden Pond to find out what he needed for a fulfilling life and what he could do without. He believed that many of the things society considered necessities were in fact merely distractions, and that the pursuit of them led people to overwork themselves and, in the process, to become unhappy. So he tried to pare his life down to the essentials. Present these ideas to your students. Then ask each of them to create a list of things that are important in their lives. They might get ideas for the list by thinking about what they spend their time doing. Lists might include such things as housing, TV, music, sports, a VCR, toys, nice clothes, a bike, and a telephone. Next, ask the children each to examine their list carefully and to put a check mark next to any items that aren't really necessary but that add significantly to the quality of their life. Have them explain why. Then have them put an X next to any items they could do without and not miss, again telling why. Finally, ask the kids what, if anything, they learned from this exercise.

Halls of fame

Tell your students the names of the five original members of the Baseball Hall of Fame: Babe Ruth, Honus Wagner, Christy Mathewson, Walter Johnson, and Ty Cobb. Next, have each student choose an area of interest and create a "Hall of Fame" for it by selecting five charter members. Have the kids present their choices to the class.

JUNE 13
activities

✳ My dinner with George

Ask your students to imagine that they had the opportunity to host a dinner party today for George Washington. What kinds of food would they serve? Whom would they invite, and why? What would they like to ask Washington about? What do they think he'd say about the current state of the nation?

🌐 Canal mapping

Have your students locate the Suez Canal on a world map and name the two major bodies of water it connects. Then ask them to name the major canal in the Americas and locate it on the world map. Which two bodies of water does it link? Why are canals important?

✒ Supreme powers

Tell your students that President Lyndon Johnson nominated Thurgood Marshall for the U.S. Supreme Court. Then have them use an almanac to find out the nine current Supreme Court justices and the presidents who nominated each of them. Some people believe a president's greatest power is the ability to nominate Supreme Court justices. Ask your students why this might be true.

✿ Spectacular space missions

When *Pioneer 10* left the solar system in 1983, it was a landmark event in aerospace history. Ask your students to imagine the kinds of space missions that might occur over the next 50 years. Have them make a list of their ideas. Then have them draw a futuristic space vehicle and describe its first-of-a-kind mission.

activities

▓ National symbol

On June 14, 1777, the Continental Congress adopted this brief resolution: "That the Flag of the united states be 13 stripes alternate red and white, and that the Union be 13 stars white in a blue field representing a new constellation." But Congress didn't make a sketch of the new flag, so people weren't sure how big the field of blue should be, how to arrange the stars, how many points the stars should have, or how wide the stripes should be. Ask your students to design their own flags based on the original resolution. Your class will be surprised by all the possible variations. Today, the size, color, and placement of each star and stripe is stipulated by executive order.

✿ Flying heroes

Tell your students that pilot John Alcock and navigator Arthur Brown flew nonstop from Newfoundland to Clifden, Ireland, despite numerous in-flight problems. For instance, an overheated exhaust pipe turned to liquid and blew away. A snowstorm caused ice to form on the airplane's instruments, and Brown had to climb out onto the wings to chip it away. And a dense fog so disoriented the men that they nearly crashed into the Atlantic Ocean. (The fog lifted suddenly, allowing Alcock to pull up after seeing he was just 100 feet above the ocean.) Challenge your students to uncover more details about this historic flight. Then encourage them to create front-page stories or television news reports about these men. Students might also like to role-play Alcock and Brown and answer classmates' questions about their adventure.

JUNE 15
activities

🧪 High-flying adventures

To mark the day that Ben Franklin used a kite to prove that lightning is an electrical charge, bring in a kite and suspend it from the classroom ceiling. Then share Tom Moran's *Kite Flying Is for Me* with your students. Next, ask the kids to write and illustrate poems about Franklin's electrifying experiment.

🖋 Young heroine

While recovering from the measles in a New York City hospital overlooking the East River, 14-year-old Mary McCann saw a steamboat on fire. Still feverish, she ran to the river and yelled encouragement to the people floundering in the water. Her courageous act helped save 20 people, including nine children, and she was awarded the Silver Lifesaving Medal by the U.S. Congress. Invite your students to design their own class medal to commemorate heroic deeds. Then, over the next month, have students clip and share newspaper articles about people who have helped others. Encourage the kids to write letters congratulating these people and to include copies of the class-designed medal.

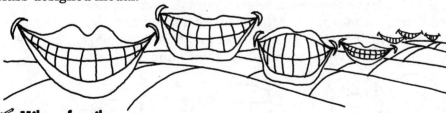

😊 Miles of smiles

Here's a fun way to celebrate Smile Power Day. In the center of a large sheet of paper, write the words "It's Great to Smile Because..." Post the paper in the hallway or outside your classroom door. Then encourage students to use this "graffiti-style" message center to complete the sentence.

BIRTHDAYS
1954 • JIM BELUSHI, American actor
1958 • WADE BOGGS, baseball star

EVENTS
1752 • BEN FRANKLIN FLEW A KITE during a lightning storm and proved that lightning is an electrical charge.

1775 • George Washington was appointed COMMANDER IN CHIEF OF THE CONTINENTAL ARMY.

1836 • ARKANSAS became the 25th state.

1844 • CHARLES GOODYEAR patented a process for vulcanizing rubber.

1854 • THE FIRST ICE CREAM FACTORY opened.

1864 • ARLINGTON NATIONAL CEMETERY was established.

1877 • Henry O. Flipper became the FIRST BLACK GRADUATE OF WEST POINT.

1889 • Congress created the NATIONAL ZOOLOGICAL PARK.

1904 • MARY McCANN HELPED SAVE 20 PEOPLE after the steamship *General Slocum* caught fire in New York's East River.

1988 • General Motors Corp.'s Sunracer established A SPEED RECORD FOR SOLAR-POWERED CARS. Its top speed: 48.712 mph.

A FRIEND IN NEED IS A FRIEND INDEED DAY

😊 SMILE POWER DAY

JUNE 16
activities

Vanishing wildlife

Tell your students that on this day in 1987, the last dusky seaside sparrow died in a wildlife preserve at Walt Disney World in Florida. Then encourage the kids to take steps to protect animals for the future. Have each child research an extinct animal, draw a picture of the animal, and write a one-paragraph report about it. Next, have the students each write a letter to their state or federal representative telling about their animal and asking for help in saving other wildlife. Have the children include their drawings and reports with the letters. Make copies for a classroom display entitled "The Extinct Zoo...What You Can Do About It." Add any responses your students receive to the display.

Risky business

Grant Burnett, a china shop owner in New Zealand, always wondered what a bull would do in a china shop. He borrowed Colonel, a 2,000-pound Hereford, and let the animal roam around the store for 3 hours. Burnett risked thousands of dollars' worth of dishes, but Colonel didn't break a thing. Ask your students to think of other descriptive animal phrases (for example, eyes like a hawk, quiet as a mouse, fish out of water, hold your horses, sly as a fox, clam up, dead as a dodo). Have them each select a phrase, then illustrate its literal and figurative meanings. Afterward, read aloud Eve Merriam's poem "Cliche," which deals with figurative and literal language. Then ask your students to write poems about their animal subjects.

16

JUNE 17
activities

 Breakfast favorites
To celebrate the birthday of George Cormack, inventor of Wheaties cereal, poll your class to find out how many students have eaten Wheaties. Do they eat it regularly? Why or why not? Next, invite your students to each name their favorite cereal, then use three adjectives to describe its taste. List all the adjectives on the board. How many different ones are there?

✿ Cooperation bee
Hold a cooperative spelling bee in your classroom. Divide the class into small groups, then have the group members—without using dictionaries—work together to correctly spell words you call out. Give each team a point for each correctly spelled word. The team with the most points at the end of a specified period wins.

✎ Celebrating the circus
Tell your students that the circus originated in ancient Rome, where it was a place for chariot races and combat between gladiators. Then have the children look up the origin of the word *circus*. (Its Latin meaning is "circle.") Next, have students brainstorm for the kinds of acts and performers found in modern-day circuses—for example, dancing elephants, trapeze artists, clowns, jugglers, bareback riders. Ask children who've been to a circus to describe the acts they saw. Finally, have your students imagine they could be a circus performer for a day, and ask them to write and illustrate stories about what they'd do.

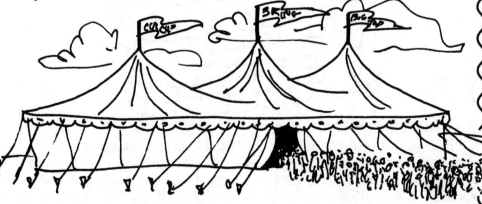

BIRTHDAYS
1870 • **GEORGE CORMACK,** inventor of Wheaties cereal
1882 • **IGOR FYODOROVICH STRAVINSKY,** Russian-American composer
1898 • **M.C. ESCHER,** German mathematician

EVENTS
1579 • **SIR FRANCIS DRAKE** landed on the California coast.
1682 • William Penn founded the **CITY OF PHILADELPHIA.**
1775 • **THE BATTLE OF BUNKER HILL,** one of the earliest engagements of the Revolutionary War, was fought near Boston.
1856 • **THE FIRST REPUBLICAN PARTY NATIONAL CONVENTION** took place in Philadelphia, Pa.
1873 • **SUSAN B. ANTHONY** was fined $100 for voting in the 1872 presidential election.
1925 • **THE FIRST NATIONAL SPELLING BEE** was held.
1972 • Five burglars were arrested at the Democratic Party headquarters in Washington, D.C. The break-in and subsequent cover-up, which came to be called **WATERGATE** after the building where the burglary occurred, ultimately led to the resignation of President Richard M. Nixon.
1979 • Richard Brown set a prone-position **SKATEBOARD SPEED RECORD** of 71.79 mph on a course at Mt. Baldy, Calif.
1991 • **PRESIDENT ZACHARY TAYLOR'S REMAINS WERE EXHUMED** (141 years after his death) in Louisville, Ky., to investigate the theory that he had been poisoned. No evidence was found to support the theory.

INDEPENDENCE DAY (Iceland)
CARNIVAL AND CIRCUS MONTH

17

JUNE 18
activities

BIRTHDAYS
1942 • ROGER EBERT, movie critic

• PAUL McCARTNEY, English musician, singer, and songwriter who was a member of the Beatles

1949 • CHRIS VAN ALLSBURG, children's author and illustrator

EVENTS
1812 • CONGRESS DECLARED WAR ON ENGLAND, marking the beginning of the War of 1812.

1823 • BRITISH SOLDIERS began wearing trousers rather than breeches.

1889 • William Richardson of Baltimore patented THE BABY CARRIAGE.

1945 • An estimated 1 million people turned out to give returning World War II general DWIGHT EISENHOWER a hero's welcome in Washington, D.C.

1983 • Sally Ride became the FIRST AMERICAN WOMAN IN SPACE.

1989 • Golfer Curtis Strange became the first man in nearly 40 years to win BACK-TO-BACK U.S. OPEN TITLES.

DRAGON BOAT FESTIVAL (China)

INTERNATIONAL PICNIC DAY

Picks and pans
Have your students discuss the kinds of things critics like Roger Ebert talk about when reviewing a movie—for example, plot development, acting, musical score, originality, humor, suspense. Then have the kids read several movie reviews in the local newspaper. Afterward, show a film and ask each student to critique it, either orally or in writing.

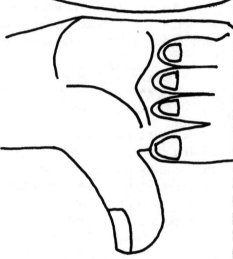

Author's special signature
Have your students look through Chris Van Allsburg's books to find Fritz, a bull terrier that appears somewhere in most of the author-illustrator's works. Ask your students why they think Van Allsburg includes Fritz. (The dog is his personal signature.) In what unique ways can your students personalize their projects? Invite the children to create their own "personal signatures" on 3×5-inch cards, then use these on future writing and art projects.

Foods from around the world
For International Picnic Day, have your class create a picnic menu with dishes from around the world. Students can work in teams to select a country, then research its typical foods. If possible, have the teams prepare their chosen dishes and share them with classmates.

JUNE 19
activities

✍ Honoring fathers

Tell your students that the mayor of Spokane, Wash., proclaimed the first Father's Day on the third Sunday in June, 1910. In 1924, President Calvin Coolidge asked that Father's Day be celebrated nationwide, but a presidential proclamation recognizing the day wasn't signed until 1966. A 1972 law made Father's Day a national holiday. If your students could name a new holiday, what would it be? Explain that when a member of Congress proposes a new holiday to the House of Representatives, he or she must get a majority of the members (218) to cosponsor the bill before it can be considered by the appropriate committee. Representatives typically make speeches to generate support for their bills, so invite your students to present arguments to the class in support of their holidays. Take a vote to see which holidays win a majority.

☞ Cartoon cat

To celebrate Garfield's birthday, give your students some background on his beginnings. Garfield's creator was cartoonist Jim Davis, who grew up on a farm with 25 cats. Davis decided to make his famous cartoon cat when he noticed there weren't any feline characters in animal comic strips. Garfield is named after Davis's grandfather. Encourage your students to bring in their favorite Garfield cartoons as well as newspaper, magazine, and pet-product pictures of cats. Also tell them to be on the lookout for descriptions of cats in literature, and to copy down ones that strike their fancy. Use the materials to make a "catty" bulletin board.

BIRTHDAYS

1903 • **LOU GEHRIG,** American baseball player
1962 • **PAULA ABDUL,** American singer
1978 • **GARFIELD,** comic-strip cat
☞

EVENTS

1586 • **ENGLISH COLONISTS SET SAIL FROM ROANOKE ISLAND** (now part of North Carolina) after failing to establish the first permanent English colony in America.
1787 • The members of the Constitutional Convention decided not to simply amend the Articles of Confederation but rather to conceive of an entirely **NEW PLAN FOR A NATIONAL GOVERNMENT.**
1846 • **THE FIRST FORMAL NINE-INNING BASEBALL GAME** was played between the New York Knickerbockers and the New Yorks at the Elysian Fields in Hoboken, N.J.
1885 • **THE STATUE OF LIBERTY** arrived in New York Harbor.
1910 • **THE FIRST OBSERVANCE OF**
✍ **FATHER'S DAY** took place in Spokane, Wash.
1976 • The U.S. spacecraft *VIKING 1* went into orbit around Mars.
1989 • Federal officials announced the creation of a **30,000-ACRE REFUGE FOR THE FLORIDA PANTHER.**

JUNETEENTH (celebration in Louisiana and Texas of the Thirteenth Amendment, which outlawed slavery)

JUNE 20
activities

BIRTHDAYS

1915 • **WALTER FARLEY**, children's author who wrote the Black Stallion books

1924 • **AUDIE MURPHY**, actor and soldier who was the most decorated American war hero in World War II

EVENTS

1782 • **THE BALD EAGLE** became the official symbol of the United States.
• **"E PLURIBUS UNUM"** became the slogan for the Great Seal of the United States.

1815 • Residents of Plymouth, Mass., reported sighting a **SEA SERPENT**.

1819 • The SS *Savannah* became the **FIRST AMERICAN STEAMSHIP TO CROSS THE ATLANTIC**.

1840 • Samuel F.B. Morse received a patent for the **TELEGRAPH**.

1863 • **WEST VIRGINIA** became the 35th state.

1963 • The United States and the Soviet Union agreed to set up a **WHITE HOUSE-KREMLIN HOT LINE**.

1977 • **THE TRANS-ALASKAN OIL PIPELINE** opened.

1984 • The Motion Picture Association of America instituted the **PG-13 RATING**, which stated that children under 13 must be accompanied by an adult.

• **MIDSOMMAR** (Sweden; on the summer solstice)

📖 Horse lover

As a child, Walter Farley wanted a horse. But his family lived in the city, and he couldn't convince his parents to let him keep a horse in the garage. His uncle—a horse trainer—encouraged him to visit stables and keep notes about his experiences. Farley used his notes years later when he wrote his first book, *The Black Stallion*. Ask your students to name an animal they'd like to own but can't for some reason. Then have them read at least two books (fiction or non-fiction) about the animal. When they've completed their reading, have them write stories in which they, through a fictional character, come to own the animal of their dreams.

Reporting on sea serpents

Ask your students to discuss how various segments of today's media might cover reports of a sea serpent sighting. Then have the class work in teams to prepare stories for the different media. For example, they could develop sensational tabloid features, serious science articles, broadcast news stories, or human interest features.

Dancing around the maypole

Tell your students that in Sweden, people celebrate midsummer by holding a daylong festival. They decorate houses, buildings, cars, trains, and buses with flowers and birch twigs. In addition, almost all the towns decorate their own maypoles. At night, the residents gather around the maypole to dance. Invite your students to decorate their classroom (or school building) to celebrate midsummer. They can even create a maypole from cardboard wrapping-paper tubes. On festival day, let them dance around the maypole to music.

JUNE 21
activities

✐ A First Lady's role

Tell your students that Martha Washington apparently didn't like the role of First Lady. She complained that it made her feel like a prisoner. Ask your students to speculate on why Mrs. Washington might have felt restricted as First Lady. How is the current First Lady handling her role? Encourage your students to research how contemporary first ladies have approached their jobs—for example, Lady Bird Johnson campaigned to beautify America, Nancy Reagan crusaded against drug abuse, and Barbara Bush promoted literacy. Then ask your students what they think is the proper role for a First Lady. Have them debate their ideas.

▥ Border states

Have your students find New Hampshire on a U.S. map. What states are located on its eastern, southern, and western borders? What country is located on its northwestern border? What states border your students' state?

❀ Wandering ways

Ask your students to share the images conjured up by the word *vagabond*. Then explain that a vagabond is someone who moves from place to place without a fixed home. Tell them that American poet Vachel Lindsay was known as "the Vagabond Poet" because he wandered throughout the United States, reciting his verse in exchange for food and lodging. Invite your students to list the pros and cons of leading a life like Lindsay's. Then have them write stories about where they'd go and what they'd do if they lived as vagabonds for a week.

BIRTHDAYS

1731 • **MARTHA WASHINGTON,** ✐ America's first First Lady
1982 • **PRINCE WILLIAM,** son of Prince Charles and Princess Diana and first in line after Charles for the British throne

EVENTS

1788 • **NEW HAMPSHIRE became the** ▥ **ninth state.**
1834 • Cyrus H. McCormick was awarded a patent for the **REAPING MACHINE.**
1948 • **THE FIRST LONG-PLAYING PHONOGRAPH RECORD was** demonstrated by Peter Goldmark.
1961 • **THE FIRST SEAWATER CONVERSION PLANT was dedicated, in** Freeport, Tex.
1963 • Bob Hayes ran the **FASTEST 100-YARD DASH EVER—9.1 sec-onds.**
1988 • **THE RUBY SLIPPERS from the** movie *The Wizard of Oz* sold for $165,000 at a movie memorabilia auction.
1991 • School 29 in Yonkers became **NEW YORK'S FIRST SCHOOL DESIGNATED AS AN URBAN WILDLIFE SANCTUARY.**

❀ **VAGABOND WEEK** (third week in June)

JUNE 22
activities

BIRTHDAYS
1757 • GEORGE VANCOUVER, British explorer for whom Vancouver, Canada, was named

1767 • KARL VON HUMBOLDT, German naturalist

1906 • ANNE MORROW LINDBERGH, American poet and essayist

EVENTS
1772 • SLAVERY WAS ABOLISHED in Great Britain.

1846 • Adolphe Sax patented the SAXOPHONE.

1868 • ARKANSAS WAS READMITTED TO THE UNION after the Civil War.

1870 • Congress established the DEPARTMENT OF JUSTICE.

1910 • ZEPPELIN AIR SERVICE began.

1939 • THE FIRST NATIONAL WATER-SKIING tournament took place.

1944 • THE G.I. BILL OF RIGHTS, providing World War II veterans with job, housing, and education benefits, was passed.

1970 • THE VOTING AGE IN THE UNITED STATES changed from 21 to 18.

1990 • The U.S. Fish and Wildlife Service declared the NORTHERN SPOTTED OWL a threatened species.

📖 Childhood writings
Anne Morrow Lindbergh kept a diary of her thoughts as a 10-year-old. She wrote about what she could see from her favorite spot—the window seat in her room. She continued to write throughout her life, publishing 13 books—some about her aviation adventures with her husband, Charles Lindbergh, others based on her diaries and letters. Ask your students to keep a diary for the rest of the month. At the end of the month, survey the class to see how many students plan to continue writing in their diary.

🏴 Younger voters
In 1970, President Nixon signed a bill lowering the voting age to 18 from 21. Ask your students if they've ever voted in an election (for instance, for student council, club, or team leaders). What qualities did they judge the candidates on? Would they consider those same things if they were voting for local, state, or national officials? Ask the kids if they think voting is a right, a privilege, or a duty. Then have them each write a paragraph defending their opinion.

⚗ Jobs vs. birds?
The decision to list the northern spotted owl as a threatened species meant that thousands of acres of public forests in the Pacific Northwest would be off limits to logging. Environmentalists hailed the move as the only way to save the owl from extinction. Loggers and the timber industry assailed it, saying that it would cost thousands of jobs in an already-depressed region. Organize a class debate on the issue of which should take precedence: saving wildlife species or saving jobs. Are the principles absolute, or would the decision depend on the number of jobs affected and the species in question? Is compromise *always* possible or even desirable?

JUNE 23
activities

Special champs

Wilma Rudolph proved she was a champion long before winning three gold medals at the 1960 Summer Olympics. When she was 4 years old, polio crippled her left leg, and doctors believed she would never again walk without a brace. But with determination and help from her family, she proved the doctors wrong.

Have your students find out about other sports heroes who have overcome difficulties, such as baseball pitchers Jim Abbott (one hand) and Monty Stratton (one leg), hockey player Bobby Clarke (diabetes), football placekicker Tom Dempsey (handless right arm and only half a right foot), and track star Jackie Joyner-Kersee (asthma).

Water from the bottom of the world

Antarctica, earth's coldest continent, has an area of about $5\frac{1}{2}$ million square miles and is covered by an ice cap that averages more than 1 mile in thickness. About 75% of the fresh water in the entire world is contained in ice and snow on this continent. Some people have suggested towing icebergs from Antarctic waters to other parts of the world to alleviate freshwater shortages. Tell your class that in the waters that surround Antarctica, icebergs the size of Connecticut (about 5,000 square miles) often break loose from the ice shelves. Then ask teams of students to consider the feasibility of transporting Antarctic icebergs to, say, Los Angeles. What strategies could be used to minimize melting in warm waters? Would the need for speed dictate that smaller icebergs be towed rather than larger ones? Or would towing several large icebergs together be most advantageous? When possible, have your students test their ideas with ice cubes and a dishpan of water.

Cheeseburger campaign

For National Cheeseburger Month, have your students create an ad campaign promoting this all-American food.

JUNE 24
activities

BIRTHDAYS

1771 • E.I. DUPONT, French-American industrialist

1916 • JOHN CIARDI, poet and children's author

1944 • KATHRYN LASKY, children's author

1949 • NADINE BERNARD WESTCOTT, children's author

EVENTS

1497 • Italian explorers JOHN AND SEBASTIAN CABOT landed on the Labrador peninsula in northeastern North America.

1541 • Spanish explorer Hernando de Soto sighted the MISSISSIPPI RIVER.

1647 • Margaret Brent appeared before the all-male Maryland Assembly and DEMANDED VOTING RIGHTS.

1930 • RADAR WAS FIRST USED to detect airplanes.

1947 • The sighting of FLYING SAUCERS was first reported, near Mt. Rainier, Wash.

1964 • COMMERCIAL PICTUREPHONE service began.

1968 • Professional baseball player Jim Northrup hit BACK-TO-BACK GRAND SLAM HOME RUNS.

1987 • Sixth-grader and pilot John Kevin Hill left Los Angeles on a 2,500-mile, CROSS-COUNTRY AIRPLANE FLIGHT.

1990 • The first CURRENCY FOR THE NEWLY REUNIFIED GERMANY was issued.

✿ Acronym names

After telling your students what an acronym is, explain that radar stands for "radio detecting and ranging." Your students might be familiar with other acronyms: AWOL, NASA, NATO, SWAT, VISTA, scuba, sonar. Challenge the kids to make up acronym phrases from the letters in their first names, your name, or the word *June* or *summer*.

❈ Honoring young heroes

As a 6th grader, John Kevin Hill piloted his own aircraft on a cross-country flight. Have your students review newspapers, magazines, and television news shows to find out about other young people who've accomplished great feats, then share their findings with the class. Next, invite the children to survey classmates and students throughout the school about their accomplishments—no matter how modest. Have them design a Hall of Fame bulletin board to celebrate these accomplishments.

⊕ Currency calculations

Introduce your students to the differences among currencies. To begin, tell them the value of the German deutsche mark relative to the U.S. dollar. Then have them calculate how many deutsche marks it would take to equal $100 U.S. dollars. Next, divide the class into groups, and give each group a supermarket circular. Have the members of each group select 20 items to buy. Then have them calculate their grocery bills in deutsche marks. For more practice, tell your students the relative values of other currencies, such as the British pound, the French franc, the Greek drachma, or the Israeli shekel, and have them calculate their grocery bills in those foreign currencies.

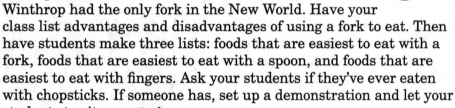

JUNE 25
activities

✿ Table manners

Tell your students that when John Winthrop left England to become the Massachusetts Bay Colony's first governor, he took his fork with him. (Even in Europe, travelers packed their forks because most inns didn't provide utensils.) For a while, Governor Winthrop had the only fork in the New World. Have your class list advantages and disadvantages of using a fork to eat. Then have students make three lists: foods that are easiest to eat with a fork, foods that are easiest to eat with a spoon, and foods that are easiest to eat with fingers. Ask your students if they've ever eaten with chopsticks. If someone has, set up a demonstration and let your students try it.

🎨 Youthful painter

While scribbling over one of her father's paintings at age 2½, Wang Yani said, "Daddy, I just want to paint." Her father soon recognized her potential, and by age 4, Yani had had her first show in Shanghai. A few years later, one of her paintings was reproduced on a postage stamp. Her works now number over 10,000. Yani's painting style is called *xieyi* (pronounced *see-air-ee*), which means "idea writing." She mixes ink and pigment to paint her favorite subjects—monkeys, trees, birds, and flowers. She often depicts herself as a monkey in her paintings. Ask your students to draw the animal they would select to represent themselves, then include it in a picture of themselves doing something they like.

BIRTHDAYS

1929 • **ERIC CARLE,** children's author and illustrator

1937 • **JANE SARNOFF,** children's author

EVENTS

1630 • **THE FORK WAS INTRODUCED IN AMERICA** by John Winthrop, governor of the Massachusetts Bay Colony.

1678 • Elena Cornaro of Venice became the **FIRST WOMAN IN THE WORLD TO GRADUATE FROM A UNIVERSITY,** the University of Padua.

1788 • **VIRGINIA** became the 10th state.

1876 • General George Custer and 225 men from the 7th U.S. Cavalry Regiment under his direct command were defeated and killed by a force of Sioux and Cheyenne Indians led by Sitting Bull, Crazy Horse, and Gall at the **BATTLE OF LITTLE BIGHORN** in Montana.

1950 • **THE KOREAN WAR** began.

1951 • CBS television presented the **FIRST COMMERCIAL COLOR BROADCAST.**

1977 • Ted St. Martin sank 2,036 **CONSECUTIVE FREE THROWS,** the most ever.

1989 • Chinese painter Wang Yani, age 14, became the **YOUNGEST ARTIST EVER TO HAVE A ONE-PERSON SHOW AT THE SMITHSONIAN.**

JUNE 26
activities

From sad to glad legends

Invite your students to write a happy ending to an originally sad legend. Tell them the story of the Pied Piper of Hamelin, who rid the German village of Hamelin of its rats. After he'd completed the task, the villagers refused to pay him the sack of gold they'd offered as a reward. So he lured all their children to a mountain, where they disappeared. Next, divide the class into small groups and have the groups brainstorm for as many happy endings as they can think of. Have them share their ideas with the class. Then ask each group to draw or write a happy-ending legend. Compile the students' work into a booklet entitled "The Pied Piper of Hamelin Revisited—A Happy Endings Collection." Use this booklet as a model for transforming other legends.

Mothers near and far

Encourage older students to read Pearl S. Buck's *The Good Earth*. Then have them compare and contrast the character of the Chinese wife and mother with their own mother or grandmother. What values do they share? In what ways do their respective societies influence or dictate their roles?

Outstanding women athletes

In honor of Babe Didrikson Zaharias, one of the greatest women athletes in history, have your students research other famous female athletes. Then have them make a list of outstanding female athletes at their school or in their community. Finally, have them design and mail certificates of recognition to these talented competitors.

Fighting drug abuse

On International Day Against Drug Abuse, invite a local substance-abuse counselor to share information with your students. Then have the kids work in teams to role-play ways they can say no to drugs.

JUNE 27
activities

✿ Rules of the road

The first traffic law applied to wagons, carts, sleighs, and other horse-drawn vehicles—prohibiting any galloping. Ask your students to speculate about why traffic laws were instituted well before the advent of automobiles and superhighways. What kinds of laws do they think might have been needed? Make a class list, then encourage the children to illustrate one of the ideas.

🎵 Making merry melodies

In honor of Mildred Hill—composer of "Happy Birthday to You"— invite your students to compose songs for other festive occasions, such as anniversaries, weddings, graduations, and holidays. Younger children can set their lyrics to familiar tunes. Older students can try making up music as well as lyrics.

✎ Sense-itive insights

Tell your students that an illness left Helen Keller deaf and blind when she was 19 months old. Before the illness, she'd been learning how to talk. But afterward, when she could no longer hear words, she lost her ability to speak and became completely cut off from the world. To help your students understand the importance of hearing and sight, have teams of students write skits and perform them in pantomime. Can the class tell what each team is portraying? Next, have team members wear blindfolds as they try to identify items through touch, smell, or (if appropriate) taste.

BIRTHDAYS

1859 • **MILDRED HILL,** composer of the 🎵 song "Happy Birthday to You"

1872 • **PAUL LAURENCE DUNBAR,** American poet

1880 • **HELEN KELLER,** American author ✎ and lecturer

1927 • **CAPTAIN KANGAROO** (real name: Bob Keeshan), American television personality

1949 • **LIONEL RICHIE,** American singer

EVENTS

1652 • **THE NEW WORLD'S FIRST TRAF-** ✿ **FIC LAW** was passed in New Amsterdam (New York City).

1922 • **THE FIRST NEWBERY MEDAL** for excellence in children's literature was awarded to Henrik Van Loon for *The Story of Mankind.*

1923 • **MIDAIR REFUELING** was first accomplished.

1978 • **THE FIRST ERASABLE BALLPOINT PEN** was patented.

1988 • **HABITAT FOR HUMANITY VOL- UNTEERS** began building 20 homes in Atlanta, Ga.

EID AL-FITR (3-day Islamic celebration of the end of Ramadan)

JUNE 28
activities

✒ Patriotic Pitcher

Mary Ludwig Hays earned the nickname Molly Pitcher by carrying pitchers of water to Continental soldiers on the battlefield. During the Revolutionary War battle of Monmouth, N.J., where her husband was fighting, she displayed rare bravery. When she realized the men were retreating—on orders from General Lee—Hays raced to the cannon where her husband had just fallen, and began firing it. General Washington arrived on the battlefield a short time later and ended the retreat. The next day, Washington gave Hays the rank of sergeant in the Continental Army. Ask your students to write newspaper stories chronicling Molly Pitcher's heroics.

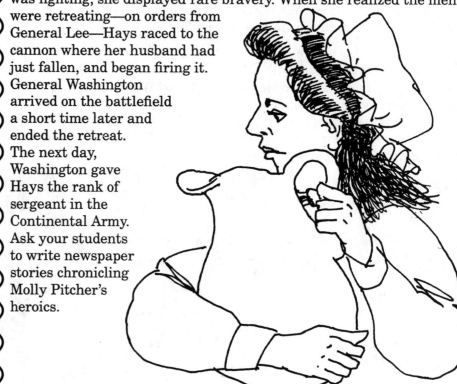

⁂ Fixing a food glut

Ask your students to imagine that their home state had a surplus of peanut butter, grape juice, and pizza. How would they eliminate the surplus? Encourage them to dream up wacky ways of selling or freely distributing the extra food statewide. Then have them illustrate their ideas.

☞ Award-winning TV shows

Make a class list of the qualities found in a good TV program. Based on this list, which three programs would your class nominate for an Emmy award? Write the names of these programs on the chalkboard, then have the class vote for the best one.

JUNE 29
activities

✹ Walk this way

Challenge your students to calculate the number of meters and kilometers covered by the Englishwoman who walked 1,000 miles in 1,000 hours. On average, how many meters per hour and kilometers per hour did she walk? Have each of your students walk a measured 50 meters as you time them with a stopwatch. Then, based on their times, have the students calculate the number of hours it would take them—if they walked continuously—to walk the same distance as the young Englishwoman.

⊘ A 7-foot feat

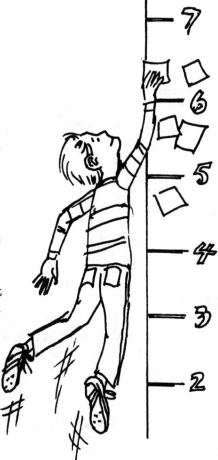

To help your students appreciate Charles Dumas's athletic feat, measure 7 feet up on a classroom wall and mark it with masking tape. Next, give each of your students a self-sticking yellow note and have them take turns jumping up and sticking the note on the wall. Which student was able to reach the highest? What was that height? How many kids were able to reach above the 7-foot mark? Remind the children that Dumas got *his entire body* above 7 feet.

⬲ Trimming the tree

Tell your students that in Appleton, England, Bawming the Thorn Day has been celebrated since 1125. On this day, Appleton residents decorate the large hawthorn tree located in the town center with ribbons, flags, and flowers. Afterward, the children of the town dance around the tree. Make a construction-paper hawthorn tree and post it on a bulletin board. Then have the students decorate it. Play some background music as the children work, then invite them to dance around the classroom when they're finished.

BIRTHDAYS

1858 • **GEORGE WASHINGTON GOETHALS**, American army officer and chief engineer of the Panama Canal
1861 • **WILLIAM MAYO**, American surgeon
1868 • **GEORGE ELLERY HALE**, American astronomer

EVENTS

1620 • Parliament PROHIBITED THE GROWING OF TOBACCO in England.
1776 • THE VIRGINIA STATE CONSTITUTION was adopted, and Patrick Henry was made governor.
1880 • A young Englishwoman completed a 1,000-MILE WALK in 1,000 ✹ hours.
1906 • Congress established MESA VERDE NATIONAL PARK in Colorado. It contains prehistoric cliff dwellings.
1956 • Charles Dumas became the FIRST ⊘ PERSON TO CLEAR 7 FEET IN THE HIGH JUMP.
1985 • Bob Brown of Boston set the YO-YO ENDURANCE RECORD at 121 hours 10 minutes.
1987 • SCIENTISTS FROM THE NEW ENGLAND AQUARIUM released three pilot whales after nursing them back to health.
1990 • The Chicago White Sox played their last game at the old COMISKEY PARK.

⬲   BAWMING THE THORN DAY (England)

BIRTHDAYS

1917 • LENA HORNE, American singer
1940 • DAVID MCPHAIL, children's
author and illustrator

EVENTS

1775 • BENJAMIN FRANKLIN was elected U.S. postmaster general.
1859 • The French tightrope walker
Charles Emile Blondin made the
FIRST TIGHTROPE CROSSING OF
NIAGARA FALLS.
1888 • ARTURO TOSCANINI, age 19,
conducted his first orchestra.
1906 • THE U.S. PURE FOOD AND DRUG
ACT was passed.
1908 • THE BIGGEST EXPLOSION EVER
RECORDED on earth took place
when a meteor struck a distant
part of Siberia.
1940 • THE U.S. FISH AND WILDLIFE
SERVICE was established.
1948 • Bell Laboratories announced the
DEVELOPMENT OF THE TRAN-
SISTOR as a substitute for radio
tubes.
1968 • RACE CAR DRIVER BOBBY
UNSER drove to the top of Pikes
Peak in a record-setting 11 minutes 54.9 seconds in the 46th
running of the Pikes Peak Auto
Hill Climb.
1985 • A NEW BASKETBALL HALL OF
FAME opened in Springfield,
Mass.

JUNE 30
activities

Friendly postcards

In honor of Ben Franklin's appointment as postmaster general, have
your students make a large postcard for a friend. Give each child a
4×6-inch plain white card. On one side, have the kids draw and color
a picture. On the other side, have them make sections for the
address and message. When they finish writing their messages and
addressing their postcards, invite the kids to design their own
postage stamps. Finally, have them deliver their postcards.

Tricky tightrope walker

Tell your students that the Frenchman Charles Emile Blondin
crossed Niagara Falls on a tightrope in just 5 minutes. Later, he
repeated his feat several times, but always with a twist. For
instance, at various times he crossed blindfolded, on stilts, in a sack,
and while carrying a man on his back. Have your students look up
the definition of "daredevil" in the dictionary. Then have them list
other people who might be considered daredevils. Their responses
might include bungee jumpers, cliff divers, race car drivers, or
trapeze artists.

Exploring books

David McPhail's first book was *The Bear's Toothache,* which was published in 1972. Afterward he wrote or illustrated over 40 books.
Gather a collection of McPhail's books for your classroom reading
corner. Invite your students to compare and contrast McPhail's more
recent books with his earlier ones. Make a class list of similarities
and differences among story themes and characters.

JULY

MONTHLONG OBSERVANCES

Anti-Boredom Month
Blueberry Month
Hitchhiking Month
National Baked Bean Month
National Hot Dog Month
National Ice Cream Month
Picnic Month
Read an Almanac Month
Recreation and Parks Month

WEEKLONG EVENTS

Music for Life Week (first week)
Special Recreation Week
  (first full week)
Be Nice to New Jersey Week
  (second week)
Space Week (week including July 20)

☆ Project of the Month: Kids' Fun Book

Celebrate Anti-Boredom Month by having your students brainstorm for fun things to do in three categories: fun for one, small-group fun, and large-group fun. Encourage the kids to think of their favorite after-school summer activities, then decide which categories they belong in. (Some activities may fit in more than one category.) Next, tell your students that they'll be publishing a book containing all their fun ideas.

Divide your class into three groups, and assign each group one of the categories. Ask the group members each to design at least two pages that illustrate, in black and white, different fun ideas for their category. Copy the pages, and assemble a copy of the "Kids' Fun Book" for each child.

EXTENDER: Your class can learn about business as well as fun. Calculate the cost of copying the "Kids' Fun Book," then decide on a fair selling price. You can advertise the book in your school or district newsletter. Have the entire class vote on how to spend the profits.

JULY 1
activities

BIRTHDAYS

1872 • LOUIS BLERIOT, French aviator who became the first person to fly an airplane across the English Channel

1961 • DIANA SPENCER, princess of Wales

• CARL LEWIS, American track star

EVENTS

1847 • THE FIRST OFFICIAL U.S. POSTAGE STAMPS were issued.

1862 • Congress established the BUREAU OF INTERNAL REVENUE.

1863 • The Civil War BATTLE OF GETTYSBURG began.

1867 • THE DOMINION OF CANADA was created.

1898 • THEODORE ROOSEVELT AND HIS ROUGH RIDERS charged up San Juan Hill during the Spanish-American War.

1941 • THE FIRST TELEVISION COMMERCIAL, sponsored by Bulova Watch, was broadcast in New York.

1963 • THE FIVE-DIGIT ZIP CODE was introduced.

1971 • THE TWENTY-SIXTH AMENDMENT was ratified, giving 18-year-olds the right to vote.

1990 • A treaty unifying the MONETARY SYSTEMS OF EAST AND WEST GERMANY became effective.

CANADA DAY
NATIONAL HOT DOG MONTH

✿ People on postage

When the first American postage stamps were issued, Benjamin Franklin appeared on the 5-cent stamp and George Washington appeared on the 10-cent stamp. Why do the children think these people were chosen? If postage stamps were being issued for the first time today, what people or images would your students want on the stamps? Have them draw and color their own "first issue" stamps.

✍ TV selling

Tell your students that the first television ad, broadcast on station WNBT in New York, lasted 10 seconds and cost $9. Ask your students how much the sponsor paid per minute. At the time, there were 4,000 TV sets in the New York area. If one person was watching each TV set when the commercial aired, how much did the sponsor pay per viewer? Ask the kids to find out how many people watch their favorite program and how much a minute of commercial time on the program costs. Then have them compare these figures with those from the first commercial.

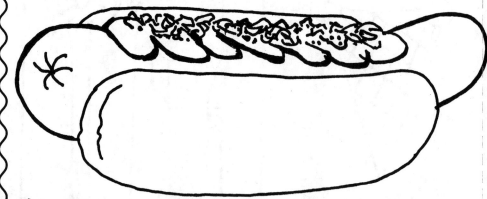

✎ Good doggies

Celebrate National Hot Dog Month with a healthy twist. Have students examine labels to determine the fat content and nutritional value of various brands of hot dogs. Then ask the kids to chart their results. Afterward, have them create truth-in-advertising poster guides to healthy hot dog eating. Display the posters in the school cafeteria.

JULY 2
activities

✒ Early judicial experiences

Tell your students that as a boy, Thurgood Marshall frequently got into trouble at school. Ironically, his punishment was to memorize parts of the U.S. Constitution. Marshall once remarked that he'd learned the entire document by heart by the time he graduated. Ask your students to write down the career paths they hope to follow. Then have them speculate on which school experiences might influence their future professions.

⬭ 40 is fabulous

Have your students celebrate Canseco's "40s feat." For the rest of July, have them keep a journal describing 40 things they did or that happened to them during the month. At month's end, have them each list their 40 things in order of greatest significance. Post the lists on a class "Top 40" bulletin board.

🍦 Flavorful ice cream

During National Ice Cream Month, have your students conduct a schoolwide survey to find out their schoolmates' favorite ice cream flavors. Ask them to create a pie chart, table, or bar graph to display their findings. What are the three most popular flavors? Afterward, have the kids brainstorm for all the known flavors of ice cream. Then have them suggest some new and unusual ones—for example, jalapeno pepper, mustard and relish, or anchovy pizza. Have them write descriptive sentences telling what these flavors would taste like. Bring in a gallon of vanilla ice cream and a variety of the students' suggested flavorings, then let the kids create. How do their new flavors taste?

BIRTHDAYS

1908 • **THURGOOD MARSHALL,**
✒ American jurist who became the first black Supreme Court justice

1919 • **JEAN CRAIGHEAD GEORGE,** children's author

1951 • **JACK GANTOS,** children's author

1964 • **JOSE CANSECO,** Cuban-born
⬭ baseball player who became the first major-leaguer to hit 40 home runs and steal 40 bases in one season

EVENTS

1776 • The Continental Congress approved the **DECLARATION OF INDEPENDENCE.**

1881 • **PRESIDENT JAMES GARFIELD WAS SHOT** by Charles Guiteau, a disgruntled office seeker. The president died of his wounds 80 days later.

1932 • Franklin Roosevelt accepted the Democratic Party's nomination for president, pledging a **"NEW DEAL FOR THE AMERICAN PEOPLE."**

1937 • American aviator **AMELIA EARHART** and her navigator, Fred Noonan, disappeared over the Pacific Ocean east of New Guinea.

1964 • President Lyndon Johnson signed the **CIVIL RIGHTS ACT OF 1964,** which guaranteed the enforcement of nondiscrimination in public accommodation, government facilities, education, and employment.

1976 • The U.S. Supreme Court ruled that the **DEATH PENALTY** was not cruel or unusual punishment.

🍦 **NATIONAL ICE CREAM MONTH**

2

JULY 3
activities

BIRTHDAYS

1878 • GEORGE M. COHAN, American playwright and composer

1962 • TOM CRUISE, American actor

EVENTS

1608 • French explorer SAMUEL DE CHAMPLAIN founded Quebec.

1775 • GEORGE WASHINGTON took command of the Continental Army in Cambridge, Mass.

1863 • THE BATTLE OF GETTYSBURG ended.

1890 • IDAHO became the 43rd state.

1991 • MOUNT RUSHMORE was finally officially dedicated on its 50th anniversary. Ceremonies in 1941 had been canceled because of World War II.

✎ COMPLIMENT YOUR MIRROR DAY

⚗ STAY OUT OF THE SUN DAY

🏳 Hallowed ground

The Battle of Gettysburg proved to be one of the most decisive battles of the Civil War as well as a defining moment in the history of the nation. After 3 days of fighting, during which both sides suffered terrible casualties, the Confederate forces were compelled to retreat, with any realistic hope of winning the war dashed. Have your students read about the battle, then imagine themselves as one of the participants, whether a famous commander or a common soldier. Ask the kids to write a letter from the participant to family members describing the events at Gettysburg.

✎ Mirror, mirror, on the wall

Place a mirror in a corner of your classroom accessible to students. Put several strips of blank paper around the mirror, then encourage the kids to write general compliments on the strips—for example, "What a great smile!" or "You look marvelous!" The comments are sure to bring smiles whenever the kids look in the mirror.

⚗ Harmful rays

Ask your students to investigate how the sun's rays affect exposed skin. Then have the kids draw posters and create advertisements (for the school PA system) warning others about the dangers of too much sun. Next, invite the children to design protective hats for people to wear outdoors. You could even challenge them to design hats for animals that spend a lot of time in the sun. For example, what type of hat would an elephant wear to protect those big, floppy ears?

JULY 4
activities

Celebrating "Satchmo"

To celebrate Louis Armstrong's birthday, play "It's A Wonderful World" for your class. Then, with the music playing in the background, have students tape their impressions of why the world is wonderful or how people can work to make it better.

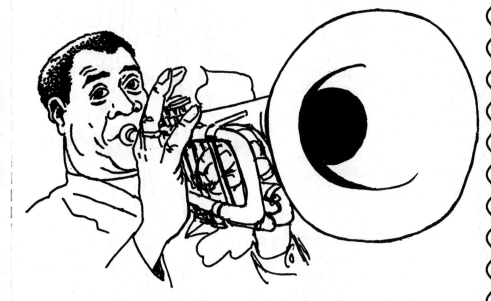

Advice for kids

Observe the birthdays of advice columnists Abigail Van Buren and Ann Landers by asking each student to write a short letter asking for advice about a typical kid problem. Collect the letters, mix them up, and distribute one to each student to answer.

Independence posters

Have each of your students create an "Independence Day Special Event" poster that features at least five local or national events. The posters' titles should incorporate the theme of independence. Ask local business or community organizations to display the finished posters.

BIRTHDAYS

1804 • NATHANIEL HAWTHORNE, American novelist

1826 • STEPHEN FOSTER, American composer

1872 • CALVIN COOLIDGE, 30th president of the United States

1900 • LOUIS ARMSTRONG, American jazz musician

1918 • ANN LANDERS AND ABIGAIL VAN BUREN, twin sisters who each wrote a popular newspaper advice column

EVENTS

1776 • The Continental Congress adopted the DECLARATION OF INDEPENDENCE.

• The Continental Congress appointed Benjamin Franklin, John Adams, and Thomas Jefferson to DESIGN A SEAL FOR THE UNITED STATES.

1826 • JOHN ADAMS AND THOMAS JEFFERSON—the second and third presidents, respectively—died.

1831 • JAMES MONROE, the fifth president, died.

• THE SONG "AMERICA" WAS INTRODUCED at a service at Boston's Park Street Church.

1960 • THE FIRST 50-STAR AMERICAN FLAG was raised at Fort McHenry, Md.

1980 • Pitcher Nolan Ryan recorded his 3,000th CAREER STRIKEOUT.

1986 • THE 100TH BIRTHDAY OF THE STATUE OF LIBERTY was celebrated with the largest fireworks display in U.S. history.

INDEPENDENCE DAY

BIRTHDAYS

1709 • ETIENNE DE SILHOUETTE, French finance minister who created shadow portraits as a hobby

1801 • DAVID G. FARRAGUT, first admiral of the U.S. Navy

1810 • PHINEAS TAYLOR BARNUM,  American showman and circus promoter

1853 • CECIL RHODES, British statesman and founder of the Rhodes scholarship

1857 • CLARA ZETKIN, German women's rights advocate and founder of International Women's Day

1958 • BILL WATTERSON, cartoonist and creator of "Calvin and Hobbes"

EVENTS

1811 • VENEZUELA proclaimed its independence from Spain.

1865 • William Booth founded the East London Revival Society (SALVATION ARMY).

• THE SECRET SERVICE was created by Congress.

1892 • A. Beard patented the ROTARY ENGINE.

1946 • THE BIKINI, designer Louis Reard's shocking new bathing suit, was first modeled.

1984 • THE STATUE OF LIBERTY'S TORCH was removed for repairs.

BE NICE TO NEW JERSEY WEEK

JULY 5 activities

Barnum's gullible public

P.T. Barnum once remarked of American audiences: "There's a sucker born every minute." What do your students think Barnum meant? As a follow-up, ask them to listen to TV advertising claims. Do these claims promise benefits they don't back up to entice the public Barnum thought was so gullible? Have the kids compile any wild claims into a class notebook as evidence of the truth of Barnum's maxim.

Bold bathing suits

Invite students to follow in bikini designer Reard's pen lines by drawing and coloring their own 21st-century bathing suits.

Classroom cartoonists

To celebrate the birth of cartoonist Bill Watterson, introduce the children to his two main characters—Calvin and Calvin's stuffed tiger, Hobbes. Read a few "Calvin and Hobbes" comic strips to the children, then ask them if they have any toys or pets they "talk" to. Give them a chance to share stories about their secret friends. Then pass out blank storyboards and have the children develop their own comic strips about themselves and these friends.

State studying

During Be Nice to New Jersey Week, encourage your students to read up on the Garden State. Then post a sheet titled "Neat Things about New Jersey." Each day, invite students to write down something interesting or unusual they learned about the state.

JULY 6
activities

A dangerous document?

After reading the Declaration of Independence, some people called it a dangerous document. Ask your students why people might have felt this way. Next, ask them to imagine that they were living in 1776. Would they have agreed with the sentiments expressed in the Declaration of Independence or remained loyal to the king? Have them write their reactions in their journals.

Thinking and talking animals

All of the animals in Beatrix Potter's stories have anthropomorphic qualities. Have your students look up the word *anthropomorphic* in the dictionary. Then invite them to tell about times when their pets (or other animals) have appeared to act like humans. Afterward, have the children write and illustrate stories about animals imbued with human qualities.

Making baseball history

Even before he hit the first home run in an All-Star game, Babe Ruth had made baseball history. During the 1927 season, he hit a record 60 home runs. In 1929, his salary climbed to $80,000 a year—more than the president of the United States earned. When Ruth was criticized for making more than the president, he reportedly quipped, "Why not? After all, I had a better year than he did." Have your students discuss what this story tells about American society. Then have them debate this question: *Does America reward its sports and entertainment stars with too much money and fame?* Encourage the kids to use concrete examples to bolster their arguments.

BIRTHDAYS

1747 • JOHN PAUL JONES, Revolutionary War hero often called "the Father of the U.S. Navy"
1866 • BEATRIX POTTER, children's author
1907 • DOROTHY CLEWES, children's author

EVENTS

1776 • THE DECLARATION OF INDEPENDENCE was announced on the front page of *The Pennsylvania Gazette.*
1885 • LOUIS PASTEUR administered the first successful antirabies inoculation to a boy who'd been bitten by a rabid dog.
1919 • A British dirigible became the FIRST AIRSHIP TO CROSS THE ATLANTIC.
1933 • Babe Ruth hit the FIRST HOME RUN IN AN ALL-STAR GAME.
1945 • Nicaragua became the FIRST COUNTRY TO ACCEPT THE UNITED NATIONS CHARTER.
1954 • ELVIS PRESLEY made his first record.
1989 • A study was released that found DANGEROUSLY HIGH CHOLESTEROL LEVELS in one-third of American adults.

JULY 7
activities

BIRTHDAYS

1887 • **MARC CHAGALL**, Russian-French artist noted for his dreamlike paintings

1906 • **SATCHEL PAIGE**, American baseball pitcher

1940 • **RINGO STARR**, English musician and member of the Beatles

EVENTS

1861 • **THE FIRST TORPEDO ATTACK** of the Civil War took place.

1923 • Warren Harding became the **FIRST U.S. PRESIDENT TO VISIT ALASKA.**

1936 • Margaret Mitchell's *GONE WITH THE WIND* was published.

1958 • President Dwight Eisenhower signed the **ALASKA STATEHOOD BILL.**

1972 • NASA announced **PLANS TO COL-LECT SOLAR ENERGY** to be used as a power source on earth.

1985 • German tennis star Boris Becker, age 17, became the **YOUNGEST PLAYER TO WIN THE WIMBLE-DON SINGLES CHAMPIONSHIP.**

1986 • Charles Stocks played 711 **HOLES OF GOLF IN 24 HOURS.**

1988 • Eleven-year-old Christopher Lee Marshall began his **FLIGHT ACROSS THE ATLANTIC.** He followed the course of his hero, Charles Lindbergh.

🌐 **FIESTA DE SAN FERMIN TANABAT (Japan)**

🎮 **VIDEO GAMES DAY**

🧪 Solar experiment

Tell your students that solar heaters typically consist of a black panel containing tubes through which water circulates. The sun heats the water as it moves through the tubes, and the hot water provides heat for buildings or homes. Ask your students why the panels are black. (Black absorbs heat.) Then have them conduct this simple experiment. Take two empty, same-size tin cans and paint the outside of one can black. Fill both cans halfway with cold water, then place them outside in the sun. Take the temperature of the water in both cans every 15 minutes. Students will find that the water in the black can becomes warmer faster.

⛳ Par for the course

Have your students calculate the average number of holes Charles Stocks played per hour, then round that number to the nearest hundredth. Then ask them to figure this out: If a round of golf consists of 18 holes, how many rounds did Stocks play in 24 hours? On average, how many rounds did he play per hour? How does this number compare with the average number of holes played per hour?

✎ Video hits

Help your students practice concise writing by having them each write just one paragraph to explain their favorite video game. Invite them to share their work with the class.

🌐 Spanish stampede

Each year in July, the city of Pamplona, Spain, honors its patron saint, San Fermin, with an 8-day festival. The highlight of the festival comes when adventurous men run through the cobbled streets to the bullring—pursued by a group of bulls. Have your students write a short, humorous poem about the running of the bulls.

JULY 8
activities

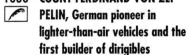 Airships and ads

Tell your students that dirigibles are also known as airships, blimps, or zeppelins (in honor of Count von Zeppelin). These vehicles have been used for passenger travel, scientific exploration, and warfare. For example, during World War II, Germany used zeppelins in air raids against Great Britain. Do your students know what dirigibles are commonly used for today? (Blimps are often used for advertising.) Ask your students to imagine they could advertise their favorite book on a blimp. What would their slogans say? Have the kids write their slogans on construction-paper blimps, then hang the blimps from the ceiling of the classroom.

Green Hornet spin-offs

To celebrate Irwin Hasen's birthday, invite your students to create a cartoon using a colorful insect of their choice as the main character. Students can create either comic strips or a single-box cartoon and use balloons for dialogue.

A long time in the saddle

To mark the day Nan Jane Aspinwall completed her horseback crossing of the United States, give your students some math problems based on this equine odyssey. If Aspinwall rode 4,500 miles in 301 days, how many miles per day did she average? At the same pace, how long would it have taken her to ride 5,000 miles? How far would she have gone if she had ridden for a full year?

BIRTHDAYS

1838 • COUNT FERDINAND VON ZEPPELIN, German pioneer in lighter-than-air vehicles and the first builder of dirigibles

1918 • IRWIN HASEN, American cartoonist who created the Green Hornet and the Green Lantern

1932 • RUSSELL EVERETT ERICKSON, children's author

EVENTS

1497 • Portuguese navigator Vasco da Gama set sail from Lisbon. His journey established a SEA ROUTE TO INDIA via the southern tip of Africa.

1629 • King Philip IV of Spain sent King Charles I of England a GIFT OF FIVE CAMELS AND ONE ELEPHANT.

1663 • King Charles II of England granted clergyman Roger Williams A CHARTER FOR RHODE ISLAND.

1776 • THE LIBERTY BELL RANG OUT IN PHILADELPHIA to announce the adoption of the Declaration of Independence.
   • THE DECLARATION OF INDEPENDENCE WAS READ TO THE PUBLIC FOR THE FIRST TIME at Philadelphia's Independence Square.

1835 • THE LIBERTY BELL CRACKED while being tolled during the funeral procession of Supreme Court Justice John Marshall.

1911 • Nan Jane Aspinwall became the FIRST WOMAN TO CROSS THE UNITED STATES ON HORSEBACK. She covered 4,500 miles in 301 days.

1976 • GERALD FORD, who had assumed the presidency upon the resignation of Richard Nixon, announced his plans to seek reelection.

BIRTHDAYS

1819 • **ELIAS HOWE, American inventor of a lockstitching sewing machine**

EVENTS

1755 • **GENERAL EDWARD BRADDOCK WAS FATALLY WOUNDED** during an attack in the French and Indian War. His aide, George Washington, escaped injury.

1776 • General George Washington summoned his troops to New York for a **READING OF THE DECLARATION OF INDEPENDENCE.**

1816 • **ARGENTINA declared its independence from Spain.**

1850 • **PRESIDENT ZACHARY TAYLOR DIED** while in office.

1872 • **THE DONUT CUTTER** was patented by J.F. Blondel.

1877 • **AMERICA'S FIRST TELEPHONE COMPANY,** Bell Telephone Company, was founded.

1893 • Surgeon Daniel Hale Williams performed the **FIRST SUCCESSFUL SURGICAL CLOSURE OF A HEART WOUND.**

1979 • *VOYAGER 2* passed Jupiter, returning photographs and scientific data.

✿ **PICNIC MONTH**

JULY 9
activities

🌐 Where in the world?

Have your students find Argentina and Spain on a world map. Then ask: In which hemispheres—and on which continents—are these two countries located? What body of water separates them? What is the capital of each country? How far is it from capital to capital?

🧪 Mother Earth's music

Tell your students that *Voyager 2* is one of two U.S. space probes that were launched in 1977. (The other probe is *Voyager 1.*) Besides their scientific instruments, both probes were equipped with special records called "Sounds of Earth"—in case of discovery by another civilization. On the chalkboard, make a list of the kinds of sounds your students would include on such a record. What would these sounds tell others about the earth and its inhabitants? Are there any particular sounds your students would *not* want to include? Why?

✿ Pretend picnic

One day this month, plan an imaginary picnic for the characters in a book your students have recently read. Encourage the kids to consider the characters' likely tastes in food, attire, and games. The children may also want to develop a "guest list" including compatible characters from other books. Assemble their ideas into a booklet.

JULY 10
activities

📖 Playing with words

Besides writing and illustrating children's books, Fred Gwynne is an award-winning stage, film, and television actor. (Your students may recall one of his TV roles—Herman in "The Munsters.") Gwynne's most popular children's books are those on wordplay. In *The King Who Rained*, he illustrates the humorous results of using the wrong homophone or homonym. Have students look up the meanings of homophone and homonym. Then divide the class into small groups, and challenge each group to collect as many homophones or homonyms as possible in a week. At week's end, have the groups each create a silly illustration depicting the literal meaning of a sentence that misuses one of their words. Post the illustrations on the bulletin board.

🇺🇸 What's in Wyoming?

Wyoming, the 44th state, may have been among the last states to join the Union, but it has experienced more than its share of firsts. For example, Wyoming is home to our nation's first national park, Yellowstone, and to the first national monument, Devils Tower. Have your students locate Wyoming on a map, then find its capital, Cheyenne. In what part of the state is this city located? Next, ask the kids to use compass directions to describe the location of Yellowstone Park and Devils Tower in relation to Cheyenne and in relation to each other.

BIRTHDAYS

1834 • **JAMES ABBOT McNEIL WHISTLER, American painter**

1875 • **MARY McLEOD BETHUNE, American educator**

1882 • **IMA HOGG, American philanthropist**

1885 • **MARY O'HARA, children's author**

1916 • **MARTIN PROVENSEN, children's author and illustrator**

1926 • **FRED GWYNNE, actor and children's author** 📖

1943 • **ARTHUR ASHE, American tennis player**

EVENTS

1220 • **LONDON BRIDGE was damaged by fire and fell down.**

1853 • Vice President **MILLARD FILLMORE assumed the presidency upon the death of Zachary Taylor.**

1890 • **WYOMING became the 44th state.** 🇺🇸

1913 • Death Valley, Calif., reached a temperature of 134° F **IN THE SHADE**—the highest ever recorded in the United States.

1929 • Congress made official the current **SIZE OF U.S. PAPER MONEY.**

1962 • *TELSTAR 1*, the first satellite to relay TV and telephone signals, was launched.

1973 • **THE BAHAMAS** gained its independence from Britain.

1991 • **BORIS YELTSIN WAS INAUGURATED as president of Russia.**

10

JULY 11
activities

Creating characters

Tell your students that a dream inspired author E.B. White to create his famous mouse character, Stuart Little. Then ask each child to create an animal character to be born or adopted into the child's own family. Next, have the kids write stories involving the reaction of their new family member to home life. Feature the stories at a class read-aloud.

Only the lonely

Involve your students in National Cheer Up the Lonely Day. First, ask them to name individuals or groups of people who may be lonely, such as senior citizens, widows, widowers, disabled people, and hospital patients. Next, have the children brainstorm for ways to cheer these people up. For example, the children might suggest giving flowers or cards to hospital patients, delivering meals to elderly shut-ins, or organizing a sing-along at a local senior citizen center. Divide the class into "children's cheer squads," and have each squad select a "mission" from the list of ideas. Enlist parent volunteers to help. Your students will not only be involved in a worthy project, they'll also derive great pride in being part of a caring community.

Population study

On World Population Day, have your students look up the meaning of the word *demography*. Then have them conduct a brief demographic study of schoolmates in their grade level. How many boys and girls are there? What are their ages? What ethnic backgrounds do they represent? Graph the results.

JULY 12
activities

Thoughts from Thoreau

Henry David Thoreau is most famous for the book *Walden,* which detailed his experiences living alone in a log cabin on Walden Pond. But he is also remembered for his essay "Civil Disobedience," which outlined the principles of nonviolent resistance later developed and used so effectively by Mahatma Gandhi and Martin Luther King, Jr. In the essay, Thoreau discussed his objections to the war with Mexico and to slavery in the United States. He concluded that he could not in good conscience support a government engaged in such policies, so he refused to pay his poll tax and was arrested. Organize a class debate on the issue of how far a citizen's obligation to obey governmental authority extends. Does the fact that the government was elected democratically mean that it is due obedience? Or is a citizen who strongly disagrees with the government's policies justified in a form of protest such as refusing to pay taxes? Should the protester be prepared to accept the legal penalties for civil disobedience? Why or why not?

Photo opportunities

Invite your students to bring in favorite photographs that they or their family members have taken. Discuss the elements to consider when taking a photograph—for example, subject, lighting, camera angle, composition. If possible, borrow a school camera and let the students take portraits of one another. The children can then make construction-paper frames for the finished prints.

Minimum-wage math

Ask your students: How much would a worker receiving the minimum wage in 1933 be paid for a 40-hour workweek? How much would the same worker be paid annually? Have the kids find out the current minimum wage in the United States, then perform the same calculations for today's minimum-wage worker.

BIRTHDAYS

100 B.C. • **JULIUS CAESAR,** Roman general and statesman
1730 • **JOSIAH WEDGWOOD,** English pottery maker
1817 • **HENRY DAVID THOREAU,** American essayist and naturalist
1854 • **GEORGE EASTMAN,** American industrialist and inventor of the Kodak camera
1895 • **BUCKMINSTER FULLER,** American engineer known for developing the geodesic dome
1917 • **ANDREW WYETH,** American artist
1937 • **BILL COSBY,** American actor and comedian

EVENTS

1808 • *The Missouri Gazette,* the **FIRST NEWSPAPER WEST OF THE MISSISSIPPI RIVER,** began publication.
1862 • Congress authorized the army **MEDAL OF HONOR** for gallantry "above and beyond the call of duty."
1870 • John W. Hyatt was granted a patent for **CELLULOID.**
1909 • Congress passed the **SIXTEENTH AMENDMENT,** which gave the federal government the power to tax incomes.
1933 • **THE U.S. MINIMUM WAGE** was set at 40¢ an hour.
1957 • Dwight D. Eisenhower became the **FIRST PRESIDENT TO FLY IN A HELICOPTER.**
1984 • New York instituted the nation's **FIRST MANDATORY SEAT-BELT LAW.**

BIRTHDAYS

1886 • **FATHER EDWARD FLANAGAN,** American priest and founder of Boys Town
1918 • **MARCIA BROWN,** children's author
1923 • **ASHLEY BRYAN,** children's poet
1940 • **PATRICK STEWART,** British actor who played Captain Picard in the TV series "Star Trek: The Next Generation"
1942 • **HARRISON FORD,** American actor
1963 • **SPUD WEBB,** 5'5" professional basketball player

EVENTS

1832 • Henry Schoolcraft discovered the **SOURCE OF THE MISSISSIPPI RIVER: Minnesota's Lake Itasca.**
1837 • **BUCKINGHAM PALACE in London** became the official residence of the British royal family.
1863 • **RIOTS AGAINST THE CIVIL WAR MILITARY DRAFT** erupted in New York.
1865 • In an editorial, Horace Greeley gave the famous advice, **"GO WEST, YOUNG MAN, AND GROW UP WITH THE COUNTRY."**
1977 • **A POWER BLACKOUT** paralyzed New York City.
1985 • A host of recording stars performed in the **LIVE AID** concerts held in Philadelphia and London, which raised $70 million for famine relief in Africa.

NIGHT WATCH DAY (eve of Bastille Day)
OBON (Japan)

JULY 13
activities

Starting over

Ask your students to speculate on why Americans might have been particularly receptive to Horace Greeley's advice in 1865. (The Civil War had just ended, and many people wanted to make a new start in life.) What advice would your students give someone who wanted to start a new life today? Have them write appropriate slogans on strips of colored construction paper. Post the slogans on a bulletin board titled "New Beginnings."

Against the odds

Using a sports almanac or other sources, have your students compile a list of the heights of 20 professional basketball players, including Spud Webb. Then have them make a graph. Discuss the results.

Blackout blues

Tell your students that during World War II, European countries routinely imposed nighttime blackouts in order to conceal their cities from enemy bombers. But the 1977 blackout in New York City was anything but routine. Make a class list of the kinds of problems New Yorkers might have faced. Then have your students suggest safety precautions they might take at home to protect themselves and their families in case of a blackout.

JULY 14
activities

✒ This land is your land

Woody Guthrie wrote more than 1,000 folk songs, including "This Land Is Your Land." Play a recording of this song for your students. Then ask them to cut out magazine pictures to illustrate the lyrics, pasting the pictures on sheets of construction paper containing the appropriate lines from the song. You might also have your students examine Guthrie's lyrics from an environmental perspective. For instance, they could use individual lines from the song to introduce reports on the ways our redwood forests and waters have been harmed.

📖 Amelia Bedelia in a pickle

Mark the birthday of author Peggy Parrish by having your students read selections from some of her Amelia Bedelia stories. Then divide the class into groups, and have the groups brainstorm for school situations in which Amelia Bedelia's literal-mindedness might get her into trouble. For instance, what would Amelia do in the computer room when she had to "boot up" or "run" a program? Have students write down their silly scenarios. Then encourage them to act out Amelia's misunderstandings.

✎ Delightful desserts

One day during Blueberry Month, invite your students to sample some fresh blueberries with sugar and cream. Then challenge the kids to write a mouth-watering description of this treat. Have them read their descriptions aloud, then hold a class vote for the best.

BIRTHDAYS

1912 • **WOODY GUTHRIE, American folk singer** ✒
1913 • **GERALD FORD, 38th president of the United States**
1927 • **PEGGY PARRISH, children's author who created Amelia Bedelia** 📖

EVENTS

1789 • **THE CITIZENS OF PARIS STORMED THE BASTILLE** and released its prisoners at the start of the French Revolution.
1865 • Edward Whymper became the **FIRST PERSON TO CLIMB THE MATTERHORN,** a mountain on the Italian-Swiss border.
1892 • **CIVIL WAR VETERANS** wounded in service were granted a $50 monthly pension.
1968 • Slugger Hank Aaron hit his **500TH HOME RUN.**
1972 • For the first time in a major league baseball game, **ONE TEAM'S CATCHER WAS THE BROTHER OF THE HOME PLATE UMPIRE.** The catcher was the Detroit Tigers' Tom Haller; the umpire, Bill Haller.

BASTILLE DAY
✎ **BLUEBERRY MONTH**

14

JULY 15
activities

BIRTHDAYS

1606 • REMBRANDT, Dutch painter

1779 • CLEMENT CLARKE MOORE, American poet who wrote "A Visit from St. Nicholas"

1903 • WALTER EDMONDS, children's author

EVENTS

1870 • Georgia became the LAST CONFEDERATE STATE READMITTED TO THE UNION.

1876 • George Washington Bradley pitched the FIRST NO-HIT GAME IN MAJOR LEAGUE HISTORY.

1912 • JIM THORPE won his 15th event at the 1912 Olympics.

1952 • THE FIRST TRANSATLANTIC HELICOPTER FLIGHT took place.

1965 • American scientists displayed CLOSE-UP PICTURES OF THE PLANET MARS taken by the *Mariner 4* spacecraft.

1975 • *Apollo* and *Soyuz* rockets blasted off for a planned RENDEZVOUS IN SPACE.

RESPECT CANADA DAY
ST. SWITHIN'S DAY (England)

Penetrating portraits

Rembrandt was one of the most influential European painters of the 17th century. While many of his contemporaries chose to paint royalty, his favorite subjects were everyday citizens of his homeland. Rembrandt aimed to portray his subjects' true personalities and tried to capture realistic facial expressions. During his career, he painted about 60 self-portraits. Show your students examples of Rembrandt's self-portraits, drawing their attention to his characteristic contrasting of light and dark. What do the children think the expressions on Rembrandt's face tell about the particular point in his life when the self-portrait was done? Ask your students to create their own self-portraits using paints, markers, colored pencils, or ink. What do their facial expressions say about them at this point in their lives?

Memorable poem

Tell your students that Clement Clarke Moore wrote "A Visit from St. Nicholas" for his six children. The poem, originally published in 1848, is still a seasonal favorite. How many of the verses can your class recall from memory? Write down your students' responses. Perhaps one child's line will trigger another's memory. Compare your students' version with the original. The kids might be surprised at how much of the poem has become a part of their literary heritage!

JULY 16
activities

🌐 Heading south

Tell your students that Roald Amundsen and the members of his South Pole expedition took enough food and fuel to last 2 years. After traveling by ship to Antarctica, they lived on the continent for a year. They used dogsleds to finally reach the South Pole. Have your students use a world map to locate the South Pole. Then explain that nearly 99% of Antarctica is covered by ice. In some areas, the ice is 16,000 feet deep—and the temperature drops to -100 degrees F. No plants or animals live in the continent's interior. Have students brainstorm for words to describe Antarctica—for example, *barren, snowy, frigid, icy, desolate.* Then ask them to write a poem about this cold continent. Afterward, discuss why they think anyone would want to explore Antarctica.

🖊 Preparing for peace

As the first secretary-general of the United Nations, Trygve Lie worked tirelessly for world peace. But his efforts could not prevent a variety of conflicts, including the Korean War. Ask your students if they think complete world peace is possible. Why or why not? What actions might countries take to move closer to peace? Have the class write a letter to the editor outlining some suggestions.

🕊 Space-y news

To celebrate Space Week, divide your class into five groups and ask each group to research what occurred during one day of *Apollo 11*'s historic mission. Have students begin with lift-off on July 16 (day 1) and continue to the famous moon walk on July 20 (day 5). Then, each day during Space Week, have the appropriate group present a news report on the day's space adventures. Students can choose to simulate a television or radio broadcast or write a newspaper article.

BIRTHDAYS

1723 • SIR JOSHUA REYNOLDS, English portrait painter
1872 • ROALD AMUNDSEN, Norwegian explorer who discovered the South Pole
1896 • TRYGVE LIE, Norwegian diplomat and first secretary-general of the United Nations

EVENTS

622 • Followers of Mohammed fled Mecca for Medina. This migration, which is termed THE HEGIRA, marks the beginning of the Muslim calendar.
1439 • AN ACT PROHIBITING KISSING was passed in England in an attempt to prevent the spread of disease.
1548 • LA PAZ, the capital of Bolivia, was founded.
1790 • THE DISTRICT OF COLUMBIA was established.
1862 • David Farragut became the FIRST REAR ADMIRAL IN THE U.S. NAVY.
1877 • A CARRIER PIGEON BEAT A TRAIN in a 70-mile race from Dover to London, England.
1935 • THE FIRST PARKING METER was installed in Oklahoma City, Okla.
1941 • JOE DIMAGGIO'S RECORD-BREAKING HITTING STREAK ENDED after 56 consecutive games.
1945 • THE FIRST ATOMIC BOMB was tested in the desert near Alamogordo, N.M. It produced a blast equivalent to the explosion of 20,000 tons of TNT.
1969 • *APOLLO 11* lifted off from Cape Kennedy, Fla. Its mission: the first manned moon landing.

🕊 SPACE WEEK
(week including July 20)

JULY 17
activities

BIRTHDAYS

1859 • LUIS MUNOZ-RIVERA, Puerto Rican patriot and poet

1932 • KARLA KUSKIN, children's 📖 author

1935 • DONALD SUTHERLAND, Canadian actor

EVENTS

1850 • THE FIRST PHOTOGRAPH OF A STAR was taken.

1897 • The steamship *Portland* arrived in Washington with the FIRST MAJOR GOLD SHIPMENT FROM THE KLONDIKE.

1938 • Pilot DOUGLAS "WRONG WAY" ⁂ CORRIGAN left New York for California. He eventually landed in Dublin, Ireland.

1954 • THE FIRST NEWPORT JAZZ FESTIVAL was held in Newport, R.I.

1975 • U.S. ASTRONAUTS AND SOVIET COSMONAUTS JOINED HANDS after linking their *Apollo* and *Soyuz* spacecrafts.

1987 • THE DOW JONES INDUSTRIAL ☼ AVERAGE CLOSED OVER 2,500 POINTS for the first time in history.

MUNOZ-RIVERA DAY
(Puerto Rico)

📖 Word lover

Author Karla Kuskin once said that her love of words was so great that she couldn't even bear to discard fortune-cookie fortunes. Have your students write their own fortunes or words of wisdom on 6-inch-long strips of adding-machine tape. Tape the strips together and post them in the hallway for others to read. Later, introduce your class to the works of Karla Kuskin by reading *The Philharmonic Gets Dressed*.

⁂ Wrong-way day

When Douglas "Wrong Way" Corrigan landed in Dublin, Ireland, he got out of his plane and asked, "Isn't this Los Angeles?" Invite your class to have a "wrong-way day." For example, students might wear their shirts backward, or you might mix up the schedule. You might also include some "wrong ways" into social studies. Have students consider how U.S. history would be different if certain events came out the "wrong way." For instance, what if the South had won the Civil War? What if the Pilgrims had landed in California?

☼ Stock market speculators

On the anniversary of the Dow Jones 2,500-point milestone, begin this (nearly) hands-on stock market activity. Divide your class into small groups, and give each group $500 in play money. Explain that for the next 2 weeks, the groups will be seeking "profit" by investing their "money" in stocks. You will be the broker. For their initial investments, groups can buy $500 worth of shares in any stock or stocks listed on the New York Stock Exchange. Each morning, bring in the business pages of the newspaper so the groups can check the previous day's closing prices. Give the groups the opportunity at this time to sell and buy stocks at the closing prices. At the end of the 2 weeks, total the value of each group's stocks to determine who earns the title of Wall Street wizards.

JULY 18
activities

Firsts in space
Have teams of students conduct research to find out about other "firsts" in space exploration—for example, the first rendezvous in space, space station, space walk, U.S. astronaut, black astronaut, woman astronaut, space shuttle. Armed with their data, the teams can each make a rocket-shaped time line depicting these important events.

Disneyland adventures
Ask any of your students who've visited Disneyland to share their experiences with the class. Encourage them to bring in park maps and souvenirs to enhance their presentations. If no students have visited Disneyland, obtain brochures from local travel agents. Share these with the class, then invite students to write about what they'd do if they could spend a day with their favorite Disney character.

Reading the almanac
Teach students how to locate information in an almanac by using the general index. Have them each identify their favorite hobby, vacation spot, or other topic, then locate it in the almanac. To test their newfound skills, have the kids list and share five facts about their topic that they gleaned from the almanac.

BIRTHDAYS
1918 • NELSON MANDELA, South African civil rights activist and longtime leader of the African National Congress
1921 • JOHN GLENN, U.S. astronaut who was the first American to orbit the earth
1954 • FELICIA BOND, children's author

EVENTS
1792 • American naval hero JOHN PAUL JONES died.
1874 • TENNIS was introduced to the United States.
1925 • The American Automobile Association DECLARED WOMEN DRIVERS TO BE AS COMPETENT AS MEN DRIVERS.
1940 • Franklin Roosevelt was NOMINATED FOR AN UNPRECEDENTED THIRD TERM.
1947 • President Harry Truman signed the PRESIDENTIAL SUCCESSION ACT.
1955 • DISNEYLAND opened in California.
1971 • Brazilian soccer star PELE ended his career with the Brazilian National Soccer Team.
1974 • Bob Gibson became the FIRST NATIONAL LEAGUE PITCHER TO STRIKE OUT 3,000 BATTERS in a career.
1980 • India became THE SIXTH NATION TO PUT A SATELLITE INTO ORBIT.

READ AN ALMANAC MONTH

18

JULY 19
activities

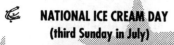

📖 Provocative poetry

Read aloud selections from Eve Merriam's *It Doesn't Always Have to Rhyme, Blackberry Ink,* and *The Inner City Mother Goose.* Have the children select their favorite poems and pick up Merriam's beat either by drawing pictures to go with the poems or by writing poems to reflect their own neighborhood experiences.

✒️ Forgotten politicians?

To mark George McGovern's birthday, have your students compile a list of unsuccessful presidential and vice presidential candidates from the second half of the 20th century. Ask each child to research the postelection career of one of these candidates, then write a one-paragraph summary on an index card. Post the cards on a bulletin board titled "American Politicians: Where Are They Now?"

🍦 Ice cream poll

To celebrate National Ice Cream Day, have each of your students ask at least 10 people the following question: "Does ice cream taste best served in a cone or in a dish?" Encourage students to create a pictograph to display the results. As a culminating activity, bring in ice cream, cones, and dishes—and invite your students to serve themselves.

JULY 20
activities

⊘ Batting for dollars

Ask your students to find out the cost of the cheapest ticket for a major-league baseball game at the park nearest their hometown. Then ask them to calculate the percentage increase in admission price since 1859.

✿ Moon memories

Have your students ask their parents or grandparents to recall where they were and what they were doing when astronaut Neil Armstrong stepped onto the moon. Your students will themselves remember other historic happenings—including, perhaps, the smashing of the Berlin Wall, the liberation of Kuwait, and the *Challenger* accident. Have the children each make a chart that consists of historic events they recall and where they were, who they were with, and what they were doing the day each event occurred.

⚗ Searching for signs of life

After landing on Mars, *Viking 1* sent back television pictures of the planet's surface. It also conducted experiments, one of which involved searching for life. The lander scooped up a soil sample, then added certain chemicals to trigger an organic reaction. None was observed. Perhaps *Viking 1* wasn't able to recognize what Martian life looks like. Or maybe the site was, indeed, devoid of life. Have your class discuss what it means to show signs of life. Make a list of places a spacecraft could land on Earth and what signs of life would be found there. Next, make a list of places on Earth that wouldn't show any signs of life—for example, inside a volcano. Take your class on an indoor field trip at school to search for signs of life. Be sure to include bacteria as a type of life.

20

BIRTHDAYS

1899 • **ERNEST HEMINGWAY,** American novelist

1920 • **ISAAC STERN,** Russian violinist

1952 • **ROBIN WILLIAMS,** American comedian and actor

EVENTS

1834 • **THE LIBERTY BELL WAS MUF-FLED** to toll the death of the Marquis de Lafayette.

1861 • At the Battle of Bull Run, the first major encounter of the Civil War, **CONFEDERATE GENERAL THOMAS J. JACKSON** gained the nickname "Stonewall."

1873 • Jesse James committed the **WORLD'S FIRST TRAIN ROBBERY,** near Council Bluffs, Iowa.

1925 • Tennessee biology teacher John Scopes was found **GUILTY OF TEACHING THE THEORY OF EVOLUTION,** which was against state law. He was fined $100.

1930 • **THE U.S. VETERANS ADMINISTRATION** was established.

1959 • The United States launched the *Savannah,* the **FIRST NUCLEAR-POWERED MERCHANT SHIP.**

1961 • U.S. astronaut Virgil Grissom became the **SECOND AMERICAN IN SPACE.** His flight lasted 16 minutes.

1969 • Astronauts Neil Armstrong and Edwin "Buzz" Aldrin **RETURNED FROM THE MOON** to the command module, manned by Michael Collins.

NATIONAL INDEPENDENCE DAY (Belgium)

JULY 21
activities

Stonewall and other nicknames

Tell your students that Confederate General Thomas J. Jackson earned the nickname "Stonewall" during the first Battle of Bull Run. Despite overwhelming odds, his brigade stood firm—"like a stone wall"—against attacks from Northern troops. Ask your students to name other prominent Americans and the actions that have earned them recognition—for example, Alexander Graham Bell, Martin Luther King, Jr., Sally Ride, Carl Lewis. What nicknames might your students give these people?

Stand-up comedy

Have your students seen Robin Williams on TV or in movies? To celebrate his birthday, ask the kids to choose a favorite comedian. Why do they like him or her? Are there any potential comedians in your class? Let those who wish prepare a short comedy skit and perform it in front of the class. Nonperformers might like to join forces with the class comics and help write the skits.

Flying in space

To mark the anniversary of Virgil "Gus" Grissom's space flight, turn off the lights in your classroom for 16 minutes. During that time—the length of Grissom's flight—ask your students to imagine what they might see or do or think about if they were flying in space. When the lights come back on, have the kids quickly write all their thoughts on scrap paper. Finally, have them use their ideas to write poems about space flight.

JULY 22
activities

✏️ Sunny flips of the tongue

Have your students look up "spoonerism" in the dictionary. Next, divide the class into pairs, and have the partners take turns reading aloud a favorite poem. Afterward, have the pairs write down their poems, intentionally transposing the initial sounds of some words. Then have them read the spoonerism-filled results.

Nature mobiles

Share some photographs of Alexander Calder's mobiles with your students. Then encourage the children to make "nature mobiles," using leaves, twigs, tree bark, and other natural objects. First, take the students for an outdoor walk to gather their objects. Next, ask them to tie or glue their objects to pieces of string cut to varied lengths, then tie the strings to coat hangers. Suspend the mobiles from the hallway or classroom ceiling.

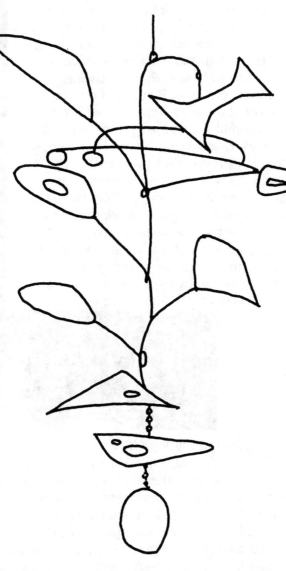

Place names

Tell your students that in 1831, the spelling of Cleaveland was changed to Cleveland to better fit into a newspaper headline. What cities, buildings, businesses, schools, or streets in your students' area are named after people? Make a class list, and note any changed spellings.

BIRTHDAYS

1822 • JOHANN GREGOR MENDEL, Austrian monk who discovered the principles of heredity

1844 • WILLIAM ARCHIBALD SPOONER, English clergyman after whom the spoonerism was named

1849 • EMMA LAZARUS, American poet who wrote the sonnet "The New Colossus," which is engraved on the Statue of Liberty

1881 • MARGERY WILLIAMS BIANCO, children's author who wrote *The Velveteen Rabbit*

1898 • ALEXANDER CALDER, American artist considered the originator of the mobile

• STEVEN VINCENT BENET, American poet

EVENTS

1587 • More than 100 English colonists founded a SECOND COLONY ON ROANOKE ISLAND off North Carolina, the site of the first attempted English colony in America. When supply ships returned 3 years later, the only trace of the colony was the word *Croatan* carved on a tree.

1796 • Moses Cleaveland, a surveyor for the Connecticut Land Co., founded CLEVELAND, Ohio.

1881 • In Seattle, Wash., Tom Clancy was ARRESTED FOR SPEEDING ON HIS HORSE. He was riding more than the legal limit of 6 mph.

1933 • American pilot Wiley Post completed the FIRST SOLO AIR CIRCUMNAVIGATION OF THE GLOBE. His flight took 7 days, 18 hours, and 45 minutes.

1975 • Congress voted to RESTORE THE AMERICAN CITIZENSHIP OF ROBERT E. LEE, who had commanded the Confederate forces during the Civil War.

22

JULY 23
activities

Classroom assembly line

Henry Ford, founder of the Ford Motor Co., believed that the average person should be able to own a car. To make this possible, he developed one of the first assembly-line production systems. The assembly line allowed Ford to produce a greater number of cars at a lower price. The process proved so successful that other manufacturers began using it. Have your students conduct an experiment to test the effectiveness of an assembly line. Bring in a couple loaves of bread, several jars of peanut butter and jelly, paper plates, and eight knives. Select two four-student groups. Tell the groups that their goal is to make 12 peanut butter and jelly sandwiches as quickly as possible. Have the members of one group work individually to make the sandwiches; have the other group devise and use an assembly-line procedure. Then see which group can make the sandwiches faster. Judge the final products for quality as well.

Seeking shooting stars

Tell your students that a meteor (also called a shooting star) is a streak of light in the sky that occurs when a meteoroid—a usually small, solid object from space—enters the earth's atmosphere and burns up. On a dark, moonless night, a careful observer might expect to see five or six meteors per hour. But at certain times of the year, when the orbit of a group of meteoroids intersects the earth's orbit, many more meteors are visible. This is called a meteor shower. Show your students a sky chart, pointing out the constellation Perseus and noting how to find it in the nighttime sky. Then encourage your students to observe the Perseid meteor shower, which begins about now but peaks around August 12. Tell them to go to a place away from bright lights, find Perseus, and note how many meteors they see in a 15- or 20-minute period.

JULY 24
activities

El Libertador

Simon Bolivar was born in Venezuela. As a child, he learned about the French and American revolutions and dreamed of the day his country would achieve independence from Spain. Bolivar became one of South America's greatest generals in the fight against Spain, managing to win independence for Bolivia, Colombia, Ecuador, Peru, and Venezuela. Have your students locate South America on a world map. Then have them find the countries that were liberated by Bolivar.

Women's rights

Tell your students that when Bella Abzug was elected to the U.S. House of Representatives in 1970, she pushed vigorously for women's rights. Ask the children to list the kinds of rights women have been fighting for since the 19th century, when women such as Elizabeth Cady Stanton and Susan B. Anthony were leading the charge. How has the women's movement progressed? Who are today's prominent feminists?

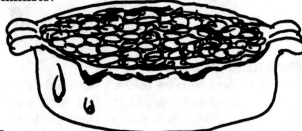

Best baked beans

Celebrate National Baked Bean Month by having your class conduct a taste test of various brands of canned baked beans. Which brand tastes best? Which tastes worst? Afterward, challenge students to create tongue twisters beginning with: "The best baked beans...."

BIRTHDAYS

1783 • SIMON BOLIVAR, South American patriot

1802 • ALEXANDRE DUMAS, French novelist

1898 • AMELIA EARHART, American aviator

1920 • BELLA ABZUG, American politician and feminist

EVENTS

1679 • NEW HAMPSHIRE became a royal colony of the British crown.

1701 • ANTOINE DE LA MOTHE CADILLAC founded a fort at the site of Detroit.

1847 • BRIGHAM YOUNG and his Mormon followers arrived at the Great Salt Lake in Utah.

1866 • Tennessee became the FIRST CONFEDERATE STATE TO BE READMITTED TO THE UNION.

1959 • U.S. vice president Richard Nixon and Soviet premier Nikita Khrushchev DEBATED THE PROS AND CONS OF CAPITALISM AND COMMUNISM on world television.

1977 • Dutch rider Henk Vink set a MOTORCYCLE WORLD RECORD by covering a 1-kilometer course in 16.68 seconds from a standing start.

PIONEER DAY (Utah)
NATIONAL BAKED BEAN MONTH

JULY 25
activities

Flying across the Channel

Tell your students that it took Louis Bleriot 37 minutes to complete his 20-mile flight. Help them appreciate Bleriot's aviation milestone by having them re-create it with paper airplanes. Have students work in teams to create a scale drawing of England, France, and the English Channel on the school playground or parking lot. They can use chalk or masking tape to lay out their design, which should use a scale of at least 1 foot to 1 mile. Have the children mark the sites of Calais, France, and Dover, England. Next, have them each make a paper airplane. Students can then take turns flying their airplanes "across the Channel."

Passport to the parks

The National Park Service offers a national parks passport book. Each time a passport holder visits a national park, the book gets stamped. Make a notebook-size version of this passport book for your students. List each national park or monument your students have visited on a separate page, and ask the kids to find an appropriate illustration or magazine photo. Then have students sign their names under the locations they've visited. Encourage those who will visit national parks or monuments in the future to send postcards for inclusion in the passport book.

JULY 26 activities

BIRTHDAYS
1856 • GEORGE BERNARD SHAW, British playwright
1892 • PEARL BUCK, American author
1897 • PAUL GALLICO, American author of *The Snow Goose*
1923 • JAN BERENSTAIN, children's author
1943 • MICK JAGGER, British rock star

Perspectives on teaching

Playwright George Bernard Shaw once observed, "Those who can, do. Those who can't, teach." Share Shaw's quote with your students. Then share this quote from Christa McAuliffe: "I touch the future; I teach." Ask your students which quote they think more accurately describes today's teachers. After they've shared their views, explain your own view of teaching. Then invite students to use these two quotes to survey family, friends, and community members about their perceptions of teaching.

Classroom rock fest

In honor of Mick Jagger's birthday, have a parent-student rock fest in your classroom. Invite parents who are fans of Jagger to bring in their favorite Rolling Stones recordings. Students also can bring in recordings by their favorite artists. After playing a sampling of the songs, ask parents and kids what they think of the other generation's musical tastes.

Native American legends

Share with your students the Hopi Indian legend of the *kachinas*—supernatural beings who leave their mountain homes for half the year to visit the tribe. The kachinas are believed to bring good health to the people and rainfall for the crops. For the Niman dance, dancers portraying kachinas sing and dance for almost the entire day. Ask your students to name other supernatural beings—for example, leprechauns and guardian angels—who come to earth and help people. Then have the children write stories featuring supernatural do-gooders of their own invention.

EVENTS
1788 • NEW YORK became the 11th state.
1847 • The West African nation of LIBERIA proclaimed its independence.
1889 • China's HWANG HO (Yellow River) flooded, leaving the surrounding countryside under as much as 12 feet of water.
1908 • THE FEDERAL BUREAU OF INVESTIGATION was created.
1920 • Oscar Swann, age 72, won a medal in rifle shooting, thus becoming the OLDEST OLYMPIC MEDALIST.
1969 • U.S. scientists examined the FIRST MOON ROCK SAMPLES.
1986 • Bicyclist Greg Lemond became the FIRST AMERICAN TO WIN THE TOUR DE FRANCE. His time for the 2,500-mile race was 110 hours, 35 minutes, 19 seconds.

HOPI NIMAN DANCE (United States)

JULY 27
activities

27

It takes teamwork
Tell your students that Orville Wright worked together with his brother, Wilbur, to build and fly the first power-driven airplane. Since the Wright brothers worked as a team, how did they decide who would fly the plane on this day in 1909? Ask your students to speculate. How do your students think Orville felt during his record-setting flight? How do they suppose Wilbur felt watching from the ground? Have each student write a narrative from the perspective of either Orville or Wilbur.

Titles of honor
Children's author Scott Corbett fulfilled a longtime wish when he joined two friends for a balloon trip. They traveled from northern Rhode Island to southern Massachusetts. Later, Corbett joked that he could sign his name "Scott Corbett, I.A. (Interstate Aerialist)." Ask your students what titles they could give themselves based on their accomplishments. Next, have them fold $8^1/_2$×11-inch sheets of construction paper in half to make "nameplates" for their desks. Have them each write their name and new title on their nameplate.

Walk the plant?
Today is Take Your Houseplants for a Walk Day. Ask your students to suggest a scientific reason why this might be a good thing to do. (Plants remove carbon dioxide from the atmosphere and generate oxygen.) What whimsical reasons can they suggest?

JULY 28
activities

📖 Character diary

Natalie Babbitt's popular book *Tuck Everlasting* deals with the theme of searching for oneself. Read it aloud to the class. As students listen, have them keep a diary of their reactions to Winnie, the main character. Following the story's conclusion, have students make collages to illustrate their reactions. They might include pictures, drawings, words, or other creative ways to capture the essence of a character who faces difficult choices

🇺🇸 Looking at legislators

Before entering politics, Senator Bill Bradley of New Jersey was a basketball star. He earned All-American honors at Princeton University, played on the 1964 U.S. Olympic team, and won two NBA championships with the New York Knicks during a 10-year pro career. Bradley said that his basketball experiences taught him lessons he could apply in his work as a legislator. In particular, he believed, he gained insights into race relations, an issue he frequently spoke on. Ask your students to list professions or personal experiences that they believe would prepare a person for a successful career in Congress. Do the kids feel Congress should contain members from diverse backgrounds? Why? Have your class write to your state's two U.S. senators, asking each about his or her previous professional experiences.

✿ Concert calculations

Tell your students that 4 years before the Watkins Glen concert, in the summer of 1969, 400,000 people attended another famous rock festival held in New York State. Ask your students to name this event (Woodstock). There were 200,000 more people at the Watkins Glen event than at Woodstock. Have students calculate this difference as a percentage increase.

BIRTHDAYS
1932 • **NATALIE BABBITT,** children's 📖 author
1943 • **BILL BRADLEY,** professional basketball player and U.S. senator 🇺🇸

EVENTS
1821 • **General Jose de San Martin proclaimed PERU'S INDEPENDENCE** from Spain.
1868 • **THE FOURTEENTH AMENDMENT,** defining U.S. citizenship and guaranteeing due process of law, took effect.
1914 • **WORLD WAR I began** when Austria declared war on Serbia.
1945 • The U.S. Senate ratified the **UNITED NATIONS CHARTER** by a vote of 89-2.
• A **B-25 BOMBER CRASHED** into the 79th floor of the Empire State Building.
1959 • Daniel Inouye of Hawaii became the **FIRST JAPANESE-AMERICAN ELECTED TO CONGRESS.**
1973 • Six hundred thousand people ✿ attended the **BIGGEST U.S. ROCK CONCERT** ever, at Watkins Glen, N.Y.
1984 • **THE SUMMER OLYMPICS OPENED** in Los Angeles. Nineteen nations, including the USSR, boycotted.

28

JULY 29
activities

BIRTHDAYS
1869 • **BOOTH TARKINGTON, American novelist**

1905 • **DAG HAMMARSKJOLD, Swedish diplomat and second secretary-general of the United Nations**

1938 • **PETER JENNINGS, Canadian-born TV journalist**

EVENTS
1778 • **A FRENCH FLEET ARRIVED AT RHODE ISLAND to help the American colonists in the Revolutionary War.**

1958 • **Congress authorized the National Aeronautics and Space Administration (NASA).**

1962 • **Seventy-five American historians and political scientists RATED U.S. PRESIDENTS as "great," "near great," "average," "below average," or "failure."**

1981 • **PRINCE CHARLES AND LADY DIANA SPENCER were married in St. Paul's Cathedral in London.**

1988 • **Javier Sotomayor of Cuba became the FIRST HIGH JUMPER TO CLEAR 8 FEET.**

• **CHINCOTEAGUE PONY PENNING (last Thursday in July)**

What's next for NASA?
As early as 1915, the U.S. government supported organized research on aeronautics. That year, a congressional resolution established the National Advisory Committee for Aeronautics (NACA). By 1958, government officials agreed that NACA's work should be extended to include the region outside earth's atmosphere—and NASA was created. Ask your students to predict how NASA's work will be extended 10 years from now. For example, what other regions or heavenly bodies might be explored? Have each student write a science fiction story describing what might happen.

Evaluating the presidents
Have your students rate all the presidents who've served in their lifetimes using the same scale as the historians and political scientists used in 1962. Ask the kids to cite specific events and presidential decisions to support their ratings.

Where the wild horses are
Tell your students that about 150 wild ponies live on Assateague Island in Virginia. These animals are descendants of colonial-era horses. Each year, the ponies are rounded up and made to swim across the inlet to Chincoteague Island, where about 40 of them are sold. Ask students to locate these two islands on a map of Virginia. How far apart are they? Invite the kids to speculate on why the ponies are rounded up annually. (With no predators, they would eventually become too numerous for the island's ecosystem to sustain.)

29

JULY 30
activities

The family car

In honor of Henry Ford's birthday, ask your students to collect data about their families' cars, including how many cars their families own, the makes and models, the colors, and the safety features, such as air bags or antilock brakes. Have students work in small groups to compile their data and design graphs illustrating the results.

Down by the bay

Tell your students that the Chesapeake Bay—which is 200 miles long and 4 to 40 miles wide—is the largest inlet on the Atlantic coast of the United States. Have the children locate the Chesapeake Bay on a U.S. map. Various rivers flow into the bay. Challenge the kids to find as many as they can. (Among the rivers are the James, York, Potomac, Rappahannock, Patuxent, and Susquehanna.)

National motto

Ask your students where the motto "In God We Trust" can be found—for example, on coins and paper currency. Then discuss the concept of mottoes and why they exist. What is your state's motto? Ask each student to adopt a personal motto, write it on a sheet of oaktag, and add a personalized border design. Tape the mottoes to the fronts of students' desks or display them on a bulletin board.

BIRTHDAYS

1863 • **HENRY FORD,** American automobile manufacturer
1947 • **ARNOLD SCHWARZENEGGER,** Austrian-born bodybuilder and actor

EVENTS

1619 • **THE FIRST REPRESENTATIVE ASSEMBLY IN THE AMERICAN COLONIES** met at Jamestown, Va., and enacted laws against drunkenness, idleness, and gambling.
1729 • **BALTIMORE TOWN** (later Baltimore) was founded by the Maryland colonial government.
1909 • **THE UNITED STATES BOUGHT ITS FIRST AIRPLANE** for $31,250.
1919 • Missouri farmer Fred Hoenemann got a temporary injunction **PROHIBITING PILOTS FROM FLYING OVER HIS FARM.**
1942 • President Franklin Roosevelt signed a bill creating the navy **WAVES** (Women Accepted for Volunteer Emergency Service).
1952 • **THE CHESAPEAKE BAY BRIDGE**—third longest in the world—opened.
1956 • Congress adopted the motto, "**IN GOD WE TRUST.**"
1971 • Apollo 15 astronauts landed on the moon. Their mission included deploying a jeeplike vehicle called a **LUNAR ROVER,** which enabled them to explore much more of the moon's surface.

30

JULY 31
activities

BIRTHDAYS

1803 • JOHN ERICSSON, Swedish-American engineer who designed the *Monitor,* the famous ironclad Civil War ship

1930 • ROBERT KIMMEL SMITH, children's author

EVENTS

1498 • Christopher Columbus first sighted TRINIDAD.

1790 • THE FIRST AMERICAN PATENT was awarded to Samuel Hopkins for his method of making potash, a substance used in the manufacture of soap and glass.

1792 • The cornerstone for the U.S. Mint—THE FIRST OFFICIAL BUILDING CONSTRUCTED BY THE U.S. GOVERNMENT—was laid in Philadelphia.

1845 • THE SAXOPHONE was officially introduced to the military bands of the French army.

1948 • President Harry Truman dedicated NEW YORK INTERNATIONAL AIRPORT at Idlewild, Queens. (It was later renamed John F. Kennedy International Airport.)

1964 • The U.S. space probe *RANGER 7* transmitted 4,308 close-up photographs of the moon before crashing. The photos showed a thousand times more detail than any previous view through telescopes on earth.

Products and patents

Explain to younger students that when a new product is invented, the inventor can apply for a special number so that no one else can take credit for the product or make money from it without the inventor's approval. Then encourage the children to look through classroom toys and supplies to find patent numbers. For homework, have them find patent numbers on household products.

Discovering cornerstones

Tell your students that besides helping support a building, a cornerstone has ceremonial and historical significance. Cornerstones typically are laid during dedication ceremonies. Many are inscribed with the date construction was begun or completed as well as with the names of those involved in the construction process—architects, builders, government officials, and so on. Some cornerstones are used as time capsules. They are hollowed out, then filled with important documents and other interesting items. Can your students find your school's cornerstone? If the school were being built today, what objects might the children include in a cornerstone time capsule? Make a class list.

International airport sweep

Engage your students in an "international airport sweep." Have each child select 10 to 15 major U.S. or international cities noted in a newspaper weather listing. Then have the kids research the names and locations of international airports in or near their selected cities. Students can use such sources as travel brochures, almanacs, city guides, and maps to find the information. Finally, have your students each map out a flight path connecting all the international airports they've chosen, then calculate the total mileage.

AUGUST

MONTHLONG
OBSERVANCES
American Arts Appreciation Month
National Catfish Month
National Sandwich Month
Romance Awareness Month
Water Quality Month

WEEKLONG EVENTS

National Smile Week
  (week beginning on the first
  Monday)
National Clown Week (first full week)
Elvis International Tribute Week
  (week ending with Aug. 16)
National Aviation Week
  (week that includes Aug. 19)

SPECIAL DAYS AND CELEBRATIONS

American Family Day (first Sunday)
Friendship Day (first Sunday)
Daughter's Day (second Sunday)

☆ Project of the Month: American Artists

Celebrate American Arts Appreciation Month by having your students learn about American painters, poets, and authors.

• Show your students prints or photographs of paintings by artists such as Andrew Wyeth, Norman Rockwell, James Whistler, Grandma Moses, and Mary Cassatt. Ask the kids to compare and contrast the artists' styles. Do the artists have favorite kinds of subjects? Post pictures your students create in a style of their own.

• Share with the class poems by such poets as Robert Frost, Emily Dickinson, Nikki Giovanni, and Jack Prelutsky. What do your students like best about the poems and their imagery? Encourage the children to memorize a favorite poem, then recite it to the class. Students might also like to illustrate their poems.

• Gather copies of books by such authors as Mark Twain, Laura Ingalls Wilder, Louisa May Alcott, and Beverly Cleary. Ask your students to read at least one book by an American writer this month, then prepare a creative book report—perhaps a mobile, an interview with the main character, or a version of the story for younger children.

EXTENDER: Create an American Artists Museum in the classroom. To design the exhibits, students can conduct further research about the artists, then prepare reports and illustrations. Invite other classes to attend.

AUGUST 1
activities

📖 At the zoo
Tell your students that Gail Gibbons was 4 years old when she created her first picture book. It was four pages long. Since then, Gibbons has written and illustrated more than 50 books. Many of her nonfiction books—including *Clocks and How They Go, New Road, Sunken Treasure,* and *Zoo*—have won awards. Before reading Gibbons's book *Zoo* to younger students, help them list the kinds of responsibilities they think a zookeeper might have—for example, feeding animals, cleaning their cages, sweeping walkways, and answering visitors' questions. Have the children compare the list of responsibilities they come up with and those mentioned in the book.

📺 Music videos for young children
In honor of MTV's premiere, invite your students to create "music videos" for younger children. Different groups of students can perform old favorites—such as "Old MacDonald Had a Farm," "Animal Fair," "If You're Happy and You Know It," and "The Hokey Pokey"—while you operate the video camera. Encourage the children to create appropriate background scenery for their performances.

AUGUST 2
activities

✿ Red-letter days

Tell your students that before on-the-street mailboxes were introduced, people had to go to the post office to mail their letters. Older students might like to investigate other postal innovations, such as postage stamps, the pony express, and airmail. Younger students will enjoy having a classroom mailbox, which you can make by cutting a slot in the top of a large cardboard box. The kids can "mail" letters to you or to classmates. And you can send letters to your students. Each week, appoint a "letter carrier" to empty the box and deliver the letters.

📖 Childhood dreams

When he was growing up, James Howe, the author of *Bunnicula* and *Howliday Inn,* often wondered about his future—where he might live, what he might do, and who his friends might be. He dreamed of many possibilities, but he never imagined he'd become a children's book author. Ask your students what they dream about. Then have them write dated letters to themselves about their dreams, seal the letters in envelopes, and give them to you. At the end of the school year, return the letters and ask the students to note how their dreams have changed, if at all. Encourage the kids to hold on to these letters for periodic "dream checking" and updating as they get older.

BIRTHDAYS

1754 • PIERRE L'ENFANT, American soldier and architect who created the city plan for Washington, D.C.

1900 • HOLLING HOLLING, children's author

1946 • JAMES HOWE, children's author 📖

EVENTS

1776 • Fifty members of the Continental Congress signed the DECLARATION OF INDEPENDENCE.

1858 • THE FIRST ON-THE-STREET MAILBOXES were installed in Boston and New York.

1909 • THE FIRST LINCOLN PENNY was issued.

1923 • PRESIDENT WARREN G. HARDING died in office.

1943 • Navy lieutenant JOHN F. KENNEDY RESCUED MEMBERS OF HIS CREW after their boat, *PT-109,* was sheared in half by a Japanese destroyer.

1977 • Congress approved a bill to establish a FEDERAL DEPARTMENT OF ENERGY.

1978 • The movie *STAR WARS* SURPASSED *JAWS* as the all-time leader in box-office receipts.

1983 • The U.S. House of Representatives voted to designate the third Monday in January a FEDERAL HOLIDAY IN HONOR OF MARTIN LUTHER KING, JR.

1990 • IRAQ invaded its neighbor to the south, Kuwait.

BIRTHDAYS

1887 • **RUPERT BROOKE, English poet**

1905 • **MAGGIE KUHN, founder of the Gray Panthers**

1926 • **MARY CALHOUN, children's author**

EVENTS

1492 • **CHRISTOPHER COLUMBUS SET SAIL from Palos, Spain, on the expedition that resulted in his discovery of America.**

1610 • **British navigator Henry Hudson entered the body of water now known as HUDSON BAY.**

1780 • **BENEDICT ARNOLD was put in charge of the fortifications at West Point, N.Y., during the Revolutionary War.**

1852 • **Harvard defeated Yale in the FIRST INTERCOLLEGIATE ROWING RACE, on Lake Winnepesaukee, N.H.**

1882 • **Congress passed a LAW TO RESTRICT IMMIGRATION, imposing a 50¢ tax on all new arrivals.**

1923 • **CALVIN COOLIDGE became the 30th president of the United States after the death of Warren G. Harding.**

1984 • **Mary Lou Retton became the FIRST AMERICAN WOMAN TO WIN THE OLYMPIC GOLD MEDAL IN THE ALL-AROUND GYMNASTICS COMPETITION.**

NATIONAL SMILE WEEK (first Monday in August through the following Sunday)

AUGUST 3
activities

Hudson's discoveries

Tell your students that between 1607 and 1611, Henry Hudson made four voyages to the New World in search of a passage to China around North America. During these voyages, Hudson discovered not only Hudson Bay but also the Hudson River and Hudson Strait. Pass out copies of a map showing the northeastern section of North America. Have students locate the bodies of water discovered by Hudson on their maps, then color them.

The way to the White House

Calvin Coolidge, like such other vice presidents as Lyndon Johnson, Harry Truman, and Theodore Roosevelt, assumed the presidency after the death of the chief executive. Challenge your students to name the only vice president to take over for a president who was still alive. (Gerald Ford, who became president when Richard Nixon resigned.) Then ask the class to predict who would become president if the president *and* the vice president were unable to serve. Have the kids check their predictions by researching the line of succession. Afterward, have them illustrate their findings with a flowchart.

When you're smiling...

To celebrate National Smile Week, hold a contest to see who can get the most people to smile. All during the week, have students nod and smile at people they meet at school, in their neighborhoods, at the grocery store, at sporting events, and so on. Encourage them to each keep scorecards noting the number of people who return their smiles. At week's end, give each child a certificate with smiley-face stickers.

NATIONAL SMILE WEEK CERTIFICATE

GIVEN TO: _____

FOR PUTTING YOUR BEST SMILE FORWARD.

AUGUST 4
activities

Coast Guard crosswords

Tell your students that the U.S. Coast Guard began with a fleet of just 10 ships, called cutters. Now the Coast Guard uses cutters, small boats, airplanes, helicopters, lighthouses, and radio beacons to carry out its many responsibilities, which include preventing smuggling; locating and rescuing victims of accidents at sea; inspecting equipment and enforcing safety rules on merchant ships; icebreaking; monitoring compliance with environmental regulations; conducting oceanographic research; and aiding navigation. Have small groups do a little reading about the Coast Guard and incorporate key terms they learn in a crossword puzzle. Then have the groups match wits by exchanging their crosswords.

Finger-puppet fairy tales

In memory of Hans Christian Andersen, get your class to read his famous fairy tales. Then have the children work in groups to create finger-puppet characters and act out the stories. After some practice, your students might perform their finger-puppet plays for younger children.

Be a clown

During Clown Week, invite your students to brainstorm for words besides *funny* to describe clowns—for example, *playful, jolly, clever, lively, amusing*. Next, have the kids come up with a list of words to describe how clowns make them feel. Their suggestions might include *cheerful, merry, lucky, delighted,* and *thrilled*. Write the words on the chalkboard. Then have students use the word lists to write poems about clowns. They can recite their works during "Be a Clown Day"—when students can come to school dressed as clowns.

BIRTHDAYS

1861 • JESSE RENO, American engineer who invented the escalator
1912 • RAOUL WALLENBERG, Swedish diplomat who is credited with saving at least 100,000 Hungarian Jews from deportation to Nazi concentration camps
1958 • MARY DECKER-SLANEY, American track star
1962 • ROGER CLEMENS, American baseball star

EVENTS

1790 • THE U.S. COAST GUARD was established.
1875 • Danish writer HANS CHRISTIAN ANDERSEN died.
1916 • The United States bought the WESTERN VIRGIN ISLANDS from Denmark.
1922 • The nation's 13 MILLION TELEPHONES WERE SILENT for a moment in tribute to Alexander Graham Bell on the occasion of his funeral.
1944 • The Nazis captured ANNE FRANK and seven others who were hiding with her in a house in Amsterdam.

   NATIONAL CLOWN WEEK (first full week in August)

AUGUST 5
activities

✒ Monumental tasks

Ask your students to explain what a monument is. Perhaps they'll suggest that a monument is a lasting symbol of a significant person, event, or ideal. Next, tell them that the Statue of Liberty, a gift to the United States from the government of France, symbolized friendship between the two nations as well as liberty under a democracy. Have your students name other local, national, or international monuments. What do these monuments honor or recognize? If your students were to have monuments symbolizing them, what would these monuments look like? Encourage each child to draw and color—or even build—a personal monument.

✺ Going halfway

Challenge your students to find other "halfway" points today. For instance, what's the halfway point of the school day, a story they're reading, lunchtime, or their bus trip home?

✉ Original greeting cards

Have your students brainstorm for all the occasions for which there are greeting cards. List these ideas on the chalkboard. Next, divide the class into small groups, and ask each group to think of occasions in people's lives for which there *aren't* any greeting cards. Finally, have each student select one of these occasions and make an appropriate greeting card. Post the cards on a bulletin board.

✐ Cutting the mustard

On National Mustard Day, conduct a survey to find out how many children like regular, spicy, or dijon mustard. On which foods do students use mustard? Do any students not like mustard at all? Have the class graph the results.

AUGUST 6
activities

🌐 Name that country

Ask your students whom Bolivia was named for (Simon Bolivar, the Venezuelan general and statesman who liberated much of South America from Spain). Then challenge the kids to think of another South American country named for a person (Colombia, named for Christopher Columbus).

☙ Contemplating peace

On Hiroshima Day, use videotapes, films, or literature to introduce students to the causes and effects of America's use of the atomic bomb on Hiroshima. After a discussion, share with students copies of books containing quotations, poetry, stories, or essays about peace. Encourage the children to review the books, then select a quotation, poem, or passage that holds meaning for them. Students can then write these words on strips of white paper. Post the strips on a bulletin board.

❊ Class sandwich book

During National Sandwich Month, help your students develop a class sandwich recipe book. Gather a collection of cookbooks, and allow your students to browse through them for sandwich recipes. Also invite the children to bring in favorite sandwich recipes from home. Your students should each copy the recipe for a sandwich they like (or would like to try) and illustrate it. Have them categorize the sandwiches—for example, meatless sandwiches, hot sandwiches, exotic sandwiches—then compile the illustrated recipes into a class book. Invite the kids to make their sandwiches at home and bring them in one day this month for a class taste test.

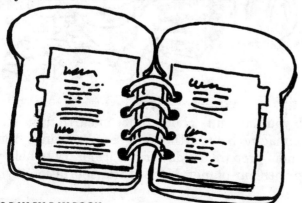

BIRTHDAYS

1809 • **ALFRED, LORD TENNYSON,** English poet
1881 • **ALEXANDER FLEMING,** British bacteriologist who discovered penicillin
1909 • **NORMA FABER,** children's author
1946 • **FRANK ASCH,** children's author
1965 • **DAVID ROBINSON,** basketball player

EVENTS

1825 • 🌐 BOLIVIA declared its independence from Spain.
1890 • CY YOUNG, baseball's winningest pitcher, appeared in his first game.
1926 • Gertrude Ederle became the **FIRST WOMAN TO SWIM THE ENGLISH CHANNEL.**
1945 • The United States dropped an atomic bomb on HIROSHIMA, Japan.
1962 • JAMAICA gained its independence after more than three centuries as a British possession.
1965 • President Lyndon Johnson signed the VOTING RIGHTS ACT, protecting the rights of black voters.

☙ **HIROSHIMA DAY**
❊ **NATIONAL SANDWICH MONTH**
PEACE FESTIVAL (Japan)

BIRTHDAYS

1742 • NATHANAEL GREENE, Revolutionary War general

1779 • CARL RITTER, German geographer considered one of the founders of modern geographic science

1903 • LOUIS S.B. LEAKEY, English anthropologist and paleontologist

1928 • BETSY BYARS, children's author

EVENTS

1782 • George Washington established the Badge of Military Merit (PURPLE HEART) to honor wounded soldiers.

1789 • THE WAR DEPARTMENT was created.

1888 • Theophilus van Kannel patented the REVOLVING DOOR.

1927 • THE INTERNATIONAL PEACE BRIDGE, commemorating long-lasting peace between the United States and Canada, was dedicated. It connects Buffalo, N.Y., and Fort Erie, Ontario.

1959 • THE UNITED STATES LAUNCHED EXPLORER VI, which took the first pictures of earth from space.

1963 • The U.N. called on the South African government to ABANDON APARTHEID.

1990 • President George Bush ordered a military buildup in the Persian Gulf following the Iraqi invasion of Kuwait. The operation was called DESERT SHIELD.

NATIONAL SCUBA DIVING DAY

AUGUST 7
activities

Geography in the news
Help your students discover how geography affects their daily lives. First, have them guess how many geographic references, maps, and charts they'll find in an edition of the daily newspaper. Then have them check their predictions by counting and clipping all the geographic references they can find from today's paper. Afterward, discuss how the news would be different without the science of geography.

Peaceful posters
To mark the dedication of the International Peace Bridge, ask your students to develop commemorative posters. Show the children photos or illustrations of the bridge. Next, have them brainstorm for images that symbolize peace, then work individually or in groups to create their posters. Make sure each poster includes the date the International Peace Bridge was dedicated and the signatures of the student-artists. Display the posters in the hallway.

Travel tips for extraterrestrials
Share with your students photographs of earth from space. Then ask the kids to imagine how earth might seem to beings from other planets. Have them prepare a 7-day travel itinerary to help the aliens get acquainted with our planet. Mode of transportation: flying saucer, of course.

AUGUST 8
activities

📖 Authors and animals

Marjorie Kinnan Rawlings's book *The Yearling* is a poignant story of growing up. In it, a young boy learns to accept the tragic necessity of getting rid of his pet deer. Ask your students how they'd feel if they had to give up their pet. Encourage them to write a story about their pet.

✑ Displaying good character

For International Good Character Day, have your students brainstorm for positive character traits. Do these traits apply to people all over the world? Next, have the kids design character-trait license plates. Ask them each to print their first name in the center of an $8\frac{1}{2}$ $\times 5\frac{1}{2}$ sheet of paper, then write their character traits along the edges to create a border. The students can tape their plates to their desks.

❋ In the middle

Are there any middle children in your class? Ask these students to describe the positive and negative aspects of holding this position in their families.

BIRTHDAYS

1763 • **CHARLES BULFINCH,** American architect who designed the state houses of Massachusetts, Maine, and Connecticut and who succeeded Benjamin Latrobe as architect of the U.S. Capitol

1799 • **NATHANIEL BROWN PALMER,** American sea captain believed to be the first explorer to sight Antarctica

1866 • **MATTHEW HENSON,** African-American polar explorer who was a member of Robert Peary's North Pole expedition

1896 • **MARJORIE KINNAN RAWLINGS,** 📖 children's author

1937 • **DUSTIN HOFFMAN,** American actor

EVENTS

1588 • Under Sir Francis Drake, **THE ENGLISH FLEET DESTROYED THE SPANISH ARMADA** off the coast of France.

1786 • **THE SILVER DOLLAR AND THE DECIMAL SYSTEM OF MONEY** were adopted by an act of Congress.

1911 • **MEMBERSHIP OF THE HOUSE OF REPRESENTATIVES** was fixed at 435.

1974 • **PRESIDENT RICHARD NIXON ANNOUNCED HIS RESIGNATION,** effective the next day.

✑ **INTERNATIONAL GOOD CHARACTER DAY**
❋ **MIDDLE CHILDREN'S DAY**

AUGUST 9
activities

9

Olympic triumphs

Tell your students that in the years preceding World War II, German leader Adolf Hitler and his Nazi propagandists proclaimed the superiority of the "Aryan race." Hitler believed that the 1936 Olympic Games held in Berlin would support his racial theories. He was wrong. Jesse Owens and nine other African-Americans—whom Hitler had called members of an "inferior race"—led a U.S. team that dominated the sprints, hurdles, and field events. Owens's brilliant performances in particular deflated the Aryan myth. Ask your students to find out the events in which Owens won medals. Then challenge them to find out the other African-Americans who won medals at the Berlin Olympics. (John Woodruff, 800-meter run; Cornelius Johnson, high jump; Ralph Metcalfe, 400-meter relay and 100-meter dash.) Have the kids use their information to make posters honoring Jesse Owens and his fellow African-American Olympians.

Family folktales

Patricia McKissack said her writing career began when she was in 3rd grade. She recalled the thrill of having a poem she'd written displayed on the bulletin board for others to read. Since she began writing professionally, McKissack has authored more than 40 children's books. One of her picture books—*Flossie and the Fox*—is based on a tale her grandfather used to tell her. (He named the characters after people in their family.) Read *Flossie and the Fox* to your students. Then ask them to share tales told to them by their grandparents or other family members. Or have them make up their own folktales based on people in their families. Compile their stories into a "Family Folktales" booklet.

AUGUST 10
activities

🏴 Statehood status

Tell your students that Missouri gained statehood only after Congress engineered the "Missouri Compromise" of 1820. This compromise, which maintained the ratio of non-slave states and slave states—allowed Missouri, a slave state, to simultaneously enter the Union with a non-slave state. Challenge your students to find out which state entered the Union with Missouri.

✿ Student-run "Smithsonian"

To celebrate the chartering of the Smithsonian Institution, invite your students to create a "mini-Smithsonian" exhibit at their school. Students can ask their families, staff members, and community members to temporarily loan appropriate items from their personal memorabilia and collections. (If items can't be loaned, students can photograph them and display the pictures.) Divide the class into teams to handle various aspects of the exhibit. Duties might include maintaining an inventory of exhibit items, preparing an exhibit catalog, designing the exhibit space, selling admission tickets, publicizing the event, installing the exhibit, and ensuring that the exhibit is guarded. Hold a by-invitation-only opening for students, their parents, and community members.

⚗ Mysterious meteorite

Ask your students to speculate about the meteorite that flew in and out of the earth's atmosphere. Where did the meteorite come from? Why didn't it hit the earth? What happened to it after it left the earth's atmosphere? Encourage the kids to conduct some background research. Then have them create fact-based science fiction stories about this mysterious meteorite.

BIRTHDAYS

1753 • EDMUND RANDOLPH, General George Washington's aide-de-camp during the Revolutionary War

1874 • HERBERT HOOVER, 31st president of the United States

1959 • ROSANNA ARQUETTE, American actress

EVENTS

1519 • THE FIRST RECORDED AROUND-THE-WORLD VOYAGE began in Seville, Spain, under the command of Ferdinand Magellan.

1821 • MISSOURI became the 24th state.

1845 • THE U.S. NAVAL ACADEMY was established at Annapolis, Md.

1846 • CONGRESS CHARTERED THE SMITHSONIAN INSTITUTION, founded with $500,000 bequeathed by English scientist James Smithson.

1949 • THE WAR DEPARTMENT was renamed the Department of Defense.

1972 • THE ONLY METEORITE KNOWN TO HAVE ENTERED THE EARTH'S ATMOSPHERE AND LEFT IT flew in over Utah and departed the atmosphere over Alberta, Canada.

AUGUST 11
activities

BIRTHDAYS

1778 • **FRIEDRICH LUDWIG JAHN,**  German teacher who invented gymnastics

1865 • **GIFFORD PINCHOT, American politician, author, and conservationist**

1908 • **DON FREEMAN, children's author and creator of Corduroy**

1921 • **ALEX HALEY, American author who wrote** *Roots* **and coauthored** *The Autobiography of Malcolm X*

1941 • **STEVEN KROLL, children's author**

1944 • **JOANNA COLE, children's author**

1953 • **HULK HOGAN, American wrestler**

EVENTS

1841 • **Former slave FREDERICK DOUGLASS spoke at his first antislavery conference.**

1877 • **THE FIRST SATELLITE OF THE PLANET MARS was discovered by Asaph Hall, director of the U.S. Naval Observatory.**

1972 • **THE LAST U.S. COMBAT TROOPS left Vietnam.**

1984 • **CARL LEWIS WON HIS FOURTH GOLD MEDAL at the Olympic Games in Los Angeles.**

THE PERSEIDS METEOR SHOWER PEAKS TONIGHT

⌀ Early phys ed

Tell your students that Friedrich Ludwig Jahn wrote books about the importance of physical education and developed rudimentary versions of today's gymnastics equipment. Are there any gymnasts in your class? Ask your students to list the kinds of physical activities they do. How often do they do these activities—daily, several times a week, weekly, biweekly? Make a class chart.

✒ Civil War dialogue

During the Civil War, Frederick Douglass tried to rally blacks to fight against the South and helped organize two black regiments for this purpose. Douglass also met with President Lincoln several times to discuss the problems of slavery. Ask your students to work in teams to conduct some background research about the life of Frederick Douglass, President Lincoln's stance on slavery, and conditions in the United States during the Civil War. Have the teams speculate about some of the things Douglass and Lincoln might have spoken about. Then have each team use its research to create a dialogue that might have occurred between the two.

📖 Corduroy corner

To celebrate Don Freeman's birthday, gather copies of his works for a special book corner. Titles might include *Corduroy, A Pocket for Corduroy,* and *Dandelion.* You might also invite the children to bring in their favorite stuffed bear—or other animal—and tell why it means so much to them.

AUGUST 12
activities

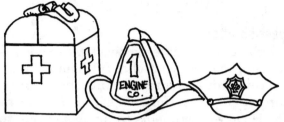

Community protectors

To mark the establishment of the first American police force, have a class discussion about how police, firefighters, and paramedics help protect us. Then write a class thank-you letter to local units of each of these groups.

Telling different tales

In honor of Robert Southey's birthday, collect several different editions of *The Three Bears*. Read one edition aloud, then divide the class into groups. Have each group read the other editions of this fairy tale, noting the similarities and differences among them. Students can then vote for the edition they think has the best illustrations, the best vocabulary, the best character delineation, or any other categories they decide on.

Book ideas

Tell your students that Ann Martin, author of the Baby-sitters Club books, draws on her own childhood experiences in many of her books. Martin says she remembers what it felt like being a kid, and she tries to put those feelings into her books. Ask your students to recall a happy, sad, frightening, confusing, or thought-provoking experience they've had during the previous year, and to write a paragraph about it. Send these paragraphs to the author as suggestions for future Baby-sitters Club books.

BIRTHDAYS

1774 • **ROBERT SOUTHEY, English poet who popularized the fairy tale** *The Three Bears*

1781 • **ROBERT MILLS, American architect and designer of the Washington Monument**

1859 • **KATHERINE LEE BATES, American author who wrote the words to "America the Beautiful"**

1880 • **CHRISTY MATHEWSON, baseball star who became one of the first five players inducted into the Hall of Fame**

1955 • **ANN MARTIN, children's author and creator of the Baby-sitters Club series**

EVENTS

1658 • **THE FIRST POLICE FORCE IN AMERICA was established in New Amsterdam, now New York City.**

1676 • **Metacomet (Philip), chief of the Wampanoag Indians, was killed, effectively ending KING PHILIP'S WAR, a bitter conflict between New England settlers and the Wampanoag tribe.**

1851 • **Isaac Singer began production of his SEWING MACHINE.**

1877 • **Thomas Edison invented the PHONOGRAPH.**

1936 • **Marjorie Gestring, age 13, became the YOUNGEST PERSON TO WIN AN OLYMPIC GOLD MEDAL in springboard diving.**

12

AUGUST 13
activities

BIRTHDAYS

1818 • **LUCY STONE, American women's rights leader**

1860 • **ANNIE OAKLEY, American markswoman**

1895 • **BERT LAHR, American actor who played the Cowardly Lion in *The Wizard of Oz***

1899 • **ALFRED HITCHCOCK, English filmmaker**

1927 • **FIDEL CASTRO, premier of Cuba**

EVENTS

1521 • **Spanish conquistador HERNAN CORTEZ captured the Aztec capital of Tenochtitlan, the site of present-day Mexico City.**

1870 • **Before starting down the Colorado River into the Grand Canyon, explorer JOHN WESLEY POWELL wrote, "We are now ready to start on our way down the Great Unknown. . . ."**

1889 • **William Gray patented the PAY TELEPHONE.**

1961 • **East Germany CLOSED THE BORDER BETWEEN EAST AND WEST BERLIN.**

1969 • **President Richard Nixon bestowed the MEDAL OF FREEDOM on Apollo 11 astronauts Neil Armstrong, Edwin Aldrin, and Michael Collins after their historic landing on the moon.**

 **INTERNATIONAL LEFT-HANDERS DAY**

13

Sharpest shooter

As a young girl, Annie Oakley showed a tremendous talent for marksmanship, beating a national rifle champion in a shooting match. She could hit a coin thrown into the air or the thin edge of a playing card at 30 paces. Her skill earned her the nickname "Little Sure Shot." Have your students think about their special talents. What nicknames might they give themselves? Have them use these nicknames as the basis of a self-portrait.

Of cowards and courage

Your students are probably familiar with Bert Lahr's portrayal of the Cowardly Lion from *The Wizard of Oz.* Ask the children to discuss what it means to be a coward. Why is it strange to see a lion act cowardly? Can they think of ways to help someone feel less afraid? Have the kids each write a paragraph telling what they do to feel less afraid in difficult situations.

Looking at lefties

On International Left-Handers Day, survey your students to see how many of them are southpaws. Have these students share the benefits and drawbacks of being left-handed with the class. Then encourage students who are right-handed to use their left hands to perform some everyday tasks—sharpening their pencils, writing, turning a light switch off and on, opening a jar, and so on. Have lefties try these tasks with their right hands.

AUGUST 14
activities

⚗ Magnetic attraction

Danish physicist and chemist Hans Christian Oersted discovered that an electrical current produces a magnetic field. On his birthday, demonstrate this principle to your students. You'll need the following materials: a 2-foot-long piece of insulated wire with the ends stripped; a 2-inch nail; a D cell battery; and some metal paper clips. Spread the paper clips on a table. Ask your students to test whether the battery, the nail, or the wire by themselves will attract the paper clips. (They won't.) Next, coil the wire tightly around the nail, leaving 2 inches of wire free at each end. Then press the stripped ends of the wire against the top and bottom of the battery. Now have your students test whether the paper clips will be attracted. (They will.) Tell your students that they've just created an electromagnet.

✺ Can you spell "fund-raiser"?

The softball marathon played in Monticello, N.Y., in 1976 lasted from 10:00 a.m. on Aug. 14 to 4 p.m. the following day. The 365-inning game, which ended in a score of 491-467, raised $4,000 for a local hospital. Why not organize a fund-raiser for your classroom? Your students can solicit pledges for a marathon spelling test. Sponsors can donate a penny per word. Have the children decide how to use the money—for example, for classroom books, dictionaries, or a field trip. Include words from all of your students' textbooks on the test. Start in the morning and continue until lunch (if feasible). Invite parent volunteers to help grade the tests. Students earn one penny for each correctly spelled word.

BIRTHDAYS

1777 • **HANS CHRISTIAN OERSTED,**
⚗ **Danish chemist and physicist who discovered the principle of electromagnetism**

1918 • **ALICE PROVENSEN, children's author**

1959 • **EARVIN "MAGIC" JOHNSON, American basketball player**

EVENTS

1511 • **MICHELANGELO'S PAINTINGS ON THE SISTINE CHAPEL CEILING** were first exhibited.

1784 • **THE FIRST RUSSIAN COLONY IN ALASKA** was founded at Three Saints Bay on Kodiak Island.

1894 • Angry at being fired, Jerry Murphy, the city jailer at Leavenworth, Kan., unlocked the prison doors and **RELEASED ALL THE PRISONERS.**

1919 • A U.S. Aeromarine flying boat dropped a bag of mail on the deck of the liner *Adriatic*. This was the **FIRST AIRMAIL DELIVERY AT SEA.**

1935 • President Franklin Roosevelt signed the **SOCIAL SECURITY ACT,** creating the nation's first system of retirement income.

1945 • **JAPAN SURRENDERED,** ending World War II.

1976 • To raise money for the
✺ Monticello, N.Y., Community General Hospital, two teams began a **MARATHON SOFTBALL GAME.**

1985 • Japan launched *Spacecraft-Planet A* on a **MISSION TO HALLEY'S COMET.**

14

AUGUST 15
activities

15

Lots of leftovers
Challenge your students to come up with zany uses for common leftovers. For instance, leftover mashed potatoes could be used to patch roads. Leftover pudding might make great finger paint. Compile students' suggestions in a class book titled "Fresh Uses for Leftovers."

Personal library plans
If your students could select 10 books for their own libraries, which titles would they pick? Have them each make a list, then group the books into genres. What's the most popular genre among your students? Combine students' lists and post as a reading reference for the kids. Have students design bookplates for books that are added to the class library.

Just relax
Ask your students to describe what they like to do for relaxation. Their responses might include sedentary activities, such as reading or watching television, as well as more active pursuits, such as playing a sport or taking a walk. Afterward, discuss why it isn't always necessary to "take it easy" in order to relax.

AUGUST 16
activities

❋ Birds of a feather

Tell your students that the Arctic tern is the champion migratory bird. This bird travels from one pole to the other, making a round-trip flight of over 20,000 miles. Divide the class into teams, and have each team learn about the migratory pattern of a different bird, such as ducks, geese, and swallows. Compare the number of miles traveled by each species on a class chart.

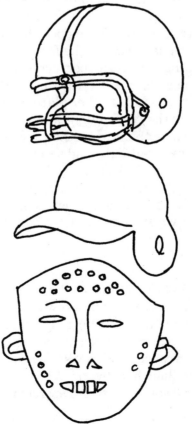

📖 Favorite games

Most of Matt Christopher's books for children are on sports topics. When Christopher was growing up, his favorite sport was baseball. Despite a lack of equipment, he and his friends played the game in his backyard, which was cement. The boys used broken broom handles and tennis balls instead of bats and baseballs. They used flat rocks to mark the bases. Ask your students if they've ever improvised in order to play a favorite game. Then have them interview their parents about favorite games they played as children. Have the kids share their information with the class.

🖋 Sports safety

Do your students think sports are safer today than in 1920, when Roy Chapman was fatally injured in a baseball game? List several sports—baseball, football, hockey, soccer—on the chalkboard. For each sport, have students identify the equipment and rules that help protect players from injury. Have any of your students ever been injured playing sports? Ask them to share their experiences. Then ask the whole class to suggest a type of equipment, rule change, or other strategy that might have prevented the injury. Afterward, invite a team coach or physical education instructor to discuss sports safety with your class.

BIRTHDAYS

1845 • **GABRIEL LIPPMAN**, French physicist and inventor of color photography

1917 • **MATT CHRISTOPHER**, children's
📖 author

EVENTS

1858 • Queen Victoria of England and President James Buchanan of the United States exchanged greetings by means of the **NEW TRANSATLANTIC CABLE.**

1861 • The federal government **PROHIBITED TRADE BETWEEN THE STATES OF THE UNION AND THE CONFEDERACY.**

1916 • The United States and Canada
❋ signed a **TREATY TO PROTECT MIGRATORY BIRDS.**

1920 • Baseball player Roy Chapman
🖋 was **HIT IN THE HEAD BY A PITCHED BALL** and died the following day. He was the only professional ballplayer to die in that manner.

1977 • Rock-and-roll idol **ELVIS PRESLEY DIED.**

AUGUST 17
activities

American folk hero
Frontiersman, scout, soldier, and politician, Davy Crockett was among the more colorful figures of his day. Have your students conduct background research about Crockett's life, then prepare a time line showing his varied adventures. What important events in U.S. history occurred during Crockett's lifetime? Have students list these events on the time line.

City mapping
Have your students find Cincinnati on a map of Ohio. In what part of the state is it located? Which geographic features might have influenced the city's location?

Enlightening poetry
Read aloud to your students from Myra Cohn Livingston's *Light and Shadow*. Ask the kids to list the places Livingston finds light—a toll bridge, the waves, a sign in a store window. Where does she discover shadows? (In the forest, leaning against a door, across stone walls.) Have students work in groups to list other places where they'd find light and shadow. Have them write their own poems about light and shadow on sheets of white construction paper, then mount the sheets on black construction paper. Display their work on the bulletin board.

Record setters
How many times in a row can your students do something? Have the kids each keep track of the number of consecutive days they complete their homework. Who's the record setter in your classroom?

AUGUST 18
activities

✿ Mountains of information

To commemorate the first successful climb of California's highest peak, divide the rest of the states among your students. Have the kids find out the highest points in their states, their elevations, and, if applicable, when they were first scaled and by whom, then write this information on slips of paper. Make sure the children sign their names on the slips they do. Collect the slips and hold a class "mountain bee" by reading aloud the information and having the kids guess which state the high point is in. Afterward, have your students record their facts on mountain-shaped sheets of construction paper scaled according to height. Arrange their work on the bulletin board to resemble a mountain range, then label the display "Mountains of Information."

✣ Thumbs down for cigarettes

To mark the anniversary of the founding of the Anti-Cigarette League, have each student choose one of the many good reasons not to smoke, think of an appropriate slogan, and create a poster.

∅ One of baseball's best

In honor of Roberto Clemente's birthday, invite your students to bring in their baseball cards. Does anyone have a Roberto Clemente card? If so, have that child share Clemente's statistics with the class. If not, encourage students to use a sports almanac to find out about Clemente's career accomplishments. Then let the kids make a poster-sized Roberto Clemente baseball card.

BIRTHDAYS

1587 • **VIRGINIA DARE, the first English child born in America**

1774 • **MERIWETHER LEWIS, American explorer and coleader of the Lewis and Clark expedition**

1934 • **ROBERTO CLEMENTE, Puerto Rican baseball player**

1937 • **ROBERT REDFORD, American actor**

1944 • **PAULA DANZIGER, children's author**

1954 • **PATRICK SWAYZE, American actor**

EVENTS

1856 • **Gail Borden patented the FIRST SUCCESSFUL MILK-CONDENSING PROCESS.**

1873 • **John Lucas, Charles Begole, and A.H. Johnson became the FIRST CLIMBERS TO REACH THE TOP OF MT. WHITNEY, the highest peak in the contiguous United States.**

1902 • **MAJOR LEAGUE BASEBALL'S FIRST UNASSISTED TRIPLE PLAY was made by Henry O'Hagen.**

1914 • **President Woodrow Wilson issued his "PROCLAMATION OF NEUTRALITY," aimed at keeping the United States out of World War I.**

1919 • **THE ANTI-CIGARETTE LEAGUE OF AMERICA was organized.**

1976 • **GERALD FORD WAS NOMINATED FOR PRESIDENT on the first ballot at the Republican National Convention in Kansas City, Mo.**

AUGUST 19
activities

Star man

John Flamsteed, who served as England's first Astronomer Royal, cataloged about 3,000 stars. Challenge teams of students to list as many stars as they can think of—along with the constellations the stars are in, if the students know—in 5 minutes. Award one point for each correct star and one point for each correct constellation. Which team is the winner?

Insect invasion

Show your students illustrations or photographs of earwigs. These insects have short, horny forewings, a pair of forceps at the end of the abdomen, and biting mouthparts. Then ask the kids to work in groups to develop a horror play titled "Invasion of the Earwigs" or a mock front page for a Stroud newspaper story on the insect invasion.

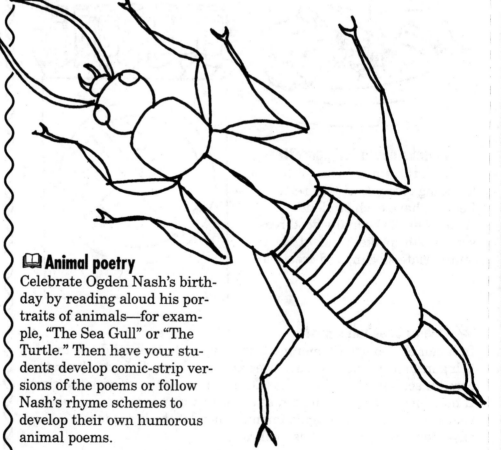

Animal poetry

Celebrate Ogden Nash's birthday by reading aloud his portraits of animals—for example, "The Sea Gull" or "The Turtle." Then have your students develop comic-strip versions of the poems or follow Nash's rhyme schemes to develop their own humorous animal poems.

AUGUST 20
activities

✏ Close continents

Vitus Bering was commissioned by Russia to find out whether Asia and North America were connected. When he sailed through the Bering Straight on his first voyage, dense fog obscured his view, and Bering didn't realize how close he was to the North American continent. On his second voyage, in 1741, he spotted Alaska. Have your students locate the Bering Strait on a map and use the map scale to determine the distance separating Asia and North America at the closest point.

✿ Whaling woes

Tell your students that during the period the *Ann Alexander* sailed, whales were hunted primarily for their blubber (a thick layer of fat beneath the skin), which was used to make oil. The oil was used as lamp fuel before the invention of kerosene. List several whale species on the chalkboard—for example, blue, finback, right, humpback, and sperm. Have groups of students each investigate the status of one of these species. (All the whales listed above are endangered.) Ask each group to draw and color a picture of its whale, then attach a paragraph describing its size, its feeding habits, and where it can be found.

✿ A large mass of bass

Can your students imagine how huge a 563-pound fish is? To help them visualize this big bass, ask each child how much he or she weighs. Add the weights together until the total reaches 563 pounds. How many children is that?

୬♀€ Museum-quality pieces?

Ask your students whether they think the first Xerox copy machine deserves a place in the Smithsonian. Why or why not? What kinds of items do they think will be in the Smithsonian 100 years from now? Make a class list.

BIRTHDAYS

1785 • OLIVER HAZARD PERRY, U.S. naval officer and hero of the War of 1812

1946 • CONNIE CHUNG, American TV reporter and anchor

EVENTS

1741 • ALASKA WAS DISCOVERED by the Danish explorer Vitus Bering.

1857 • After being harpooned by the crew of the whaling ship *Ann Alexander,* A WHALE ATTACKED and destroyed the vessel.

1912 • THE PLANT QUARANTINE ACT went into effect, placing restrictions on the entry of plants into the United States.

1934 • THE COMIC STRIP "LI'L ABNER" first appeared.

1940 • Winston Churchill paid TRIBUTE TO THE ROYAL AIR FORCE by saying, "Never in the field of human conflict was so much owed by so many to so few."

1968 • James McAdam, Jr., snagged the LARGEST SEA BASS ON RECORD—563 pounds.

1977 • The unmanned spacecraft *VOYAGER 2* was launched. Its destinations were Jupiter, Saturn, Uranus, and Neptune.

1985 • THE ORIGINAL XEROX COPY MACHINE was donated to the Smithsonian Institution's National Museum of American History.

20

AUGUST 21
activities

Explaining an eclipse
Have your students investigate what happens during a solar eclipse, then make diagrams showing the position of the sun, moon, and earth. Afterward, ask the kids to imagine that they were living in Spain or Portugal during the total eclipse of the sun in 1560. Have them write down their thoughts as if they were composing a diary entry for that day.

Hawaiian volcanoes
Have your students locate Hawaii on a map, then ask them to locate and find out about its significant volcanoes. Haleakala, on the island of Maui, is the largest dormant volcano in the world. Its crater is 7 miles long and 2 miles wide. Diamond Head, an extinct volcano, is located on the island of Oahu. Mauna Loa and Kilauea, on the island of Hawaii, are still active. Have students research the differences between active, dormant, and extinct volcanoes. Then use their information to make a class chart.

Beginning of the end of the USSR
The leaders of the Soviet coup surrendered in the face of widespread public resistance and the refusal of key army units to obey their orders. They'd failed to take into account the changes that several years of democratic reforms had brought to Soviet society. And they hadn't arrested the Russian president, Boris Yeltsin, who rallied the people of Moscow and convinced army units to oppose the conspirators. Although Mikhail Gorbachev returned to office after the coup, his power had eroded. Within 6 months the Soviet Union no longer existed as a political entity, having been replaced by the Commonwealth of Independent States (CIS). Challenge your students to research the republics in the CIS. What are their boundaries? What are their capitals? Who are their leaders? What ethnic groups do they embrace, and what are their populations?

AUGUST 22
activities

⌹ Classroom concert-goers

Celebrate the music of Claude Debussy by inviting your students to become classroom concert-goers. Select 20 to 40 minutes' worth of Debussy recordings, then have the children relax and listen. If they wish, students can draw pictures, write poems or stories, or simply jot down thoughts inspired by this master's music.

☀ Sampling soaps

To mark the anniversary of William Sheppard's patent for liquid soap, collect—or invite the children to bring in—a variety of brands of liquid soap. Then divide the kids into groups of "soap samplers," and have them compare and contrast the various soaps for quality of suds, texture, cleaning power, scent, color, and price. Review each group's ratings, then design a class "Soap Seal of Approval." Students can extend their study of liquid soap into the realm of video or audio advertising. Have the kids develop a commercial for their selected super soap. Record or videotape their presentations.

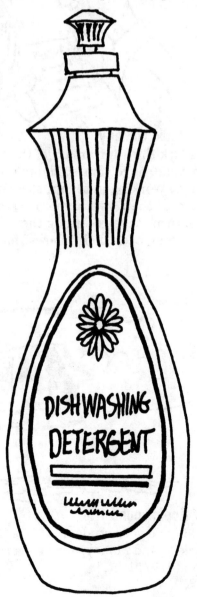

📖 Fact and (science) fiction

In honor of Ray Bradbury's birthday, share with your students his classic short story "The Veldt." Then ask the kids to note how many of the inventions, technologies, and appliances described in this story written in the 1950s exist today. Discuss how Bradbury and other science fiction writers are able to correctly predict the invention and use of new technologies. Then have students review recent newspapers to find current technological breakthroughs. Invite them to write their own science fiction stories incorporating these new technologies.

BIRTHDAYS

1862 • **CLAUDE DEBUSSY**, French musician and composer ⌹

1920 • **RAY BRADBURY**, American science fiction writer 📖

• **DENTON COOLEY**, American surgeon who was a pioneer in the area of heart transplant operations

1934 • **H. NORMAN SCHWARZKOPF**, American general and commander of Operation Desert Storm

1949 • **DIANA NYAD**, American marathon swimmer

EVENTS

1762 • Ann Franklin, Benjamin Franklin's sister-in-law, became the **FIRST FEMALE EDITOR OF AN AMERICAN NEWSPAPER**, *The Mercury* of Newport, R.I.

1851 • The yacht *America* won the **FIRST AMERICA'S CUP RACE.**

1865 • William Sheppard patented **LIQ-** ☀ **UID SOAP.**

1881 • Clara Barton established the **FIRST CHAPTER OF THE AMERICAN ASSOCIATION OF THE RED CROSS.**

1902 • Theodore Roosevelt became the **FIRST PRESIDENT TO RIDE IN A CAR.**

1991 • In Moscow, a **14-TON STATUE OF FELIX DZERZHINSKY,** the founder of the Soviet KGB, was dismantled while a crowd of 10,000 cheered.

AUGUST 23
activities

Personalized comics

In honor of Ernie Bushmiller's birthday, share with your students several installments of the "Nancy" comic strip. Then give each child a 3-inch-wide strip of plain paper to fold into fourths. Invite the kids to create comic strips with themselves as the title character.

Radio comedy

To mark the anniversary of the first time comedians were heard on the radio, have your students produce their own "radio" comedy shows. Working in teams, students can gather joke and riddle books or create their own humorous stories and dialogue. Have the teams take turns tape-recording their funny material in another room. Then play back their "shows" for a "radio audience" of classmates.

Rapid round-trip

Challenge your students to use their calculators to figure out Hackett and Moneypenny's average speed on their record-setting round-trip flight.

AUGUST 24

-tivities

☀💡 Wonders of waffles

How many of your students enjoy eating waffles for breakfast? Ask the children if the waffles they typically eat are freshly made—with a waffle iron—or frozen. What other breakfast foods do they enjoy? Make a chart of class breakfast favorites. Then challenge students to rate the nutritional values of these foods against the nutritional value of waffles. Have them use their information to create posters, which can be displayed in the school cafeteria.

✿ A swimmer's challenge

Since Matthew Webb first swam the English Channel in 1875, many others have repeated his feat. Have students locate the English Channel on a map of Europe. Where is its narrowest point? (Between Dover, England, and Calais, France, the Channel is only about 20 miles wide.) Next, have students do research to find out how many hours it has taken swimmers since Webb to cross the Channel. Plot the results on a graph.

✈ Coast-to-coast questions

Have your students use their math and geography skills to determine the mileage from Los Angeles to Newark, N.J. At approximately what speed was Amelia Earhart traveling? Recently, it took about 5 hours and 45 minutes to make a transcontinental flight. Can your students calculate the approximate speed at which modern jets travel?

BIRTHDAYS

1960 • **CAL RIPKEN, JR.,** professional baseball player
1965 • **MARLEE MATLIN,** American actress

EVENTS

79 • **MT. VESUVIUS ERUPTED,** destroying the Roman cities of Pompeii and Herculaneum.

1814 • **BRITISH SOLDIERS INVADED WASHINGTON** and burned the Capitol and the White House.

1869 • Cornelius Swartout patented the
☀💡 **WAFFLE IRON.**

1875 • Matthew Webb began the FIRST
✿ **SUCCESSFUL SWIM OF THE ENGLISH CHANNEL** from Dover, England. He reached Calais, France, 21 hours and 45 minutes later.

1887 • The United States established a **SCIENTIFIC OBSERVATION POST IN GREENLAND.**

1932 • Amelia Earhart became the FIRST
✈ **WOMAN TO MAKE A NONSTOP FLIGHT ACROSS THE UNITED STATES,** from Los Angeles to Newark, N.J. The trip took 19 hours and 5 minutes.

1959 • Hiran Fong was sworn in as the **FIRST CHINESE-AMERICAN IN THE SENATE.**
• Daniel Inouye was sworn in as the **FIRST JAPANESE-AMERICAN MEMBER OF THE HOUSE OF REPRESENTATIVES.**

1987 • **WEST GERMANY OPENED ITS FIRST WIND-ENERGY PARK.** Its 30 windmills generate up to 2 million kilowatt hours of electricity a year.

1992 • **HURRICANE ANDREW** tore through densely populated areas of southern Florida, becoming the costliest natural disaster in U.S. history.

24

AUGUST 25
activities

BIRTHDAYS
1836 • **BRET HARTE,** American author
1918 • **LEONARD BERNSTEIN,** American composer and conductor
1927 • **ALTHEA GIBSON,** tennis star who became the first African-American to win a major U.S. title

EVENTS
1718 • **THE CITY OF NEW ORLEANS** was founded by Jean Baptiste la Moyne.
1825 • **URUGUAY** declared its independence from Brazil.
1829 • The government of Mexico rejected President Andrew Jackson's **BID TO BUY THE MEXICAN STATE OF TEXAS.**
1916 • **THE NATIONAL PARK SERVICE** was established within the Department of the Interior.
1921 • **THE UNITED STATES SIGNED A PEACE TREATY WITH GERMANY,** officially ending World War I hostilities between the two nations.
1944 • **ALLIED FORCES LIBERATED PARIS,** ending the Nazis' 4-year occupation of the French capital during World War II.
1989 • U.S. government officials announced a $65 million aid package to help the government of Colombia fight the drug trade.

KISS-AND-MAKE-UP DAY
UFO DAY

25

Future parks
Have your students brainstorm for ways parks of the future may be different from today's parks. List the kids' ideas on the board, then divide the class into small groups. Have each group develop a plan for a futuristic park. Groups might create maps, three-dimensional models, dioramas, murals, or advertisements for their park. Display their work in the school media center.

The changing face of Europe
Have your students compare and contrast maps of pre- and post-World War I Europe. What differences do they notice?

Next, show the kids post-World War II and contemporary maps of Europe. Can anyone give an overview of the political conditions that gave rise to all the changes?

Flying saucer fun
On UFO Day, get your students' imaginations soaring. Welcome them in the morning with some "outer space" music—perhaps the theme from *2001: A Space Odyssey.* Next, have them each write a letter inviting an alien to visit your classroom. How might they "mail" these letters? Afterward, read aloud a science fiction story. Finally, divide the class into groups. Give each group a paper bag filled with ordinary objects and discarded items—screws, twist ties, paper cups, bottle tops, plastic sandwich bags, old keys, erasers, aluminum foil, and so on. Then challenge each group to create a UFO from the materials. Let the kids suspend their UFOs from the classroom ceiling.

AUGUST 26
activities

✦ Kindergarten then and now

Celebrate the opening of the first U.S. kindergarten by having older students visit your school's kindergarten class. Before the visit, have each student write a story about a favorite kindergarten memory. Then have the kids buddy up with kindergartners and share their stories. Afterward, they can help their "little buddies" write and illustrate stories about *their* favorite kindergarten activities. Post all the stories in the hallway under a banner titled "The Best of Kindergarten."

🇺🇸 Voting rights

Ask your students to speculate on what the word *suffragist* means. Then have them check a dictionary. Can they name famous American suffragists, such as Elizabeth Cady Stanton, Susan B. Anthony, and Lucy Stone?

⊘ Out of their league?

Have your students name sports besides baseball that are regularly broadcast on television. List these sports on the chalkboard. Are women's sports equally represented? Why or why not? Invite your students to write letters to network and cable television officials stating their opinions about the media's coverage of women's sports.

BIRTHDAYS

1740 • **JOSEPH MICHEL MONTGOLFIER,** French balloonist

1838 • **JOHN WILKES BOOTH, American** actor who assassinated Abraham Lincoln

1873 • **LEE DE FOREST, American inventor** who made important contributions to the development of radio and television

1906 • **ALBERT SABIN, Russian-American microbiologist** who developed an oral polio vaccine

1935 • **GERALDINE FERRARO, American politician** who, as the Democratic candidate for vice president in 1984, became the first woman to run on a major party's national ticket

EVENTS

1498 • **MICHELANGELO** was commissioned to create the *Pieta.*

1873 • **THE FIRST U.S. PUBLIC SCHOOL ✦ KINDERGARTEN** was established.

1920 • **THE NINETEENTH AMENDMENT** 🇺🇸 went into effect, giving women the right to vote.

1939 • The Cincinnati Reds and the ⊘ Brooklyn Dodgers played in the **FIRST TELEVISED MAJOR LEAGUE BASEBALL GAME.**

1974 • Russian cosmonaut Lev Demin became the **FIRST GRANDFATHER IN SPACE,** aboard *Soyuz 15.*

WOMEN'S EQUALITY DAY

26

AUGUST 27
activities

27

✿ Classroom performances
To celebrate the first theatrical performance in the colonies, have small groups of students perform a dramatic reading, skit, play, or puppet show.

▬ Oil drilling and spilling
Since the first U.S. oil well was drilled, Americans have experienced the benefits—and hazards—of using oil. One major hazard is an oil spill, which can occur when oil is being transported. In 1989, for example, the tanker *Exxon Valdez* spilled 240,000 barrels of oil in Alaska's Prince William Sound. To help students understand the difficulties of cleaning up an oil spill, have them conduct this simple experiment. Give small groups a shallow pan filled with water and some eyedroppers, straws, paper towels, cotton balls, and spoons. Add about $\frac{1}{4}$ cup of vegetable oil to the pans. Ask the group members to clean up the "spill" with the materials they were given, and discuss the results. Then have the groups research the kinds of techniques used to clean up real-life oil spills.

⚗ Killer wave
The Krakatoa explosion produced what may have been the loudest noise in earth's history and left a 600-foot-deep hole under Sunda Strait where the island had once been. It also created a 120-foot-high tidal wave that killed 36,000 people. Use an almanac and a map of the United States to determine which cities might be covered with water if a 120-foot tidal wave struck the eastern or western coasts. How many people live in those cities? Then have your students examine topography maps to get a rough estimate of how much land would be lost if the water level rose 120 feet. Using this information, have the kids create a new U.S. map showing the post-tidal-wave coastline.

AUGUST 28
activities

📖 Wise-guy stories

Caldecott medalist Roger Duvoisin introduced children to Petunia the silly goose in 1950. Many of his Petunia stories tackle important philosophical questions. Ask your students to discuss how they can tell if someone is smart, then read aloud *Petunia*. Petunia thought that carrying a book would make her wise. Invite your students to create stories in which the main character finds or wears something that makes others think he or she is wise.

✨ Delaying tactic

Have your students look up the meaning of the word *filibuster*. Why is this technique used? Do your students think filibusters should be permitted in the Senate? Why or why not?

✏️ Dreams day

Tell your students that Martin Luther King, Jr., helped organize the 1963 March on Washington—the largest civil rights demonstration in U.S. history. During this demonstration, King gave his famous "I Have a Dream" speech. Share a film of King giving this speech, or have students take turns reading the text of it aloud. Discuss which of King's dreams have come true. What dreams do the children have for America, their school, their families, or themselves? Have them each write their dreams on strips of paper, then post the strips under these categories on a bulletin board.

BIRTHDAYS

1904 • ROGER DUVOISIN, children's
📖   illustrator
1926 • PHYLLIS KRASILOVSKY, children's author
1958 • SCOTT HAMILTON, American figure skater

EVENTS

1609 • English navigator Henry Hudson discovered the DELAWARE BAY.
1830 • THE FIRST AMERICAN-BUILT LOCOMOTIVE, the *Tom Thumb*, lost a race with a horse-drawn stagecoach.
1922 • THE FIRST RADIO COMMERCIAL was aired.
1957 • Senator Strom Thurmond of
✨   South Carolina set a FILIBUSTER RECORD by talking for 24 hours and 18 minutes.
1963 • MARTIN LUTHER KING, JR.,
✏️   spoke to 200,000 people at the Lincoln Memorial in Washington, D.C.
1968 • British scientists using sonar detected several HUGE OBJECTS MOVING THROUGH THE WATER OF LOCH NESS in Scotland.
1989 • Disney Productions purchased the Muppets for $100 million.

"I HAVE A DREAM" DAY

AUGUST 29
activities

BIRTHDAYS

1632 • JOHN LOCKE, English philosopher

1811 • HENRY BERGH, founder of the American Society for the Prevention of Cruelty to Animals (ASPCA)

1915 • INGRID BERGMAN, Swedish actress

1920 • CHARLIE PARKER, American jazz saxophonist considered a founder of the bebop style

1958 • MICHAEL JACKSON, American singer

EVENTS

1835 • The city of MELBOURNE, AUSTRALIA, was founded.

1884 • H.J. Webb completed a 898-MILE TRICYCLE RIDE across Scotland.

1929 • THE AIRSHIP *GRAF ZEPPELIN* completed a circumnavigation of the globe in record time: 21 days, 7 hours, 26 minutes.

1966 • THE BEATLES GAVE THEIR LAST LIVE PERFORMANCE, at Candlestick Park in San Francisco.

1971 • Hank Aaron became the FIRST NATIONAL LEAGUE BASEBALL PLAYER TO DRIVE IN 100 RUNS IN EACH OF 11 SEASONS.

1982 • British explorers Sir Ranulph Fiennes and Charles Burton successfully completed the FIRST AERIAL CIRCUMNAVIGATION OF THE GLOBE by way of the North and South Poles.

29

Natural rights

Tell your students that John Locke had a profound influence on Thomas Jefferson's writing of the Declaration of Independence. Locke identified three rights of man similar to those Jefferson included in the Declaration: life, liberty, and property. Ask your students to track how these rights are being maintained today. For 1 week, have them review newspapers, magazines, and radio and television broadcasts for actions by local, state, and federal governments that affect these rights. Do the kids feel government is doing its job? What government actions might be taken to further protect these rights?

Animal rights

Celebrate ASPCA founder Henry Bergh's birthday by having a class discussion about humane treatment of animals. Children who own pets can provide dos and don'ts of pet care. For example, don't keep a large dog confined in a small area (bathroom, laundry room) for long periods; do take the dog for frequent walks. With older children, you can broaden the discussion to include farm and wild animals also.

Sensational singer

On singer Michael Jackson's birthday, play some of his hits or screen a couple of his music videos. Explain that in addition to music, Jackson's interests include promoting worldwide peace and intergroup harmony. Then invite your students to design birthday cards reflecting the pop star's personality or areas of special concern.

AUGUST 30
activities

✎ Ted Williams math

Boston Red Sox star Ted Williams was one of the greatest hitters in baseball history. Among his many other batting feats, Williams was the last man to hit over .400 in a season, posting a .406 batting average in 1941. Explain to your students that batting averages are computed by dividing a player's total number of hits by his total number of at bats, and carrying the division to three decimal places. Thus Williams's .406 batting average means that he got hits 40.6% of the times he was up. Projected over the course of 1,000 at bats, he'd have gotten 406 hits. Now pose this math problem for your students to do as quickly as possible in their heads: With his batting average of .406, how many hits would Williams have gotten if he'd had 600 at bats? Have kids raise their hands as they finish the problem. Call on students until someone gives you the correct answer (243 or, rounding up, 244). Then discuss the kids' strategies. Did anyone solve the problem by taking half of 406 (203, or the number of hits Williams would have gotten in 500 at bats), and adding 40.6 (the number he'd have gotten in 100 at bats)?

📖 Inspirations for writing

Donald Crews drew on childhood experiences as inspiration for his book *Freight Train*. During summer vacations, Crews used to take the train from his home in New Jersey to his grandparents' farm in Florida. His grandparents' porch was only 150 yards from the railroad tracks. Crews liked to sit on the porch and watch the freight trains roll by, counting their cars to pass the time. Share the book *Freight Train* with your students. Then invite the class to make a freight train to record the books they read for 1 month. Post a construction-paper train engine on a bulletin board. Then give each child several construction-paper freight cars. Have your students write the titles of books they finish reading on the freight cars, then attach the cars to the train engine.

BIRTHDAYS

1797 • MARY SHELLEY, English author whose best-known work is *Frankenstein*

1901 • ROY WILKINS, American civil rights leader

1909 • VIRGINIA LEE BURTON, children's author

1918 • TED WILLIAMS, American baseball player ✎

1938 • DONALD CREWS, children's 📖 author and illustrator

EVENTS

1682 • WILLIAM PENN sailed from England to America to take over a tract of land—Pennsylvania—granted to him by the king.

1780 • General BENEDICT ARNOLD secretly promised to surrender the American fort at West Point, N.Y., to the British.

1830 • THE BALTIMORE AND OHIO RAILROAD abandoned the horse-powered locomotive for trains powered by steam.

1970 • ABRAHAM ZAPRUDER, who filmed the assassination of President John F. Kennedy, died.

1983 • Lt. Col. Guion S. Bluford, Jr., became the FIRST AFRICAN-AMERICAN ASTRONAUT IN SPACE.

1984 • The space shuttle *DISCOVERY* blasted off on its maiden voyage.

AUGUST 31
activities

BIRTHDAYS

1786 • **MICHEL EUGENE CHEVREUL,** French chemist who invented margarine

1870 • **MARIA MONTESSORI,** Italian 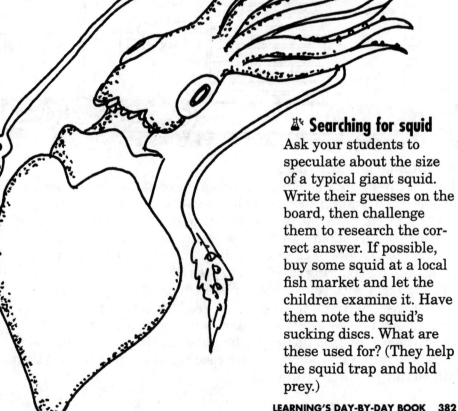 educator

1945 • **ITZHAK PERLMAN,** Israeli violinist

• **VAN MORRISON,** Irish singer and songwriter

1955 • **EDWIN MOSES,** American track star

EVENTS

1881 • **THE FIRST MEN'S TENNIS SINGLES CHAMPIONSHIPS were** held in Newport, R.I.

1886 • **THE FIRST RECORDED MAJOR EARTHQUAKE in U.S. history** rocked Charleston, S.C.

1954 • **HURRICANE CAROL hit New** England, New York, and New Jersey, causing $500 million in damage.

1955 • **THE FIRST SOLAR-POWERED CAR was demonstrated.**

1964 • **THE BUREAU OF THE CENSUS** announced that California had surpassed New York as the most populous U.S. state.

1980 • **Poland's SOLIDARITY trade** union was founded at the port city of Gdansk.

1982 • **THE FIRST GIANT SQUID CAP-TURED ALIVE was taken near** Bergen, Norway.

Nontraditional schools

Teacher Maria Montessori was unhappy with the way young children were educated, so she started her own school. Ask your students to research the backgrounds of Montessori and others who had to create their own schools or programs to meet specific needs—for example, Booker T. Washington, Howard Gardner, Lucy Calkins, Nancie Atwell, Sylvia Townsend-Warner, and Christopher Whittle. Students also can scan newspapers and magazines for information about contemporary school experiments, including for-profit schools, business-run schools, and magnet schools. Encourage the kids to clip pertinent articles and share their information with the class.

California, here they come

Renowned for its pleasant weather, miles of beaches, job opportunities, and laid-back life-style, California became a magnet for Americans from other parts of the country. Have your students compare the population of their state with that of California, the nation's largest. Also challenge the kids to find countries that have fewer citizens than California.

Searching for squid

Ask your students to speculate about the size of a typical giant squid. Write their guesses on the board, then challenge them to research the correct answer. If possible, buy some squid at a local fish market and let the children examine it. Have them note the squid's sucking discs. What are these used for? (They help the squid trap and hold prey.)